# Hangups From Way Back

Historical Myths and Canons

R. Bausch

# Hangups From Way Back

Historical Myths and Canons
Volume I
Second Edition

Frederick Gentles
Melvin Steinfield

San Diego Mesa College

Canfield Press
San Francisco
A Department of Harper & Row, Publishers, Inc.

O world of men, what is your happiness?
A painted show. Comes sorrow and the touch—
a wet sponge—blots the painting out.
And this moves pity, sadder still than death.

                                    —AESCHYLUS

HANGUPS FROM WAY BACK: Historical Myths and Canons, Volume 1, Second Edition. Copyright © 1970, 1974 by Frederick Gentles and Melvin Steinfield.

**Library of Congress Cataloging in Publication Data**

Gentles, Frederick, comp.
  Hangups from way back.

  Includes bibliographies.
  1. Civilization—History. 2. History—Errors, inventions, etc. I. Steinfield, Melvin, joint comp.
II. Title.
CB59.G43   1974   901.9   74-1191
ISBN 0–06–382785–9

Design by Michael Rogondino
Illustrations by Robert Bausch

74 75 76 10 9 8 7 6 5 4 3 2 1

# Contents

Contents

Contents

Contents

Contents

# Preface

The blame for student criticism of the lack of relevance in their education—for their feeling that what they are studying somehow does not relate to the world they live in—must be shared by teachers and the books they use. Although teachers of world and Western civilization defend their courses—justifiably—as being necessary to an understanding of today's world, it is clear many have failed to communicate history's relevance. Obviously, more effective teaching tools are needed.

This book attempts to demonstrate this relevance. And what is more relevant today than the way man handles myth, an idea that seems eternal but is actually only transient? "A myth," as Ashley Montagu observes, "is something which is in fact not true, but in which we believe and act upon as if it were true." Myths later become canons—that is, rules, regulations, and laws, the correct and accepted ways of doing things. We build our cultures on myths; indeed, myths are necessary for the stability of a culture. All of us live by myths and canons, taking them for reality. And for certain myths that man has held dear, he has become involved, frustrated, paranoid, and even vicious.

Here we are concerned with some ideas that have caused endless controversy and bloodshed throughout history. The intoxicating, man-made idea is the myth, the canon, the hangup. By seeing how myths have determined man's behavior in the past and how some of them are still with us, perhaps we can better resist their influence. It is, of course, not enough to simply *say* that history is relevant; it must be shown. The selections in each chapter, therefore, focus on those basic patterns of intellectual, social, political, military, and economic history—the myths—that especially pertain to today's problems.

When the first edition of *Hangups From Way Back* appeared in 1970, America had just experienced a decade of violence over issues of race and war. Men had also first walked on the moon and surgeons had successfully transplanted hearts, but despite these optimistic technological developments the search for world peace was clouded by the specter of thermonuclear holocaust.

In the four years since, the world has changed dramatically. President Nixon, known for two decades for rigid anti-Communism, traveled to China and the Soviet Union in order to wind down the cold war and the Vietnam war. The Strategic Arms Limitations Talks made significant progress in reducing the arms race. With the first significant steps toward a resolution of the conflict in the Middle East, the possibility of world-wide peace seemed attainable.

But science and technology, once viewed as panaceas, are now seen as encompassing very real limitations and dangers. Pollution, technology's unexpected child, threatens to choke civilization before the year 2000. The energy crisis suddenly shocked the Western world late in 1973 and threatened permanently to change economies and life styles dependent on the continuing availability of all natural resources. More critics began to question the idea that progress means unrestricted economic growth. The Watergate scandals and the resignation of Vice President Agnew embarrassed an administration elected on a strong law and order platform. No doubt, the repercussions of all these will continue both at home and abroad for many years to come.

Though these recent events have created an upheaval in the flow of history, mankind's traditional hangups persist. In this second edition, then, we have updated some of the essays and reading selections while still retaining the basic approach, which we feel is just as relevant today as it was in 1970. We have added three chapters to Volume 1: "Women in the Ancient World," "Art and Life," and "The Protestant Reformation and the Capitalist System." In Volume 2, we have added two chapters: "Napoleon, the Man and the Myth" and "The Emergence of the Masses."

It is impossible to acknowledge every individual who assisted in the development of this book, but a few names do stand out for the magnitude of their contribution. The entire Canfield Press staff—especially publisher and history editor Jack Jennings and production editor Gracia Alkema—offered expert assistance in many ways. We are also grateful to Brian Williams for the copy editing and to Robert Bausch for the illustrations. In addition, thanks are due our colleagues at Mesa College, particularly Arelene Wolinski and Carolyn Pickering. We would also like to express our appreciation of Francis J. Moriarty of Franklin Pierce College in Rindge, New Hampshire, and of Sandra K. Craig for preparing the questions that appear at the end of each chapter. Of course, the authors assume responsibility for all interpretations in their essays and any errors that might appear in the book.

*Frederick Gentles*

*Melvin Steinfield*

# Hangups From Way Back

Historical Myths and Canons

# 1

# Some Concepts
# of Man and Society

If you love must you also hate? Some people say yes, it is instinctual; others say no, we learn to love and hate. In other words, we may be programmed for peace and programmed for violence, and there has been a lot of both on this small planet far out from the center of our Milky Way Galaxy. It is with the hate and violence in the world today—and the possibility of greater violence tomorrow, now that man possesses the ultimate weapons—that the following essay is concerned. The author believes the student beginning a study of civilization should know something about the twentieth-century viewpoints of man's behavior so that he can analyze and interpret the men and events of history.

# Love and Hate on Planet III

Frederick Gentles

On the moon's Sea of Tranquility is a plaque with the names of the American Apollo 11 astronauts and President of the United States Richard Nixon, plus the legend: WE CAME IN PEACE FOR ALL MANKIND. This ideal of peace has been a goal of mankind since the earliest days of civilization. From time to time in history, man seems to have realized the dream, but the world has been a violent one too—at the time of the 1969 moon landing a cartoonist pictured a shattered earth posted with a battered placard with the caption: HERE MAN FIRST SET FOOT ON THE PLANET EARTH, # % 00 B.C. WE CAME IN PEACE FOR ALL MANKIND. It was signed by man, *Adam*, and by woman, *Eve*.[1]

Why is it we have not achieved the permanent peace and order long desired? Is it man's nature that he loves but also hates and fears his fellow men? Is he naturally so aggressive and self-interested that he will always try to destroy others—and very likely himself?

In the "nature versus nurture" debate some scientists say these violent traits are innate—an inborn part of man's "nature"—and there isn't much we can do except try to redirect these instincts so they will not harm others. Other scientists say man's nature is actually "nurtured"—he has learned to be what he is because of conditioning processes in his society. Some people, they say, are conditioned to be aggressive and some to be passive, some to love and some to hate.

Despite all the studies on the nature of man, there is obviously, considering the intensity of violence in the world, a scandalous gap between our ability to scamper about on the moon and our ability to solve great domestic and foreign problems. As far as learning how

3

to control ourselves and solve age-old problems, we are still in the Middle Ages. One factor is that men are set apart in rather isolated groups all over the world and grow up with many different ideas about the values and meaning of life. Thus, we are all provincials, even those living in the big cities.

Members of an old religious order claim that if they can direct a child's mind for seven years, his religious thinking will be determined for the rest of his life. Of course, the training of a child in *any* particular culture will usually result in his behavior reflecting the customs and values of that culture. A Greek thinks as a Greek, a Roman as a Roman, and a clansman as a clansman. Consider for a moment what has determined your thinking—family and friends? neighborhood and nation? newspapers, television, books, magazines? It is difficult to rise above the parochialism of one's own village, state, or country and think in larger terms; even one of the Apollo 11 astronauts, when in the vicinity of the moon, said he felt homesick for the earth. However, with the perspective of space and time, together with knowledge and understanding, one can hope to rise above local and narrow paths of thought, in spite of the gravitational pull of the old neighborhood.

Two cases illustrate how the trauma of sudden change can affect thinking and routine. Although the examples involve what might be called simple people, there is no reason to believe the rest of us are any less immune to the shock of cultural change.

After the British forbade headhunting in the Eddystone Islands in the last century, the "primitives" demonstrated less of an interest in life, and their population dwindled. Before, each individual and village had a certain amount of "spirit power," and they added to this by taking heads from neighboring villages. With the new "civilized" law, there was no longer head power or so much spirit power, and a major institution of the culture was destroyed. After all, what was the fun in life if one couldn't go headhunting?

In another instance, the natives of a village in India found the essence of their culture destroyed when American technicians piped running water into their huts. Since the well had been the social center of the village, the people became unhappy—they no longer saw their old friends and life was dull at home all day. They decided, therefore, that the village must be restored to its old ways and that the pipe system must go. It went.

As a creature of habit, man may be trained to believe in all sorts of ideas, even absurd ones. These ideas become a part of his life, and existence becomes meaningless without them. Indeed, he may be willing to die for what he believes in, whether it be headhunting, village wells, or apple pie.

Although historians generally believe that knowledge of self and understanding of life is revealed through the study of man and his institutions, some scientists now urge that it may be through the study of the biological structure of the cell and the nature of animal behavior. This is a controversial area among scientists, and students of history should at least be aware of it, if only to remind themselves that human affairs involve *both* biological and environmental factors. Accordingly, a brief description follows of the so-called "nature versus nurture" controversy.

Biochemists have intensively studied the make-up of the single cell, and results indicate that the nature of a Clyde Barrow, a Mahatma Gandhi, or a Charlie Brown is tied, at least in part, to his genes. The nucleus of the fertilized cell in the mother carries information from both parents which leads to the development of such particulars as skin, eye, and hair color, mental capacity, nervous characteristics, height, susceptibility to various diseases, and memory capabilities in the new individual. These inherited characteristics are sometimes very important factors in the behavior of individuals and groups.

As an example of the importance of body chemistry in the behavior of an individual, the story is told of Sir Walter Raleigh, traveling on Roanoke Island in 1585 in the New World, coming to a fork in the road and taking the right turn, which lead off to the legendary Tabac Indians. Here he was offered the peace pipe, which he enjoyed so much that he took it with him back to England. Soon all of England and then the whole world was smoking the delicious weed of the Tabac Indians; moreover, there were many wars, and much history was made after this time. But, so one popular version of this tale goes, had Sir Walter taken the turn to the *left,* he would have come upon another tribe, the Mari Wanna Indians. They too would have offered him the peace pipe; he would have taken their weed back to England to spread the habit throughout the world—and, in that case, there would have been no history worth mentioning for nearly 400 years. Instead, according to the marijuana converts, there would have been beautiful people living in beautiful harmony. Although the story is fanciful, the point is that the body chemistry can be changed, and with the change can come changes in behavior. Chemicals can tame a man and make him docile, or they can make him vicious and violent—and the stimulant and the tranquilizer are fashions in our time.

*Homo homini lupus*—"man is a wolf to man"—is a phrase used

by some scientists who see man behaving in ways like animals. In his *Civilization and Its Discontents,* psychoanalyst Sigmund Freud used the phrase to emphasize man's animal nature, then asked:

> Who, in the face of all his experience of life and history, will have the courage to dispute this assertion? As a rule this cruel aggressiveness waits for some provocation or puts itself at the service of some other purpose, whose goal might also have been reached by milder measures. In circumstances that are favorable to it, when the mental counter-forces which ordinarily inhibit it are out of action, it also manifests itself spontaneously and reveals man as a savage beast to whom consideration towards his own kind is something alien. Anyone who calls to mind the atrocities committed during the racial migrations or the invasions of the Huns, or by the people known as Mongols under Jenghiz Khan and Tamerlane, or at the capture of Jerusalem by the pious Crusaders, or even, indeed, the horrors of the recent World War—anyone who calls these things to mind will have to bow humbly before the truth of the view.*[2]

Freud, who scorned to distinguish between a culture and a civilization, wrote this in a book published in Vienna in 1930. There have been a few wars since then, and there have been the Hitlers and the Stalins and the massacre of millions from Indonesia to Biafra.

In another book, *The Future of an Illusion,* Freud says that civilization has to be protected against the individual and that every individual is virtually an enemy of civilization. "It is remarkable [he writes] that, little as men are able to exist in isolation, they should nevertheless feel as a heavy burden the sacrifices which civilization expects of them in order to make a communal life possible."[3] In other words, he says, man can't live contentedly either with or without his fellow man; man is simply discontent, and arguments are of no avail against his passions.

Civilization, Freud continues, is built upon coercion and upon renunciation of instinct. All men contain destructive and antisocial attitudes; these trends in a great number of people determine the collective nature of their society. Furthermore, educating man toward a life of reason and kindness is unlikely because the ability of the masses to absorb education is limited. Freud sees hostility, protest, and revolt ahead, especially where a society accepts great inequalities between privileged and underprivileged.

Ethologists, who study animal behavior in the natural habitat, think man has important lessons to learn from the animal kingdom. The extremes of brutal behavior do not belong to animals but to man; it is man who is the beast. While there is fighting among animals, most of it is ritual, and there are appeasement ceremonies by both victor and vanquished. Animals habitually kill only for food; they do not slaughter their own kind, or any other kind, in wholesale numbers.

Konrad Lorenz, the director of the Max Planck Institute for Behavioral Physiology in Bavaria and an eminent naturalist and zoologist, believes that "Expert teaching of biology is the one and only foundation on which really sound opinions about mankind and its relation to the universe can be built."[4] In his best-selling book *On Aggression*, he says that the same aggressive instincts that help preserve life may also destroy it if carried to extremes. As with Freud, he appeals for some redirection of our aggressive instincts; man has become so self-centered and so possessive that these traits could destroy him. Lorenz still has hopes, however, that man's knowledge and his humor will save him.

In *The Territorial Imperative*,[5] a follower of Lorenz, Robert Ardrey, makes the point that the drive for the acquisition of territory is common to men and animals. This drive often brings individuals and societies into conflict, depending upon which aspect of our dual nature is uppermost. Ardrey defines this duality as the code of *amity,* in which there is a capacity for love, kindness, friendship, generosity, sympathy, and so forth; and the code of *enmity,* in which there is a pronounced capacity to hate, to be cruel, to destroy. Ardrey thinks this amity–enmity is basic to man's nature because of his animal-inheritance. And man, he says, is a willing subject to this dual code. We love our friends, and we hate our enemies. Some of us say, no, we don't hate our enemies, we just hate the things they stand for. At any rate, we are willing to kill them.

Rats, as men, are exceptions in the animal world to killing their own species in great numbers. While a rat will seldom kill another rat in his own pack, one pack will mercilessly attack and kill members of another pack. Evidently there is a process by which rats as well as men distinguish between murder and war.

In a war, people of one nation will kill people of another even though they are of the same religion, the same race, and even having the same language and culture. Only an imaginary line separates them. An idea separates them. People, tribes, and nations are always drawing lines—and rat packs, apparently, draw them too.

But men are not rats, says Professor David Krech, who calls himself a rat-brain psychologist: "It is not true that a brain is a brain is a brain. The rat is a rat and he hath a rat's brain; the child is a child and he hath a child's brain—and each, according to my hypothesis, requires its own educational nutrient."[6] He believes that the study of language and how it is acquired may provide understanding of the basis of our mental life. Being human, he says, means that people have the power of cognition or knowing.

Which brings us at last to the other side of the nature-nurture controversy. The idea that man has a brain with acquisitive or perceptive powers not characteristic of other animals leads other scientists to object strenuously to the Lorenz school's emphasis on nature. That school, they believe, is dangerous—man might simply accept his aggressive and destructive ways, pass them off as natural, and go on committing outrageous deeds upon his fellow man. Instead, man is what he has sensed in life. Man experiences, man learns. This is the empiricism of Locke and Hume, who believed that all knowledge is founded upon experience. This is nurture, and Alexander Pope was right, they say, in his *Essay on Man*, when he wrote, "The proper study of mankind is man." If man is programmed for violence, it is not programming done by instincts but programming done very largely by fellow man. Witness the Eddystone Islander with his headhunting and the civilized man with his warfare.

In *Patterns of Culture*,[7] Ruth Benedict described three cultures. In one the orientation of life was toward peace and serenity, in the two others toward conflict and aggressiveness. The Zuñi of New Mexico live in a society where the emphasis is on harmony and the quiet, peaceful life. The Dobu in eastern New Guinea, however, live in one where conflict with fellow man is the essence of being—one may steal, kill children, maim one's neighbor, and commit other deeds that our Western society would consider crimes. The whole atmosphere of the Dobu culture is one of hostility and fear.

In the Kwakiutl Indian culture of the Pacific Northwest, the drive in life was for one to accumulate possessions so that he might gain prestige by giving to others so that they too might possess. This was the acquisitive society par excellence. The Kwakiutl orientation recalls that of the American "robber barons" of the nineteenth century, who accumulated massive wealth and then set up foundations to distribute it for charitable and cultural purposes. The Carnegie, Rockefeller, and Morgan foundations still help support science, medicine, colleges and universities, museums, and so on.

One of Miss Benedict's purposes in writing the book was to suggest that cultures have different orientations and that those individuals who demonstrate or who object to the traditions of their particular culture are not necessarily and fundamentally evil in not conforming to the set standards of their society. At the moment, long hair, sideburns, beards, and sandals represent a challenge to the traditional ways in our society.

The way of life that emphasizes harmony and peace, like the Zuñi's, is called *Apollonian*, after Apollo, the Greek god of beauty and harmony. Apollo 11 astronauts landed in the moon's Sea of Tranquility, "in peace for all mankind"; Apollo 12 landed in the Ocean of Storms —a perfect, if unconscious, symbolism for man's other side, conflict, called *Dionysian* after the Greek god of wine. Although Dionysius (Bacchus in Rome) could be kind and gentle as he went about his world teaching the cultivation of the vine, this perfect peace alternated with revelry, orgy, cruelty, and suffering, and after harvest time, Dionysius descended to the underworld, where he was the only god who was tortured. He has been called the tragic god, and the Dionysian-type societies named after him re-enact this same rhythm of life: peace, love, conflict, cruelty, and often violent death. But Dionysius' resurrection in the spring each year also represented hope for mankind, and there was a great festival (Bacchanalia) celebrating the new life.

According to Claude Lévi-Strauss, the French anthropologist:

> No society is perfect. Each has within it, by nature, an impurity incompatible with the norms to which it lays claim; this impurity finds outlet in elements of injustice, cruelty, and insensitivity. . . . It will eventually become plain that no human society is fundamentally good; but neither is any of them fundamentally bad; all offer their members certain advantages, though we must bear in mind a residue of iniquity, apparently more or less constant in its importance.[8]

What he has to say about the imperfections and inconsistencies of societies applies to individuals as well, and with both individuals and societies, declared purposes and objectives are often inconsistent with actual day-to-day living. The United States is certainly one of the freest countries in the world; even so, to what extent has its people really lived up to the ideals of the Declaration of Independence and the Bill of Rights? With liberty and justice for all or with liberty and justice for some? Of course, there are greater inconsistencies between claims and practices about justice in the Soviet Union, the Republic of South Africa, and many other countries one could name. What Lévi-Strauss seems to suggest is that we are a world-community of sinners.

Some people and some cultures have more readily accepted change in their patterns than others. Progress may be thought of as two kinds: *circular progress*, where there is little change in the political, social, and economic institutions from one generation to another, and *linear progress*, where people have been willing to make changes in their institutions in order to improve and refine their ways of living. The mind of the primitive (his is not a primitive mind, however) seeks order and in order finds safety. He hesitates to change; he fears the unknown, though change, if meaningful, will be assimilated into the traditional culture. Usually, however, he is the most conservative of the conservatives.

The mind of civilized man, beginning with the Sumerians, seeks change, a way of thought that has culminated in several Herculean and portentous events of the twentieth century: the Bomb, the Pill, the moon landing, and, of course, TV. Politically, socially, and economically, however, linear progress has left something to be desired. There is a marked cultural lag between scientific progress and progress that involves man's ability to get along with his fellow man and to supply everyone with the necessary goods of life.

Linear progress may be described as a line inclined upward from right to left, conservative to liberal. One student suggested that the line might better be described with a spiral running through it, since change comes gradually, and we maintain a circular progress with our traditions and customs while change is going on. Another student suggested that the spiral should turn to the left for the liberals and to the right for the conservatives.

At any rate, the symbolism of circle, line, or spiral can stand for the progress of a society or the progress of an individual. Some individuals experience linear progress up through high school and then settle down to circular progress for the rest of their lives at an eight-to-five job fifty weeks a year, with TV from six to bedtime. Others may go on through college and then settle down to a routine. Routine, however, is not just a behavioral pattern of Western Civilization; in one fashion or another, it is universal. Meanwhile, the battle of the bumper stickers goes on among those who are pretty well satisfied with the status quo and those who are not. One example of the recurring conflict: AMERICA: LOVE IT OR LEAVE IT answered by AMERICA: CHANGE IT OR LOSE IT.

Rapid and marked change is an unsettling experience for the psyche. It leads to bewilderment and sometimes to violence, say Ivo and Rosalind Feierabend and Betty Nesvold in their studies on the aggressive habits of nations.[9] Their analyses of the internal stability of

84 countries between 1948 and 1965—riots, revolutions, assassinations, strikes, and demonstrations were considered with other data—showed the following scores:[10]

| | |
|---|---|
| Finland | 0 |
| Luxembourg | 0 |
| Japan | 32 |
| USSR | 81 |
| United States | 97 |
| Union of South Africa | 158 |
| Indonesia | 190 |

They found that violence tended to increase when social achievement failed to keep pace with social expectations. That is, on the chart of a society of rising expectations, the actual achievement line turned at a point and started to descend in what is called the "J-curve." The greater this gap between expectations and achievement, the more likely it is that violence will occur.

The J-curve is applied by another author, James C. Davies, to account for the French Revolution, the American Civil War, the Nazi Revolution, and the Black uprisings in America. In all these cases, there was a long period in which the lines of expectation and achievement rose together on the charts, but when achievements failed to keep pace and the gap widened, violence broke out.[11]

What hope is there for survival of the species or of civilization in the light of man's behavior? Oswald Spengler, in the *Decline of the West*, said there was none—that it was already too late for Western Civilization because the decay was so far advanced. He viewed societies as being organic in nature, each with a vigorous springtime of growth and development, a summertime of maturity, an autumn of decline, and a winter of decay and death. Western society, Spengler thought, was in its wintertime, and only a few gloomy decades remained before the non-white races of the world would take over and build on the ruins of the West. To Spengler, as to his contemporary, Freud, World War I was proof of this decay.

In 1968 a London newspaper ran a series of articles on the so-called "Savage American," describing the history of violence in America prior to the assassinations of Martin Luther King and Robert Kennedy. Another newspaper followed with a series on "The Politics of Hate in America." Communists, Birchers, KKK, labor groups, businessmen, the poor, the middle class—all hate and fear some other individuals and groups they consider evil and dangerous. They have been conditioned by newspapers, television, neighborhoods, friends, and so on, to think and behave in ways common to the group. They firmly believe in their righteousness. Perhaps it should be put: *we* firmly believe in *our* righteousness. Given other conditions we could think in ways quite contrary to our present views and be equally positive. No wonder Shakespeare wrote, "What fools these mortals be!" No wonder Pilate asked, "What is truth?"

Viewed from space the earth is such a beautiful blue and white planet! By 2001 we may have discovered what Mars is all about. Will we have discovered ourselves? This book is one endeavor, at least, to see ourselves in the perspective of time and recurrent problems.

### Notes

1 Cartoon by Paul Conrad, *Los Angeles Times,* July 17, 1969.

2 Sigmund Freud, *Civilization and Its Discontents* (New York: W. W. Norton, 1962), pp. 58–59.

3 Sigmund Freud, *The Future of an Illusion* (Garden City, N.Y.: Doubleday-Anchor, 1964), p. 3.

4 Konrad Lorenz, *On Aggression* (New York: Harcourt, Brace & World, 1966), p. 298.

5 Robert Ardrey, *The Territorial Imperative* (New York: Atheneum, 1966).

6 David Krech, "Psychoneurobiochemeducation," *California Monthly,* June-July 1969, p. 18.

7 Ruth Benedict, *Patterns of Culture* (New York: Mentor, 1951). This book is one of the classics in cultural anthropology.

8 Claude Lévi-Strauss, *Tristes Tropiques* (New York: Atheneum, 1965), p. 385.

9 Ivo K. Feierabend, Rosalind L. Feierabend, Betty A. Nesvold, "Social Change and Political Violence: Cross-National Patterns," in *Violence in America, Historical and Comparative Perspectives*, Hugh Davis Graham and Ted Robert Gurr, eds. (New York: Signet, 1969), p. 606.

10 *Ibid.*, p. 626.

11 James C. Davies, "The J-Curve of Rising and Declining Satisfactions as a Cause of Some Great Revolutions and a Contained Rebellion," in Graham and Gurr, *ibid.*, p. 671 ff.

The magic of King Solomon's ring that enabled that wise king to talk with animals is a very real one, says Nobel laureate ethologist Konrad Lorenz, though it is not really necessary to have a ring or use magic in such communication. "Without supernatural assistance, our fellow creatures can tell us the most beautiful stories, and that means true stories, because the truth about nature is always far more beautiful even than what our great poets sing of it, and they are the only magicians that exist." In his charming book King Solomon's Ring, Lorenz interprets some important messages to us from the animal kingdom.

# King Solomon's Ring

Konrad Z. Lorenz

Once the social order of rank amongst the members of a colony is established it is most conscientiously preserved by jackdaws, much more so than by hens, dogs or monkeys. A spontaneous reshuffling, without outside influence, and due only to the discontent of one of the lower orders, has never come to my notice. Only once, in my colony, did I witness the dethroning of the hitherto ruling tyrant, Goldgreen. It was a returned wanderer who, having lost in his long absence his former deeply imbued respect for his ruler, succeeded in defeating him in their very first encounter. In the autumn of 1931, the conqueror, "Double-aluminium"—he derived this strange name from the rings on his feet—came back, after having been away the whole summer. He returned home strong in heart and stimulated by his travels, and at once subdued the former autocrat. His victory was remarkable for two reasons: first, Double-aluminium, who was unmated and therefore fighting alone, was opposed in the struggle by both the former ruler and his wife. Secondly, the victor was only one and a half years old, whereas Goldgreen and his wife both dated back to the original fourteen jackdaws with which I started the settlement in 1927.

The way in which my attention was drawn to this revolution was quite unusual. Suddenly, at the feeding tray, I say, to my astonishment, how a little, very fragile, and, in order of rank, low-standing lady sidled ever closer to the quietly feeding Goldgreen, and finally, as though inspired by some unseen power, assumed an attitude of self-display, whereupon the large male quietly and without opposition vacated his place. Then I noticed the newly returned hero, Double-aluminium, and saw that he had usurped the position of Goldgreen, and I thought, at first, that the deposed despot, under the influence of his recent defeat, was so subdued that he had allowed himself to be intimidated by the other members of the colony, including the aforesaid young female. But the assumption was false: Goldgreen had been conquered by Double-aluminium only, and remained forever the second in command. But Double-aluminium, on his return, had fallen in love with the young female and within the course of two days was publicly engaged to her! Since the partners in a jackdaw marriage support each other loyally and bravely in every conflict, and as no pecking order exists between them, they automatically rank as of equal status in their disputes with all other members of the colony; a wife is therefore, of necessity, raised to her husband's position. But the contrary does not hold good—an inviolable law dictates that no male may marry a female that ranks above him. The extraordinary part of the business is not the promotion as such but the amazing speed with which the news spreads that such a little jackdaw lady, who hitherto had been maltreated by eighty percent of the colony, is, from today, the "wife of the president" and may no longer receive so much as a black look from any other jackdaw. But more curious still— the promoted bird knows of its promotion! It is no credit to an animal to be shy and anxious after a bad experience, but to understand that a hitherto existent danger is now removed and to face the fact with an adequate supply of courage requires more sense. On a pond, a despot swan rules with so tyrannical a rule that no other swan, except the wife of the feared one, dares to enter the water at all. You can catch this terrible tyrant and carry him away before the eyes of all the others, and expect that the remaining birds will breathe an audible sigh of relief and at once proceed to take the bath of which they have been so long deprived. Nothing of the kind occurs. Days pass before the first of these suppressed subjects can pluck up enough courage to indulge in a modest swim hard against the shores of the pond. For a much longer time, nobody ventures into the middle of the water.

But that little jackdaw knew within forty-eight hours exactly what she could allow herself, and I am sorry to say that she made the fullest use of it. She lacked entirely that noble or even blasé tolerance which jackdaws of high rank should exhibit toward their inferiors. She used every opportunity to snub former superiors, and she did not stop at gestures of self-importance, as high-rankers of long standing nearly always do. No—she always had an active and malicious plan of attack ready at hand. In short, she conducted herself with the utmost vulgarity.

You think I humanize the animal? Perhaps you do not know that what we are wont to call "human weakness" is, in reality, nearly always a pre-human factor and one which we have in common with the higher animals? Believe me, I am not mistakenly assigning human properties to animals: on the contrary, I am showing you what an enormous animal inheritance remains in man, to this day.

And if I have just spoken of a young male jackdaw falling in love with a jackdaw female, this does not invest the animal with human properties, but, on the contrary, shows up the still remaining animal instincts in man. And if you argue the point with me, and deny that the power of love is an age-old instinctive force, then I can only surmise that you yourself are incapable of falling a prey to that passion.

A strange thing this "falling in love." The metaphor expresses the physical process with a drastic sense of realism—an audible bump, and you are in love! It would be impossible to symbolize it more aptly. And in this connection, many higher birds and mammals behave in exactly the same way as the human being. Very often even in jackdaws the "Grand Amor" is quite suddenly there, from one day to the next—indeed most typically, just as in the case of man, at the moment of the first encounter. Marlowe says:

> The reason no man knows, let it suffice,
> What we behold is censured by our eyes.
> Where both deliberate, the love is slight;
> Who ever loved, that loved not at first sight?

This famous "love at first sight" plays a big role in the life of wild geese and jackdaws and this may be most impressive for the observer. I know of a whole number of cases where love and troth were plighted on the occasion of the first meeting. The continual presence of the loved one is not so conducive to this state of mind as one might at first imagine. It can even be disadvantageous. At any rate, a temporary parting may achieve that which was hindered by years of intimacy. In the case of wild geese, I have repeatedly noticed that a betrothal was pledged when two fairly close friends met again after a fairly long separation. Even I myself have been affected by this quite typical phenomenon—but that is another story.

. . .

An enormous old timber wolf and a rather weaker, obviously younger one are the opposing champions and they are moving in circles round each other, exhibiting admirable "footwork." At the same time, the bared fangs flash in such a rapid exchange of snaps that the eye can scarcely follow them. So far, nothing has really happened. The jaws of one wolf close on the gleaming white teeth of the other who is on the alert and wards off the attack. Only the lips have received one or two minor injuries. The younger wolf is gradually being forced backwards. It dawns upon us that the older one is purposely maneuvering him towards the fence. We wait with breathless anticipation what will happen when he "goes to the wall." Now he strikes the wire netting, stumbles . . . and the old one is upon him. And now the incredible happens, just the opposite of what you would expect. The furious whirling of the grey bodies has come to a sudden standstill. Shoulder to shoulder they stand, pressed against each other in a stiff and strained attitude, both heads now facing in the same direction. Both wolves are growling angrily, the elder in a deep bass, the younger in higher tones, suggestive of the fear that underlies his threat. But notice carefully the position of the two opponents; the older wolf had his muzzle close, very close against the neck of the younger, and the latter holds away his head, offering unprotected to his enemy the bend of his neck, the most vulnerable part of his whole body! Less than an inch from the tense neck-muscles, where the jugular vein lies immediately beneath the skin, gleam the fangs of his antagonist from beneath the wickedly retracted lips. Whereas, during the thick of the fight, both wolves were intent on keeping only their teeth, the one invulnerable part of the body, in opposition to each other, it now appears that the discomfited fighter proffers intentionally that part of his anatomy to which a bite must assuredly prove fatal. Appearances are notoriously deceptive, but in his case, surprisingly, they are not!

. . .

Whatever may be the reasons that prevent the dominant individual from injuring the submissive one, whether he is prevented from doing so by a simple and purely mechanical reflex process or by a highly philosophical moral standard, is immaterial to the practical issue. The essential behavior of the submissive as well as of the dominant partner remains the same: the humbled creature suddenly seems to lose his objections to being injured and removes all obstacles from the path of the killer, and it would seem that the very removal of these outer obstacles raises an insurmountable inner obstruction in the central nervous system of the aggressor.

And what is a human appeal for mercy after all? Is it so very different from what we have just described? The Homeric warrior who wishes to yield and plead mercy, discards helmet and shield, falls on his knees and inclines his head, a set of actions which should make it easier for the enemy to kill, but, in reality, hinders him from doing so. As Shakespeare makes Nestor say of Hector:

> "Thou has hung thy advanced sword i' the air,
> Not letting it decline on the declined."

Even today, we have retained many symbols of such submissive attitudes in a number of our gestures of courtesy: bowing, removal of the hat, and presenting arms in military ceremonial. If we are to believe the ancient epics, an appeal to mercy does not seem to have raised an "inner obstruction" which was entirely insurmountable. Homer's heroes were certainly not as soft-hearted as the wolves of Whipsnade! In any case, the poet cites numerous instances where the supplicant was slaughtered with or without compunction. The Norse heroic sagas bring us many examples of similar failures of the submissive gesture and it was not till the era of knight-errantry that it was no longer considered "sporting" to kill a man who begged for mercy. The Christian knight is the first who, for reasons of traditional and religious morals, is as chivalrous as is the wolf from the depth of his natural impulses and inhibitions. What a strange paradox!

Of course, the innate, instinctive, fixed inhibitions that prevent an animal from using his weapons indiscriminately against his own kind are only a functional analogy, at the most a slight foreshadowing, a genealogical predecessor of the social morals of man. The worker in comparative ethology does well to be very careful in applying moral criteria to animal behavior. But here, I must myself own to harboring sentimental feelings: I think it a truly magnificent thing that one wolf finds himself unable to bite the proffered neck of the other, but still more so that the other relies upon him for this amazing restraint. Mankind can learn a lesson from this, from the animal that Dante calls "la bestia senza pace." I at least have extracted from it a new and deeper understanding of a wonderful and often misunderstood saying from the Gospel which hitherto had only awakened in me feelings of strong opposition: "And unto him that smiteth thee on the one cheek offer also the other." (St. Luke VI, 26). A wolf has enlightened me: not so that your enemy may strike you again do you turn the other cheek toward him, but to make him unable to do it.

When, in the course of its evolution, a species of animals develops a weapon which may destroy a fellow-member at one blow, then, in order to survive, it must develop, along with the weapon, a social inhibition to prevent a usage which could endanger the existence of the species. Among the predatory animals, there are only a few which lead so solitary a life that they can, in general, forego such restraint. They come together only at the mating season when the sexual impulse outweighs all others, including that of aggression. Such unsociable hermits are the polar bear and the jaguar and, owing to the absence of these social inhibitions, animals of these species, when kept together in Zoos, hold a sorry record for murdering their own kind. The system of special inherited impulses and inhibitions, together with the weapons with which a social species is provided by nature, form a complex which is carefully computed and self-regulating. All living beings have received their weapons through the same process of evolution that molded their impulses and inhibitions; for the structural plan of the body and the system of behavior of a species are parts of the same whole.

> "If such be Nature's holy plan,
>    Have I not reason to lament
>    What man has made of man?"

Wordsworth is right: there is only one being in possession of weapons which do not grow on his body and of whose working plan, therefore, the instincts of his species know nothing and in the usage of which he has no correspondingly adequate inhibition. That being is man. With unarrested growth his weapons increase in monstrousness, multiplying horribly within a few decades. But innate impulses and inhibitions, like bodily structures, need time for their development, time on a scale in which geologists and astronomers are accustomed to calculate, and not historians. We did not receive our weapons from nature. We made them ourselves, of our own free will. Which is going to be easier for us in the future, the production of the weapons or the engendering of the feeling of responsibility that should go along with them, the inhibitions without which our race must perish by virtue of its own creations? We must build up these inhibitions purposefully for we cannot rely upon our instincts. Fourteen years ago, in November 1935, I concluded an article on "Morals and Weapons of Animals" which appeared in a Viennese journal, with the words, "The day will come when two warring factions will be faced with the possibility of each wiping the other out completely. The day may come when the whole of mankind is divided into two such opposing camps. Shall we then behave like doves or like wolves? The fate of mankind will be settled by the answer to this question." We may well be apprehensive.

In this article, British anthropologist Geoffrey Gorer says that man may be a killer, but it is not because of his instincts. Why, then, does man take pleasure in killing? Why does he hate? Gorer compares rat packs to the nation-state and speaks of the advantages of the nation-state over the territory of the clan and the tribe. What are the advantages? What are the disadvantages of the large nation?

# Man Has No "Killer" Instinct

Geoffrey Gorer

One of the most persistent and widespread beliefs about "human nature" held by men of goodwill in most of the advanced societies in the world is that human beings are "naturally" peaceful and gentle, considerate of their fellow human beings and unwilling to hurt or kill them save under the (assumedly) exceptional conditions of war.

This belief in the essential gentleness of "human nature" can only be maintained by a wilful blindness that refuses to recognize the evidence which history, social anthropology, the daily newspapers and television so constantly provide of man's willingness to hurt and kill his fellows, and to take pride and pleasure in so doing.

In recent months we have read detailed accounts and seen gruesome pictures of Ibos and Hausas gleefully slaughtering one another in Nigeria, of massacres of Indonesians and Chinese in Java and other islands of the archipelago, of Chinese youngsters with red armlets self-righteously humiliating their elders, not to mention both sides in Vietnam. If we try to console ourselves by claiming that most of these slaughters and humiliations were the acts of people who were not civilized and not Christian, this consolation should be short-lived. The Boers and white Rhodesians claim Christian justification for the ill-treatment of their fellow citizens with darker skins; the pictures of the school at Grenada, Miss., are surely not forgotten; and no recorded "uncivilized" nation has equaled the systematic humiliation and slaughter practiced by Christian Germany and her allies a bare generation ago.

All known societies make a distinction between murder—the killing of a member of one's own group—and the killing of outsiders. We can understand murder for jealousy or gain or safety, however much we reprobate and punish it; we think it "rational." But when somebody kills without a "rational" motive—nurses in a dormitory, students from a university tower, policemen in a street—we are puzzled, disturbed and fascinated. The murder of eight nurses or three policemen will hold our attention over longer periods and with more intensity than the slaughter of masses of Javanese.

Contemporary psychological science is at a loss to account for people killing one another without a "rational" motive, according to our standards; an implicit hypothesis in all Western thinking, both scientific and popular, is that man has built-in instincts against killing except under extreme provocation. When people in our own societies kill without a "good reason" we tend to use the term "psychopath"; but this is really a scientific-sounding confession of ignorance and impotence.

Sometimes this pseudo-explanation is applied to killers in other societies; but more frequently the Malayan term "running amok" is used. In Malaya, and some other societies, individuals may suddenly start killing strangers, and amok is the Malayan term for this kind of behavior. This is, however, a description, not an explanation.

Some people reject the hypothesis that man is naturally peaceable and instead, invoke the hypothesis of a "killer instinct" as an aspect of man's hereditary endowment. This "instinct" is held to be normally under strong restraint in "civilized societies" but capable of erupting in "psychopathic" individuals and nearer the surface in "savage" societies. Were there evidence for such an "instinct" it would offer a sort of explanation for the joy of killing, for which there is such plentiful evidence; but I will argue that this is an unnecessary hypothesis.

The most important statement, almost without question, about this aspect of human nature made in this century is that contained in the recent book of the ethologist Konrad Lorenz, translated into English under the title, "On Aggression." He shows that all the carnivores, the mammals which kill other species for their food, have innate inhibitions (instincts, if the term be preferred) against killing members of their own species, with two exceptions—rats and men. The animals with potentially lethal teeth, claws or horns can be automatically stopped from pressing an attack on a fellow member of the species by signs of submission, either flight or some physical analogue to raising the hands or showing the white flag. Once the species-specific signs of submission are made, the attacker automatically halts; he literally *cannot* kill his defeated rival.

Dr. Lorenz argues that there is an evolutionary connection between the large carnivores' lethal physical equipment and the innate inhibitions against using this physical equipment on fellow members of the same species. In comparison, man is physically ill-equipped; his teeth and nails are not adapted to killing large animals of other species; and even his strong and clever hands could seldom be used on healthy beasts. It has indeed been argued that very early man, away from the seacoasts, relied on carrion for his protein. Since man is so physically ill-equipped for killing, he did not acquire the built-in inhibitions against killing other men as part of the evolutionary protection of the species, as wolves or tigers did for their co-specifies. And then he invented weapons.

To avoid confusion, it should be emphasized that for all carnivores, including man, killing other species of animals for food is innately of a different nature from killing members of the same species for rivalry or jealously or pleasure. In animals, there is no connection between hunting and ferocity toward members of their own species; ethology gives no support to the arguments of tender-minded human beings that man would be less ferocious if he abstained from eating meat.

The Latin proverb, *homo homini lupus*—man is a wolf to man—has been taken over by nearly every society which derives its customs, laws or language from ancient Rome. This is a libel on the wolf, which is a gentle animal with other wolves. Ethologically more appropriate would be *homo homini mus rattus*—man is a rat to man—for, exceptionally among carnivores, rats do sometimes kill other rats. In his mating and child-rearing patterns, in his vision, and in some other aspects, man resembles birds more than he does other mammals; but in his treatment of his own species there is an uncomfortably close analogy with rats.

Rats live in packs or hordes; and (still following Dr. Lorenz) they do not fight seriously with, much less kill, members of the same pack. But they are quite merciless to members of alien packs; they kill them slowly and painfully and (if one wishes to be anthropomorphic) they seem to get pleasure from so doing. They share our lack of built-in inhibitions against killing members of the same species.

The analogy with human beings is almost total. Human beings also live in packs (in most cases the pack is the society) and the killing of other members of the pack is always forbidden (save, occasionally, under carefully defined rules) and typically subject to very severe sanctions; but this ban and these sanctions do not usually apply to members of other packs. As is well known, very many primitive tribes have only a single word to designate members of the tribe and human beings; they alone are fully human, members of other packs are (so to speak) subhuman, and killing them is not murder. This primitive type of rat-thinking is never far below the surface, even among the civilized and sensitive.

Where human beings differ from rats is in their very varying definitions of who shall be included within the pack. Usually, the pack is the society or tribe, people who speak the same language (typically unique to the tribe) and between whom real or suppositious bonds of kinship can be traced; but there are variants in both directions.

The smallest packs known to me are those described by Dr. and Mrs. Ronald M. Berndt, who studied four contiguous language groups in the Eastern Highlands of New Guinea. Here the people one should not kill are certain specified kinfolk and a few relations of one's wife or wives. Everyone else, irrespective of ancestry or language, was fit prey for the "deadly game" of death, for only by killing can a man earn power and prestige. The dead were eaten and, in the case of women, raped either before or after death.

The only reason why these packs had not exterminated one another before the Australians pacified the area a bare decade ago is that they practiced a policy of preservation of human game. They seldom killed more than they could eat, and left the temporarily weak in peace to breed. The gleeful, guiltless accounts that Dr. and Mrs. Berndt gathered from the participants in these orgies of slaughter, cannibalism and rape read like a nightmare vision of human savagery.

New Guinea also contains one of the relatively few tribes described by anthropologists in whom the joy of killing seems to be completely absent. These are the Arapesh, studied by Dr. Margaret Mead and Dr. Reo Fortune. They will be discussed in more detail subsequently.

For most of humanity, the tribe is the unit within which killing is considered murder, and outside which killing may be a proof of manhood and bravery, a pleasure and a duty. Such killing may be done by individuals—head-hunters, scalp-collectors, as part of a vendetta or raid—or by groups; in the latter case the killing is called "warfare." The differences in quality and scope between tribal warfare and modern war between nation-states are so great that it might be useful if different words were used for the two activities.

The nation-state was invented after the Neolithic revolution, less than 10,000 years ago; and this is a very short period in man's evolutionary history. One of the advantages of the nation-state is that it greatly extended the area within which killing would be murder; a number of tribes were brought under the same law and equally protected from mutual slaughter. This amalgamation is not now an easy one, as the sad condition of contemporary Nigeria or Indonesia demonstrates; and it probably was no less difficult in the past. There are no reliable contemporary records of the establishment of the first nation-states, mostly along the great rivers of Asia and North Africa; by the time adequate historical records commence, a dominant group had succeeded in preserving peace among the component tribes. The pack was successfully extended to include and protect most of the inhabitants of a given geographical area, even though slaves and captives were usually excluded.

The nation-state is really the last successful human invention for extending the size of the pack, within which killing is murder. In the past 4,000 years a number of religions have been founded which would include all believers inside the pack; but no religion has commanded worldwide allegiance; and regularly the outcasts, infidels, untouchables, heathen or heretics could all be humiliated or killed with added pleasure and self-righteousness, because they were members of the devil's pack.

The founders of the great world religions, Gautama Buddha, Jesus, Lao-Tzu, Mohammed, all seem to have striven for a worldwide brotherhood of man; but none of them could develop institutions which would include the enemy, the unbeliever, and give him the same protection from anger, hatred and the lust for killing which they decreed within their own congregations.

Within the last century and a half, various millennial ideologies—democracy, Socialism, the Communist internationals, the United Nations—have taken over the goal of the traditional religions: the establishment of a world-wide brotherhood of man, a single pack. They have been no more successful than their predecessors in protecting the enemy, the unbeliever, from the horrible results of righteous anger.

In recent centuries, most men of goodwill have at least paid lip-service to the ideal of a universal brotherhood with equal protection for all, whatever might be their actual behavior or that of their compatriots. But this century has seen a most sinister recrudescence of rat-pack ideology, in which human status is denied to all persons who do not share one's hypothetical ancestry or visible skin color: Fascism, Nazism, white supremacy, black power all justify hatred and contempt for those outside the pack; and recent history shows how easily, how very easily, this justified hatred and contempt develop into humiliation, torture and killing.

The evidence could be endlessly multiplied to demonstrate that man, as a species, has no inhibitions against killing his fellow men who do not belong to the same pack, however the pack may be defined, and often gets intense pleasure and a sense of pride from so doing. But to admit this is not the same as positing a "killer instinct" as part of man's hereditary endowment. There is no logical reason for hypothesizing such an instinct, and indeed some arguments, to be advanced shortly, against doing so.

Because men have no innate instinctual inhibitions against hurting and killing other members of their species, this offers some human beings a potential source of intense pleasure, as do incest, homosexuality and other sexual deviations. Man has no built-in inhibitions against these sources of pleasure either; did he possess them, laws would be unnecessary. Whether any of these pleasures will be sought, how frequently, and by whom, depends on the values of a specific society at a given time and the vicissitudes of individual lives.

Because man can and does gain intense pleasure from humiliating, hurting and killing his fellows, the speculative novels of the Marquis de Sade are extremely important documents, whatever their literary qualities. Save in a directly sexual situation (when he relished flagellation), de Sade was an affectionate, humane and very courageous man. In his 13-year-long solitary confinement he looked without flinching into the deepest recesses of his unconscious fantasies and reported, in fictional form, the pleasures to be derived from the unfettered exercise of power over one's fellow men and women.

De Sade linked these pleasures with the pleasures of sex; this was the only metaphor which contemporary science made available to him and it was congenial to his temperament. Even so, there are many episodes in the novels when power is used for its own sake— power to humiliate, hurt or kill—without any overt sexual gratification. De Sade wished to portray "the spasms of man's loathsome heart and fearful passions" because he was convinced that only by acknowledging the truth about human nature, as he saw it, could a safe and just society be built.

Classical psychoanalysis has in good part confirmed de Sade's pessimistic diagnosis of "man's loathsome heart." Freud always maintained the central position in his theory of the Oedipus complex; and the little Oedipus had murder in his heart, the killing of his father—a point which many contemporary psychoanalysts tend to gloss over. According to the findings of the late Melanie Klein and her followers, the inchoate hatred and rages of very young children produce wishes which, when translated into verbal metaphors,

parallel the fantasies of de Sade: cannibalism, poisoning, eviscera-
tion, castration, murder.

The history of civilized nations in the century and a half since de
Sade's death also confirms his pessimistic diagnosis of human behavior. Although he placed no bounds on his imagination, we have
been witnesses to far greater horrors than de Sade could dream of;
man can be an even more savage monster than he guessed. It is possible that, had de Sade's diagnosis of human potentialities been taken
consistently into account, the fanatics, torturers and murderers would
have had less impunity in the indulging of their fearful passions.

There are, however, a few rays of hope, a few societies where
men seem to find no pleasure in dominating over, hurting or killing
the members of other societies, where all they ask is to be at peace
and to be left in peace. These societies are, of course, small, weak,
technologically backward, and living in inaccessible country; only so
could they survive the power-seeking of their uninhibited neighbors.

Among these gentle societies are the Arapesh of New Guinea,
mentioned earlier; the Lepchas of Sikkim in the Himalayas (whom
I studied); and, most impressive of all, the pygmies of the Ituri rain-
forest in the Congo, studied by Colin Turnbull. These small societies
(there are several others) living in the most inaccessible deserts and
forests and mountains of four continents, have a number of traits in
common, besides the fact that they do not dominate over, hurt or kill
one another or their neighbors, though they possess the weapons to
do so. Many of them, including the pygmies and the Lepchas until a
couple of generations ago, rely almost exclusively on hunting for
their protein food.

What seem to me the most significant common traits in these
peaceful societies are that they all manifest enormous gusto for
concrete physical pleasures—eating, drinking, sex, laughter—and
that they all make very little distinction between the ideal characters
of men and women, particularly that they have no ideal of brave,
aggressive masculinity.

Men and women have different primary sexual characteristics—a
source of endless merriment as well as of more concrete satisfactions—and some different skills and aptitudes. No child, however,
grows up with the injunctions, "All real men do . . . " or "No
proper woman does . . . ," so that there is no confusion of sexual
identity: no cases of sexual inversion have been reported among
them. The model for the growing child is of concrete performance
and frank enjoyment, not of metaphysical symbolic achievements or
of ordeals to be surmounted. They do not have heroes or martyrs to

emulate or cowards or traitors to despise; their religious life lacks significant personalized gods and devils; a happy, hard-working and productive life is within the reach of all.

As far as the history of these small tribes can be reconstructed, they have always chosen to retreat into ever more inaccessible country rather than stand their ground and fight with invaders. There is no reason to suppose that their psychological or physiological potentialities are different from those of their more aggressive neighbors, but their values certainly are; for them peace and the absence of quarreling and jealousy are far more important than a reputation for bravery and virility. And while the tribes are not broken up, it is likely that these values will continue to prevail. When the tribes are broken, individuals, unsupported by the traditional ethics, might easily revert to rat-pack mentality. Save that they have so far survived, these small tribes have not been conspicuously successful in the struggle for existence and terrain against more ruthless neighbors. Nevertheless, they may offer a paradigm of ways to diminish the joy of killing in the uninhibited human race.

By contrast, the cannibals in the New Guinea Highlands have a highly aggressive ideal of masculinity; and so, in general, do all the peoples who prize the martial virtues and self-righteously kill their enemies or their "inferiors." The New Guinea Highlanders frankly enjoy sex, especially if it approximates to rape; but many other martial societies repudiate all sensual pleasure as unworthy of a Real Man. If our gods and heroes are killers—Lords of Hosts, warriors, successful revolutionaries—and if masculinity is demonstrated by the willingness to give and take "punishment," then the joy of killing is always likely to re-emerge.

It seems possible that the youth international, which has developed nearly the whole world over in the last generation, has inarticulately sensed the necessity to redefine the concepts of a "real man" and "a true woman" if we are not to destroy ourselves completely. The long hair, dandified dress and pleasantly epicene features (which so infuriate their elders) are a physical repudiation of the ideal of aggressive masculinity which has been traditional in all their societies in recent generations, and which is still maintained by the conventional and the neo-Fascists (white supremacists, Empire loyalists, Birchites and the like) in the same societies.

Even idiotic slogans such as "Make love, not war" (as if the two activities had ever been incompatible!) and the use of drugs make the same point. Mankind is safer when men seek pleasure than when they seek the power and the glory.

If the members of the youth international—the beats and the swingers, the *provos* and the *stilyagi*—maintain the same scale of values and the same sex ideals 20 years hence when they themselves are middle-aged and parents, then they may, just possibly, have produced a permanent change in the value systems and sex roles of their societies, which will turn the joy of killing into an unhappy episode of man's historic past, analogous to human sacrifice, which ascribed joy in killing to the gods also.

The attempts to devise a social unit more inclusive than the nation-state, a brotherhood of man, have all been unsuccessful to date. It is just possible that the youth international, with its emphasis on shared sensual pleasure and its repudiation of the ideal of truculent "manliness," may succeed where the grandiose schemes of idealists have always failed. For man has no "killer instinct"; he merely lacks inhibitions.

What is there about violence and violent sports that is so attractive to so many people? We have our much talked about violence on television, our long attraction for the gun, our history of the Wild West, and our gangsters and ganster movies. Stimulation and excitement is headlined on both the front page and the sports page. Bob Oates, "Los Angeles Times" staff writer, surveys the sports world and the nearby academic world in search of answers.

# Violent Sports: Furious Tribal Instincts Freed?

Bob Oates

The invitation had come from the coach of the San Diego Chargers; "Let's put it on the screen." And now, as he turned on the lights, Sid Gillman was smiling. "Beautiful," he said.

In the movie, three linebackers had assaulted a quarterback, knocking him down and out.

Gillman said, "I have never known a football player who didn't want to hit you with everything he had. Hitting is the nature of the animal and the game."

In the country today, this is a popular view. The more violent sports, from hockey to auto racing, are attracting more attention each year. Every football coach endorses, and teaches, violence.

"But I am convinced there is right and wrong violence," Gillman said, pointing to a newspaper headline. "I'm in favor of the football kind—not the Harvard campus kind."

This also is a popular view in America.

A contradiction of the era is that whereas violence is deplored on streets and campuses, it seems to be admired and encouraged in stadiums.

Why? Are humans instinctively violent? In their sports preferences, are the American people expressing socially unacceptable impulses in acceptable ways? Or is there another explanation for the expanding interest in rougher sports?

The answer may be in two parts:

1—Most psychologists and sociologists believe that man's disposition to violence is not an instinct. Rather, it is learned. The thing that distinguishes man, they say, is a capacity for generalized learning. And in recent years he has been conditioned to appreciate both the fury and the science of more active games.

2—Athletes and sports fans alike are attracted by the interplay of both elements: (a) the violence and (b) the science (skills, techniques and ability founded on training, discipline and experience).

A sport which tends to be one-sided—emphasizing skills without much savagery, or vice versa—engages the attention of fewer Americans than a sport based on the combinations.

The essential interest comes from the art and science of each sport. The excitement comes from the violence: from athletes testing their skills in situations of "the right kind."

Both elements are illustrated in professional football.

Says all-pro Merlin Olsen of the Rams: "Frankly, what I like about football is that it gives me a chance to demonstrate my ability and courage at the same time. I've never cared for non-contact games of skill—but I don't get any kick, either, out of beating up a guy just for the hell of it. I need a reason to hit him."

"In football," he says, "you've got to intimidate a man physically and dominate him intellectually. You have to show him who's boss and who's smarter. That's the challenge, and I love it."

Along with most football players, Olsen accepts rather than revels in the violence. But he doesn't underestimate it.

"Aggressiveness," he says, "is what puts football in tune with the times, more so than baseball or other sports. This is an aggressive country. Our economic system is the most aggressive in the world. School kids are taught to compete aggressively for scholarships. Aggression is all over television and the newspapers. It's only natural that the most aggressive games are the best liked."

What it may come down to is that a rough sport is a picturesque example of the "American way."

Lance Alworth, for instance, and Rudi Nureyev are men of similar skills and size, although one is a pro football player for the Chargers and the other a ballet dancer. To American spectators, Rudi is interesting—whereas Lance is both interesting and exciting.

Alworth's thing is Nureyev's thing in a setting of violence. The slim Alworth as an all-pro pass receiver is grace in action—but his stage is a booby trap. It can and has blown up under him.

Alworth moves elegantly through a mine field of roughnecks; he extends his great talent along the brink of a total wipeout.

And it is this that draws Alworth, and the spectators, to football.

In Los Angeles, ice hockey is the newest major league manifestation of this kind of art and malice—though an ineffective team has held down the crowds that illustrate the point more convincingly elsewhere.

Says Larry Regan, general manager of the Kings:

"The most violent hockey team usually wins. Hitting is half of this game, and a collision gets the crowd on its feet every time. But the other half—speed and skating—is just as vital.

"Hockey," says Regan, "is the only sport in which to play it skill-fully, you have to learn another skill first—skating. Any American boy can swing a bat or carry a football or a hockey stick. The trick in hockey is not just to put a stick on a baseball or a golf ball or a puck —but to do this when you're speeding along on a sheet of ice, or cutting sharply, and all the time keeping yourself balanced on two little blades one-eighth of an inch thick. And at the same time, keep-ing your eye open for a guy who wants to bust you heels over tea kettle."

Boys and men alike are attracted to hockey by these double chal-lenges to ability and inner fortitude—and much the same is true of boxing, although this sport is better known for violence than skill.

Boxing is widely considered to be the prima facie example of the most violent thing one man can do to another without a weapon. Under supervision in a licensed ring, however, this is a sport less violent than football, according to promoter Aileen Eaton of the Olympic.

"A 200-pound quarterback," says Mrs. Eaton, "is fair game for a 290-pound defensive lineman. We'd never allow that in boxing. Be-fore a match is made, the whole object is to get athletes of even weight, even strength and even ability.

"This is the only sport," she says, "that is so concerned about those things—in terms of injury and punishment. In football, certainly, the object sometimes seems to be just the opposite."

Boxing also is the one sport in which the goal is to knock another human being senseless. This is the aspect which repels non-boxing fans. But in the majority, those who like boxing are probably no more bloodthirsty than the average of the rest of us.

"Violence is the least part of boxing," Mrs. Eaton insists. "The appeal is a pair of well-matched athletes on their own in a small ring—with no help coming from a defensive platoon or a home-run hitter batting fourth. Who's the better man? That's boxing."

That's automobile racing, too—in the judgment of those who com-pete in one of America's fastest-rising sports.

The late Tony Bettenhausen once said that the appeal of an In-dianapolis ride rests on its "extended challenge" to each man to prove himself.

"Any good motorist can navigate one turn," he said. "The challenge is 200 laps: you alone against determined men and machinery."

Machine racing remains under fire in this country both for its "unnecessary" risks (Bettenhausen was killed testing a race car at Indianapolis) and for its "unhealthy" stimulus to the race public. But those who have studied race crowds for many years doubt the charge that the typical race fan is "blood-thirsty."

Says former Ram linebacker Les Richter: "The race driver balances on the fringe of disaster, of total tragedy. You're there to see him dance on the fringe, not go over. The 'almost' accident is the thrill, not the tragic accident."

Richter, now the president of Riverside International Raceway, was regarded as the roughest linebacker of his time. He once provoked a Coliseum opponent to take off his helmet and swing it like a hammer on Richter's head. Richter speaks as a two-sport expert when he says:

"Football fans are there to see John Unitas with his back to the wall—facing a violent end at the hands of Deacon Jones—and they want Unitas to stand there and take it. They want him to try for a touchdown pass instead of taking the easy way out and running off with the ball.

"It is the same in racing. The thrill is watching human beings weave through murderous traffic at 150 m.p.h. with their life in their two hands. But if a man is hurt, everybody feels it; everybody hurts."

Richter expands on this thought with a theory about sports crowds that may be definitive.

"Every sports fan, including me," he says, "is a Walter Mitty. He puts himself in the car or on the hockey rink and wishes he were brave enough to do what he is seeing. Bravery is the pull."

Psychologists agree in general that athletes and spectators are "psychologically similar." Thus it is likely that the rise of public interest in the more violent games (as compared with the more passive games: baseball, soccer, track and field, etc.) is due in part to the public's growing appetite for (or tolerance of) violence.

There are other reasons. Speaking of team sports as a whole, their overall appeal probably rests to a large extent on their entertainment value and two other things:

1—The fan identifies with the hometown team and when it wins, he is happier. He feels better. HE is a winner.

2—When his team loses, it wasn't the fan who lost the game. The spectator, who was only mentally engaged on the field, can now dissociate himself from the players and blame them. They are now "bums."

Accordingly, the fan is invincible. He can win, but he can't lose.

In this context, the violent side of sports is an extra dimension—a bonus thrill.

The lure, in some respects, is synthetic: hockey fans hope to see sticks in the air and blows landed, but sociologists can find no proof that they are ecstatic when skulls are fractured.

At baseball games the fans may holler, "Stick it in his ear." They may implore the pitcher to knock the batter down.

"But the fans don't really mean it," says Bill Rigney, the manager of the California Angels.

"They're just blowing off steam," Rigney believes. "Nobody wants to see a player beaned."

Curiously, the introduction of the protective batting helmet in recent years may have changed baseball in subtle ways—and not entirely for the better. Batting, to begin with, is something more than "the most difficult sports skill to master," as Ted Williams calls it. It is an act of bravery. A man standing at the plate with a bat, but without a helmet, commits his life to the accuracy of the bullet throwers of the major leagues.

But put him under a helmet and some of the fear leaves him, and some of the concentration, too.

Says Rigney: "I often think they get careless standing there under those magical hats. They don't have to think about getting hurt any more, and pretty soon they aren't even thinking about what they're doing. If the pitchers would brush them back more often, they'd be doing them a favor.

"But baseball today frowns on the brushback pitch," Rigney sighs. "It used to be that a manager could sit in a dugout and yell to his pitcher, 'Knock him down.' But no more. Today, the rules forbid it."

The irony is that as the rest of the world grows more violent, baseball, which has never been the most savage national pastime, gets safer. It has the helmet now and more scruples.

It has been speculated that the sport is losing ground for this reason. In a national poll (the Harris Survey) last month, football was listed as the "favorite sport" of more Americans (31%) than any other. Baseball, second with 28%, had never been out of the lead before. Five years ago when baseball was first with 40%, football had 25%.

In the nominally non-contact game of basketball, acts of physical aggression have a different meaning.

Says Jerry West, the Laker star :"In the NBA, the first thing you have to show the old pros is that you can 'take it.' "

Answering a question about [former] UCLA All-American Lew

Alcindor's professional future, West says:

"Much depends on how Lew handles the rough stuff. He will be shouldered, elbowed and stepped on. Big men will drive through him if they can. I think Lew can take it, but we'll have to wait and see."

Track and field is the perfect example of the one-sided non-violent sport demanding the most carefully refined skills.

Says USC track coach Vern Wolfe: "In our sport, if a runner so much as steps in front of another runner, he is disqualified. I guess the most exciting thing that ever happened to us was the day a shot putter wound up and punched another shot putter in the nose."

There is a correlation between lack of violence and lack of public interest in track—and also in such sports as swimming, diving, tennis and golf.

Coach Wolfe, speaking for the artists of the non-contact sports, says: "They work just as hard as football men. And they have just as many skills. They have everything but the crowds."

In some sports, it has been shown that sex appeal is box office—when combined with violence. Hockey and wrestling are examples.

Says Regan of the Kings: "Women love hockey, and many come unescorted. They like to get close to big, strong men who do violent, masculine things. There isn't as much sex appeal in football, where the field is far away. It's hard for a girl to identify herself with a faceless man. In hockey you can almost touch the man. When he's hit, you can see the expression change on his face."

On wrestling nights at the Olympic, where simulated violence is continuous, there also is a large proportion of women, many unescorted. It has been suggested that some are sexually attracted.

An oddity of wrestling is that its fans are among the most violent in sports and its participants among the least.

Soccer, in one sense, is like wrestling. There isn't much genuine violence in soccer, yet it provokes violent outbursts in the crowd. In Peru, a moat around the field separates fans and athletes. In other countries there are chain-link fences.

And there may be another link—between the non-violence of soccer and its furious fans, who, herded into a packed stadium, achieve no emotional release from the game because nobody has been beaten up.

Social scientists are not united on this explanation. But most of them appear to be in agreement with Mike Ditka and other football players that the action of a forceful game serves as an outlet for tensions.

Ditka, now with the Dallas Cowboys, feels "more calm" in the autumn pressures of the football season than he does in the winter and spring. He doubts the popular notion in America that acts of violence "stimulate" aggressors to more aggressions.

"A lot of football players," says Ditka, "build up anxieties in the off-season because they have no outlet for them. I'm most relaxed when I'm playing football. If I'm not getting rid of my energy this way, I blow it off in some way that isn't proper in this society."

Many hockey and football fans might make a similar self-analysis.

Says a USC psychologist, Dr. Donald J. Lewis: "Most of us get a release out of a controlled, forceful spectacle like football."

Lewis concedes that public interest in violence is rising. So is research on the subject on the torn campuses of the nation, where the usual starting point is a question: Were the agitators (or the football players) born violent?

Psychology's answer: There is no evidence that violence is transmitted in the genes from one generation to the next.

Dr. Lewis says, "The only instincts—or at least the only unlearned reactions built into the nervous system—are, first, the drives for sex, food, water and oxygen; second, the need for activity and rest after activity; avoidance of pain. Some psychologists might add one or two things to the list and some would subtract one or two."

It is clear to most scientists that there is no inborn, powerful need for violence as such.

A belief widely persists, nonetheless, that there is a "fighting instinct" in man. Otherwise, why do athletes and spectators tend to choose violent games of skill over non-violent games of skill?

Social scientists hold in general that "man is mostly what he learns to be." In an aggressive environment he is aggressive. Introduced to games combining skill and aggression, he likes the combination.

Psychology approaches the subject from a viewpoint explained by USC's Dr. Lewis in a comment on the effects of televised violence: "Each man's reaction is determined by his social training. For a small percentage, violence leads to violence. For others, it is a cathartic. The majority simply adapts to it—and the more violence, the more widely tolerated."

Psychology finds, furthermore, that aggression is related to frustration. Dr. Lewis says:

"If any organism (including man) is blocked or thwarted in its efforts to reach any instinctive goal, it flails out immediately. This is a basic attempt to remove one frustration. But the form this takes is purely learned. A man can say 'gol-darn it' in a letter to the editor or he can put on a football uniform. These are both expressions of aggression."

In sports terms, the interest in violence often is not so much "learned" as "taught" (or coached). This has been the contribution of such men as Vince Lombardi, former Green Bay Packer coach now with the Washington Redskins, and Punch Imlach, coach of the Toronto hockey team.

A pertinent comment is found in anthropology. Dr. Sally Carrighar, a British anthropologist, writes:

"Aggressiveness can be taught . . . It also intensifies when it is exercised and atrophies when it is not . . . When men began to settle in communities, they learned the irritations of being crowded . . . With words they could incite hatred against neighboring tribes.

"A leader—coveting power or property—could, with propaganda, instill in his subjects admiration for warlike attitudes."

In American sports, it will be recalled that for nine years in Green Bay, coach Lombardi "instilled in his subjects admiration for warlike attitudes."

Moreover, "coveting power and property," he admitted that he incited hatred against neighboring tribes.

Football is a good modern example of man's tribal pulls to both cooperation and aggression. A football team is a cooperative of 40 men. And the mainspring of the game is violence.

"Cooperation is teamwork," says San Diego's coach Gillman, "and only two things mean more: courage and skill."

The essay at the beginning of this chapter tried to simplify some aspects of man's behavior. But things are not that simple, as the following article indicates. Human behavior is undergoing greater analysis in the 1970s, and the deeper the probing, the more complex human behavior seems to be. Perhaps, this article suggests, there can be no Utopia but only a discovery of ourselves. Man must make society, and he—with a small "h"—is imperfect.

# The Rediscovery of Human Nature

**Time** magazine

> I believe that the day has come when we can combine sensory deprivation with drugs, hypnosis and astute manipulation of reward and punishment to gain absolute control over an individual's behavior.—James V. McConnell

A behaviorist speaking. In the past four decades the heady belief has grown that people can be molded by simply deciding what they should be and then manipulating their behavior, as though the world were a laboratory and man a rat or a pigeon. No one has done more to advance the notion than B. F. Skinner, Harvard psychology professor and author of the bestselling *Beyond Freedom and Dignity*. . . . Those who claim to leave man "free," Skinner believes, are merely abandoning him to uncontrolled forces in his environment. To Skinner, observable behavior is the only reality and belief in an "inner man" is mere superstition. "Something going on inside the individual, states of mind, feelings, purposes, expectancies"—all these, Skinner insists, are no more than fictions.

Freudianism, the other dogma of the era, is very much concerned with what is going on inside the individual. To Freud, man was, in fact, buffeted about by internal, unconscious drives. These frequently caused neuroses, which, to be sure, could be alleviated by psychoanalysis. Repressed sexuality was a major problem in Freud's day, and he was not particularly concerned with other concepts of neurosis, like the feeling of meaninglessness that is so prevalent today. "I have always confined myself to the ground floor and basement of the edifice called man," Freud once wrote to a friend. As for religion, Freud put it in "the category of the neurosis of mankind."

The psychoanalysts and the behaviorists still man the academy. For all their differences, what do they have in common? They share a reductive, limited view of man, according to the humanistic psychologists working today, who consider themselves a "third force" knocking at the academy gates. In sociology and anthropology, other challenges are being made to long-held beliefs. The challenges add up to a new regard for human intractability—and potentiality. There is a sneaking reappearance of the old notion that certain fixed elements in man (once unscientifically known as "human nature") are not susceptible to environmental changes. That notion obviously has major political overtones, since traditionally liberalism has posited that man is almost infinitely changeable, if not perfectible, while conservatives tend to believe that man is man, and that he has an irreducible core of evil (another nonscientific term).

The best-known humanistic psychoanalyst is Rollo May. Although May feels that psychology owes a debt to Freud for his emphasis on the "irrational, repressed, hostile and unacceptable urges" of a man's past, he also believes that Freud's approach leaves out much that is most human. At the same time, May warns that the behaviorists must beware lest they create a totally mechanical society. "My faith is that the human being will be rediscovered," says May. With this rediscovery, he hopes, will come a new emphasis on love, creativity, music and all the other qualitative, introspective experiences.

These are among the experiences stressed in the "human-potential movement," . . . which includes Esalen and other growth centers. But, writes May in his new [1973] book *Power and Innocence*, "the human-potential movement has fallen heir to the form of innocence prevalent in America, namely that we grow toward greater and greater moral perfection." Evil is present in everyone, along with good, May insists, and one should grow toward greater sensitivity to both.

Anyone is a utopian, says May, who believes "that when we develop a society which trains us rightly, we'll all be in fine shape." He does not agree that "it is society's fault that we are what we are." For one thing, there will always be strong individuals who will step forth from "the conditioned mass." Just as evil is a distinguishing characteristic of human beings, so too is the capacity to rebel, to fight against bureaucracy or loss of integrity. In man's relationship to society, May believes, a new ethic is needed for our age—"an ethic of intention, based on the assumption that each man is responsible for the effects of his own actions."

Just as the behaviorist establishment in psychology has long centered its attention on environmental influences on man, so too have the leading figures in anthropology. From the days of Franz Boas, most American anthropologists have been cultural relativists, seeing each society as distinctive and trying to show how man's feelings and thoughts were shaped by the way he lived. Anthropologists did not believe in a narrowly fixed, hereditary human nature. Early in her career, Margaret Mead, for example, set out to show how even the notions of maleness and femaleness vary from place to place. As she explained later: "It was a simple—a very simple—point to which our materials were organized in the 1920s, merely the documentation over and over of the fact that human nature is not rigid and unyielding." Linguists Edward Sapir and Benjamin Whorf contributed to cultural relativism by stating that different linguistic groups conceive reality in different ways, that the way they think shapes the language they speak and vice versa.

Mead subsequently modified her views, and other anthropologists and linguists came along with different notions. Noam Chomsky contends that the way people learn languages and the structure of those languages are basically the same the world over. Claude Lévi-Strauss, the French structuralist, gathered thousands of myths from different cultures and demonstrated that beyond their great diversity were even greater similarities. At the deepest level, believes Lévi-Strauss, there is an implacable pattern ingrained in the human intellect and this pattern has not changed since primitive times.

To humanists and others who believe that both man and society are perfectible, Lévi-Strauss extends small comfort. "Humanism has failed," he believes. "It has lent itself to excusing and justifying all kinds of horrors. It has misunderstood man. It has tried to cut him off from all other manifestations of nature." He is gloomy about the population explosion, the pollution of air and water and "the destruction of living species, one after another." Like many another student of past societies, he admires those primitive cultures that struck a balance between man and his natural environment.

Two other scholars with a nostalgia for primitive societies are Rutgers' Lionel Tiger and Robin Fox (who met, ironically enough, at the London Zoo). They too believe in implacable, ingrained patterns of behavior that they call "biogrammar." "A species is what it is because of the pattern of successful adaptation built into its genes," they wrote in *The Imperial Animal*. "It is programmed to grow and develop in a highly specific way." Aggression is central to man's emotional evolution and survival. And the mother-infant bond is essential. "Nature intended mother and child to be together." Add the authors: "The human mother is a splendid mammal —the epitome of her order."

Tiger and Fox have been called everything from fascist to sexist to simply "unpersuasive." They are not surprised. "You don't go up to someone who has taught cultural relativism for 40 years and say, 'Sorry, old chap, but you're wrong,' and expect to be loved," says Fox philosophically. He believes that they are being criticized primarily on political grounds.

The critics "think we should be striving for the good and the right and the true."

Tiger and Fox are preaching that man's survival as a species depends on finding out what kind of creature he is. "What is proposed here is not a kind of determinism," they insist. "To those who think that the law of gravity interferes with their freedom, there is nothing to say. To most sensible people, this law is simply something that has to be taken into account in dealing with the world . . . In the behavioral sphere, we may be ignoring laws just as fundamental." Man must learn from his animal heritage, or evolution will be as ruthless with him as it was with the dinosaurs, say the anthropologists who are laying their bets on the biological roots of man's behavior.

A similar conclusion has been reached by a former Harvard professor of government. "We have tended to suppose that every problem must have a solution and that good intentions should somehow guarantee good results," philosophized Henry Kissinger not long ago. "Utopia was seen not as a dream but as our logical destination if we only traveled the right road. Our generation is the first to find that the road is endless, that in traveling it we will find not utopia but ourselves."

Many sociologists are making the same discovery. For them, and for some anthropologists and psychologists as well, a long-held vision of a utopia engineered by human minds has begun to fade. The new mood is one of bitter resignation for many. Others are hopeful that man can apply his newly found will to the realization of his limited but inherent potential. To these optimistic pragmatists, the idea that man is made by society is giving way to the notion that society has to be made by men, with all the personal responsibility and travail that the task entails.

The evolution and development of man's use of language, fire, leisure, and aggression is the subject for debate between Dr. L. S. B. Leakey and Mr. Robert Ardrey. One leans toward the so-called nature school of man's aggression, as developed by Konrad Lorenz; the other leans toward the nurture school of Ashley Montagu and Geoffrey Gorer. Do you agree that the biggest enemy of mankind is not the person but the name? That is, that it is not the individual that is hated so much as the idea he presents to another through language? Language may help unify man, but it also divides him and is a basic cause of aggression.

# Aggression and Violence in Man

Louis Leakey and Robert Ardrey

ARDREY: . . . You will understand that you have before you two of the most opinionated men of the 20th century. Happily, we like each other, and this may ruin the evening as far as I'm concerned. If with this subject of violence you really expect that both of us are going to be carried out on stretchers, having annihilated ourselves by the end of the evening, taken on separate stretchers to separate hospitals, I would suggest you go and get a refund on your ticket immediately. Because we're not going to do it. We like each other and we ritualize our aggressions. May we hope that a few others do, too. . . .

LEAKEY: . . . First of all I think we should cover one or two points on which I know we do not disagree, but just for the sake of the audience, so they will realize what we mean by "man." I don't want them to think we are confining "man" to *Homo sapiens*, because that would cut out a great deal of our argument, and I take it, Robert, that you would agree for this evening at any rate that "man" is in the hominids. The creatures who are our ancestors go way back to *kenyapithecus*, right through our cousins the australopithecines, to the present day. Will you agree?

ARDREY: You can't disagree, because it is a continuous line. You would never be able to find the moment when you could say the animal ended and the man began.

LEAKEY: So we agree on that particular point entirely. And the other thing we have to agree upon, which is very vital indeed, is that we are not discussing aggression in terms of the attacks that man and near-man and proto-man make on animals of other genera of species for the sake of food. That is not aggression in the sense that we are discussing it tonight.

From "Aggression and Violence in Man." A Dialogue between Dr. Louis Leakey and Mr. Robert Ardrey. © 1971 L. S. B. Leakey Foundation, 1100 Glendon Avenue, Los Angeles, California 90024.

Lions eat zebras, but that is not aggression. That is hunting food. And you do agree that we are not discussing that tonight?

ARDREY: Yes. The difficulty with that is you're going to have to say the aggression of the stockyards, where you kill cattle for beef and so on. That is not aggression, obviously, as we have had to kill for food. I agree entirely, although I have a little thing I might ask you about some time.

LEAKEY: But on the whole, you agree we are not going to discuss aggression in the attack form. We are really concerned with where a creature of one species attacks another of his same species, whether it is in australopithecus or in man today or in the past. So we have now eliminated two important things we do agree on, so we won't discuss either of those any further at all.

Now from there, I think we start to disagree a bit, because from my point of view I look at man and man's ancestors as creatures which until they became what Huxley and I call psycho-social men—when they were purely animal men, were like the animals themselves, and not, as far as I can see, aggressive or violent to each other. I will explain a little bit why I think that is so. I think they definitely did not have either the opportunity or the time or the means of any form to be really aggressive against their own species. This was chiefly because (a) there were too few of them on the ground, there was plenty of territory for them not to squabble; and (b) they were still not living in close contact with each other. I believe the beginning of living close together came at a much later date (which I shall discuss in a minute), and I think that is something which was linked with a change from—the animal—at the beginning, and psycho-social man—the man who developed fire, speech, abstract thought and religion, burying his dead, and magic. And I believe, although I don't think Robert would agree on this, that was the turning point at which we, man—. We had been man before that, we had been *Homo sapiens* before that. We were still *Homo sapiens* in the animal, and before that *Homo sapiens* with ancestors *Homo habilis* and his cousins the australopithecines that Dart found in South Africa and we now are finding in East Africa, too. And before that, back to *kenyapithecus wickerii*. I don't believe personally, which is where I think we will disagree, that any of those forms of man, in the widest sense, were aggressive and violent to each other. They hadn't the time, they hadn't the leisure, and I have a horrid suspicion that one of the reasons why we have become aggressive to each other more and more in an ever-increasing way is because we have turned to a way of life which throws us more and more together into great masses of people and gives us more and more leisure to think up things like jealousy, hatred, and malice, and then practice them.

At this point I'll ask Robert if he agrees with what I've said so far. I think he wants to throw some questions at me now about our earliest hominids.

ARDREY: Unfortunately, we do love each other, but we do get into trouble. You have, for example, Peking man—*Homo erectus*—who was evidently a head hunter. You find no body bones at Choukoutien, and you have heads with the underneath hollowed out to extract the brains, or at least most authorities accept it as such. You have a great deal of mayhem in the history of the developing man, but which is personal. You see, if you want to make a line between organized violence and personal violence, I'd say, absolutely, you don't get much organized violence until fairly recent times. Personal violence you get a lot. You can go back a long way and you'll find that somebody clobbered somebody. I think this is like murder today, where two-thirds of murders are committed between people who know each other. And I think we had the same old instincts in the old days. But what I am more concerned about is organized violence, which we have had in more recent times. I think it is perfectly natural for a man to get mad at his wife and hit her over the head and kill her, or vice versa. But this is one of the things that happens that you call "human," and which started early. Did or did not *homo habilis* get conked on the top of the head?

LEAKEY: I'll answer that right away. *Homo habilis* had a hole on the top of his head, the first *habilis* we ever got—the youngster, the 11-year-old. But I have never stated that he was murdered. As far as I am concerned that hole in his head was definitely a sign of death by violence. Whether it was from falling out of a tree or being hit accidentally by a fellow schoolboy (if you can call it that), or whether it was deliberate killing, I don't know. I personally do not think at that stage people were killing each other seriously because they were angry with each other. But it is an open question—I can't prove it.

ARDREY: No, you can't. However, there is a very clean-cut case which is Vertezollos man in Hungary, which was the first known *Homo sapiens* —unless maybe your new one is a bit earlier. But they are the same age— 300,000 to 400,000 years ago—and he was definitely killed by one of the stone implements that lay beside him. His head was caved in by it, and that was the first known *Homo sapiens*. . . . You do have evidence of violence all through, though. I mean, Monte Circeo man and the Neanderthals with his head cut off, and brains hollowed out, and mounted around stones. You have these things, you have evidence of violence. I don't take them all that seriously. We were dangerous animals. We were dangerous to each other. But I don't think this relates necessarily to the modern problem of violence as we know it, which is group violence, organized violence, war, etc.

LEAKEY: I agree. I'd like to take you up on two things. First, I would like to discuss very briefly the Choukoutien man. It is true that there is some evidence of Choukoutien cannibalism, but at the same time Choukoutien is one of the exceptions of the rest of mankind because they were already living in a cave. In other words, there was a cave and they were living in close communities because caves were rare.

ARDREY: May I interrupt to say this is Peking man, as he is more commonly known—say 300- to 500,000 years ago. Peking man with a brain two-thirds the size of our own.

LEAKEY: Yes, Peking man is certainly an exception in that, surprisingly, he had fire. I don't think he had made fire, but I think he was catching wild fire and domesticating it. The evidence shows he had discontinuous fire and he was in caves. And when you start living side by side in the small area of one cave with a lot of different families, then your jealousies are going to start and your hostilities between each other are going to start. My argument is that if you go back to *Homo habilis*, or to early *Homo sapiens*, he was not in a position to really be hostile. He was living in very, very small groups, and, as far as I can see, he did not have *the leisure*, I repeat, *he did not have the leisure* in which to develop hostilities to his fellow man. Too much of his time was taken up with other business.

ARDREY: I agree; he was too busy surviving. And separation was very important, because as hunters they had to live quite far apart in groups. They could not have been next door neighbors because there wouldn't have been enough animals.

LEAKEY: Until you get to visit the caves of Dordogne, where they had moved into cave living, cave dwelling, which gave them shelter from the wind and the cold which they had never had before in the open. But, at that point, they were certainly in much closer communities as far as living was concerned, and they were going out farther to hunt. And I still put that down to the discovery that man could make fire himself. Have you ever thought about the significance of the making of fire in relation to human speech? I have thought about it a great deal in the last few years. I have been out on a number of occasions with hunting tribes in Tanganyika. And to my great surprise they were silent pretty well the whole day long from dawn to dark because they were either hunting, or after they made a kill, they were still not going to talk because they might make a second kill—it might be their lucky day. From dawn to dark, when they got back to camp they talked. But while they were out, their only talk was of essential things, like meat, stone—concrete things. And I was foolish; I thought that the women of the tribe, because they were food gathering, would be chatter, chatter, chattering all day long, because the nuts, berries, and fruits would not run away. But I had overlooked the fact that they, too, always had their eye for meat which they would find. They have bifocal vision.

ARDREY: Is this people like the Hadza?

LEAKEY: Yes, the Hadza. I went out with the women, and I found they didn't talk, either. Of course, they talk at night—talk, talk, talk, and the men talk, too. But they didn't talk by day. They had bifocal vision; they would come around a bush, and there would be a baby Grant's gazelle or Thompson's gazelle lying on the grass, which they could see with their television and bifocal vision. And the other animals couldn't. A dog would go right past if he wasn't on the right side of the wind. But humans, no. And so they didn't talk while hunting or food gathering. But once you got fire, then after you come home in the evening, the men and women first are cooking, then in the shelter of a cave they can talk and talk until 11 o'clock at night. And *that* to me is the beginning of our real aggression, because then was the time they began to invent words for and began to think about horrible things like hatred and malice and war—things that before had never been in their consciousness.

ARDREY: This reminds me of a very funny joke. That the Aswan Dam in Egypt was going to light up all the villages and would reduce the birth rate, because all the people will have something else to do! I don't know—they will be able to talk or play dominoes, or something. But I agree; the fire makes a focus at night which you wouldn't have otherwise and encourages you to communicate and tell the story of what happened during the day.

LEAKEY: And you thus get speech. And with the arrival of real speech, although it has done a great many beautiful things, at the same time it has done certain awfully bad things, because it gave us time and leisure to invent ideas and some of those ideas, I am afraid, were the causes of our aggression.

ARDREY: So much communication is *this* kind of communication. And so much of communication as languages developed has made it absolutely impossible to understand what somebody else thinks. This is part of our problem today. Speech is not all fine. You hear some beautiful things from beautiful anthropologists about how it makes mankind one. I don't see any part of it. I agree with you down to the bottom on that.

LEAKEY: I don't think speech was present at all early. I think possibly you would regard the proto-men, hominids, and the early things like *habilis* as maybe having speech. I think they had rather more words than the chimpanzees do. Jane [Goodall, author of a book about chimpanzees] has now, with the help of one of our sound machines, got about 80 different sounds. I imagine our ancestors had three or four times that number, but not speech in my sense. I am trying to get you to agree with me that really the fundamental was speech and it was very late.

ARDREY: No, I don't think so. I think speech in moderately, not elaborate, but grammatical form emerged at a fairly early date—let's say before the big brain, in your *Homo habilis* stage because of the necessity of transmitting the social wisdom—the wisdom of the hunter—to the young. I don't think the hunter needed it so badly, but I do think there was a tremendous necessity for the young hunter—the hunter-to-be—to learn verbally from his elders the ways of the wild animals of different forms, which vary so much. So I have a feeling that speech started at a very early date, but perhaps it did not become too sophisticated until later on.

LEAKEY: I would disagree with you there. I would agree that *Homo habilis* definitely had the *potential* . . . for speech of a far greater quality than any chimpanzee or any near-man had—even more than the australopithecines. *Homo habilis* had a speech potential created by the muscles of the root of the lower jaw. This was two million years ago. He had the potential, but I don't think he had developed that potential because he didn't have the leisure. I cannot see men or women, until they have fire, being able to develop speech to any degree—at least not abstract speech—because of having been out with these people. Until you have fire, when you come home in the evening you just sit. And those who are not cooking or cutting up the meat and getting ready to go to bed, are listening, listening. Elephants can stampede past; snakes can come wiggling up where they lie—they are not in caves. *Only* when they have got fire. Cave living is late, apart from Peking man, and fire is late. I put the whole development of articulate speech in relation to abstract ideas as late.

ARDREY: Are you getting at something with articulate speech—you developed the capacity for articulate violence along with articulate speech?

LEAKEY: Yes. Between man and man.

ARDREY: You could unite groups with speech against others. Something that was impossible before you had speech?

LEAKEY: Exactly. You could stir up emotions.

ARDREY: That's a very interesting idea.

LEAKEY: To me it's one of the key points.

ARDREY: The regular use of fire was about 40,000 years ago. The sporadic use of fire went back to Choukoutien man, 300,000 to 400,000 years. But regular use of fire, meaning control, so you could make a fire, about 40,000. So this would mean that this began only about 40,000 years ago.

LEAKEY: Yes, that's what I think, and that's why I disagree with you.

I can't see it any earlier. Going back to that, once you had fire, you moved into caves, and once you moved into caves, you had freedom and leisure. But with that came concentrated groups. The number of caves in the Dordogne valley that we have both seen were limited. And for the first time I think the people went in large numbers in one and the same place to sleep and to live, although not to hunt. They had to hunt separately. I think that was a key point, as I've called it in my recent lectures, the "Last Milestone in Human Evolution."

. . .

LEAKEY: But we were scavenging and you can scavenge. Many times I've seen a kill with only vultures and jackals and no bigger animals on the kill at all. They didn't scavenge all the time; they'd kill other things and hunt other things, and they had nuts and berries as well. They were omnivorous, but I don't believe in the earlier days we were anything but scavengers; insofar as we date meat at all.

ARDREY: Well, it's a big difference, but in a way it doesn't all matter that much, because we're going back so far. We're talking now about 1- to 2 million years ago. This isn't even recent in my terms. If we go back 500,000 years ago to *Homo sapiens*, the big-brain man, there isn't much question about what went on. They were definitely hunters. What we do know is that for only 10,000 years have we had any control of our food supply and have we not been dependent on wild food. I believe you and I agree that we didn't live much on spinach. This is a fashionable point of view much promoted in American anthropology. Lettuce is great for diets, but not for men who have to work for a living. We had the necessity of living off meat. We had to get it somehow. We undoubtedly scavenged whenever we could, but we could not survive 365 days of the year hoping someone would leave some meat around. So we had to be able to hunt and kill. The basis of the hunting hypothesis is that the necessity lay on us for selective survival to be able to dare to go in to attack. And, unhappily, about 10,000 years ago we domesticated cereals, we domesticated cattle, goats, sheep, and so on. I say "unhappily" because in the new book *The Imperial Animal* by these ethnologically named anthropologists, Robin Fox and Lionel Tiger—a marvelous book, incidentally—they go back to this date when we got control of our food supply and say, "Was it good or was it bad? We have sure had enough trouble since." Overpopulation, because suddenly we've got so much more food and we have so many more children and all of a sudden we begin to get the conflict of things which is important. This is where your idea and mine link together so interestingly, because your language thing meant greater differences between human beings, and my weapon thing says these differences could be enforced so much more violently. And here these two ideas come together. I go with this entirely. Now we come to the point of the food supply. And it is vegetable food supply, but fortunately by that time we had invented cooking. If you ever ate some raw spaghetti you'd find out that you have to be able to cook this stuff. But by this time we had controlled fires. And now comes the population explosion, and the problem of conflicting groups for space, for areas, for food supply, and all that came in about 5,000 to 10,000 years ago. About then we all really began to get into trouble. But here are two points that add up: language, which made possible beliefs of inordinately irrational order, and . . . food, which made possible inordinately too many people. This was more or less the road, as I see it, which is in our line. But, of course, from that time on you really had the possibilities of violence beautifully stated. The foundations, like the walls of Jericho, were there in front of us, to proceed and to perfect, and we have perfected them as no other species of the living world.

LEAKEY: Now, Robert, this brings us to a most terribly important thing. We can't leave our friends here thinking that you and I believe that we have become so violent now that there is no hope for the future. I personally don't believe this at all. I think we have reached a point where we certainly have a very short time in which to make up our minds what we are going to do. We can, because we're the only animal (and I say "animal" advisedly) who, amongst his evolutionary developments, developed a brain and a precision grip. And, if we do not want to destroy ourselves in the very near future, we can and we must today set to work jointly, and all together—over the whole world—say to each other and to our leaders, "We are not prepared to have destruction of men and the whole beauty of the arts, of the music that we have inherited from our forefathers. We insist on changing direction now!"

ARDREY: I find an interesting thing. I have never known an evolutionist who was a pessimist. It's very curious! You say you are not?

LEAKEY: I am not.

ARDREY: And part of the reason is that life has a way of solving its own problems. Now, you may have to go through dreadful things to get to the solution. You know, "Things have to get worse before they get better"—that sort of thing. It's never going to be easy. But there is an idea that has come up in recent years that I think is marvelous. The man responsible is up at Stanford. He is a clinical psychiatrist named David Hamburg. He's done a lot of work with Washburn at Berkeley. . . . They have an idea which is marvelous. I have always made a good deal out of instinct. . . . The Hamburg hypothesis is quite simply this: Forget about instinct when you get up into the higher animals in which learning is so important. Never have the idea that people go by learning and animals by instinct. It grades so gradually—read Jane Goodall's book, *In the Shadow of Man*, about the chimpanzees. The greatest book ever written on animal observation. I urge you to read it. And you will see how much the chimp has to learn—why it takes so long to grow up, because it has so much to learn. Ten years of observation before it becomes an adult.

Now what happens to us—and with chimps also, as far as that's concerned—is Hamburg's thesis. Evolution makes easy to learn that which is of survival value. Evolution makes it difficult to learn that which is not survival value. Think how quickly you learn language and how long it takes to learn the multiplication tables, which have no survival value in our evolutionary history. But language has. So we learn—bingo!—between the ages of two and three. Says Hamburg, it also makes it pleasurable to learn those things that are of survival value. Go back into the hunting past and think of the necessity of being able to hunt and all that. The violence and all was pleasurable. Now it is maladaptive. It's murder. Now, what is it we are up against? You can learn to be inimical. Kids can wind up in trouble or kids can wind up angels. But you have got to work on them, because it is easier to learn to be a murderer than it is to be a peacemaker.

LEAKEY: I entirely agree, and consequently we have to take steps now. I absolutely agree with you that we are not, as evolutionists, pessimists. We know the potential of men, and somehow, in some way, in the very near future, because we only have a very short time to go now, either we will be destroyed by overpopulation, pollution, etc., or we are going to save the world for our future generations—for our children and grandchildren and great-grandchildren. One or the other. And I think we have to do it now. That is the lesson from our study of the past.

## Questions

1 How do Sigmund Freud, Konrad Lorenz, and Robert Ardrey account for people's drives and behavior? Would you consider their views of human nature optimistic or pessimistic? Do you agree with them?

2 Define **circular progress** and **linear progress.** Have all societies tried to attain linear progress? Is it possible for a society to maintain linear progress indefinitely?

3 What does Konrad Lorenz think we can and should learn from the social relationships of the animal kingdom?

4  If, as Goeffrey Gorer claims, man has no "killer" instinct, why then does man kill? What does Gorer see as the solution, the way to end killing? Is there any evidence that this is happening or could happen?

5  Bob Oates links the aggressive environment in which we live to our seeming preference for "violent" sports such as football and hockey. How do you explain the recent popularity of such a "nonviolent" sport as tennis?

6  Do you see the new interest in the study of man's biological roots (as opposed to the study of the influence on man of his environment) as an example of circular progress or linear progress?

7  To what developments in primitive societies do Robert Ardrey and Louis Leakey attribute the beginnings of violence and aggression? Do the benefits of "civilization" outweigh the drawbacks of violence? Would it have been possible to develop "civilized" societies without simultaneously developing aggression?

# 2

# The Brilliant
# Beginnings of Civilization

R. Bausch

Men become absorbed in a fixed idea about head-hunting or burning crosses and are so sure that they have the truth that they consider others as lost souls. We are all subject to the hangup of a fixed idea, and as civilized people we have been hung up on certain ideas and issues from ages past. The first civilizations had varied but definite ideas about material goods and government. In seeing them deal with the problems of goods and services we see something of ourselves.

# A Few Old Hangups From the Bronze Age

Frederick Gentles

Some five hundred years ago Machiavelli said that what has happened in the modern world happened first in ancient times. There is, he said, a genuine resemblance of things present to things past, and the reason for this is that man has ever had the same passions. Civilized man, indeed, has gone round and round with the same old issues from the Bronze Age to the present, and these issues—and passions— are as vital and as unsettled in the present world as they were in the old.

From the beginnings of civilization in ancient Mesopotamia and Egypt, man has been concerned not only about his larger relations with god and country but also with such immediacies as the power of government over his affairs. He has been troubled about local states' rights versus a larger centralized authority. He has worried about taxes, justice, wealth, security, power, and prestige. He has been caught up with the man-made institution of property. Should property be common to all, concentrated in the hands of a few, or privately held but widely distributed?

In hanging on to ideas about these problems, man has often become a true believer, letting the ideas dominate his thinking and life-style unto death; so many of the ideas he lives by are taken as truth when in fact they are myth. "A myth," Ashley Montagu reminds us, "is something which is in fact not true, but in which we believe and act upon as if it were true." A myth is a convenient belief. The problems are old; only the characters and the sets are changed from one age to another. There are, as Machiavelli said, present resemblances to things past.

As record-keeping man appears out of the haze of prehistory, we find him concerned primarily with practical matters such as barley and beer, turnips and onions, sheep and cattle, and the buying and selling of property, slaves, and fields. He has harnessed the Tigris and Euphrates in order to produce regularly and abundantly, and he has invented such practical gadgets as the plow, the wheel, wagons, boats, and copper and bronze implements for tools and weapons. This was, indeed, a remarkable new frontier and a great society that began to take form in the Sumeria of five thousand years ago. Over 90 percent of the tablets discovered in this ancient land pertain to business transactions of private individuals or to bureaucratic governmental agencies administering social or community property. Businessmen and bureaucrats appear at a very early time in history.

It has been suggested by some scholars that a basic inspiration for the development of writing was the need to keep track of property, and that this was accomplished in the land of two rivers (Mesopotamia) by scratching symbols and numbers of sheep, barley, or other property on clay tablets. The temple gods (with priests acting in their names), the kings, and the nobles had extensive property holdings, and there is abundant evidence of property transactions among the common people. The large holdings of temples, kings, and nobles were worked by serfs and slaves or were leased to tenant farmers who gave up a good percentage of their produce as rent. Thus, the old institution of tenant-farming that has plagued both Eastern and Western civilizations through long ages, began with the first civilized peoples. There have been government-imposed land reforms ever since, many of them resulting from peasant protest and revolt, but, typically, land always seems to flow back to the few who charge exorbitant rents and keep the masses poor. America, too, has its poor tenant-farmers and share-croppers.

One gathers from reading about the Sumerians that the great temples were used as much for business undertakings as for religious purposes. The priests at Lagash, for instance, supervised not only tenant farmers but also bakers of bread, brewers of beer, clerks, smiths, spinners, weavers, and other artisans in a communal-type operation that eventually resulted in wealthy priests taking advantage of poor workers by paying them low wages, overcharging for burials, and treating the communal property as their own. The temple accounts of the goddess Bau in Lagash have been preserved almost intact and report that in her temple worked twenty-one bakers who were assisted by twenty-seven female slaves, twenty-five brewers with six slaves assisting, forty women preparing wool from the goddess's flocks, female spinners and weavers, a male smith, and other artisans working with tools provided by the temple. In addition, Bau had a personal estate worked by tenant-farmers and wage-earners.[1] In this brief but well-kept record, we find we are already in the age of socialism, free enterprise, specialization, bureaucracy, and—with Bau importing a stud bull from the mountains to cross with her lowland cattle—scientific farming. And all this long before 2000 B.C.

Goods and gods were not far apart. To a great many people, they are one and the same, then and now. The priests had their vested interests and maintained their power by perpetuating the myths, which, of course, became reality to people living out the symbolism of gods and goddesses, rites and sacrifices. Kings, frequently in competition with priests, perpetuated their power with the help of myths, police, and soldiers.

There was a form of socialism in the temple economy, but a socialism that operated a bit differently from modern concepts of the term. There was also a form of capitalism, both private and temple, that operated in ways unique to the Sumerians and their successors, the Old Babylonians. Samuel Noah Kramer, in the article following this essay, says that even the poor owned farms, gardens, houses, and cattle in a mixed economy that was socialistic, capitalistic, and state-controlled. There was even the idea of the pooling of resources to form a type of corporation separate from the state.

> The degree of the trader's freedom of disposition and individual financial responsibility and initiative can not yet be established with any clarity. Only from Ur of the early Old Babylonian period have we evidence that the importers of copper from beyond the Persian Gulf transacted their business by pooling their funds and by sharing the risks, the responsibility, and the profits. These texts repeatedly mention the *karu*, a merchant organization with a seat and a legal status of its own, outside the city proper.[2]

No name is given for the company. (Could it be Anaconda?) In any case, capitalism and socialism were taking form and people were reacting to them just as they do now to Wall Street and Red Square.

From the records and from the codes of law, it is obvious there was much class conflict in the ancient world of the Near East. Gordon Childe says that:

> The surplus produced by the new economy was, in fact, concentrated in the hands of a relatively small class. Such concentration was doubtless necessary for the accumulation of absolutely small individual contributions into reserves sufficient for the great tasks imposed on civilized society. But it split society into classes and produced further concentration in the new economy. For it limited the expansion of industry and consequently the absorption of the surplus rural population.[3]

Shades of Karl Marx and Sigmund Freud! It was Marx in the *Communist Manifesto* who claimed that the great conflicts of history were due to the creation of classes, and it was Freud who said that civilization's discontents were due to man's inability to satisfy all his selfish desires.

As a respected Sumerologist, Kramer is also particularly interested in behavioral patterns, and in 1958 he wrote an article entitled "Love, Hate, and Fear: Psychological Aspects of Sumerian Culture" in which he described the motivations and values of that society whose settlements date from about 4500 B.C. down to about 1750 B.C. Although marriage might be for love, he said, it was also a business affair in which the almighty shekel counted in making the nuptial arrangements. There was also divine love, love of country and city-state, love of family, friends, and last, but definitely not least—self. Although much of it was probably pure love, it is obvious that some of it was tainted with material motives. The Sumerians loved possessions; possessions added meaning to life.

Kramer believes that hatred played a dominant role in Sumerian behavior because the political, economic, and educational institutions were characterized by aggressive competition and conflict between individuals. Even the gods displayed hatred, and stories were told of the laying of curses upon the cities of Sumer by enraged deities. Foreigners were frequently hated, and there was even cause to fear and hate those in one's family or town, and, of course, those who were rulers. Many letters have been found filled with protest, cutting remarks, and general invective. The Sumerians placed great stress on ambition, success, prestige, and honor. There was competition, and there was love, hate, and fear in ancient Sumeria. These were the beginnings of the civilized games that civilized people play.

Though the Sumerian was a materialist, he was deeply involved spiritually with both his religion and his state, which were considered nearly one and the same at one time and rather separate at another. At one time there was a conflict between temple and palace, and at another time the king came to control the temple and there was a close association of god and country. A fierce loyalty led, at least in part, to fierce wars between the city-states. The worst catastrophe that could befall a city was to have the enemy destroy the holy places; the flag is such a sacred symbol among nations today. Lamentations deploring the destruction of the cities were composed by survivors of the persistent and bitter conflicts among our ancestors.

Warfare with its soldiers and armaments became an institution for protecting the city-state and enlarging its boundaries, for bloating its ego and gratifying its lust for wealth. One city or another succeeded in dominating the battlefields of Sumer, but, as in the nation-states of Western society, its domination lasted only until decline and decay set in. There was a power struggle between Ur and Nippur; the victor was named King of Kish. There was a border dispute between Umma and Lagash; the King of Kish arbitrated a settlement. The treaty of peace was violated; the Ummaites burned and looted Lagash. It reads like our daily paper. Says Kramer:

> Sad to say, the passion for competition and superiority carried with it the seed of self-destruction and helped trigger the bloody and disastrous wars between the city-states and to impede the unification of the country as a whole, thus exposing Sumer to the external attacks which finally overwhelmed it. All of which provides us with but another historic example of the poignant irony inherent in man and his fate.[4]

What are the attitudes of people toward local control of their political, economic, and social affairs when there is a challenge by a giant national organization? The people of the United States have acted and reacted to the issue of states' rights versus federalism from the time of the Constitutional Convention on. From 1787 to the Civil War on through to the New Deal and Nixon's New Federalism, this issue has always divided the country. Why? In ancient Egypt there were about forty-four states. How did the Egyptians face this issue?

Egypt never had the concept of city-state; it instead developed around provinces called *nomes*, each ruled by a governor, or *nomarch*. There were about twenty-two nomes each in Upper and Lower Egypt, and the history of that land is one of wars between those wanting unification and those wanting local independence. First Upper and Lower Egypt were unified separately as two rival kingdoms, and then about 3100 B.C. the two were brought together under one king, or *pharaoh*. There were at least three political loyalties of the people: to the nome, to Upper or Lower Nile cultures, and to Egypt's king. From time to time one or another took precedence in claiming the prime loyalties of subjects; however, for the better part of 2000 years, the idea of king-power prevailed, largely because the pharaoh was considered as a god and because he had priests, police, and military might to maintain his law and order. As late as King Tutankhamen (King Tut, about 1350 B.C.) there appear two symbols on his beautiful gold crown—the vulture, representing Upper Egypt of the south and the cobra, representing Lower Egypt of the northern Nile delta. Sectionalism persisted in Egypt as it persists in the U.S.A.

Despite its isolation from neighboring peoples and its achievement of stability over a very long period, Egypt, like America, was a polyglot nation of many foreigners and racial mixtures. In the south there was a mixture of black Nubians of the Sudan with brown-skinned peoples of the desert. Queen Nefertiti was a striking Eurasian, while Queen

Tiy, the daughter of two prominent Thebans of Upper Egypt, was a Nubian beauty. The delta was a land of foreigners from Asia and Mediterranean lands, and because of the differences in culture between north and south there was discrimination and conflict. The discrimination seems to have been based on differences in culture rather than on skin color, possibly because there was little difference in color between the black-skinned people with wooly hair and the swarthy people from the desert and Asia. Even today, the people of North Africa and of the Holy Land of Judaism, Christianity, and Islam are predominantly dark-skinned. Could it be that Abraham, Moses, the prophets, Christ, Paul, and Mohammed were all very dark people? Professor Pierre Montet of the College de France has an excellent description of races in Egypt as he interprets them from inscriptions, paintings, and statues.[5]

For all their physical and cultural differences, however, the Egyptians considered themselves a nation apart and felt very proud, even superior. Besides isolation, two other compelling reasons for unity in the disunity of Egypt are the success of the king in persuading the people to think of him as the godhead and the conquest and occupation of Egypt by foreigners. Though Hans Kohn in his excellent book *The Idea of Nationalism* does not speak of the idea in Egypt as he does in Israel and Greece, many Egyptologists insist there was the idea of nationalism in Egypt.

There was a feeling of being an Egyptian over and above that of being loyal to the pharaoh. Just before 1700 B.C., the Hyksos from Asia overran Egypt and imposed such a harsh rule over the land for almost 200 years that they were ardently hated by all who could call themselves Egyptians. It was at this point that a great national feeling developed; it approached in intensity modern-day romantic nationalism, where people experience a strong national bond despite sectional or provincial ties. They were proud to be Egyptians, and they hated the barbaric and inferior foreigners. Myths, canons, and hangups had already developed around the institution of nationalism.

After the Hyksos were driven out, the Egyptians created a military-imperialistic state to seek empire in Asia and Africa. The Empire Period led to an oxerextension of resources, to a military hierarchy to go with the entrenched civil and ecclesiastical hierarchies (not entirely unlike the three dominant institutions in Latin American history of church, nobility, and military), and to the decline and decay of a brilliant culture. The gods, and the pharaoh as god, were questioned by larger numbers than ever before. Self-interest became the rule, with increasing violence and the breakdown of law, order, and justice.

Professor John A. Wilson says that:

> The great effort of building up and maintaining a new organism such as an empire of remote frontiers, required national unity, and, in the first surge of vengeful patriotism after the Hyksos, that unity was formed out of the devoted fervor of all Egyptians. However, the burden of maintenance was of indefinite time, and the fruits of empire were not shared equally by all. Of course, the wealth pouring into Egypt affected everybody in some degree, but it also created and widened a gap between the governing class and those who were governed. Those who took the lead in the national adventure became increasingly powerful and wealthy. As time went on, they did not need to march with the armies but were tied down at home with their increasing investments and local concerns. . . . There was a class cleavage, and it was no longer possible—theoretically and exceptionally— to move upward in the social scale. That high value set upon the individual Egyptian, down to the ordinary peasant, in the early Middle Kingdom was a thing of the distant past.[6]

And so Egypt, as other civilized nations, fell into decline and decay and was overrun and conquered by Persians, Greeks, Romans, Arabs, Turks, French, and British.

This seems to be the story of our civilized lives from the beginning of our civilized time: We rise to great heights of wealth and beauty only to descend to depths of corruption, worshipping the material gadgets of our own creation. Not truth, not beauty, not even the gods deter the personal ambition that so often brings about personal destruction.

Why?

### Notes

1 Gordon Childe, *What Happened in History* (Baltimore, Md.: Penguin, 1961), pp. 94–95.

2 A. Leo Oppenheim, *Ancient Mesopotamia, Portrait of a Dead Civilization* (Chicago: University of Chicago Press, 1964), p. 91.

3 Childe, *op cit.*, p. 99.

4 Samuel Noah Kramer, *The Sumerians, Their History, Culture and Character* (Chicago: University of Chicago Press, 1963), p. 268.

5 Pierre Montet, *Eternal Egypt* (New York: New American Library, 1964).

6 John A. Wilson, *The Burden of Egypt, An Interpretation of Ancient Egyptian Culture* (Chicago: University of Chicago Press, 1965), p. 186.

Was man free in the first civilization of which we have record? Professor Muller of Indiana University—answers yes but a qualified yes, for man is never entirely free in any culture. In Sumeria in the third century B.C., the gods, the upper classes, urbanization, and wealth worked both to give freedom and to take it away. Can men be free but slaves at the same time? Consider.

# Freedom in the Ancient World

Herbert J. Muller

A student of freedom should not be distressed by the implication that we cannot wholly explain the rise of civilization, any more than we can the work of genius. We could explain it only if history were completely governed by determinate laws, or by the will of a God whose designs were completely known. As it is, a historian must recognize the deep, impersonal processes of social change, with consequences always unintended and unforeseen by men, just as no group of early Sumerians sat down and planned a civilization; but he is not obliged to conclude that unplanned developments are wholly involuntary, automatic, or predetermined. Instead of ultimate causes, he may be content to specify the essential conditions and factors of civilization, the frame of necessities within which man's power of choice operates. Assuming sufficient natural resources (such as are not available to Eskimos or Bedouins), it requires an adequate technology to provide an economic surplus. More basically, it requires creative thought, first to design and build up the technology, then to employ the surplus in the cultivation of aesthetic, intellectual, spiritual interests. On both counts it requires a great deal of co-operation and organization, in particular a division of labor. The temple records of Sumer disclose that the city god had a staff of "divine" servants—a butler, a coachman, a musician, a gamekeeper, a sheriff, etc. He had a much larger staff of human servants, including brewers, bakers, smiths, clerks, and female spinners and weavers. There can be no civilization without many such specialists, to provide both its material and its spiritual goods.

Hence the Sumerian city was no longer a homogeneous community. Although many or perhaps most of its people still worked in the surrounding fields, many were artisans of various kinds. Over them were administrators, served by scribes; under them were slaves; around them were professional merchants, including visitors or settlers from other cities. The records of the city indicate that it was comprised of different linguistic and cultural stocks. The land of Sumer as a whole was similarly diversified. It had a basically uniform culture, it recognized common gods, its people identified themselves as the "black-headed" people; but it was made up of a congeries of city-states, each under its own god, behind its own walls.

Now, as we are all too familiar with the problems of civilized life, we may be disposed to overlook the positive goods it brought to man, goods we now take for granted. Immediately it brought material abundance, reflected in an immense increase in population. Man was no longer at the mercy of the annual flood, the scorching wind, the periodic drought; by trade and by the surplus stored in his granaries he could tide over the lean years. He had achieved a measure of supremacy over nature. If he was still close to it, likely to work in the fields, the landscape about him was his own creation too; he had made these well-watered gardens and fields, just as his ancestors had created the very land on which his city stood. He could enjoy the imported goods that made up for the deficiencies of nature in his own region. In Sumer he was very conscious of the pleasures of abundance.

The inevitable constraints imposed by the more complex life of civilization may likewise obscure the positive gains in freedom. Life in the city was much more varied, colorful, and stimulating than life in the village. It provided much more scope for creative ability, much more opportunity for self-realization. The young in particular might enjoy such opportunities; whereas education in the village trained the child to do and to be just like his father, education in Sumer might train him to do something different or to become something better. "Better" might not mean more contented—freedom has never been a guarantee of contentment. As [philosopher Alfred] Whitehead said, civilization comes down to a program for discontent. But its justification comes down to the only possible reasons why it is better to be a man than an oyster, an intelligent man than a moron, an educated man than an illiterate, a free man than a slave. It lies in the expansion, refinement, and enrichment of man's distinctive consciousness, the realization of his distinctive capacities for knowing, feeling, striving, and creating.

In the city the restrictions on him were also means of realizing more real freedom in thought and practice. With specialization of labor a man was tied down to his job, no longer self-sufficient; but at the same time he was relieved of the necessity of growing his own food and taking care of all his material needs. He might realize his creative potentialities more fully by sticking to one vocation, while sharing in the more abundant material and spiritual goods that obviously accrued to the community as a whole. (Today he may enjoy as well the sentimental illusion of self-sufficiency by hunting his own game, building his own cabin, or like Thoreau going "back to nature"—in order to become a sophisticated writer, and forget that no great artist has ever been self-sufficient.) If for the same reason man became dependent upon the city, bound to it, he was no more bound than the villager had been, and he evidently stayed in it by conscious preference. The always crowded, restless, noisy, wicked city would in time be deplored by many writers, denounced by many more preachers; and it would always remain the mecca of bright, ambitious young men from the countryside. It stimulated intelligence, perhaps even increased brain power; there is some evidence that native intelligence declines in a stable environment. The interdependence of civilized life by no means prohibits independence of spirit, but requires more of it.

Above all, the notorious wickedness of the city was a sign of more moral and intellectual freedom—and not merely for dissolute spirits. The homogeneous village had no serious moral problems because it bred an unthinking acceptance; morality was pure custom, bound by taboo. The heterogeneous city created moral problems by creating moral consciousness. Men began thinking about the relation of man to man, not merely of man to nature or the gods. Right conduct became a matter of conscious choice, personal responsibility. The Sumerians formulated a moral code, setting up such ideas as truthfulness, righteousness, justice, compassion, and mercy. They began trying to hold up even their gods to these high standards, as villagers could hardly dream of doing—the gods of nature are plainly as amoral as the weather, having no concern whatever for justice. Sumerian kings repeatedly boasted of how they had protected the poor from the rich, restored justice, and abolished iniquity.

Their boasts, however, give away the sad truth. Justice was never restored for long, iniquity never abolished at all. We must now consider the problems that came with civilization—problems due not so much to the sinful nature of man as to the nature of the city. "Friendship lasts a day" ran a Sumerian proverb; "kinship endures forever."[1] The heterogeneous city was no longer held together by the bonds of kinship. Even the family was unstable. "For his pleasure: marriage," ran another proverb; "on his thinking it over: divorce." Hence the Sumerians could no longer depend on the informal controls of custom or common understanding that had sufficed to maintain order in the village. They had to supplement custom by political controls, a system of laws, backed by both force and moral persuasion. In this sense the city created the problem of evil. Here, not in Eden, occurred the Fall.

More specifically, the rise of civilization forced the social question that is still with us. By their great drainage and irrigation system the Sumerians were able to produce an increasing surplus of material wealth. The question is: Who was to possess and enjoy this wealth? The answer in Sumer was to be the inevitable one: Chiefly a privileged few. The god who in theory owned it all in fact required the services of priestly bailiffs, and before long these were doing more than their share in assisting him to enjoy it, at the expense of the many menials beneath them. Class divisions grew more pronounced in the divine household, as in the city at large. The skilled artisans of Sumer, whose work in metals and gems has hardly ever been surpassed, became a proletariat, unable to afford their own products. "The valet always wears dirty clothes" noted the Sumerian scribe. Other proverbs dwelt on the troubles of the poor:

> The poor man is better dead than alive;
> If he has bread, he has no salt,
> If he has salt, he has no bread.

The poor have not always been with us. As a class, they came with civilization. There was also the new type of the slave: victors in war had discovered that it was even more profitable to domesticate human captives than other types of animals. And outside its walls the city created still another type of man—the peasant. The villager had been preliterate, on a cultural par with his fellows; the peasant was illiterate, aware of the writing he did not know, aware of his dependence on the powers of the city, and liable to exploitation by them. Altogether, the urban revolution produced the anomaly that would become more glaring with the Industrial Revolution. As the collective wealth increased, many men were worse off, and many more felt worse off, than the neolithic villager had been.

Similarly the great irrigation system posed a political problem: Who would control the organization it required, exercise the power it gave? The answer was the same—a privileged few. As the temple estate grew into a city, the priesthood needed more secular help, especially in time of war. Sumerian legend retained memories of some sort of democratic assembly in the early cities, but it emphasized that after the Flood "kingship descended from heaven." The gods had sent kings to maintain order and to assure the proper service of them upon which the city's welfare depended. This was not a pure heavenly boon, judging by the Sumerian myth of a Golden Age before the Flood: an Eden of peace and plenty in which there was no snake, scorpion, hyena, lion, wild dog, wolf—"There was no fear, no terror. Man had no rival." At any rate, the divinely appointed king ruled as an absolute monarch, and might be a terror. With him descended a plague of locusts—the tax collectors. Again civilization meant an anomaly: as the collective achieved much more effective freedom, many individuals enjoyed less freedom than prehistoric villagers had.

In Sumer these problems were aggravated by a profounder paradox. All along, we have seen, man had come to depend more and more on supernatural means of power as he extended his own power over nature. Now, with the most triumphant demonstration of his creative powers, he became convinced of his utter dependence upon the gods, his utter powerlessness without them. The monumental architecture of the Sumerians exemplifies this crowning paradox. The ziggurat, which inspired the Hebrew myth of the Tower of Babel, was by no means the symbol of human presumption that Jehovah mistook it for—it was a symbol of abject subservience. Sumerian myth taught that man had been created simply to be the slave of the gods; he did all the dirty work, that they might rest and freely enjoy. They got the credit for all the highest achievements of the Sumerians. They also got the prime benefits, since the works of the city were dedicated to the promotion of their welfare, not man's welfare.

Such servility is still understandable. If men had made a world really their own in the walled city, life in it was never actually secure, as its very walls indicated. Other cities might attack it, natural disaster might still strike. Sometimes the floodwaters got out of control; then its inhabitants were more helpless than the prehistoric villagers, who could pick up their simple belongings and move on to new pastures. Always they had to deal with the problems created by the more rapid change in their society, and before long they knew that it might be change for the worse; they began experiencing the cycle of rise and fall that would ever after recur in civilized societies, as it does not in primitive ones. Meanwhile the individual in particular could no longer know his world so well as the villager had known it, nor have an illusion of mastery. He was more dependent on a social system that was growing more complex, on powers that were growing more remote and impersonal. He had a more vivid sense of the temporal, the perishable, the mortal—of a gulf between man and deity, if not an opposition between culture and nature. The Sumerians paid the price of their livelier, fuller consciousness. Reflection leads man to an awareness of strictly insoluble problems, mysteries that remain unfathomable even after religion has provided a solution; for faith itself—and still more the felt *need* of faith, the insistence of the godly that man *must* have faith—testifies to a painful mystery.

As it was material success that the Sumerians chiefly sought from their gods, they could remain aggressively devoted to the pursuit of wealth, pleasure, and worldly prestige. Their religion was doubtless a positive inspiration, given all the great works executed in its name. Looking back from our vantage point, we can always see that men have acted on mistaken beliefs; so we must guard against the illogical but common conclusion that the beliefs counted for nothing, and that the "real" cause of their doings must have been something different (usually more discreditable). But considered either as illusion or as a positive power, the religion of the Sumerians gives a melancholy cast to their achievement. If on the face of their record it did not crush their spirit, it remained a constant source of anxiety. It brought little apparent spiritual freedom or peace of mind.

While believing that everything depended upon the gods, the Sumerians felt that the gods could never really be depended upon. They might insist that the gods were just, but in their hearts they knew differently. Their myths told how the gods could be violent in wrath, could be irresponsible (especially when they had had too much beer), could be simply heedless. In effect the Sumerians acknowledged that the divine will was inscrutable. The gods might send floods or droughts, or even let their own city be destroyed by enemies, for reasons that their unhappy worshipers could never fathom. Nor did it always help that every man had a personal god whom he might plead to, or bribe to get favors from the higher gods. (The favorite seal of the Sumerians represents this good angel introducing a worshiper to a god.) At best these were favors, not rights to be earned by righteousness; and the personal god too might fall down on his job. In general, the Sumerians had come to conceive of a cosmic order that was comparable to the order they had established in their own state, and that therefore was not a secure, clearly rational, consistently lawful order. The gods themselves were insecure, limited in power, in a cosmos that had not been created by an Almighty, but had arisen out of chaos by heavenly violence.

At this stage the whole development may be summed up by a document in which appears the first recorded use of the word "freedom." In the twenty-fourth century B.C. King Urukagina of Lagash, the first social reformer known to history, issued decrees revealing that the Sumerians were still conscious of lost liberties: he "established the freedom" of his citizen-subjects by restoring their ancient rights. In the name of Ningirsu, the god of Lagash, he rid the city of the ubiquitous tax collectors; he put a stop to the practices of the high priest, who was treating the god's property as his own and the god's servants as his personal slaves; he made a special covenant with Ningirsu to protect widows and orphans from "men of power." But the god evidently did not approve of his deeds. He allowed King Urukagina and his city of Lagash to be overwhelmed by the king of another city, after a reign of less than ten years. The scribe who gratefully recorded the reforms of Urukagina did not complain of the ingratitude of Ningirsu; he took for granted the arbitrary ways of the god. He brings us back to the basic mentality of the Sumerians, who accomplished so much in spite of the inscrutable gods, but always in the name of the gods. In his new man-made world, man was not yet really conscious of himself as a maker. Neither did he become so in any other of the civilizations of the ancient East.

### Note

1 This and subsequent translations from the Sumerian are by Samuel Noah Kramer, in *From the Tablets of Sumer*.

We see reflections of ourselves in the peoples of the ancient lands of
Sumer and Egypt. They too were once hung up with problems of socialism,
capitalism, social justice, goods and gods. They were involved with the
problem of states' rights versus centralized government. History, it is said,
repeats itself. "The fact is a testimony to human stupidity," said
Edith Hamilton, the eminent classical scholar. And yet, she said, history is
really a chart to guide us. In this selection, Kramer shows that the people
of Lagash 4500 years ago had many of the same problems about
material things that people have today. What was the need for tax reform
then? What is the need in the United States today?

# The First Case of Tax Reduction

Samuel Noah Kramer

The first recorded social reform took place in the Sumerian city-
state of Lagash in the twenty-fourth century B.C. It was directed
against the abuses of "former days" practiced by an obnoxious and
ubiquitous bureaucracy, such as the levying of high and multifarious
taxes and the appropriation of property belonging to the temple. In
fact, the Lagashites felt so victimized and oppressed that they threw
off the old Ur-Nanshe dynasty and selected a ruler from another family
altogether. It was this new *ishakku*, Urukagina by name, who restored
law and order in the city and "established the freedom" of its citizens.
All this is told in a document composed and written by the Urukagina
archivists to commemorate the dedication of a new canal. To better
understand and appreciate the contents of this unique inscription,
here is a background sketch of some of the more significant social,
economic, and political practices in a Sumerian city-state.

The state of Lagash, in the early third millennium B.C., consisted
of a small group of prosperous towns, each clustering about a temple.
Nominally the city of Lagash, like the other Sumerian city-states, was
under the overlordship of the king of the entire land of Sumer. Actually its secular ruler was the *ishakku*, who ruled the city as the
representative of the tutelary deity to whom, in accordance with the
Sumerian world view, the city had been allotted after the creation.
Just how the earlier *ishakku's* came to power is uncertain; it may well
be that they were selected by the freemen of the city, among whom
the temple administrators (*sanga's*) played a leading political role. In
any case, the office became hereditary in time. The more ambitious
and successful of the *ishakku's* naturally tended to augment their

From *History Begins at Sumer* by Samuel Noah Kramer (Garden City, N.Y.:
Doubleday Anchor, 1959), pp. 45–50. Reprinted by permission of Dr. Samuel
N. Kramer.

power and wealth at the expense of the temple, and this led at times to a struggle for power between temple and palace.

By and large, the inhabitants of Lagash were farmers and cattle breeders, boatmen and fishermen, merchants and craftsmen. Its economy was mixed—partly socialistic and state-controlled, and partly capitalistic and free. In theory, the soil belonged to the city god, and therefore, presumably, to his temple, which held it in trust for all the citizens. In actual practice, while the temple corporation owned a good deal of land, which it rented out to some of the people as sharecroppers, much of the soil was the private property of the individual citizen. Even the poor owned farms and gardens, houses and cattle. Moreover, because of Lagash's hot, rainless climate, the supervision of the irrigation projects and waterworks, which were essential to the life and welfare of the entire community, necessarily had to be communally administered. But in many other respects the economy was relatively free and unhampered. Riches and poverty, success and failure, were, at least to some extent, the result of private enterprise and individual drive. The more industrious of the artisans and craftsmen sold their handmade products in the free town market. Traveling merchants carried on a thriving trade with the surrounding states by land and sea, and it is not unlikely that some of these merchants were private individuals rather than temple representatives. The citizens of Lagash were conscious of their civil rights and wary of any government action tending to abridge their economic and personal freedom, which they cherished as a heritage essential to their way of life. It was this "freedom" that the Lagash citizens had lost, according to our ancient reform document, in the days before Urukagina's reign. It was restored by Urukagina when he came to power.

Of the events that led to the lawless and oppressive state of affairs, there is not a hint in the document. But we may surmise that it was the direct result of the political and economic forces unloosed by the drive for power that characterized the ruling dynasty founded by Ur-Nansho about 2500 B.C. Inflated with grandiose ambitions for themselves and and their state, some of these rulers resorted to "imperialistic" wars and bloody conquests. In a few cases they met with considerable success, and for a brief period one of them actually extended the sway of Lagash over Sumer as a whole, and even over several of the neighboring states. The earlier victories proved ephemeral, however, and in less than a century Lagash was reduced to its earlier boundaries and former status. By the time Urukagina came to power, Lagash had been so weakened that it was a ready prey for its unrelenting enemy to the north, the city-state of Umma.

It was during these cruel wars and their tragic aftermath that the citizens of Lagash found themselves deprived of their political and economic freedom. In order to raise armies and supply them with arms and equipment, the rulers found it necessary to infringe on the personal rights of the individual citizen, to tax his wealth and property to the limit, and to appropriate property belonging to the temple. Under the impact of war, these rulers met with little opposition. Once domestic controls were in the hands of the palace coterie, its members were most unwilling to relinquish them, even in peacetime, for the controls proved highly profitable. Indeed, our ancient bureaucrats devised a variety of sources of revenue and income, taxes and imposts, that might well be the envy of their modern counterparts.

But let the historian who lived in Lagash almost 4,500 years ago, and was therefore a contemporary of the events he reports, tell it more or less in his own words: The inspector of the boatmen seized the boats. The cattle inspector seized the large cattle, seized the small cattle. The fisheries inspector seized the fisheries. When a citizen of Lagash brought a wool-bearing sheep to the palace for shearing, he had to pay five shekels if the wool was white. If a man divorced his wife, the *ishakku* got five shekels, and his vizier got one shekel. If a perfumer made an oil preparation, the *ishakku* got five shekels, the vizier got one shekel, and the palace steward got another shekel. As for the temple and its property, the *ishakku* took it over as his own. To quote our ancient narrator literally: "The oxen of the gods plowed the *ishakku's* onion patches; the onion and cucumber patches of the *ishakku* were located in the god's best fields." In addition, the more important temple officials, particularly the *sanga's*, were deprived of many of their donkeys and oxen and of much of their grain.

Even death brought no relief from levies and taxes. When a dead man was brought to the cemetery for burial, a number of officials and parasites made it their business to be on hand to relieve the bereaved family of quantities of barley, bread, and beer, and various furnishings. From one end of the state to the other, our historian observes bitterly, "There were the tax collectors." No wonder the palace waxed fat and prosperous. Its lands and properties formed one vast, continuous, and unbroken estate. In the words of the Sumerian historian, "The houses of the *ishakku* and the fields of the *ishakku*, the houses of the palace harem and the fields of the palace harem, the houses of the palace nursery and the fields of the palace nursery crowded each other side to side."

At this low point in the political and social affairs of Lagash, our Sumerian historian tells us, a new and god-fearing ruler came to the fore, Urukagina by name, who restored justice and freedom to the long-suffering citizens. He removed the inspector of the boatmen from the boats. He removed the cattle inspector from the cattle, large and small. He removed the fisheries inspector from the fisheries. He removed the collector of the silver which had to be paid for the shearing of the white sheep. When a man divorced his wife, neither the *ishakku* nor his vizier got anything. When a perfumer made an oil preparation, neither the *ishakku*, nor the vizier, nor the palace steward got anything. When a dead man was brought to the cemetery for burial, the officials received considerably less of the dead man's goods than formerly, in some cases a good deal less than half. Temple property was now highly respected. From one end of the land to the other, our on-the-scene historian observes, "There was no tax collector." He, Urukagina, "established the freedom" of the citizens of Lagash.

But removing the ubiquitous revenue collectors and the parasitic officials was not Urukagina's only achievement. He also put a stop to the injustice and exploitation suffered by the poor at the hands of the rich. For example, "The house of a lowly man was next to the house of a 'big man,' and the 'big man' said to him, 'I want to buy it from you.' If, when he (the 'big man') was about to buy it from him, the lowly man said, 'pay me as much as I think fair,' and then he (the 'big man') did not buy it, that 'big man' must not 'take it out' on the lowly man."

Urukagina also cleared the city of usurers, thieves, and murderers. If, for instance, "a poor man's son laid out a fishing pond, no one would now steal its fish." No wealthy official dared trespass on the garden of a "poor man's mother," pluck the trees, and carry off their fruit, as had been their wont. Urukagina made a special covenant with Ningirsu, the god of Lagash, that he would not permit widows and orphans to be victimized by the "men of power."

How helpful and effective were these reforms in the struggle for power between Lagash and Umma? Unfortunately, they failed to bring about the expected strength and victory. Urukagina and his reforms were soon "gone with the wind." Like many another reformer, he seemed to have come "too late" with "too little." His reign lasted less than ten years, and he and his city were soon overthrown by Lugal-zaggisi, the ambitious ruler of nearby Umma, who succeeded in making himself the king of Sumer and the surrounding lands, at least for a very brief period.

The Urukagina reforms and their social implications made a profound impression on our ancient "historians." The text of the documents has been found inscribed in four more or less varying versions on three clay cones and an oval-shaped plaque. All of them were excavated by the French at Lagash in 1878. They were copied and first translated by François Thureau-Dangin, the . . . painstaking cunei-formist. . . . However, the interpretation of the Urukagina reforms in the present volume is based on a still unpublished translation of the document prepared by Arno Poebel, the leading Sumerologist of our time.

Freedom under law, it should now be evident, was a way of life not unknown to the Sumerians of the third millennium B.C. Whether laws had already been written down and promulgated in the form of codes in Urukagina's day is still uncertain; at least no law codes from that period have as yet been recovered. But that proves little. For a long time the oldest law code known was one dating back to about 1750 B.C., but only recently three earlier codes have come to light. The oldest of these is the code of the Sumerian ruler Ur-Nammu; it dates from the end of the third millennium B.C. It was excavated in 1889–1900, but it was not until 1952 that it was identified and trans-lated, and even then more or less by accident.

Pa-ser was a reform mayor of Thebes near the end of Egypt's greatness
as a civilization. He could not prove his charges of graft and corruption
in the handling of tomb robberies, but the record of his attempt shows that
hypocrisy is not confined to the twentieth century. Here Professor Wilson
relates one of the consequences of the tyranny of corrupt government:
a military coup that results in another tyranny, a police state. Can you
give some recent examples? Watergate? The resignation of Vice-President
Spiro Agnew and his light sentence?

# Where Is the Glory?

John A. Wilson

When his rival Pa-wer-aa heard that Pa-ser had promised five new
accusations about tomb robbery, the Mayor of Western Thebes seized
the initiative and asked the Vizier for a new investigation: "I have
heard the words which this Mayor of Thebes spoke to the people of
the great and august necropolis . . . and I report them to my lord, for
it would be a crime for one in my position to hear something and con-
ceal it. But I do not know the bearing of the very serious charges which
the Mayor of Thebes says that (his informants) made to him. I really
cannot understand them, but I report them to my lord, so that my lord
may get to the bottom of these charges." Pa-wer-aa then put Pa-ser
further in the wrong by pointing out that the latter had accepted information which ought to have gone directly to the Vizier.

The Vizier acted promptly on Pa-wer-aa's report. On the very next
day a new commission of inquiry sat in the Temple of Amon. The
Vizier himself presided, and the High Priest of Amon lent his dignity
to the court. Among the officials on the bench was Pa-ser himself, sitting on the hearing on his charges. Three wretched prisoners were
introduced, but before any testimony was heard, the Vizier made an
opening statement which was so heavy with authoritative indignation
that it choked off all debate: "This Mayor of Thebes (Pa-ser) made
certain charges to the supervisors and necropolis workers (day before
yesterday), in the presence of the Royal Butler and Secretary of
Pharaoh, Nes-Amon, making statements about the great tombs which
are in the Place of Beauty; even though, when I myself—the vizier
of the land—was there with the Royal Butler and Secretary of Pharaoh, Nes-Amon, we inspected the tombs . . . and found them unin-
jured, so that all that he has said was found to be false. Now, see, the

From *The Burden of Egypt: An Interpretation of Ancient Egyptian Culture*
by John A. Wilson (Chicago: University of Chicago Press, 1966), pp. 286–
288. © 1951 by the University of Chicago. All rights reserved. Published 1951.

coppersmiths stand before you. Let them tell all that happened." Naturally, after so biased an opening statement, the coppersmiths felt no obligation to support Pa-ser's charges. "They were questioned, but the men were found to know no tomb in the Place of Pharaoh about which the Mayor had spoken the words. He was placed in the wrong about it. The great officials released the coppersmiths. . . . A report was drawn up; it is deposited in the Vizier's archives."

One can imagine Pa-ser sitting on the bench and hearing his charges swept aside by his superiors. He was completely outmaneuvered by those who wanted no disturbance of the evil status quo. The aftermath of the case is interesting. After this trial, we never hear another word about Pa-ser, the Mayor of Thebes. He drops out of the record. On the other hand, his wily rival, Pa-wer-aa, was still Mayor and Chief of Police in Western Thebes seventeen years later, seventeen years in which the tomb robberies in his district continued in crescendo. Fifteen months after this trial, one of the tombs in the Queens' Valley was found smashed to bits by robbers. In all the documents of investigation there was not a single defendant of high position. Only the little men, the stonemasons and coppersmiths and farmers, were caught. Why?

The deposition of the stonemason Amon-pa-nefer gives us the answer. He and his gang were the looters of the tomb of Sebek-em-saf. He described the tunneling into the tomb and the exciting first view of the jewel-laden "god lying at the rear of his burial-place." When the mummies of the pharaoh and of his queen had been stripped of the gold and silver and costly stones, the thieves set fire to the coffins. "And we made the gold which we had found on these two gods—from their mummies, amulets, ornaments, and coffins—into eight shares. And twenty *deben* of gold fell to each one of the eight of us, making 160 *deben* of gold, without dividing the rest of the furniture(?)." The total of gold from this tomb was nearly 40 lb. Troy, each robber taking 5 lb., which was no small amount for a peasant.

Amon-pa-nefer continued: "Then we crossed over to Thebes. And after some days, the agents of Thebes heard that we had been stealing in the west, so they arrested me and imprisoned me at the Mayor of Thebes' place. So I took the twenty *deben* of gold that had fallen to me as (my) share, and gave them to Kha-em-Opet, the District Clerk of the harbor at Thebes. He let me go, and I joined my companions, and they made up for me another share. And I, as well as the other robbers who are with me, have continued to this day in the practice of robbing the tombs of the nobles and people of the land who rest in the west of Thebes. And a large number of the men of the land rob them also."

Twenty *deben* of gold—nearly two kilograms or five Troy pounds—was a very large bribe. Not only did this stonemason walk out of imprisonment, but he was permitted to continue his robberies. What happpened to the records of his arrest? Probably that District Clerk of the Theban harbor did not retain all of the twenty *deben*; the bribe went on up high enough to choke off any inquisitiveness about the failure of legal procedure. The long and sorry record of the tomb robberies of the Twentieth Dynasty is a story of higher officials evading their duties because they were gaining personal advantage out of such evasion. It was a cynical rejection of the content of *maᶜat* and a retention of so much of the form of *maᶜat* as would make an impressive documentary show. The unimportant little people who were threatened and beaten and tortured by examining magistrates were the sacrifices for the responsible officers who were examining them. Here the Egyptian spirit reached bottom.

A century after these tomb robberies had come to their climax the state finally took action to protect the sacred persons of those gods who had once been kings. Furtively they took the royal mummies to a secret pit in the necropolis and there stacked them up like cordwood: thirty in one room. Since they were already stripped of treasure they rested undisturbed for nearly three thousand years. But the damage had already been done when the priest-kings of the Twenty-first Dynasty gave them this inglorious reburial.

In the struggle for power in the Egyptian state, the pharaoh never regained the ground lost by the Amarna heresy. But it was not the High Priest of Amon nor the Vizier who won out. It was not a member of the family which held the high priesthood, Ramses-nakht and Amen-hotep and their relatives, who took over the control of Upper Egypt. It was the army which snatched the power at the end of the Ramesside period. A certain Heri-Hor, of obscure parentage, served in the army and finally rose to the position of Viceroy of Nubia and Commander of the Army. Rather abruptly in the last years of Ramses XI, the final king of the Twentieth Dynasty, Heri-Hor appeared in Thebes as Vizier for Upper Egypt and High Priest of Amon. The implication is strong that there was an army coup to seize power from the ruling clique, and the ecclesiastical role of the new military dictator, Heri-Hor, was assumed by him in order to gather all the reins into his own hands. Very soon the Ramesside pharaohs faded out of sight, unwept and unhonored, the last of a line of true claimants to the dignity of god-emperor. After an interval Heri-Hor took to himself the crown, passing the viziership and the high priesthood to his son, but he was also scrupulous to make his son Commander of the Army, because the control of the state lay in the exercise of police power. Heri-Hor did not attempt to rule all of Egypt. Merchant princes at the northern capital, Tanis, set up a dynasty of their own, so that the rule was divided between Upper and Lower Egypt. Never again was ancient Egypt to enjoy a firmly united land for any length of time. The inner dynamic power was dead in the organism.

Economics and religion played a central role in the rise and development of the remarkable Egyptian civilization that lasted nearly 3000 years, all before the time of Caesar and Christ. The material achievements in agriculture, bread, and beer, and metal, stone, and art were intertwined with the mysterious spirits of both lower and upper worlds. One sees a civilization busy with the everyday pursuits of living that is not unlike that in neighboring Sumeria—or even in twentieth-century Kalamazoo, Michigan.

# Ancient Egypt Lives

### The Columbia History of the World

The first agricultural settlements on high ground along the Nile and the Faiyûm, probably established in the fifth millennium, reveal no surprises. The villagers cultivated barley of the Mesopotamian type, emmer, and flax. They raised livestock and used pottery, flint tools, and some copper articles. Life of the same kind continued in Nubia as late as the third millennium, but in Egypt two new powers appeared around 3000 which for the next 3,000 years determined the style of Egyptian life: the pharaoh and hieroglyphs.

In predynastic times pictorial representations of hunt and battle show warriors who are equal. Then, suddenly, representations appear in which a giant bestrides his own men and his adversaries, single-handedly destroying the enemy or digging a canal. He is the pharaoh, and his name is written alongside the picture in hieroglyphs. For instance, the images of fish and of chisel, read in Egyptian as Nar-Mer, give the name of a pharaoh. Yet, the impression that the hieroglyphs and the pharaoh emerge together may be erroneous, since the texts of the same period written on papyrus have disappeared and the prehistory of the Egyptian writing remains unknown. The hieroglyphic signs were and remained pictorial: a man leaning on a walking stick meant old age. Various supplementary signs made hieroglyphic writing capable of expressing any thought. Egyptian writing, like Hebrew and Arabic, did not indicate vowels, so we do not know exactly how the words were pronounced. Different scholars have had different theories and in accordance with these have inserted vowels in Egyptian names for the convenience of modern readers; thus it is not uncommon to find in different texts quite different spellings of the same name.

The first representations of the pharaohs show them wearing, now the

From pp. 70–74 and 79–81 in *The Columbia History of the World*, edited by John A. Garraty and Peter Gay. Copyright © 1972 by Harper & Row, Publishers, Inc. By permission of Harper & Row, Publishers, Inc.

white crown of the south, now the red crown of lower Egypt. It seems that the ruler of the south conquered the Delta. Thereafter there was in principle only one pharaoh. (This term comes to us through the Bible; it meant "palace" in Egyptian.) The history of Egypt became the story of the pharaohs. Its three millennia are divided among thirty dynasties, the last of which reigned between 378 and 342 B.C. The first two dynasties laid the foundation of the pharaonic civilization. The third settled in Memphis, near modern Cairo, immediately south of the delta, and here, about 2600, the kings erected the pyramids. For the whole period of the "Old Kingdom," from the unification of Egypt to the last pharaoh of Memphis (Eighth Dynasty), the Egyptian king lists counted 955 years.

During this millennium the pharaohs reclaimed brackish lagoons in the Delta and papyrus swamps in upper Egypt, where the rich hunted aquatic birds. About 2600 a royal officer founded twelve villages in the Delta. Storehouses where grain was laid up for the use in lean years covered the land. Barley or emmer bread and beer from barley remained the basic foods. ("Barley and beer" often meant any kind of salary.) Vegetables, particularly onions, supplemented the diet. Grapes and wine are first mentioned under the Second Dynasty (twenty-ninth to twenty-seventh centuries). Some 300 years later, under the Fourth Dynasty, there were five varieties of wine from the Delta, several sorts of beers, and some twenty bread products. A repast found in the grave of a noble lady of the Second Dynasty consisted of eight courses, from barley porridge to fresh fruits. Agricultural techniques remained simple. A wooden hoe was sufficient for the muddy ground and a small plot. From the Second Dynasty on, a light plow drawn by cattle aided the farmer. The houses were built of mud bricks, although those of the wealthy must have been quite comfortable. As early as the Second Dynasty, tombs were equipped with bathrooms for the next life of the owner.

Egypt abounded in excellent stone, from limestone, the building material of the pyramids, to porphyry and granite. In the first centuries of the third millennium the manufacture of heavy vessels made of hard stone was prodigious both in quantity and in workmanship. We still cannot understand how an Egyptian craftsman with his flint-pointed drill could hollow out rock crystal to make jars with sides as thin as paper. The use of stone for building was apparently more difficult. The tomb of the last pharaoh of the Second Dynasty was the first entirely lined with limestone. Stone vessels were for the wealthy, but the common use of the potter's wheel from about 2600 made pottery available to all. In the pit burials of the poor a clay cup for water and a dish for bread comforted the dead. The Egyptians imagined that the god Khnum fashioned men on a potter's wheel. Thus a technical device, invented within the historical period, could become the material for a myth.

The use of copper became more and more widespread during the third millennium. Toward the end of it the payments to workers, besides food and linen, often included copper utensils. From about 2750 copper tools, hardened by skillful hammering, facilitated large exploitation of quarries and the use of stone for building. Copper points for arrows were in use by 2100, and in a book written about 2000, the picture of a copper implement is a sign of an artisan.

However, flint tools and weapons, which could be easily and cheaply replaced, continued to be employed well into the second millennium. Flint was a native material; copper had to be brought from faraway lands. For the same reason, bronze, which required tin as well as copper, was not used for weapons and tools before the sixteenth century, a millennium later than in Mesopotamia, though the alloy is stronger and easier to cast than copper.

. . .

The pyramids express the self-confidence of self-centered Egypt. The Great Pyramid, built in the middle of the twenty-sixth century, covers more than 13 acres and remains one of the largest buildings in the world. For almost 4,500 years it was also the tallest (over 480 feet). It was erected without machinery or scaffolding by the sweat of perhaps 100,000 workers and the ingenuity of Egyptian engineers who used levers and ropes. Men and cattle drew sledges up brick ramps to make a pile of some 2,300,000 limestone blocks weighing about two and a half tons each. The sides of the pyramid were oriented according to the four cardinal points, and the maximum error was about one-twelfth of a degree. Each side was to be 756 feet long at the base, and the maximum error was only a few inches.

Some 2,100 years later, Egyptian priests told Greek travelers that Cheops, the Pharaoh of the Great Pyramid, reduced the people to misery for his project. In fact, the annual working season for the building of the pyramids was presumably the late summer, when the Nile flooded and farming stopped. At that time the stones could be carried over water to the site of the pyramid. Since the mobilized peasants were paid in kind, the building of the pyramids was also a kind of relief work system. Modern man may ask whether the capital and labor extended in erecting the enormous funerary complex centered on the royal pyramid could not have been better devoted to low-cost housing. The same question, however, can be asked about Gothic cathedrals or the Temple of Jerusalem.

The first need of any social system is to create incentives to make people do more work than that required by their immediate wants. As Adam Smith writes: "The desire of food is limited in every man by the narrow capacity of the stomach," but the desire for "conveniences and ornaments" is unlimited. When Smith wrote (1776), conspicuous consumption was, perhaps, the main lever of production. As he put it, with the greater part of the rich people the chief enjoyment of wealth consisted in the parade of riches. But Adam Smith wrote at the dawn of the Industrial Revolution. In earlier and poorer societies religion provided the incentive for works of economic supererogation; it raised common labor to the dignity of a ritual gesture. The Sumerian king is represented carrying on his head a basket with bricks for the foundation of a temple. When men of Lagash had to repair a canal, it was the canal of their god Ningirsu.

In Egypt, the pharaoh, a "great god" himself, linked mortal men to the eternal. He was represented on the temple walls worshiping the gods and associating with them, "the servants of the gods" (priests, in our terms) were his delegates, and none of his subjects were ever pictured in association with a deity. The common people needed the pharaoh for eternal salvation, since the offerings without which the deceased could not exist were officially the pharaoh's gift: he alone had the key to the afterlife. His eternal life in the pyramid, thus, was directly related to the well-being of every Egyptian. Princes and courtiers were entombed around the royal pyramid, and images of their tenants and servants appeared on the walls of these tombs, so that their names, too, were "established forever." Through this living chain of hope the humblest worker on the Great Pyramid participated in the sacrament of pharaonic immortality just as men who raised the Gothic cathedrals labored in the hope of the enternal reward for their pains.

. . .

The New Kingdom (about 1550–1200) was a period of military expansion, that is, of enrichment. War was, until the Industrial Revolution, the fastest and the most direct way of capital accumulation. Booty and, afterward, the tribute of conquered lands stimulated the economy. The skill of captured and enslaved craftsmen sustained the economic growth. That the pharaohs extended the boundaries of Egypt in accordance with the command of gods was not surprising. The pharaoh Sesostris I, in the twentieth century, said of the sun-god of Heliopolis: He makes himself rich when he makes me conquer. The great hall of the Karnak temple, a forest of 144 stone shafts, each 50 feet high, cool on the hottest day, the two colossi of reddish sandstone, each 70 feet high, the treasury of the tomb of Tutankhamen, or the mighty obelisks of Thutmose III that now stand in Istanbul, Rome, London, and New York, thus fulfilling his hope that his name might endure forever and ever—all these wonders were paid for with the plunder of Nubia and Syria. The simplest soldiers profited from a successful campaign. They were "drunk and anointed with oil every day as at a feast in Egypt."

We do not know how much of the new wealth percolated to the nameless toilers of Egypt who had no means to erect tombs. But documents show that the bastinado and the shout of the taskmaster, "The rod is in my hand, be not idle!" were only a part of the real life. For instance an official reported about 1230 that three peasants of a royal domain ran away after having been beaten by the manager, and now there were none to till the royal land. The workmen at the royal tombs lived in pleasant two-room houses which were gaily decorated (dancing girls, protective spirits), and at least some of them read the perennial classics. They received decent salaries in kind, had a lunch break, three days of rest monthly, plus many days off on the occasions of festivals: they rejoiced until sunset at the accession of a new pharaoh. Disputes among them were settled by judges from their village. They even went on strike, "because of hunger and thirst" when rations were in arrears. And they had their own burial chambers in the mountain near their village. But they were a privileged, hereditary group.

Yet these glimpses of real life are rare. Equally rare is evidence about technical advances during the New Kingdom: the yoke resting on the necks of the cattle (it was previously lashed to the horns), wheeled cars, shadoofs for watering gardens, bellows for blacksmiths, the introduction of a new breed of rams and also of the chicken, "a bird that gives birth every day," and so on. Our sources, the eulogies of the dead and the self-praises of the pharaohs, speak to posterity and hence are not directly concerned with the routine of life.

For the same reason we know little about the meanings of changes which suddenly become visible. Experience taught the Egyptians that even pyramids cannot protect the corpse; therefore—many concluded—let us eat, drink, and be merry. But why did a scribe of the New Kingdom, like Horace and Horace's imitators in later ages, proclaim that literary works outlive the pyramids? In the sixteenth century Egyptian scribes began to visit ancient monuments as sightseers. One scribbled on a wall: "I have visited the pyramid of Zoser. It is beautiful." Why was he so much concerned about the present? Again, we can understand that affluence brings self-indulgence. Women in diaphanous dresses and unclad dancing girls people the decorations of the tombs in the fourteenth century. Yet in the no less affluent thirteenth century scantily clothed girls disappear from the walls—in one reused tomb such figures were repainted to show them decently dressed—and funerary subjects replaced the optimistic scenes of eternal happiness. The deceased now was not enjoying a festival in his garden, but praying prostrated under a palm.

How are we to understand the strangest figure of Egyptian history, the pharaoh Ikhnaton, who about 1370 undertook to reform the religion of Egypt? After his death, some fifteen years later, his memory was damned, his residence city, which we call Amarna, about 160 miles south of modern Cairo, abandoned, and the old faith restored. The artificialities of Amarna art, which appeal to modern taste, and the anachronistic interpretation of Ikhnaton as a forerunner of Jesus, have made the name of this deformed and sullen pharaoh well known. He is described as the first monotheist. In fact, he proclaimed the solar disk as his own deity. Ikhnaton means: "Serviceable to the sun disk." He addresses the disk as, "Thou sole god, like to whom there is none other." In the language of polytheism this would mean that the god in question was the preferred one, but Ikhnaton worshiped no other god. The essential novelty of his theology was the doctrine that he alone knew the god and was its sole image on the earth. In private houses as well as in the tombs at Amarna sculptured icons expressed the new "Doctrine of Life": Ikhnaton and his family prayed to the sun. Its rays blessed them. His subjects prayed to him. The reform was not monotheistic but egocentric; only its intolerance was monotheistic. Throughout Egypt the names of the other gods were obliterated. According to Egyptian belief the destruction of the name destroyed the person. We need not wonder why Egypt did not revolt. The army remained faithful to the legitimate pharaoh.

The natural path of Egyptian expansion lay up the Nile. Between 1550 and 1450 the pharaohs of the New Kingdom, following in steps of their predecessors, colonized and Egyptianized the gold-producing land of Nubia, advancing the frontier to the fourth cataract. The savages to the south could not endanger the pharaonic forces. Despite some setbacks, Egypt held the greater part of Nubia securely almost to the end of the second millennium, and when the southern province finally became independent its rulers remained the devoted protégés of Amon-Re of Thebes.

The materialistic Sumerian civilization was a small one, but it had its troubles with goods, services, money, and taxes. The American civilization is the wonder of the world with its trillion-dollar-a-year economy, but it is in trouble from the national to the state and local governmental levels. The very size of the economy, the bulging population, shortages of natural resources, and the need to conserve land, water, air, and energy, as well as people, make burdensome demands upon government at all levels. Death and higher taxes are the only certainties in today's world.

# Money

Time magazine

Can a nation with a trillion-dollar economy be running out of money? That startling question is forcing itself upon every government official who must shape a budget, from President Nixon down to the head of the smallest local mosquito-abatement district. By most measures of private wealth, the U.S. is the world's richest country. But in terms of its ability to pay for the public services—health care, education, welfare, garbage pickup, pollution control, police and fire protection—that make the life of its citizens pleasant, or at least tolerable, or in some cases even possible, the country seems almost to be going broke.

This anomaly has come as a bitter shock. Americans have long thought that they had the resources to accomplish practically any goal that they set for themselves. Political liberals have argued for years that economic growth could pay for a vast improvement in housing, health care and education programs, and leave an ample margin for tax cuts besides. Only a few years ago, liberals and conservatives alike thought that the major question of public finance was how best to use the "peace dividend" of $30 billion a year they expected the U.S. to collect once the Viet Nam War ended.

Today, that *hubris* has been drowned in a rising sea of red ink. In 1970, federal, state and local governments spent $60 billion more than they took in, and the deficit certainly yawned even wider last year. Meanwhile, taxes keep going up and up. Though federal taxes have been reduced since 1960, the cuts have been offset by severe increases in state and city income taxes, sales taxes,, property taxes, Social Security taxes and "sin" taxes on liquor and cigarettes. Between 1960 and 1970, the tax burden on each American man, woman and child almost doubled, from

$711 to $1,348. Many Americans, worried about just what will be taxed next, could echo the Beatles' song, *Taxman*:

If you drive a car, I'll tax the street,
If you try to sit, I'll tax your seat,
If you get too cold, I'll tax the heat,
If you take a walk, I'll tax your feet.

The higher taxes and higher spending have brought little if any improvement in public services. In many cases, the nation's streets are dirtier, its mass transit more decrepit, its public hospitals more understaffed, its streets more crime-ridden today than in decades. The knowledge that they are paying more and more for less and less service has bred in many citizens a suspicion that they are being cheated, and has fanned a mood for rebellion.

In Connecticut, an outburst of voter anger frightened the state legislature last August [1971] into repealing an income tax that had been passed just six weeks before; that was a hollow victory for the rebellious citizens because the lawmakers were quickly forced to impose some of the nation's highest taxes on sales (6½%), on gasoline (10¢ per gal.) and on cigarettes (21¢ per pack). In Kansas City, voters last December [1971] defeated a property tax increase that civic leaders of both parties had campaigned hard for on the grounds that it was urgently needed to improve the city's schools. Across the country, citizens last year voted down 65% of all bond issues proposed to build new schools, hospitals, sewage plants and other facilities *v.* an average of a 30% turndown rate during the 1960s and a mere 8% in 1947.

The voter rebellion has considerable justification. The U.S. urgently needs radical reforms in the way that it collects, apportions and spends tax money. But for the moment, the taxpayer revolt is only tightening an already merciless squeeze on the budgets of most of the nation's 81,299 governmental units. At a time when public officials should be planning to finance the pollution-control, mass-transit and slum-rebuilding programs of the future, they are having to struggle to stretch present revenues to cover immediate spending needs. Increasingly, they are failing.

The failure has been most conspicuous in Washington. Richard Nixon, who in the past has zealously denounced federal deficits, now admits that he is likely to run up the biggest three-year red-ink totals that the U.S. has ever experienced outside of the World War II period: an estimated $87 billion for fiscal years 1971 through 1973. The President argues persuasively that the deficits are necessary to spur a lagging economy. Even so, he has felt obliged to limit some programs that his Administration earlier had labeled top priority. For instance, the Labor Department has kept the number of people in its manpower-training programs below

1.3 million, although the persistence of a nearly 6% unemployment rate cries out for a greater effort to help provide the jobless with marketable skills.

Still, the Federal Government is in much better budgetary shape than many states and cities. For the most part, Washington has only been delaying or underfinancing desirable programs, rather than cutting back on absolutely essential spending. No such statement can be made about many states and cities. . . .

A result of the bias in favor of the private economy has been a persistent refusal by Americans to tax themselves heavily enough to pay for public services. Though almost every American feels oppressed by taxes, the U.S. is in fact one of the most lightly taxed of all the industrial nations. Total U.S. tax collections equal only 31% of the country's gross national product *v.* 33% in Germany, 37% in Canada, 41% in Sweden and 43% in Britain. By no coincidence, most of these nations enjoy higher-quality health care, recreational facilities, mass transit and many other services than the U.S. does. Japan is the only major industrial nation where taxes account for a smaller share of G.N.P. (16%) than they do in the U.S., at least partly because Japan's tax system was designed by American occupation authorities after World War II. . . .

Although the income tax is fair enough in principle—rates rise with ability to pay—the way in which it actually operates is not. Because of elaborate deductions and exemptions, hardly anyone pays the rate that theoretically applies to his salary bracket. The deductions and exemptions excessively favor married couples over single people, homeowners over renters, large families over small, receivers of dividends and stock market profits over people who live by wages alone. Congress narrowed some of the loopholes in 1969, with the result that the number of people who paid no tax whatever on incomes of $200,000 or more declined from 300 in 1969 to 112 in 1970 (before final audit). Simultaneously, though, Congress has piled on new tax breaks. The latest, enacted last year [1971] in a bow to Women's Lib, is a child-care deduction for working mothers in families with incomes up to $27,000 a year. . . .

In the end, though, no amount of administrative reform is likely to save Americans from the necessity of paying higher taxes. The nation is not running out of money so much as it has misallocated its resources so badly that it now faces a staggering bill for the public services that citizens have a right to expect. Tax and governmental reforms can and must apportion that bill more fairly; to the extent that the taxpayers' revolt is a protest against inequity, it is only too justified. Americans, however, will have to get used to the idea that a greater portion of the country's wealth must be devoted to the public sector if they are to enjoy clean air, safe streets and better health and education. Paying the bill cannot be made pleasant. By reflecting on the observation of Justice Oliver Wendell Holmes that taxes are the price of civilization, it can perhaps be made at least tolerable.

## Questions

1 In the essay Professor Gentles views the institution of property as one of the basic determinants of the direction of civilized societies. Could civilization have developed without the concept of private ownership? Does civilization produce benefits apart from property? Do you think that the development of civilization from Sumeria to America has benefitted only the few?

2 Three thousand years before Christ a king of Lagash effected tax reform and ended the exploitation of the poor by the rich. But after less than ten years the reformer and his city were overrun. Do you conclude that a just kingdom is a weak kingdom? Is there a lesson for contemporary politicians?

3 John Wilson's account of dishonest officials in the Twentieth Dynasty of Egypt reminds us that the contemporary world has no monopoly on political malpractice. Does power invariably corrupt? Can you name rulers or public servants whom you believe to be honest and who work for the public welfare?

4 The **Time** magazine article "Money" states that although a revolt of U.S. taxpayers is justified because tax funds have been misallocated for so many years, taxpayers will have to adjust to the idea that they must pay more for public services. How would you go about convincing the public of this necessity?

# 3

# Civil Disobedience in Western Civilization

Although the turbulent political protests of the 1960s have given way to a more orderly set of social changes in the 1970s, the potential for renewed outbreaks of massive civil disobedience remains high. The revolutionary implications of the women's liberation movement, the unresolved grievances of ethnic minorities (which formed the original motivation for the protests of the past decade), and increased citizen awareness in the post–Ralph Nader, post-Watergate period of the mid-1970s . . . these are just a few of the sparks that could set off another series of radical campaigns to speed up the changing of the American system. Should this happen, the protestors will no doubt refer to the long tradition of civil disobedience in Western civilization. This introductory essay surveys some of the historical highlights in the development of justifications for disobedience to the laws of the society. Though centuries have passed since the origins of Western civilization, the central question remains the same now as way back then: "Is there a higher law?"

# Is There a Higher Law Than the Constitution?

Melvin Steinfield

The usual propaganda fed by the entrenched elders of society to younger minds questioning the right of the state to prohibit marijuana usage, alcohol consumption, or any other victimless activity labeled "criminal" by the law is:

"If you don't like the law, you should work through the system to change it." "A society would be in chaos if everyone could write his own law." "We must abide by the established laws, and keep our laws up to date by changing them by proper procedures." "Meanwhile, everyone should obey the laws they don't like until they are changed."

From the point of view of law and order, that may be the most practical advice anyone could give. But from the point of view of justice, that may sometimes present a painful dilemma.

Consider the experience of the Vietnam war. While they waited for a change in draft laws, the bombing authorization laws, and appropriation laws that supplied money for the war, concerned Americans found their opposition to the war bumping up against legally constituted governmental authority. The result: America was torn as it had not been since the Civil War. The hawks favored continuing, even escalating, the war; the doves favored promptly reducing, or even ending, the American involvement.

The bodies of Vietnamese burned with napalm impelled many Americans to ask, Is there a higher law than the laws of society? Some argued that to disobey even one law would weaken respect for all laws. Others argued that to kill people in Vietnam was just as immoral as Nazi concentration-camp executions, that individuals had to answer to their consciences, not to their draft board or to the FBI.

The antiwar movements brought forth some new names—names like Daniel Ellsberg, the government-employed consultant who revealed the "top secret"–labeled Pentagon Papers to the press, and the Berrigan brothers, who protested the draft by pouring their own blood over Selective Service System files. To the opponents of the Vietnam war, Ellsberg, the Berrigans, and others were heroes in the best tradition of civil disobedience. They were following their consciences, not the fallible laws of society. To the defenders of law and order, who happened most of the time to support the American involvement in Vietnam, antiwar protests that went beyond legal demonstration and petition were endangering the entire foundation of society.

This embittered division of America dramatically illustrated the vitality of an idea first presented to the West by the lips of a woman—the heroine of Sophocles' classic Greek play *Antigone*, who argued that eternal justice supersedes any laws made by men on earth. When man-made law is unjust, she felt, then men and women have the right to disobey it. To Antigone, there was no point in waiting to try to change the law, because her dead brother's body needed to be buried right then. Creon, the tyrant, had ruled that her brother's traitorous action in fighting against his own city-state was sufficient grounds for prohibiting his honorable burial, but Antigone did not feel bound to accept the edict. The first reading in this chapter shows some of this conflict as presented in a dialogue between Antigone and her antagonist, Creon.

During the American Civil War, another important highlight in the history of civil disobedience was reached. The horrible injustice and cruelty of slavery stimulated many Americans to question the validity of the laws and of the government that upheld them. One questioner was Henry David Thoreau, who wrote a famous essay on civil disobedience, excerpts of which appear in the readings. Thoreau advocated defiance of unjust laws, and spent a day in jail for refusing to pay his poll tax as a protest against his government's support of slavery as an institution. As a measure of his defiance, there is the famous exchange between Thoreau and the essayist and poet Ralph Waldo Emerson: "What are you doing in jail, Henry?" "What are you doing *out* of jail, Ralph?"

Thoreau's life and essay exerted inestimable influence upon Mohandas Gandhi (1869–1948), the famous political, social, and religious leader of India. And Thoreau and Gandhi both were definite influences upon Martin Luther King, Jr. and the entire nonviolent protest movement of the American civil rights revolution. Lunch-counter sit-ins, for example, openly and nonviolently defied the unjust laws of the segregated society;

other recent demonstrations protested the failure of government to end the disparity between the laws in theory and in application.

Since the end of the Second World War, American society has been undergoing the most serious and sustained challenges to the stability of its cultural canons and social institutions. A very important role in the protest movements against the established myths and traditions has been played by individuals and groups who show the influence of the spirit of Antigone, Thoreau, Gandhi, and King.

Until the Watergate scandals of 1973, the best known cases of civil disobedience were by protestors on the liberal left seeking to reform laws that restricted civil liberties and to promote a humane society. Yet this was not always the case; there was, for instance, the massive resistance to integration in both the North and the South. Often, in defiance of court orders, American Whites openly indicated they had no intention of obeying the "unjust laws that intruded upon their rights." To liberals, this was an ironic twist of the knife of civil disobedience, because the tactic was being employed to stop integration. But those on the other side argued that the government was trying to compel something contrary to the wishes of the (white) people.

The final article in this chapter discusses the civil disobedience question with reference to Watergate. The Watergate conspirators believed that they were acting in good conscience to save the country from evil influences. Thus, were they not acting the same as the Berrigans and others by their willingness to disobey law in the interests of a "higher law?" One important difference between the Watergate conspirators and the others, however, is that the Haldemans and Erlichmanns carried out their intention clandestinely, all the while supporting a "law and order" administration, whereas the Berrigans and Ellsberg were open about their methods.

And so we have come full circle. The question still is, "Is there a higher law?" But that is only the half of it. If there is a higher law, who is to say what it is? Is it right to harbor a fugitive slave against the pursuers who seek to return him to slavery but wrong to withhold paying income tax because the funds go to support the war?

If there is a higher law, and we can all agree on what it is, then perhaps draft resisters should be honored instead of made scapegoats. For the real heroes are the ones who courageously defied the unjust laws and practices of society, not blindly obeyed them merely because they were labeled as law.

"I was only doing my duty" pleaded Adolf Eichmann, the Nazi leader who was responsible for administering the concentration-camp deaths of several million people. Should he have resisted?

What do you think?

Sophocles, one of the world's greatest dramatists, produced a lasting symbol of the superiority of divine law to man-made law. Antigone voices her feelings in a sharp exchange with Creon, who represents the State, in the selection below. Do you find the issues relevant today? With whom do you tend to identify, Antigone or Creon?

# The Woman Who Started It All

Sophocles

CREON: And thy prisoner here—how and whence hast thou taken her?

GUARD: She was burying the man; thou knowest all.

CREON: Dost thou mean what thou sayest? Dost thou speak aright?

GUARD: I saw her burying the corpse that thou hadst forbidden to bury. Is that plain and clear?

CREON: And how was she seen? how taken in the act?

GUARD: It befell on this wise. When we had come to the place,—with those dread menaces of thine upon us,—we swept away all the dust that covered the corpse, and bared the dank body well; and then sat us down on the brow of the hill, to windward, heedful that the smell from him should not strike us; every man was wide awake, and kept his neighbor alert with torrents of threats, if any one should be careless of this task.

So went it, until the sun's bright orb stood in mid-heaven, and the heat began to burn: and then suddenly a whirlwind lifted from the earth a storm of dust, a trouble in the sky, and filled the plain, marring all the leafage of its woods; and the wide air was choked therewith: we closed our eyes, and bore the plague from the gods.

And when, after a long while, this storm had passed, the maid was seen; and she cried aloud with the sharp eye of a bird in its bitterness,—even as when, within the empty nest, it sees the bed stripped of its nestlings. So she also, when she saw the corpse bare, lifted up a voice of wailing, and called down curses on the doers of that deed. And straightway she brought thirsty dust in her hands; and from a shapely ewer of bronze, held high, with thrice-poured drink-offering she crowned the dead.

We rushed forward when we saw it, and at once closed upon our quarry, who was in no wise dismayed. Then we taxed her with her past and present doings; and she stood not on denial of aught,—at

From *The Antigone* by Sophocles, translated by Richard C. Jebb (Cambridge: Cambridge University Press, 1891).

once to my joy and to my pain. To have escaped from ills one's self is a great joy; but 'tis painful to bring friends to ill. Howbeit, all such things are of less account to me than mine own safety.

CREON: Thou—thou whose face is bent to earth—dost thou avow, or disavow, this deed?

ANTIGONE: I avow it; I make no denial.

CREON: (*To* GUARD) Thou canst betake thee whither thou wilt, free and clear of a grave charge.                    (*Exit* GUARD.)

(*To* ANTIGONE) Now, tell me thou—not in many words, but briefly—knewest thou that an edict had forbidden this?

ANTIGONE: I knew it: Could I help it? It was public.

CREON: And thou didst indeed dare to transgress that law?

ANTIGONE: Yes; for it was not Zeus that had published me that edict; not such are the laws set among men by the Justice who dwells with the gods below; nor deemed I that thy decrees were of such force, that a mortal could override the unwritten and unfailing statutes of heaven. For their life is not of to-day or yesterday, but from all time, and no man knows when they were first put forth.

Not through dread of any human pride could I answer to the gods for breaking *these*. Die I must,—I know that well (how should I not?)—even without thy edicts. But if I am to die before my time, I count that a gain: for when any one lives, as I do, compassed about with evils, can such an one find aught but gain in death?

So for me to meet this doom is trifling grief; but if I had suffered my mother's son to lie in death an unburied corpse, that would have grieved me; for this, I am not grieved. And if my present deeds are foolish in thy sight, it may be that a foolish judge arraigns my folly.

CHORUS: The maid shows herself passionate child of passionate sire, and knows not how to bend before troubles.

CREON: Yet I would have thee know that o'er-stubborn spirits are most often humbled; 'tis the stiffest iron, baked to hardness in the fire, that thou shalt oftenest see snapped and shivered; and I have known horses that show temper brought to order by a little curb; there is no room for pride, when thou art thy neighbor's slave.—This girl was already versed in insolence when she transgressed the laws that had been set forth; and, that done, lo, a second insult,—to vaunt of this, and exult in her deed.

Now verily I am no man, she is the man, if this victory shall rest with her, and bring no penalty. No! be she sister's child, or nearer to me in blood than any that worships Zeus at the altar of our house, —she and her kinsfolk shall not avoid a doom most dire; for indeed I charge that other with a like share in the plotting of this burial.

And summon her—for I saw her e'en now within,—raving and not mistress of her wits. So oft, before the deed, the mind stands self-convicted in its treason, when folks are plotting mischief in the dark. But verily this, too, is hateful,—when one who hath been caught in wickedness then seeks to make the crime a glory.

ANTIGONE: Wouldst thou do more than take and slay me?

CREON: No more, indeed; having that, I have all.

ANTIGONE: Why then dost thou delay? In thy discourse there is nought that pleases me,—never may there be!—and so my words must needs be unpleasing to thee. And yet, for glory—whence could I have won a nobler, than by giving burial to mine own brother? All here would own that they thought it well, were not their lips sealed by fear. But royalty, blest in so much besides, hath the power to do and say what it will.

CREON: Thou differest from all these Thebans in that view.

ANTIGONE: These also share it; but they curb their tongues for thee.

CREON: And art thou not ashamed to act apart from them?

ANTIGONE: No; there is nothing shameful in piety to a brother.

CREON: Was it not a brother, too, that died in the opposite cause?

ANTIGONE: Brother by the same mother and the same sire.

CREON: Why, then, dost thou render a grace that is impious in his sight?

ANTIGONE: The dead man will not say that he so deems it.

CREON: Yea, if thou makest him but equal in honour with the wicked.

ANTIGONE: It was his brother, not his slave, that perished.

CREON: Wasting this land; while *he* fell as its champion.

ANTIGONE: Nevertheless, Hades desires these rites.

CREON: But the good desires not a like portion with the evil.

ANTIGONE: Who knows but this seems blameless in the world below?

CREON: A foe is never a friend—not even in death.

ANTIGONE: 'Tis not my nature to join in hating, but in loving.

CREON: Pass, then, to the world of the dead, and, if thou must needs love, love them. While I live, no woman shall rule me.

Written in 1849, "On Civil Disobedience," from which the following
selection was taken, represents the distillation of a lifetime of critical
thinking by a famous American, who is also known for his "Walden."
Thoreau says that justice, rather than power, is the state's reason for being.
Is his argument about revolution and civil disobedience logical? Is it workable?

# Casting Your Whole Vote

Henry David Thoreau

How does it become a man to behave toward this American government to-day? I answer, that he cannot without disgrace be
associated with it. I cannot for an instant recognize that political
organization as *my* government which is the *slave's* government also.

All men recognize the right of revolution; that is, the right to
refuse allegiance to, and to resist, the government, when its tyranny
or its inefficiency are great and unendurable. But almost all say that
such is not the case now. But such was the case, they think, in the
Revolution of '75. If one were to tell me that this was a bad government because it taxed certain foreign commodities brought to its
ports, it is most probable that I should not make an ado about it,
for I can do without them. All machines have their friction, and
possibly this does enough good to counterbalance the evil. At any rate,
it is a great evil to make a stir about it. But when the friction comes
to have its machine, and oppression and robbery are organized, I
say, let us not have such a machine any longer. In other words, when
a sixth of the population of a nation which has undertaken to be
the refuge of liberty are slaves, and a whole country is unjustly
overrun and conquered by a foreign army, and subjected to military
law, I think it is not too soon for honest men to rebel and revolu-
tionize. What makes this duty the more urgent is the fact, that the
country so overrun is not our own, but ours is the invading army. . . .

It is not a man's duty, as a matter of course, to devote himself
to the eradication of any, even the most enormous wrong; he may
still properly have other concerns to engage him; but it is his duty,
at least, to wash his hands of it, and, if he gives it no thought longer,
not to give it practically his support. If I devote myself to other
pursuits and contemplations, I must first see, at least, that I do not
pursue them sitting upon another man's shoulders. I must get off
him first, that he may pursue his contemplations too. . . .

From *Writings* by Henry D. Thoreau (Boston: Houghton Mifflin, 1906),
Vol. IV.

Unjust laws exist: shall we be content to obey them, or shall we endeavor to amend them, and obey them until we have succeeded, or shall we transgress them at once? Men generally, under such a government as this, think that they ought to wait until they have persuaded the majority to alter them. They think that, if they should resist, the remedy would be worse than the evil. But it is the fault of the government itself that the remedy *is* worse than the evil. *It* makes it worse. Why is it not more apt to anticipate and provide for reform? Why does it not cherish its wise minority? Why does it cry and resist before it is hurt? Why does it not encourage its citizens to be on the alert to point out its faults, and *do* better than it would have them? Why does it always crucify Christ, and excommunicate Copernicus and Luther, and pronounce Washington and Franklin rebels? . . .

Under a government which imprisons any unjustly, the true place for a just man is also a prison. The proper place to-day, the only place which Massachusetts has provided for her freer and less desponding spirits, is in her prisons, to be put out and locked out of the State by her own act, as they have already put themselves out by their principles. It is there that the fugitive slave, and the Mexican prisoner on parole, and the Indian come to plead the wrongs of his race, should find them; on that separate, but more free and honorable ground, where the State places those who are not *with* her, but *against* her,—the only house in a slave State in which a free man can abide with honor. If any think that their influence would be lost there, and their voices no longer afflict the ear of the State, that they would not be as an enemy within its walls, they do not know by how much truth is stronger than error, nor how much more eloquently and effectively he can combat injustice who has experienced a little in his own person. Cast your whole vote not a strip of paper merely, but your whole influence. A minority is powerless while it conforms to the majority; it is not even a minority then; but it is irresistible when it clogs by its whole weight. If the alternative is to keep all just men in prison, or give up war and slavery, the State will not hesitate which to choose. . . .

From Antigone to Thoreau to Gandhi to Martin Luther King, Jr., there is a common spiritual bond: the belief that unjust laws must be defied nonviolently. Is this idea beginning to exert a greater influence upon Western man in the twentieth century than in earlier times? As you think about the following passages from Dr. King's 1963 letter, some questions to keep in mind are: Do you think Dr. King's letter is the high point of the Antigone tradition? Is the civil rights movement the beginning of the end for Hammurabi-type rigidity in laws?

# Letter From Birmingham Jail

Martin Luther King, Jr.

You may well ask: "Why direct action? Why sit-ins, marches and so forth? Isn't negotiation a better path?" You are quite right in calling for negotiation. Indeed, this is the very purpose of direct action. Nonviolent direct action seeks to create such a crisis and foster such a tension that a community which has constantly refused to negotiate is forced to confront the issue. It seeks so to dramatize the issue that it can no longer be ignored. My citing the creation of tension as part of the work of the nonviolent-resister may sound rather shocking. But I must confess that I am not afraid of the word "tension." I have earnestly opposed violent tension, but there is a type of constructive, nonviolent tension which is necessary for growth. Just as Socrates felt that it was necessary to create a tension in the mind so that individuals could rise from the bondage of myths and half-truths to the unfettered realm of creative analysis and objective appraisal, so must we see the need for nonviolent gadflies to create the kind of tension in society that will help men rise from the dark depths of prejudice and racism to the majestic heights of understanding and brotherhood.

The purpose of our direct-action program is to create a situation so crisis-packed that it will inevitably open the door to negotiation. I therefore concur with you in your call for negotiation. Too long has our beloved Southland been bogged down in a tragic effort to live in monologue rather than dialogue.

. . .

We have waited for more than 340 years for our constitutional and God-given rights. The nations of Asia and Africa are moving with jetlike speed toward gaining political independence, but we still creep at horse-and-buggy pace toward gaining a cup of coffee at a lunch counter. Perhaps it is easy for those who have never felt the stinging darts of segregation to say, "Wait." But when you have seen vicious mobs lynch your mothers and fathers at will and drown your sisters and brothers at whim; when you have seen hate-filled policemen curse, kick and even kill your black brothers and sisters; when you see the vast majority of your twenty million Negro brothers smothering in an airtight cage of poverty in the midst of an affluent society; when you suddenly find your tongue twisted and your speech stammering as you seek to explain to your six-year-old daughter why she can't go to the public amusement park that has just been advertised on television, and see tears welling up in her eyes when she is told that Funtown is closed to colored children, and see ominous clouds of inferiority beginning to form in her little mental sky, and see her beginning to distort her personality by developing an unconscious bitterness toward white people; when you have to concoct an answer for a five-year-old son who is asking: "Daddy, why do white people treat colored people so mean?"; when you take a cross-country drive and find it necessary to sleep night after night in the uncomfortable corners of your automobile because no motel will accept you; when you are humiliated day in and day out by nagging signs reading "white" and "colored"; when your first name becomes "nigger," your middle name becomes "boy" (however old you are) and your last name becomes "John," and your wife and mother are never given the respected title "Mrs."; when you are harried by day and haunted by night by the fact that you are a Negro, living constantly at tiptoe stance, never quite knowing what to expect next, and are plagued with inner fears and outer resentments; when you are forever fighting a degenerating sense of "nobodiness"—then you will understand why we find it difficult to wait. There comes a time when the cup of endurance runs over, and men are no longer willing to be plunged into the abyss of despair. I hope, sirs, you can understand our legitimate and unavoidable impatience.

. . .

I must make two honest confessions to you, my Christian and Jewish brothers. First, I must confess that over the past few years I have been gravely disappointed with the white moderate. I have almost reached the regrettable conclusion that the Negro's great stumbling block in his stride toward freedom is not the White Citizen's Counciler or the Ku Klux Klanner, but the white moderate, who is more devoted to "order" than to justice; who prefers a negative peace which is the absence of tension to a positive peace which is the presence of justice; who constantly says: "I agree with you in the goal you seek but I cannot agree with your methods of direct action"; who paternalistically believes he can set the timetable for another man's freedom; who lives by a mythical concept of time and who constantly advises the Negro to wait for a "more convenient season." Shallow understanding from people of good will is more frustrating than absolute misunderstanding from people of ill will. Lukewarm acceptance is much more bewildering than outright rejection.

I had hoped that the white moderate would understand that law and order exist for the purpose of establishing justice and that when they fail in this purpose they become the dangerously structured dams that block the flow of social progress. I had hoped that the white moderate would understand that the present tension in the South is a necessary phase of the transition from an obnoxious negative peace, in which the Negro passively accepted his unjust plight, to a substantive and positive peace, in which all men will respect the dignity and worth of human personality. Actually, we who engage in nonviolent direct action are not the creators of tension. We merely bring to the surface the hidden tension that is already alive. We bring it out in the open, where it can be seen and dealt with. Like a boil that can never be cured so long as it is covered up but must be opened with all its ugliness to the natural medicines of air and light, injustice must be exposed, with all the tension its exposure creates, to the light of human conscience and the air of national opinion before it can be cured. . . .

. . .

Before closing I feel impelled to mention one other point in your statement that has troubled me profoundly. You warmly commended the Birmingham police force for keeping "order" and "preventing violence." I doubt that you would have so warmly commended the police force if you had seen its dogs sinking their teeth into unarmed, nonviolent Negroes. I doubt that you would so quickly commend the policemen if you were to observe their ugly and inhumane treatment of Negroes here in the city jail; if you were to watch them push and curse old Negro women and young Negro girls; if you were to see them slap and kick old Negro men and young boys; if you were to observe them, as they did on two occasions, refuse to give us food because we wanted to sing our grace together. I cannot join you in your praise of the Birmingham police department.

It is true that the police have exercised a degree of discipline in handling the demonstrators. In this sense they have conducted themselves rather "nonviolently" in public. But for what purpose? To preserve the evil system of segregation. Over the past few years I have consistently preached that nonviolence demands that the means we use must be as pure as the ends we seek. I have tried to make clear that it is wrong to use immoral means to attain moral ends. But now I must affirm that it is just as wrong, or perhaps even more so, to use moral means to preserve immoral ends. Perhaps Mr. Conner and his policemen have been rather nonviolent in public, as was Chief Pritchett in Albany, Georgia, but they have used the moral means of nonviolence to maintain the immoral end of racial injustice. As T. S. Eliot has said: "The last temptation is the greatest treason: To do the right deed for the wrong reason."

Philip Berrigan is a Catholic priest who was one of a small group of antiwar protesters who threw blood on the draft board's files in the Baltimore Customs House in October 1967 and who smeared napalm on draft records in Catonsville, Maryland, in May 1968. While serving a jail sentence for these deliberate acts of civil disobedience, he penned the following words.

# Resistance to the War

Philip Berrigan

There was no conspiracy, as the government suspected. There was only a group of friends, trying to validate themselves as a community, by a decision for peace.

I make no pretension in calling this a "Letter from a Baltimore Jail." Many of you remember Martin Luther King's "Letter from a Birmingham Jail." Together we cherish the man and the martyr. As I recall, Dr. King's letter silenced his critics, most of whom were Christians and some of whom were Catholics. I do not intend that, nor do I hope for it. I ask you merely to ponder events with me and then to make whatever response you choose. As our President [Lyndon Johnson] says, "Let us reason together." So, a letter from a Baltimore jail, written with all the esteem and love I can muster.

Many of you have been sorely perplexed with me (us); some of you have been angry, others despairing. (One parishioner writes of quarreling with people who thought me mad.) After all, isn't it impudent and sick for a grown man (and a priest) to slosh blood—wasn't it duck's blood—on draft files; to terrorize harmless secretaries doing their job; to act without ecclesiastical permission and to disgrace the collar and its sublime office? And then, while convicted and awaiting sentence, to insult a tolerant government by bursting wildly into another draft board with a larger troop of irresponsibles—forcibly seizing the records, forcibly carrying them outside, there to burn them with napalm? With smiles and jubilation? Disgusting, frenzied, violent; many of you wrote or told us that.

You had trouble with blood as a symbol—uncivilized, messy, bizarre. *Time, Newsweek,* and the Catholic Church lent their impressive authority. You had trouble with the war—had it really gotten so bad that men had to do that? You had trouble with departures from legitimate dissent, from law and order itself. You had trouble with napalm as a symbol—what's that got to do with it? You had trouble with us calling violence nonviolence, and the press calling nonviolence violence. You had trouble with destruction of property; with civil disobedience; with priests getting involved, and getting involved this much. Let's face it: Perhaps half of you had trouble with us acting at all.

You'll forgive me for interpreting, but it has a certain legitimacy here. My friends and I have had long dealings with the press, and we think it generally reflects the attitudes of the people. We have read our mail and have spoken to—and listened to—hundreds of audiences around the country. We have talked to congressmen, cabinet members, military and intelligence men in Washington, and to state and local officials. We have spoken to servicemen on trains, buses, and planes; we have written to relatives in Viet Nam. We have experienced war firsthand, several of us; we have served Church and country abroad, several of us. And one of us (my brother) spent a week in Laos and another in Viet Nam negotiating the release of three American fliers. We have learned, finally, from the peace movement—its rhetoric, aims, convictions, criticisms of us. Pardon us for interpreting.

Let me share with you an analogy to introduce mutual concerns. Imagine, if you will, a tiny community of sixteen people, relatively isolated, exclusive, and self-sufficient. Its leader is leader for the simple reason that he owns more than the rest put together. Because he does, the others work for him, making him richer as they make themselves poorer. Naturally there is fear on his part, discontent on the others'. The rich man hires guards and intelligence; he resolves to protect his person and property. He often exhorts them, telling them of the honor of their role, carefully avoiding terms like "mercenary" and "spy." When unrest develops, it is ferreted out, condemned as godless, subversive, and hostile to law and order. Then it is crushed.

### A Wealthy and Powerful Nation

Another analogy, if you please. A nation that counts its wealth in dollars had two billionaires, six half-billionaires, and 153 multimillionaires with more than one hundred million each. Paradoxically, this nation had also many poor—ten million who hungered, twenty million inadequately fed. Many of the rich, thinking undoubtedly of other services to the nation, pay no taxes, while the poor pay upwards of fourteen percent (I must banish this dirty thought resolutely: If the rich do not draft the law, they certainly apply it!) And the citizens' attitude toward dollars is so curious that in their land of freedom and equality, five percent of the people control twenty percent of the wealth; at the other end, twenty percent control five percent. And that's what somebody calls the symmetry of injustice.

Need I remind you that my clumsy analogies depict—as through a glass darkly—our beloved country, abroad and at home? Need I remind you that wealth can be legislated abroad—NATO, SEATO, CENTO, OAS—as it is at home in graduated income tax, oil-depletion allowances? And if legislation fails, unrest can be militarized: Viet Nam, the Dominican Republic, Newark, Detroit. Need I remind you that wealth is such a priority with us that we both add to it by war production (defense budget, eighty billion dollars plus) and protect it by war (Viet Nam, Thailand, Laos, Guatemala, Bolivia, Peru)?

Need I remind you that the United States maintains its wealth by an imperial economy—foreign investments totaling seventy billion dollars in 1967, eighty percent of all the foreign investments in the world? (Another dirty thought that I must banish resolutely: Empires have always valued power more than wisdom, survival more than justice.)

Need I remind you that law legislated for the few equals lawlessness for the many, and that lawlessness rests not so much on crime in the streets as on crimes at the top? Need I remind you that conscription reflects national injustice more than the ghetto, simply because it plays a more deadly deceit upon its victims. "Tell my soldiers what they really fight for," said Frederick the Great, "and the ranks would be empty in the morning."

As for the blood, it was ours: the FBI made sure of that. Our greatest mistake was technical incompetence, not getting enough of it. You showed an odd fascination with blood, my friends. You worried the point as a puppy worries a rubber bone, and with as much profit. Surely men foolhardy enough to do such a stunt would be foolhardy enough to take their own blood?

We were painfully educated by people concentrating on blood while neglecting its meaning. Blood is life—the Bible says so; lose enough or shed enough, and death results. Blood is redemption (freedom) also, depending on how it is shed; the contrast between Cain and Christ shows that. Our point was simply this: We could claim no right to life or freedom as long as the Viet Nam war—U Thant [former UN Secretary General] calls it one of the most barbarous in history—deprives Americans and Vietnamese of life and freedom. If we said no to the war, we could say yes to its victims, and to sharing their predicament.

What of official disobedience, you wonder, and disgrace to the priesthood? The answer depends on one's frame of reference, I suppose. Is a Christian Christ's man, or the state's; is the Church a community of belief or a spiritual spa? If the first in both cases, I have honored the priesthood and have been obedient to the Church. One must deal, it seems, with two realities—the Church as Christ's body, and the Church as the body of man. Which has the higher reality? If you say the first, then the first must be the benchmark, and the other found and served. One cannot interpret Christ by interpreting man. One rather says what man can be because of what Christ is.

You claim we disregard legitimate dissent at the expense of law and order. Quite the contrary. My brother and I have had experience with legitimate dissent for ten years, the Melvilles nearly as long in Guatemala, Tom Lewis and David Eberhardt nearly as long. We have seen legitimate dissent first ridiculed, then resisted, then absorbed. To become, in effect, an exercise in naïveté.*

### The Usefulness of Legitimate Dissent

If society can absorb lawlessness, or protests against lawlessness, without redress, it suggests its own insensitivity to injustice. Law and order tend to become a figment because law and justice become harder to attain. With ineffectual grievance machinery, there is little hope of redress. Which may explain why legal scholars say the Constitution must allow civil disobedience to check itself in keeping with the balance it constructs among the three branches of the federal government.

In point of fact, we have experienced intimately the uselessness of legitimate dissent. The war grows in savagery, more American coffins come home, Vietnamese suffering would seem to have passed the limits of human endurance. Astute and faithful men, including congressional doves, say we can't win in Viet Nam without World War III. Others disagree, saying that World War III has begun, that it is merely a question of time before one side or the other employs nuclear weapons. We have nuclear weapons in Viet Nam; we have carried them over the Chinese mainland; China is a nuclear power; Russia and China have not dissolved their mutual-defense treaty. These are not debatable items by either side.

In face of these facts, for some Americans to ask others to restrict their dissent to legal channels is asking them to joust with a windmill. More than that, it is to ask them for silent complicity with unimaginable injustice, for political unrepresentation, for voicelessness in the fate that

*Editor's note: These references are to fellow members of the "Catonsville nine," the group which put napalm on the draft records at Catonsville, Maryland, in May, 1968.

threatens everyone. God would never ask that of any man; no man can ask it justly of other men.

In turn, we destroyed property; indeed, the people's property. Ah, there's the rub. The Jews had their golden calf, Americans have their own property. Its misuse and disparity is our most sinister social fact; its international pursuit has brought us to grips with the world. Scripture calls the love of money the root of all evil, a judgment true enough to require respectful attention. The Lord said that renouncing possessions and following Him were the two criteria of discipleship, so mutually reliant in fact that the absence of one cancels the other. In contrast, no people have cherished and celebrated property as we have, even to the point of obsessions and orgy.

Americans would not quarrel with destroying German gas ovens or the Nazi and Stalinist slave camps. We would not quarrel with violent destruction of war matériel threatening us. But let the issue become nonviolent destruction of "weapons for defense"—hydrogen bombs; germ cultures at Fort Detrick, Maryland, cluster-bomb units, Stoner rifles, Selective Service files—and the issue suffers an abortive death. Americans know, with a kind of avaricious instinct, that property like this serves as insurance policy to private property. As our President [Johnson] says, "They want what we have, and we're not going to give it to them."

Friends, countrymen, such is our case. It may be overassertive and presumptuous in spots. That is for you to judge. But here it is, and here we take our stand, because, obviously, it is the best one we have. Disagree as you might, one thing you must acknowledge—our stand disrupts our lives, removes our liberty, exiles us for a considerable time from our friends, our communities, our country, our church—from everything we love so passionately. What of your stand? It costs most of you neither risk nor loss, except perhaps your integrity, your country's welfare, your Christianity. Perhaps your immediate gain may be your long-term loss.

In closing, there is one request we make. We can fairly predict that our government will show flexible leniency if we prove ourselves contrite. We can't be contrite at this point, not seeing reasons to be so. For you to point out our errors firmly and patiently would be a great service, truly in the spirit of the Gospel. It could restore to us confidence in our government and our church, and could return us to our families, friends, and assignments. It could as well allow us a constructive part in building the Great Society—instead of a destructive share in tearing it down. In all humanity, we plead for your help.

Love and peace and gratitude
In Christ
Fr. Philip Berrigan, S.S.J.

If it is all right for liberals to violate the laws to protest something they believe is morally wrong, isn't it all right for conservatives to do the same? That is one question discussed in the following article, written during the time of the 1973 Watergate hearings by the United States Senate.

# Watergate and Conscience

John Cogley

During his testimony at the Senate Watergate hearings, Jeb Stuart Magruder mentioned the fact that one of his professors at Williams College was William Sloane Coffin, Jr. who was later the chaplain at Yale University and an activist leader in the opposition to the Vietnam war. Magruder, in answer to a question by Senator Howard Baker of Tennessee, suggested that although he now recognizes the error of his ways, during the 1972 Presidential election campaign, in his own mind, he was invoking a code of ethics similar to that practiced by Dr. Coffin, by Daniel and Philip Berrigan, and other high-minded opponents of the war. Like them, Magruder said, he knowingly broke the law, but was impelled by politico-moral considerations to do so. Was his case so different from theirs, then?

The protest leaders believed the nation was being hopelessly corrupted by the war. Magruder claimed that he came to the conclusion that a Nixon defeat would represent not only a calamity for the Administration but a disaster for the nation: a McGovern victory, he said he had been given reason to believe, would open the gates to a group of professed revolutionaries (some of whom had already made written threats on the lives of officials) and could conceivably represent a fatal danger to the American system of government. In this sense, Magruder implied, he was motivated by conscience and sober political judgment quite the same as that of Dr. Coffin and the Berrigans. If he now believes he did wrong, therefore, he was wrong because he adopted their basic ethical system.

Was there any fundamental difference between them? Both supposedly broke the law in order to serve a higher cause. Coffin, like the Berrigans, wanted to save America from the Magruders in the White House; Magruder wanted to save it from the Coffins and Berrigans on the streets. Both, for quite different reasons, put their private judgment above the public law.

From "Private Judgment: Above the Law?" by John Cogley. Reprinted with permission from the August, 1973, issue of the *Center Report*, a publication of the Center for the Study of Democratic Institutions, Santa Barbara, California.

Magruder, of course, may have been merely rationalizing, but let us take his testimony on face value, at least for purposes of discussion.

There are, it must be said right off, some very important differences in the two cases. For example, no one has ever accused Coffin or the Berrigans of perjury in a courtroom. Magruder has confessed that he lied under oath. Coffin and the Berrigans were not entrusted with political power, though their private power to affect public opinion was certainly not negligible. Magruder had easy access to the sources of power. The protesters made no secret of their desperation about the immorality of the war; Magruder kept careful silence about his belief that the progress of politics-as-usual could possibly lead to national disaster. Unlike Magruder, the protesters were candid about their dissent; they did not appear to be supporting a system they were secretly subverting. If Coffin and the Berrigans were subverting the war effort, Magruder, hypocritically, was subverting the most important enterprise of a free people, their electoral process.

These differences are significant, perhaps even critical. Still, I don't believe the abstract issue is settled once they are noted. The larger issue of individual conscience versus democratic decision, as represented by the law, remains.

It is a difficult problem and one not likely to be solved once and for all by us or by any other group. In actual cases, a great deal depends on the factual context of the situation. All I propose is to suggest some general questions, which are certain to be controversial.

One way of handling the problem, of course, is to abolish it by completely exalting the will of the people, expressed in the laws, above anyone's individual conscience. Then there really is no serious ethical question: the democratic decision (the known will of the majority) is taken to be the only absolute. The conscientious objector, once he becomes sure that he is in the minority, is free to continue by lawful means to protest against the majority decision and to do all he can to change it, to castigate the majority *and* the government for their moral blindness, and to repudiate them in ringing moral terms. All the avenues of legal protest remain open to him. But, according to this reasoning, insofar as the C.O. is bound by laws (even laws he considers unjust) he has no moral choice but to obey them: there is no claim more binding than the one which expresses the will of the majority. That majority, in its beneficence, may take account of conscientious objection and the dissenter is certainly free to take advantage of whatever legal provisions are made for him. But to do this requires no basic conflict between conscience and law. The status of the C.O. *qua* C.O. is as law-abiding as that of the drafted infantryman. If the solution to the problem is found via this route, the problem largely disappears. Talk about a higher law is finally meaningless if the law of the land is looked upon as the highest of all.

Another approach is illustrated by those who openly break the law in order to test it, and who are willing to take their punishment. This technique was employed on occasion by Martin Luther King, Gandhi, and other reformers. With it, calculated disobedience becomes an overt, even a friendly political act. It is widely admired and often succeeds in its basic purpose of getting laws changed. There is a great deal to be said for it. Nevertheless, it involves a contradiction: if I believe a law is unjust (in the classic sense of the term), then I believe it is not binding on me or anyone else and that it may even be morally reprehensible for me to obey it. To cooperate with the authorities in enforcing it by making myself available for arrest, in the final analysis, amounts to conferring upon an unjust law a kind of back-handed legitimacy; therefore, if I go to jail, I should do so kicking and screaming.

When Daniel Berrigan eluded the F.B.I. for months, he cut a kind of Scarlet Pimpernel figure—which was the way his defiance was generally reported by the press. It fit in with the Berrigans' special style of liturgizing protest and also invoked one of the romantic traditions of Daniel's order (the Jesuit hidden in the "priest's hole" while Elizabeth's men search in vain for him). It is just possible, though, that Father Berrigan may also have been impelled by the logic of his long training in consistent behavior. That logic would conceivably hold that one doesn't resist a law as unjust and then cooperate freely in its enforcement.

A third approach to solving the problem of conscience versus law is to absolutize the individual conscience and relativize the democratic will of the majority. A decision made on this basis inevitably smacks of arrogance and self-righteousness and calls up the specter of anarchy. For these reasons alone, it is not particularly appealing. The people who practice it are bound to be suspect. No one wants the stability of society to be ultimately dependent on the subjective moral judgments of individual citizens—especially moralistic hard heads. We all recognize that it can be dangerous, leading to lawlessness, violence, and fatal disturbances, as well as encouraging monomaniac zealots and fanatics. One would hesitate, then, to say a good word for it, except for the fact that some lonely men and women—and some of them *have* been moralizing prigs—have been right when whole peoples have been wrong. After the war, to cite one case, we honored those who were not law-abiding citizens in Nazi Germany and sent to jail or put to death some who were.

Now I am quite aware of the dangers involved in reducing ethical quandaries to the *argumentum ad Hitler*, but with the Nazi experience still relatively fresh in our memory, I do not believe that many of us would want to put our approval on obeying the law under any and all circumstances—any law, anywhere, anytime.

But, the argument can be made, Hitler's laws were so egregiously inhuman and unambiguously evil that the Nazi case marked an exception to the general rule. In a nation like the United States, where the laws are generally humane and are ultimately the product of a democratic decision, the Nuremberg logic is inapplicable. Here—the argument is made—by far the greater evil is risked by the refusal to obey even bad laws; one should be content to do one's damndest to change them by legal means. According to this moral calculus, Magruder (presuming he meant what he said in his testimony), Coffin, and the Berrigans are almost equally culpable because they all took the law into their own hands and thereby tore at the very fabric of society. In contrast, a "good German" who set out to destroy Nazi society would not be particularly reprehensible since that society did not incarnate law at all but only moral anarchy.

If I believed that society was simply the sum of its parts, I think I would go along with the notion that since the situation in the United States is totally different from the one that prevailed in Nazi Germany, the conscience versus law question here should be settled by insisting that final moral authority be ceded to the will of the majority.

I still have a problem, however. I am stuck with the notion that society is made up of *persons*, and I choose that word precisely. As a person, each citizen has his or her own conscience, each has his or her own private ends and purposes, each in an important sense is morally autonomous. In this accounting of what it means to be a citizen in a democracy, the person does not exist to serve the society; society exists to serve the person. (Of course, the person actually does serve society, but that is not his basic *raison d'etre*. He supports society not in the way an individual stone sustains a building, but rather in the unique way the members of a human community enrich each other's human possibilities.)

This means that when the person is asked to betray himself by resisting his own conscience, in order to go along with the majority, he has no moral choice but to say no. To some it may even mean that active opposition (or subversion if you will) is required, and that they have to *act* against the majority decision in order to overturn what they take to be evil-doing (e.g., legalized racism or war) carried out in their name. The point here, of course, is that one doesn't cease to be a member of society because one disapproves of what is being done in the name of society, even when the evildoing has the approval of the majority. For it is precisely as a member of society, not as an outcast who freely accepts excommunication, that one feels justified in actively subverting the evil deeds of the majority. In this sense, one's act is not truly antisocial, though it may well be illegal. Wasn't it precisely as a German that Dietrich Bonhoeffer made his decision to participate in the plot to kill Hitler? I presume too that it was consciously as an American, not as a dropout, a self-excommunicate, or an enemy agent, that William Sloane Coffin took his stand.

I confess that I wish I could accept one of the simple, if not simplistic, answers to the basic questions I have tried to outline, but they all finally leave me unsatisfied.

To go the "majority always rules" route, without serious qualifications, strikes me as simply an avoidance of the problem of good and evil. Too many horrors have been carried out too recently with the approval of too many political majorities for that escape.

Nor can I take seriously the politics-and-morality-have-very-little-to-do-with-one-another route, though one still hears it said that "there is no morality in politics: they are two separate realms." You don't have to invoke Aristotle on the link between politics and ethics to see through that particular idiocy. If politics is not an enterprise involving constant moral judgments, morality means nothing but social convention, and the horrors of Dachau, Buchenwald, Hiroshima, and Vietnam can be brushed aside as mere examples of unconventional political behavior.

Finally, I can't really accept the view that, in the final analysis, political democracy is no more than a form of warfare between the majority and a dissenting minority and that just about anything goes, as long as the dissenters are sincere and conscientious. Too many kooks and monsters have been sincere and conscientious for that solution to offer any comfort.

In short, I have no really satisfying answer to the questions I have asked myself.

## Questions

1 Is the term **civil disobedience** now being used by dishonest people to legitimize and ennoble their dubious actions?

2 How would you determine that a law was unjust? Is there such a thing as an eternal moral code?

3 "How does it become a man to behave toward this American government? I answer that he cannot without disgrace be associated with it." Are Thoreau's question and answer valid today? If so, does it then follow that those who support the government are at best misguided and at worst evil?

4 In "Letter from Birmingham Jail" Martin Luther King, Jr., stated that he wished to foster "tension," which he believed would lead to negotiations for a better life for American black persons. Did he see tension as destructive or constructive? Who would be most likely to handicap his plan, white moderates or groups such as the Ku Klux Klan?

5 Father Philip Berrigan, obviously pointing to the U.S., asserts that "empires have always valued power more than wisdom, survival more than justice." Does this observation seem accurate? Is he saying that a just government could not survive? Which is more important—survival or justice?

6 Can you offer satisfactory answers to John Cogley's questions about "Watergate and Conscience"? Is he asking the correct questions?

# 4

# Self-Fulfillment
# in Ancient Greece

R. Bausch

The following essay tries to show that the culturally conditioned classical Greek was hampered in his efforts to realize personal ambitions because of two significant taboos. Do you see any interesting parallels or contrasts between the realities of self-fulfillment in ancient Athens and contemporary America?

# Polis and Hubris: Two Greek Hangups

Melvin Steinfield

If residents of most large cities in America were asked to indicate the tallest buildings in the downtown section, they would have to point to the pathetic clusters of bank and insurance buildings that scratch the clouds like a conspiracy of King Kongs. They could not even imagine the huge chunk of pride most Athenian citizens of the Golden Age felt when they guided a visitor to their Acropolis. For though the Greeks built no skyscrapers, they possessed a sense of community that was reflected in the quality of their public buildings. They had an identification with the *polis* (city) that is rarely attained in the typical American metropolis or megalopolis.

Men of every succeeding civilization have admired with awe what the Greeks accomplished in their Golden Age. Again and again they have returned to study the Greek achievement in order to gain insight into solving the problems of their own time. But they never recaptured quite the degree of identification with the city-state possessed by Greeks, particularly the Athenians.

Nor was man ever again haunted as much as the Athenians were by the strange taboo known as *hubris* (pride). For it was in the environment of the city-state, and the many demands it imposed, that the concept of hubris functioned to hinder individual self-fulfillment. The relationship of both hubris and polis to the Greek achievement will be discussed later. Here it is important to note that individual self-fulfillment was a vital part of the Greek vision of happiness. It was an especially important goal for the Athenian of the fifth century B.C.

It is also an important goal for Americans of the twentieth century A.D. In fact, one of the most relevant questions a student can ask himself today is: What kinds of obstacles will the society I live in place before my goals of self-fulfillment? Looking at the world less cynically, he might ask such questions as: How much will I be permitted to develop my potential as a complete human being with my own distinct personality?, or, How free am I to express myself in words and actions? He might wonder: Are we as free as the Athenians of the Golden Age?

To some, America is the land of freedom and unlimited opportunity in which a "rugged individualist" who dedicates himself to hard work is practically assured of success at whatever he attempts. This attitude is based upon a traditional faith in America as the land of golden opportunity, which goes back to the days of the Puritan settlers. It is reinforced by the Horatio Alger stories of rags-to-riches and with slogans such as "the sky's the limit."

But not everyone shares this optimism. Many of the student-protest movements of the past few years have stressed the dehumanizing and impersonal nature of our society. It is not just the war in Vietnam or racism at home, they say, but a society that has gone mad in the pursuit of power and materialistic things while ignoring the human values of our Western heritage. According to this view, America is on the verge of committing the same kind of hubris that the ancient Athenians did. Furthermore, claim those who are not impressed with the Puritan concept, the individual is being overwhelmed by a massive, technologically oriented society that has undergone unprecedented change in a short time. His individuality and his humanity are not cultivated in a polis-type atmosphere. Rather, they are buried at the bottom of a mass society. Many individuals are wondering about their role in an overpopulated world.

Where does this leave historians and others who are trying to make an intelligent study of the past in order to add to their understanding of the present and of ourselves? If students of the same college generation can differ so markedly in their interpretations of the opportunities and limitations of their own society, is it so surprising that historians find themselves challenged by the enormous difficulty of describing accurately the way people of a previous era lived? How much do we really know about the Greeks after all? And particularly, what percentage of that is relevant to the critical issues of today?

Another challenge to understanding the past or the present is the unfortunate fact that the stated values of a society do not always correspond to the actual reality of that society. Practices tend to fall short of values (see the article by Levine following this essay). Because there is often a disparity between the proud claims of public officials and the way it really is for many of the people in a society, students of history must be alert to the danger of being deluded into judging a society merely by taking at face value its claims and ideals.

This caution is especially important to the student of ancient

Greek history. If one were to judge only by the claims of its leaders, Athens during the Golden Age was a model society for individual self-fulfillment. Most historians today agree that individualism was treasured as a major value of the Greek heritage. Mottoes such as *Know thyself,* or *Man is the measure of all things* symbolize the great attention focused by the Greeks on the question of individuality. Aristotle wrote about "actualizing one's potentiality" and his teacher, Plato, pondered the issue of a just society in which every individual can play his proper and just role.

One of the most important sources of belief in the cult of individualism in classical Greece is Thucydides' *History of the Peloponnesian War.* Thucydides warns his readers not to regard the speeches he reports as verbatim accounts, but rather "while keeping as closely as possible to the general sense of the words that were actually used, to make the speakers say what, in my opinion, was called for by each situation." The following statements by Pericles, the leader of Athens, are excerpted from his Funeral Oration, which is reprinted in its entirety in the readings.

> Our constitution is called a democracy because power is in the hands not of a minority but of the whole people. When it is a question of settling private disputes, everyone is equal before the law; when it is a question of putting one person before another in positions of public responsibility, what counts is not membership of a particular class, but the actual ability which the man possesses. No one, so long as he has it in him to be of service to the state, is kept in political obscurity because of poverty. . . . Taking everything together then, I declare that our city is an education to Greece, and I declare that in my opinion each single one of our citizens, in all the manifold aspects of life, is able to show himself the rightful lord and owner of his own person, and do this, moreover, with exceptional grace and exceptional versatility.[1]

But Pericles' boast about Athens must not hide the fact that in the middle of the fifth century B.C. one-third of the population of Athens consisted of slaves; women did not vote, serve on juries, or hold office; and the privileges of "democracy" were confined to an aristocracy of adult males. As in other countries, there was a democracy of the few and the claims of universal democracy were simply not true.

Apart from the obvious omissions in Pericles' speech, there were two cultural patterns of classical Greece that inhibited the individual's desire for unrestrained freedom of expression and development. One of these was the taboo against immoderate success, and, what is worse, immoderate boasting about that success (hubris). Hubris, and the punishment that goes along with it, nemesis, is a recurring theme in Greek thought from Homer to the Golden Age.

According to the doctrine of hubris, excessive pride or arrogance will be punished by nemesis, a vindictive type of revenge. Thus if a man brags arrogantly about his wealth, he can expect to encounter financial disaster before long. To boast about one's success in life is an unpardonable sin to ancient Greeks because it carries the pre-sumption that man entirely controls his own destiny and that he alone is completely responsible for his success. This ignores the importance of fate, moderation, and polis in Greek life. As C.M. Bowra states, in *The Greek Experience*:

> Unbridled arrogance shocked the Greeks morally, politically, and aesthetically. It was, in their view, quite different from legitimate ambition, since this was possible only with a large degree of self-control and even of self-sacrifice. At all periods from the Heroic Age to the fourth century, arrogance was regarded as the worst of evils, because it made chaos of all attempts to achieve balance and harmony in the self and because it scorned the social obligations on which the city-state depended.[2]

There are many examples in Greek literature of individuals committing the sins of hubris and suffering as a consequence some sort of nemesis. For example, the god Prometheus defies Zeus and gives man fire. Because he refused to accept a limitation on what he might do, because his actions went beyond the bounds of restraint and moderation, Prometheus, even though he is a god, must suffer retribution. In this particular case, the nemesis was to be bound to a rock while vultures ate away at his liver by day. (Since he was immortal, he could not die; his liver grew back at night so that the process could be repeated daily.)

Why was Prometheus bound to the rock? He defied Zeus by giving man fire and other means of increasing his freedom and his conquest of nature. The Chorus of *Prometheus Bound,* by Aeschylus, sings a warning to the Athenians in the Amphitheatre:

> But thee, Prometheus, racked
> With anguish infinite,
> I shudder to behold:
> For Zeus thou dost defy—self-willed—
> Revering overmuch the sons of men.
> For tell me, O my friend,
> How, rendering unto them

> This thankless service, art thou helped?
> Can short-lived mortals mend thy plight?
> Seest thou not the feeble helpless state,
> Shadowy as a dream, whereto are bound
> The purblind race of men?
> No human counsels shall avail
> To pass the bounds of that great harmony
> Which Zeus ordains.
> So am I taught, Prometheus, by the sight
> Of this thy ruined state.[3]

The message is clear: "No human counsels shall avail to pass the bounds of that great harmony which Zeus ordains."[4] For the individual to overstep his bounds is to invite disaster.

Another example of hubris in Greek thought can be found in Homer's *Odyssey*. After Odysseus kills his wife's suitors, his old nurse is about to gloat over his success, but he is aware of the sin of boasting. He chides her with: "It is an unholy thing to boast over slain men."

Odysseus is not the only major character in the Homeric poems who deals with hubris. Achilles, the hero of the *Iliad,* arrogantly asserts that the Greeks will beg him to fight for them as soon as they realize his importance on the battlefield: ". . . the day is coming when Achaeans one and all will miss me sorely, and you in your despair will be powerless to help them as they fall in their hundreds to Hector killer of men. Then, you will tear your heart out in remorse for having treated the best man in the expedition with contempt." Achilles had just committed hubris—he dared think of himself as the best in the expedition. As fans of the *Iliad* know, it is Achilles who starts tearing his own heart out with remorse over the death of his best friend, Patrocles. Patrocles' death was Achilles' punishment for having committed hubris.

Both Herodotus and Thucydides, famous Greek historians of the fifth century B.C., are conscious of hubris and its importance in the Greek scheme of values. Herodotus tells of the rich and powerful Lydian King Croesus who supposes that he is the happiest of men, thus bringing into play the forces of nemesis that will destroy the basis for his arrogance. (This is powerfully and explicitly described in Herodotus' *History of the Persian War.* The famous section on Croesus and Solon is included in the readings.)

Thucydides also devotes considerable space to listing and analyzing instances of hubris. For example, during the War Debate at Sparta, he has one of the Spartan kings say:

"Slow" and "cautious" can equally well be "wise" and "sensible." Certainly it is because we possess these qualities that we are the only people who do not become arrogant when we are successful and who in times of stress are less likely to give in than others. We are not carried away by the pleasure of hearing ourselves praised. . . .[5]

The Athenians, however, had become arrogant after the Persian Wars, according to Thucydides. The Melian Dialogue is a clear example of the growing imperialistic sentiment in Athens and how it corrupted the older values of moderation. The powerful Athenians inform the Melians that they must become their allies or face destruction. The Melians plead to be allowed to remain neutral, but the Athenians say they cannot afford to allow this because their prestige would suffer and it would create the appearance of weakness on their part. This hard line was typical of the attitude that had infected the Athenians after they let their success in the Persian Wars go to their heads. And as it turned out, there was a nemesis—the Athenians lost the Greek civil war, known as the Peloponnesian War.

Pericles' Funeral Oration came at the peak of Athenian power and glory, the end of the first year of the Peloponnesian War. He commits hubris by arrogantly boasting about Athens' preeminence in the Greek world of 431 B.C.: "Mighty indeed are the marks and monuments of our empire which we have left. Future ages will wonder at us, as the present age wonders at us now."

Poor Pericles failed to abide by the rules of restraint. He committed hubris by virtue of his immoderate boasting. He failed to act humbly to set limits to what Athens should hope to achieve, allowing himself freedom from restraint. His nemesis was not long in coming. Within a few weeks, the plague broke out in Athens, Pericles died, and there followed a long series of disasters for the hubris-committing Athenians.

The examples could continue almost indefinitely, but the point should be amply illustrated by now: a Greek was faced each day with the culturally ingrained attitude that he must not allow himself to be carried away with his own success. He must remember that there are forces beyond his control that are responsible for his success. To brag about great achievement, or even to strive too far, is to defy the will of the gods, to flaunt fate, to commit hubris.

Polis is the second of the two Greek hangups that have the effect of limiting self-development and expression. It is, like hubris, a major element of the Greek life-style. Polis means city-state, but it is much more; it is a way of life. When Aristotle opened his *Politics* with "Man is a political animal," he meant it as only classical Greeks could mean it: man is an animal who by nature lives in a polis.

The individual Greek citizen must never forget his relationship to the community; that is the pervasive meaning of polis. That is why Plato and Aristotle always dealt with the subject of justice for the individual in the context of the polis. The two simply could not be separated. That is why exile was such a severe punishment in ancient Greece. For to be cut off from one's community meant that his fellow citizens held him in low regard, and that was a fate worse than death. Death with honor, especially if it occurred while fighting on behalf of one's city-state, was one of the greatest blessings that could befall a man. But dishonor was worse than death. Thus we find that a public burial with full state honors is at one end of the spectrum, and exile is at the other end. These are the extremes of reward and punishment in Greek polis life. Polis was a hangup, then, because it imposed a continuous responsibility on every Greek citizen to think and act with the best interests of the community always as a main consideration. Individual aspirations were frequently dampened by the pressure of this concept, though it did inspire men to make great sacrifices on behalf of the state.

Consider the behavior of Hector in the *Iliad* when he realized that he was no match for Achilles and that he faced imminent death: "But now my death is upon me. Let me at least not die without a struggle, inglorious, but do some big thing first, that men to come shall know of it."

Or listen to the reasons that Solon offers to explain why a relatively obscure Athenian by the name of Tellus was considered one of the happiest persons in the world: "First, his city was prosperous and he had fine sons, and lived to see children born to each of them, and all these children surviving . . . ."[6] In other words, he lived in a prosperous community and he contributed to the prosperity of the community. An individual's happiness is always related to the condition of his community as well as to the manner of his death: ". . . and secondly, after a life, which by our standards was a good one, he had a glorious death. In a battle with the neighboring town of Eleusis, he fought for his countrymen, routed the enemy, and died like a soldier; and the Athenians paid him the high honor of a public funeral on the spot where he fell."[7]

Thus the concept of polis embodied a sense of community identification that the individual never lost. Nor could he ever escape it.

A prosperous city was something to be happy about. Conversely, no matter how well one's personal fortunes might be going, if his polis were in trouble, he could not be content.

How much freedom did the typical aristocratic Athenian of the Golden Age enjoy? How much of a dampening effect did his sense of awareness of hubris and polis exert on his enthusiasm for individual achievement? Did he willingly accept or grudgingly observe these restraints? It is difficult to answer these questions. On the whole, it would appear that polis and hubris were two values that exerted a tremendous influence upon the daily lives of ancient Greeks. Whether the Greeks themselves were fully conscious of the extent to which their actions were shaped and conditioned and restricted by these values is impossible to ascertain.

What is certain is that every society has its particular hangups. The individual who wants to gather some extra dimensions of comparison with his own life-style would be wise to consider the restraints upon self-fulfillment in ancient Greece. What is truly remarkable is that, despite these restraints, the Greek achievement was phenomenal. Or maybe because of them?

## Notes

1 Thucydides, *History of the Peloponnesian War*, translated by Rex Warner (Baltimore, Md.: Penguin, 1956), pp. 117, 119.

2 C. M. Bowra, *The Greek Experience* (New York: New American Library, 1959), p. 102.

3 Aeschylus, *Prometheus Bound*, translated by Robert Whitelaw, in Lane Cooper, ed., *Fifteen Greek Plays* (New York: Oxford University Press, 1943), p. 17.

4 Homer, *The Iliad*, translated by E. V. Rieu (Baltimore, Md.: Penguin, 1954), p. 29.

5 Thucydides, *op. cit.*, p. 59.

6 Herodotus, *The Histories*, translated by Aubrey de Selincourt (Baltimore, Md.: Penguin, 1954), p. 24.

7 *Ibid.*

The following commencement address was delivered at Harvard University in June 1969. It is a valuable source for pinpointing the clash of values in contemporary America. It also underscores the difficulty of accurately interpreting a society's character. Pericles made certain statements about the nature of Athenian values and the possibilities for individual self-fulfillment. Does this mean that the values were actually realized? What about self-fulfillment of American ideals? Do you share Levine's concern?

# The Disparity Between Ideals and Practices

Meldon E. Levine

The streets of our country are in turmoil. The universities are filled with students rebelling and rioting. Communists are seeking to destroy our country. Russia is threatening us with her might. And the republic is in danger. Yes, danger from within and without. We need law and order! . . . without law and order our nation cannot survive. . . .*

These words were spoken in 1932 by Adolf Hitler.

We have heard almost every one of those assertions used this year in this country as justifications for repressing student protests. Instead of adjudicating the legitimate causes of the dissatisfaction, our political and social leaders have searched for explanations which deny either the validity or the pervasiveness of the dissent.

Our society cannot afford to deny this conflict any longer. You cannot expect it to go away by suppressing it. For it is a conflict inherent in our consciences—one which exists because you have taught us what America should stand for.

What is this protest all about?

It is not a protest to subvert institutions or an attempt to challenge values which have been affirmed for centuries. We are *not*—as we have been accused—conspiring to destroy America. We are attempting to do precisely the reverse: we are affirming the values which you have instilled in us and which you have taught us to respect.

You have told us repeatedly that trust and courage were standards to emulate. You have convinced us that equality and justice were inviolable concepts. You have taught us that authority should be guided

*Editor's note: For two years beginning in 1969 this statement was widely quoted by speakers who wanted a shock effect comparison with American law-and-order advocates, until somebody pointed out that there is no evidence Hitler ever really made these remarks.

by reason and tempered by fairness. *And we have taken you seriously.*

We have accepted your principles—and have tried to implement them. But we have found this task to be less than easy. Almost every one of us has faced the inflexibility and the insensitivity of our system.

To those who would argue that the system has been responsive, there is a one-word answer: Vietnam. It is not a weakness but a strength of American education that enables us to understand the absurdity of the premises which control our policy in Vietnam and which threaten to embroil us elsewhere.

We have tried every possible peaceful means to change our disastrous course. We have signed petitions. We have written to our congressmen. We have had teach-ins. We have marched. We have reasoned with anyone who would listen. And, in 1968, after years of peaceful protest and after the American people had spoken in primary after primary in favor of a change, we were not even given a choice on Vietnam.

We have grown weary of being promised a dialogue. What we urgently need is a meaningful response.

Our experience with Vietnam reflects the type of frustration we face every time we press for change. We are told to follow "the system." But when I look at that "system," I see rules—but not understanding. I see standards—but no compassion.

And although our complaints are more with society than with the university, the university itself is not an illogical target. Some students believe it contributes to oppressive social policies and most of us feel that it has become, in an unresponsive system, the only means whereby we can focus attention on the most serious injustices which continue to infect our nation.

And the university too has tenaciously resisted change. Six years ago, I was elected president of the student body at Berkeley. I ran on a moderate platform—one calling for educational reform, increased university involvement in the community, and student participation in academic decision-making.

Since that time, I have received degrees at Berkeley, at Princeton, and at Harvard. And I have heard my fellow students raise the same issues—time and again. And time and again, I have witnessed the university's response: A committee will be formed, and the issues will be discussed.

Year after year, the result is the same. And eventually the tactic of setting up committees is discredited. They come to be seen as a device to buy time rather than to make changes; an opportunity to stall until another class of undergraduates leaves the school, removing that particular thorn from the university's side as they go.

Thus, the university and the society respond the same way to our appeals for change: A direct confrontation of ideas is refused and the issues raised are avoided. But explaining the issues away won't make them go away. And the frustration which comes both from the issues themselves and from the continual denial of their existence touches all segments of the campus.

If anyone still doubts the depth of the conviction, I ask him to witness the intensity with which it is felt. I ask him to review the efforts of my classmates. These efforts were pursued not as a sacrifice, though sacrifices were made; not as a risk, though risks were involved; not to gain praise, though praise they deserve, but because this was *necessary* to achieve the ideals which you have held forth for us.

They chose to work with poor people in Appalachia and with black people in Mississippi and in urban ghettos. They persevered in calling attention to the injustices in Vietnam, despite accusations of disloyalty to their country. And when the price was raised to include physical danger, they exhibited courage and did not waver—in Chicago, in Berkeley, and in Cambridge.

Now, for attempting to achieve the values which you have taught us to cherish, your response has been astounding. It has escalated from the presence of police on the campuses to their use of clubs and of gas. At Berkeley in May, the state ordered a helicopter to gas the campus from the sky and ordered the police to shoot protesters from the street. Whether the victims had themselves engaged in violence seems to have made little difference.

When this type of violent repression replaces the search for reasonable alternatives, Americans are allowing their most fundamental ideals to be compromised.

What do you think that response does to students?

It drives the wedge even deeper. It creates solidarity among a previously divided group, committing the uncommitted and radicalizing the moderates.

I have asked many of my classmates what they wanted me to say in this address. "Talk with them about hypocrisy," most of them said. "Tell them they have broken the best heads in the country, embittered the most creative minds, and turned off their most talented scholars. Tell them they have destroyed our confidence and lost our respect. Tell them that, as they use the phrase, 'law and order' is merely a substitute for reason and an alternative to justice."

Continuing to explain the conflict away will only serve to heighten the frustration. It can no longer be denied. Once you recognize that it pervades the campuses—that it affects more than a discontented few—how will you respond?

So far, we have been unable to understand your response. You have given us our visions and then asked us to curb them. You have offered us dreams and then urged us to abandon them. You have made us idealists and then told us to go slowly.

We have been asking for no more than what you have taught us is *right*. We can't understand why you have been so offended. But as the repression continues, as the pressure increases, as the stakes become higher and the risks greater, we can do nothing but resist more strongly and refuse more adamantly. For it would be unthinkable to abandon principle because we were threatened or to compromise ideals because we were repressed.

We are asking that you allow us to realize the very values which you have held forth. And we think you should be *with us* in our quest.

The following excerpt from Herodotus' "History of the Persian War" contains significant statements about Greek values. Solon personifies the wise Greek philosopher who expounds with great wisdom the nature of true happiness. He stands in sharp contrast with Croesus, who violates many Greek rules of good behavior. Observe carefully how Croesus commits hubris and notice the vindictive nature of the nemesis that befalls him as a consequence.

# Defining the Good Life

Herodotus

Solon left home and, after a visit to the court of Amasis in Egypt, went to Sardis to see Croesus.

Croesus entertained him hospitably in the palace, and three or four days after his arrival instructed some servants to take him on a tour of the royal treasuries and point out the richness and magnificence of everything. When Solon had made as thorough an inspection as opportunity allowed, Croesus said: "Well, my Athenian friend, I have heard a great deal about your wisdom, and how widely you have traveled in the pursuit of knowledge. I cannot resist my desire to ask you a question: who is the happiest man you have ever seen?"

The point of the question was that Croesus supposed himself to be the happiest of men. Solon, however, refused to flatter, and answered in strict accordance with his view of the truth. "An Athenian," he said, "called Tellus."

Croesus was taken aback. "And what," he asked sharply, "is your reason for this choice?"

"There are two good reasons," said Solon, "first, his city was prosperous, and he had fine sons, and lived to see children born to each of them, and all these children surviving; and, secondly, after a life which by our standards was a good one, he had a glorious death. In a battle with the neighboring town of Eleusis, he fought for his countrymen, routed the enemy, and died like a soldier; and the Athenians paid him the high honor of a public funeral on the spot where he fell."

All these details about the happiness of Tellus, Solon doubtless intended as a moral lesson for the king; Croesus, however, thinking he would at least be awarded second prize, asked who was the next happiest person whom Solon had seen.

"Two young men of Argos," was the reply; "Cleobis and Biton.

From *The Histories* by Herodotus, translated by Aubrey de Sélincourt (Penguin Classics, 1954), pp. 23–29. Copyright © the Estate of Aubrey de Sélincourt, 1954.

They had enough to live on comfortably; and their physical strength is proved not merely by their success in athletics, but much more by the following incident. The Argives were celebrating the festival of Hera, and it was most important that the mother of the two young men should drive to the temple in her ox-cart; but it so happened that the oxen were late in coming back from the fields. Her two sons therefore, as there was no time to lose, harnessed themselves to the cart and dragged it along, with their mother inside, for a distance of nearly six miles, until they reached the temple. After this exploit, which was witnessed by the assembled crowd, they had a most enviable death—a heaven-sent proof of how much better it is to be dead than alive. Men kept crowding round them and congratulating them on their strength, and women kept telling the mother how lucky she was to have such sons, when, in sheer pleasure at this public recognition of her sons' act, she prayed the goddess Hera, before whose shrine she stood, to grant Cleobis and Biton, who had brought her such honor, the greatest blessing that can fall to mortal man.

"After her prayer came the ceremonies of sacrifice and feasting; and the two lads, when all was over, fell asleep in the temple—and that was the end of them, for they never woke again.

"The Argives had statues made of them, which they sent to Delphi, as a mark of their particular respect."

Croesus was vexed with Solon for giving the second prize for happiness to the two young Argives, and snapped out: "That's all very well, my Athenian friend; but what of my own happiness? Is it so utterly contemptible that you won't even compare me with mere common folk like those you have mentioned?"

"My lord," replied Solon, "I know God is envious of human prosperity and likes to trouble us. . . . You can see from that, Croesus, what a chancy thing life is. You are very rich, and you rule a numerous people; but the question you asked me I will not answer, until I know that you have died happily. Great wealth can make a man no happier than moderate means, unless he has the luck to continue in prosperity to the end. Many very rich men have been unfortunate, and many with a modest competence have had good luck. The former are better off than the latter in two respects only, whereas the poor but lucky man has the advantage in many ways; for though the rich have the means to satisfy their appetites and to bear calamities, and the poor have not, the poor, if they are lucky, are more likely to keep clear of trouble, and will have besides the blessings of a sound body, health, freedom from trouble, fine children, and good looks.

"Now if a man thus favored dies as he has lived, he will be just the one you are looking for: the only sort of person who deserves to be called happy. But mark this: until he is dead, keep the word 'happy' in reserve. Till then, he is not happy, but only lucky.

"Nobody of course can have all these advantages, any more than a country can produce everything it needs: whatever it has, it is bound to lack something. The best country is the one which has most. It is the same with people: no man is ever self-sufficient—there is sure to be something missing. But whoever has the greatest number of the good things I have mentioned, and keeps them to the end, and dies a peaceful death, that man, my lord Croesus, deserves in my opinion to be called happy.

"Look to the end, no matter what it is you are considering. Often enough God gives a man a glimpse of happiness, and then utterly ruins him."

These sentiments were not of the sort to give Croesus any pleasure; he let Solon go with cold indifference, firmly convinced that he was a fool. For what could be more stupid than to keep telling him to look at the "end" of everything, without any regard to present prosperity?

After Solon's departure Croesus was dreadfully punished, presumably because God was angry with him for supposing himself the happiest of men. It began with a dream he had about a disaster to one of his sons: a dream which came true. He had two sons: one with a physical disability, being deaf and dumb; the other, named Atys, as fine a young man as one can fancy. Croesus dreamt that Atys would be killed by a blow from an iron weapon. He woke from the dream in horror, and lost no time in getting his son a wife, and seeing to it that he no longer took the field with the Lydian soldiers, whom he used to command. He also removed all the weapons—javelins, spears and so on—from the men's rooms, and had them piled up in the women's quarters, because he was afraid that some blade hanging on the wall might fall on Atys' head.

The arrangements for the wedding were well in hand, when there came to Sardis an unfortunate stranger who had been guilty of manslaughter. He was a Phrygian, and related to the Phrygian royal house. This man presented himself at the palace and begged Croesus to cleanse him from blood-guilt according to the laws of the country (the ceremony is much the same in Lydia as in Greece): and Croesus did as he asked. When the formalities were over, Croesus, wishing to know who he was and where he came from, said: "What is your name, stranger, and what part of Phrygia have you come from, to take refuge with me? What man or woman did you kill?"

"Sire," the stranger replied, "I am the son of Gordias, and Midas was my grandfather. My name is Adrastus. I killed my brother by accident, and here I am, driven from home by my father and stripped of all I possessed."

"Your family and mine," said Croesus, "are friends. You have come to a friendly house. If you stay in my dominions, you shall have all you need. The best thing for you will be not to take your misfortune too much to heart." Adrastus, therefore, took up his residence in the palace.

Now it happened just at this time that Mount Olympus in Mysia was infested by a monstrous boar. This tremendous creature used to issue from his mountain lair and play havoc with the crops, and many times the Mysians had taken the field against him, but to no purpose. The unfortunate hunters received more damage than they were able to inflict. As a last resource the Mysians sent to Croesus. "Sire," the messengers said, "a huge beast of a boar has appeared amongst us, and is doing fearful damage. We want to catch him, but we can't. Please, my lord, send us your son with a party of young men, and some dogs, so that we can get rid of the brute."

Croesus had not forgotten his dream, and in answer to this request forbade any further mention of his son.

"I could not send him," he said; "he is just married, and that keeps him busy. But I will certainly send picked men, with a complete hunting outfit, and I will urge them to do all they can to help rid you of the animal."

This answer satisfied the Mysians; but at that moment Atys, who had heard of their request, entered the room. The young man, finding that Croesus persisted in his refusal to let him join the hunting party, said to his father: "Once honor demanded that I should win fame as a huntsman and fighter; but now, father, though you cannot accuse me of cowardice or lack of spirit, you won't let me take part in either of these admirable pursuits. Think what a figure I must cut when I walk between here and the place of assembly! What will people take me for? What must my young wife think of me? That she hasn't married much of a husband, I fear! Now, father, either let me join this hunt, or give me an intelligible reason why what you're doing is good for me."

"My son," said Croesus, "of course you are not a coward or anything unpleasant of that kind. That is not the reason for what I'm doing. The fact is, I dreamt that you had not long to live—that you would be killed by an iron weapon. It was that dream that made me hasten your wedding; and the same thing makes me refuse to let you join in this enterprise. As long as I live, I am determined to protect you, and to rob death of his prize. You are my only son, for I do not count that wretched cripple, your brother."

"No one can blame you, father," Atys replied, "for taking care of me after a dream like that. Nevertheless there is something which you have failed to observe, and it is only right that I should point it out to you. You dreamt that I should be killed by an iron weapon. Very well: has a boar got hands? Can a boar hold this weapon you fear so much? Had you dreamt that I should be killed by a boar's tusk or anything of that sort, your precautions would be justified. But you didn't: it was a weapon which was to kill me. Let me go, then. It is only to hunt an animal, not to fight against men."

"My boy," said Croesus, "I own myself beaten. You interpret the dream better than I did. I cannot but change my mind, and allow you to join the expedition."

The king then sent for Adrastus the Phrygian, and said to him: "Through no fault of your own, Adrastus, you came to me in great distress and with an ugly stain on your character. I gave you ritual purification, welcomed you to my house, and have spared no expense to entertain you. Now I expect a fair return for my generosity: take charge of my son on this boar-hunt; protect him from footpads and cut-throats on the road. In any case it is your duty to go where you can distinguish yourself: your family honor demands it, and you are a stalwart fellow besides."

"Sire," Adrastus answered, "under ordinary circumstances I should have taken no part in this adventure. A man under a cloud has no business to associate with those who are luckier than himself. Indeed I have no heart for it, and there are many reasons to prevent my going. But your wishes make all the difference. It is my duty to gratify you in return for your kindness; so I am ready to do as you ask. So far as it lies in my power to protect your son, you may count on his returning safe and sound."

When Adrastus had given his answer, the party set out, men, dogs, and all. They made their way to Olympus and kept their eyes open for the boar. As soon as they spotted him, they surrounded him and let fly with spears—and then it was that the stranger—Adrastus, the very man whom Croesus had cleansed from the stain of blood— aimed at the boar, missed him, and struck the king's son. Croesus' dream had come true.

A messenger hurried off to Sardis, and Croesus was told of the encounter with the boar and the death of his son. The shock of the news was dreadful; and the horror of it was increased by the fact that the weapon had been thrown by the very man whom the king had cleansed from the guilt of blood. In the violence of his grief Croesus prayed to Zeus, calling on him as God of Purification to witness what he had suffered at the hands of his guest; he invoked him again under his title of Protector of the Hearth, because he had unwittingly entertained his son's murderer in his own house; and yet again as God of Friendship, because the man he had sent to guard his son had turned out to be his bitterest enemy.

Before long the Lydians arrived with the body, followed by the unlucky killer. He took his stand in front of the corpse, and stretching out his hands in an attitude of submission begged the king to cut his throat there and then upon the dead body of his son.

"My former trouble," he said, "was bad enough. But now that I have ruined the man who absolved me of my guilt, I cannot bear to live."

In spite of his grief Croesus was moved to pity by these words.

"Friend," he said, "as you condemn yourself to death, there is nothing more I can require of you. Justice is satisfied. This calamity is not your fault; you never meant to strike the blow, though strike it you did. Some God is to blame—some God who long ago warned me of what was to happen."

Croesus buried his son with all proper ceremony; and as soon as everything was quiet after the funeral, Adrastus—the son of Gordias, the grandson of Midas: the man who had killed his brother and ruined the host who gave him purification—convinced that he was the unluckiest of all the men he had ever known, stabbed himself and fell dead upon the tomb.

In this famous passage from Thucydides' History of the Peloponnesian War, Pericles, the ruler of Athens, delivers his Funeral Oration. For the most part, the speech recounts the blessings of living in Athens as perceived by the Athenians themselves. Strong claims are made for the advantages to the individual and for the superiority of Athens over Sparta as far as the general way of life is concerned and other insights into the mind of the Athenians are given. The arrogant tone of boasting was an act of immoderation and was destined to bring suffering upon the proud Athenians. One wonders whether the Athenian youth shared Pericles' description of the Great Society. Maybe they noticed wide disparities between the claims and the realities, as did Levine in his speech on American ideals and practices.

# Athens, the School of Hellas

Thucydides

Many of those who have spoken here in the past have praised the institution of this speech at the close of our ceremony. It seemed to them a mark of honor to our soldiers who have fallen in war that a speech should be made over them. I do not agree. These men have shown themselves valiant in action, and it would be enough, I think, for their glories to be proclaimed in action, as you have just seen it done at this funeral organized by the state. Our belief in the courage and manliness of so many should not be hazarded on the goodness or badness of one man's speech. Then it is not easy to speak with a proper sense of balance, when a man's listeners find it difficult to believe in the truth of what one is saying. The man who knows the facts and loves the dead may well think that an oration tells less than what he knows and what he would like to hear: others who do not know so much may feel envy for the dead, and think the orator over-praises them, when he speaks of exploits that are beyond their own capacities. Praise of other people is tolerable only up to a certain point, the point where one still believes that one could do oneself some of the things one is hearing about. Once you get beyond this point, you will find people becoming jealous and incredulous. However, the fact is that this institution was set up and approved by our forefathers, and it is my duty to follow the tradition and do my best to meet the wishes and the expectations of every one of you.

I shall begin by speaking about our ancestors, since it is only right

From History of the Peloponnesian War by Thucydides, translated by Rex Warner (Baltimore, Md.: Penguin, 1956), pp. 116–123. Reprinted by permission of The Bodley Head.

and proper on such an occasion to pay them the honor of recalling what they did. In this land of ours there have always been the same people living from generation to generation up till now, and they, by their courage and their virtues, have handed it on to us, a free country. They certainly deserve our praise. Even more so do our fathers deserve it. For to the inheritance they had received they added all the empire we have now, and it was not without blood and toil that they handed it down to us of the present generation. And then we ourselves, assembled here today, who are mostly in the prime of life, have, in most directions, added to the power of our empire and have organized our State in such a way that it is perfectly well able to look after itself both in peace and in war.

I have no wish to make a long speech on subjects familiar to you all: so I shall say nothing about the warlike deeds by which we acquired our power or the battles in which we or our fathers gallantly resisted our enemies, Greek or foreign. What I want to do is, in the first place, to discuss the spirit in which we faced our trials and also our constitution and the way of life which has made us great. After that I shall speak in praise of the dead, believing that this kind of speech is not inappropriate to the present occasion, and that this whole assembly, of citizens and foreigners, may listen to it with advantage.

Let me say that our system of government does not copy the institutions of our neighbors. It is more the case of our being a model to others, than of our imitating anyone else. Our constitution is called a democracy because power is in the hands not of a minority but of the whole people. When it is a question of settling private disputes, everyone is equal before the law; when it is a question of putting one person before another in positions of public responsibility, what counts is not membership of a particular class, but the actual ability which the man possesses. No one, so long as he has it in him to be of service to the state, is kept in political obscurity because of poverty. And, just as our political life is free and open, so is our day-to-day life in our relations with each other. We do not get into a state with our next-door neighbor if he enjoys himself in his own way, nor do we give him the kind of black looks which, though they do no real harm, still do hurt people's feelings. We are free and tolerant in our private lives; but in public affairs we keep to the law. This is because it commands our deep respect.

We give our obedience to those whom we put in positions of authority, and we obey the laws themselves, especially those which are for the protection of the oppressed, and those unwritten laws which it is an acknowledged shame to break.

And here is another point. When our work is over, we are in a position to enjoy all kinds of recreation for our spirits. There are various kinds of contests and sacrifices regularly throughout the year; in our own homes we find a beauty and a good taste which delight us every day and which drive away our cares. Then the greatness of our city brings it about that all the good things from all over the world flow in to us, so that to us it seems just as natural to enjoy foreign goods as our own local products.

Then there is a great difference between us and our opponents, in our attitude toward military security. Here are some examples: Our city is open to the world, and we have no periodical deportations in order to prevent people observing or finding out secrets which might be of military advantage to the enemy. This is because we rely, not on secret weapons, but on our own real courage and loyalty. There is a difference, too, in our educational systems. The Spartans, from their earliest boyhood, are submitted to the most laborious training in courage; we pass our lives without all these restrictions, and yet are just as ready to face the same dangers as they are. Here is a proof of this: When the Spartans invade our land, they do not come by themselves, but bring all their allies with them; whereas we, when we launch an attack abroad, do the job by ourselves, and, though fighting on foreign soil, do not often fail to defeat opponents who are fighting for their own hearths and homes. As a matter of fact none of our enemies has ever yet been confronted with our total strength, because we have to divide our attention between our navy and the many missions on which our troops are sent on land. Yet, if our enemies engage a detachment of our forces and defeat it, they give themselves credit for having thrown back our entire army; or, if they lose, they claim that they were beaten by us in full strength. There are certain advantages, I think, in our way of meeting danger voluntarily, with an easy mind, instead of with a laborious training, with natural rather than with state-induced courage. We do not have to spend our time practicing to meet sufferings which are still in the future; and when they are actually upon us we show ourselves just as brave as these others who are always in strict training. This is one point in which, I think, our city deserves to be admired. There are also others:

Our love of what is beautiful does not lead to extravagance; our love of the things of the mind does not make us soft. We regard wealth as something to be properly used, rather than as something to boast about. As for poverty, no one need be ashamed to admit it: the real shame is in not taking practical measures to escape from it. Here each individual is interested not only in his own affairs but in the affairs of the state as well: even those who are mostly occupied with their own business are extremely well-informed on general politics—

this is a peculiarity of ours: we do not say that a man who takes no interest in politics is a man who minds his own business; we say that he has no business here at all. We Athenians, in our own persons, take our decisions on policy or submit them to proper discussions: for we do not think that there is an incompatibility between words and deeds; the worst thing is to rush into action before the consequences have been properly debated. And this is another point where we differ from other people. We are capable at the same time of taking risks and of estimating them beforehand. Others are brave out of ignorance; and, when they stop to think, they begin to fear. But the man who can most truly be accounted brave is he who best knows the meaning of what is sweet in life and what is terrible, and then goes out undeterred to meet what is to come.

Again, in questions of general good feeling there is a great contrast between us and most other people. We make friends by doing good to others, not by receiving good from them. This makes our friendship all the more reliable, since we want to keep alive the gratitude of those who are in our debt by showing continued goodwill to them: whereas the feelings of one who owes us something lack the same enthusiasm, since he knows that, when he repays our kindness, it will be more like paying back a debt than giving something spontaneously. We are unique in this. When we do kindnesses to others, we do not do them out of any calculations of profit or loss: we do them without afterthought, relying on our free liberality. Taking everything together then, I declare that our city is an education to Greece, and I declare that in my opinion each single one of our citizens, in all the manifold aspects of life, is able to show himself the rightful lord and owner of his own person, and do this, moreover, with exceptional grace and exceptional versatility. And to show that this is no empty boasting for the present occasion, but real tangible fact, you have only to consider the power which our city possesses and which has been won by those very qualities which I have mentioned. Athens, alone of the states we know, comes to her testing time in a greatness that surpasses what was imagined of her. In her case, and in her case alone, no invading enemy is ashamed at being defeated, and no subject can complain of being governed by people unfit for their responsibilities. Mighty indeed are the marks and monuments of our empire which we have left. Future ages will wonder at us, as the present age wonders at us now. We do not need the praises of a Homer, or of anyone else whose words may delight us for the moment, but whose estimation of facts will fall short of what is really true. For our adventurous spirit has forced an entry into every sea and into every land; and everywhere we have left behind us everlasting memorials of good done to our friends or suffering inflicted on our enemies.

This, then, is the kind of city for which these men, who could not bear the thought of losing her, nobly fought and nobly died. It is only natural that every one of us who survive them should be willing to undergo hardships in her service. And it was for this reason that I have spoken at such length about our city, because I wanted to make it clear that for us there is more at stake than there is for others who lack our advantages; also I wanted my words of praise for the dead to be set in the bright light of evidence. And now the most important of these words has been spoken. I have sung the praises of our city; but it was the courage and gallantry of these men, and of people like them, which made her splendid. Nor would you find it true in the case of many of the Greeks, as it is true of them, that no words can do more than justice to their deeds.

To me it seems that the consummation which has overtaken these men shows us the meaning of manliness in its first revelation and in its final proof. Some of them, no doubt, had their faults; but what we ought to remember first is their gallant conduct against the enemy in defense of their native land. They have blotted out evil with good, and done more service to the commonwealth than they ever did harm in their private lives. No one of these men weakened because he wanted to go on enjoying his wealth: no one put off the awful day in the hope that he might live to escape his poverty and grow rich. More to be desired than such things, they chose to check the enemy's pride. This, to them, was a risk most glorious, and they accepted it, willing to strike down the enemy and relinquish everything else. As for success or failure, they left that in the doubtful hands of Hope, and when the reality of battle was before their face, they put their trust in their own selves. In the fighting, they thought it more honorable to stand their ground and suffer death than to give in and save their lives. So they fled from the reproaches of men, abiding with life and limb the brunt of battle; and, in a small moment of time, the climax of their lives, a culmination of glory, not of fear, were swept away from us.

So and such they were, these men—worthy of their city. We who remain behind may hope to be spared their fate, but must resolve to keep the same daring spirit against the foe. It is not simply a question of estimating the advantages in theory. I could tell you a long story (and you know it as well as I do) about what is to be gained by beating the enemy back. What I would prefer is that you should fix your eyes every day on the greatness of Athens as she really is, and should fall in love with her. When you realize her greatness, then reflect that what made her great was men with a spirit of adventure, men who knew their duty, men who were ashamed to fall below a certain standard. If they ever failed in an enterprise, they made up their minds that at any rate the city should not find their courage lacking to her, and they gave to her the best contribution that they could. They gave her their lives, to her and to all of us, and for their own selves they won praises that never grow old, the most splendid of sepulchers— not the sepulcher in which their bodies are laid, but where their glory remains eternal in men's minds, always there on the right occasion to stir others to speech or to action. For famous men have the whole earth as their memorial: it is not only the inscriptions on their graves in their own country that mark them out; no, in foreign lands also, not in any visible form but in people's hearts, their memory abides and grows. It is for you to try to be like them. Make up your minds that happiness depends on being free, and freedom depends on being courageous. Let there be no relaxation in face of the perils of the war. The people who have most excuse for despising death are not the wretched and unfortunate, who have no hope of doing well for themselves, but those who run the risk of a complete reversal in their lives, and who would feel the difference most intensely, if things went wrong for them. Any intelligent man would find a humiliation caused by his own slackness more painful to bear than death, when death comes to him unperceived, in battle, and in the confidence of his patriotism.

For these reasons I shall not commiserate with those parents of the dead, who are present here. Instead I shall try to comfort them. They are well aware that they have grown up in a world where there are many changes and chances. But this is good fortune—for men to end their lives with honor, as these have done, and for you honorably to lament them: their life was set to a measure where death and happiness went hand in hand. I know that it is difficult to convince you of this. When you see other people happy you will often be reminded of what used to make you happy too. One does not feel sad at not having some good thing which is outside one's experience: real grief is felt at the loss of something which one is used to. All the same, those of you who are of the right age must bear up and take comfort in the thought of having more children. In your own homes these new children will prevent you from brooding over those who are no more, and they will be a help to the city, too, both in filling the empty places, and in assuring her security. For it is impossible for a man to put forward fair and honest views about our affairs if he has not, like everyone else, children whose lives may be at stake. As for those of you who are now to old to have children, I would ask you to count as gain the greater part of your life, in which you have been happy, and remember that what remains is not long, and let your hearts be lifted up at the thought of the fair fame of the dead. One's sense of honor is the only thing that does not grow old, and the last pleasure, when one is worn out with age, is not, as the poet said, making money, but having the respect of one's fellow men.

As for those of you here who are sons or brothers of the dead, I can see a hard struggle in front of you. Everyone always speaks well of the dead, and, even if you rise to the greatest heights of heroism, it will be a hard thing for you to get the reputation of having come near, let alone equalled, their standard. When one is alive, one is always liable to the jealousy of one's competitors, but when one is out of the way, the honor one receives is sincere and unchallenged.

Perhaps I should say a word or two on the duties of women to those among you who are now widowed. I can say all I have to say in a short word of advice. Your great glory is not to be inferior to what God has made you, and the greatest glory of a woman is to be least talked about by men, whether they are praising you or criticizing you. I have now, as the law demanded, said what I had to say. For the time being our offerings to the dead have been made, and for the future their children will be supported at the public expense by the city, until they come of age. This is the crown and prize which she offers, both to the dead and to their children, for the ordeals which they have faced. Where the rewards of valor are the greatest, there you will find also the best and bravest spirits among the people. And now, when you have mourned for your dear ones, you must depart.

It must have been impossible for a Greek of the classical period to think of self-fulfillment solely in terms of selfish satisfactions. Happiness for the individual was inseparable from happiness or the general well-being of the community. In the following selection from Plato's Republic, temperance and justice are treated as two of four essential ingredients in the Utopian society.

# The Search for Utopia

Plato

Two virtues remain to be discovered in the State—first temperance, and then justice which is the end of our search.

Very true.

Now, can we find justice without troubling ourselves about temperance?

I do not know how that can be accomplished, he said, nor do I desire that justice should be brought to light and temperance lost sight of; and therefore I wish that you would do me the favor of considering temperance first.

Certainly, I replied, I should not be justified in refusing your request.

Then consider, he said.

Yes, I replied; I will; and as far as I can at present see, the virtue of temperance has more of the nature of harmony and symphony than the preceding.

How so? he asked.

Temperance, I replied, is the ordering or controlling of certain pleasures and desires; this is curiously enough implied in the saying of "a man being his own master"; and other traces of the same notion may be found in language.

No doubt, he said.

There is something ridiculous in the expression "master of himself"; for the master is also the servant and the servant the master; and in all these modes of speaking the same person is denoted.

Certainly.

The meaning is, I believe, that in the human soul there is a better and also a worse principle; and when the better has the worse under control, then a man is said to be master of himself; and this is a term of praise: but when, owing to evil education or association, the better principle, which is also the smaller, is overwhelmed by the greater mass of the

From The Republic, Book IV, by Plato, from The Dialogues of Plato, Vol. 1, translated by B. A. Jowett (New York: Random House, 1892, 1920), pp. 693–698.

worse—in this case he is blamed and is called the slave of self and un-principled.

Yes, there is reason in that.

And now, I said, look at our newly-created State, and there you will find one of these two conditions realized; for the State, as you will acknowledge, may be justly called master of itself, if the words "temperance" and "self-mastery" truly express the rule of the better part over the worse.

Yes, he said, I see that what you say is true.

Let me further note that the manifold and complex pleasures and desires and pains are generally found in children and women and servants, and in the freemen so called who are of the lowest and more numerous class.

Certainly, he said.

Whereas the simple and moderate desires which follow reason, and are under the guidance of mind and true opinion, are to be found only in a few, and those the best born and best educated.

Very true.

These two, as you may perceive, have a place in our State; and the meaner desires of the many are held down by the virtuous desires and wisdom of the few.

That I perceive, he said.

Then if there be any city which may be described as master of its own pleasures and desires, and master of itself, ours may claim such a designation?

Certainly, he replied.

It may also be called temperate, and for the same reasons?

Yes.

And if there be any State in which rulers and subjects will be agreed as to the question who are to rule, that again will be our State?

Undoubtedly.

And the citizens being thus agreed among themselves, in which class will temperance be found—in the rulers or in the subjects?

In both, as I should imagine, he replied.

Do you observe that we were not far wrong in our guess that temperance was a sort of harmony?

Why so?

Why, because temperance is unlike courage and wisdom, each of which resides in a part only, the one making the State wise and the other valiant; not so temperance, which extends to the whole, and runs through all the notes of the scale, and produces a harmony of the weaker and the stronger and the middle class, whether you suppose them to be stronger or weaker in wisdom or power or numbers or wealth, or anything else. Most truly then may we deem temperance to be the agreement of the naturally superior and inferior, as to the right to rule of either, both in states and individuals.

I entirely agree with you.

And so, I said, we may consider three out of the four virtues to have been discovered in our State. The last of those qualities which make a state virtuous must be justice, if we only knew what that was.

The inference is obvious.

The time then has arrived, Glaucon, when, like huntsmen, we should surround the cover, and look sharp that justice does not steal away, and pass out of sight and escape us; for beyond a doubt she is somewhere in this country: watch therefore and strive to catch a sight of her, and if you see her first, let me know.

Would that I could! but you should regard me rather as a follower who has just eyes enough to see what you show him—that is about as much as I am good for.

Offer up a prayer with me and follow.

I will, but you must show me the way.

Here is no path, I said, and the wood is dark and perplexing; still we must push on.

Let us push on.

Here I saw something: Halloo! I said, I begin to perceive a track, and I believe that the quarry will not escape.

Good news, he said.

Truly, I said, we are stupid fellows.

Why so?

Why, my good sir, at the beginning of our inquiry, ages ago, there was justice tumbling out at our feet, and we never saw her; nothing could be more ridiculous. Like people who go about looking for what they have in their minds—that was the way with us—we looked not at what we were seeking, but at what was far off in the distance; and therefore, I suppose, we missed her.

What do you mean?

I mean to say that in reality for a long time past we have been talking of justice, and have failed to recognize her.

I grow impatient at the length of your exordium.

Well then, tell me, I said, whether I am right or not: You remember the original principle which we were always laying down at the foundation of the State, that one man should practice one thing only, the thing to which his nature was best adapted;—now justice is this principle or a part of it.

Yes, we often said that one man should do one thing only.

Further, we affirmed that justice was doing one's own business, and not being a busybody; we said so again and again, and many others have said the same to us.

Yes, we said so.

Then to do one's own business in a certain way may be assumed to be justice. Can you tell me whence I derive this inference?

I cannot, but I should like to be told.

Because I think that this is the only virtue which remains in the State when the other virtues of temperance and courage and wisdom are abstracted; and, that this is the ultimate cause and condition of the existence of all of them, and while remaining in them is also their preservative; and we were saying that if the three were discovered by us, justice would be the fourth or remaining one.

That follows of necessity.

If we are asked to determine which of these four qualities by its presence contributes most to the excellence of the State, whether the agreement of rulers and subjects, or the preservation in the soldiers of the opinion which the law ordains about the true nature of dangers, or wisdom and watchfulness in the rulers, or whether this other which I am mentioning, and which is found in children and women, slave and freeman, artisan, ruler, subject,—the quality I mean, of every one doing his own work, and not being a busybody, would claim the palm—the question is not so easily answered.

Certainly, he replied, there would be a difficulty in saying which.

Then the power of each individual in the State to do his own work appears to compete with the other political virtues, wisdom, temperance, courage.

Yes, he said.

And the virtue which enters into this competition is justice?

Exactly.

Let us look at the question from another point of view: Are not the rulers in a State those to whom you would entrust the office of determining suits at law?

Certainly.

And are suits decided on any other ground but that a man may neither take what is another's, nor be deprived of what is his own?

Yes; that is their principle.

Which is the just principle?

Yes.

Then on this view also justice will be admitted to be the having and doing what is a man's own, and belongs to him?

Very true.

Think, now, and say whether you agree with me or not. Suppose a carpenter to be doing the business of a cobbler, or a cobbler of a carpenter; and suppose them to exchange their implements or their duties, or the same person to be doing the work of both, or whatever be the change; do you think that any great harm would result to the State?

Not much.

But when the cobbler or any other man whom nature designed to be a trader, having his heart lifted up by wealth or strength or the number of his followers, or any like advantage, attempts to force his way into the class of warriors, or a warrior into that of legislators and guardians, for which he is unfitted, and either to take the implements or the duties of the other; or when one man is trader, legislator, and warrior all in one, then I think you will agree with me in saying that this interchange and this meddling of one with another is the ruin of the State.

Most true.

Seeing then, I said, that there are three distinct classes, any meddling of one with another, or the change of one into another, is the greatest harm to the State, and may be most justly termed evil-doing?

Precisely.

And the greatest degree of evil-doing to one's own city would be termed by you injustice?

Certainly.

This then is injustice; and on the other hand when the trader, the auxiliary, and the guardian each do their own business, that is justice, and will make the city just.

I agree with you.

We will not, I said, be over-positive as yet; but if, on trial, this conception of justice be verified in the individual as well as in the State, there will be no longer any room for doubt; if it be not verified, we must have a fresh inquiry. First let us complete the old investigation, which we began, as you remember, under the impression that, if we could previously examine justice on the larger scale, there would be less difficulty in discerning her in the individual. That larger example appeared to be the State, and accordingly we constructed as good a one as we could, knowing well that in the good State justice would be found. Let the discovery which we made be now applied to the individual—if they agree, we shall be satisfied; or, if there be a difference in the individual, we will come back to the State and have another trial of the theory. The friction of the two men rubbed together may possibly strike a light in which justice will shine forth, and the vision which is then revealed we will fix in our souls.

That will be in regular course; let us do as you say.

I proceeded to ask: When two things, a greater and less, are called by the same name, are they like or unlike in so far as they are called the same?

Like, he replied.

The just man then, if we regard the idea of justice only, will be like the State?

He will.

And a State was thought by us to be just when the three classes in the State severally did their own business; and also thought to be temperate and valiant and wise by reason of certain other affections and qualities of these same classes?

True, he said.

And so of the individual; we may assume that he has the same three principles in his own soul which are found in the State; and he may be rightly described in the same terms, because he is affected in the same manner?

Certainly, he said.

The women's liberation movement in America has made it increasingly clear that Western Civilization has a long tradition of suppressing women, generally confining them to the role of watcher rather than doer. Still, women have achieved, and Sappho of Lesbos is just one example of outstanding accomplishment in the face of sexist restrictions. There was a world of difference between Athens and Sparta, just as there has been a world of cultural differences between women and men in our Western heritage that only now is beginning to be seriously challenged. In the following passage, the regimentation of Sparta is shown to have been a decisive factor in hindering development of strong individualistic traits among women and men alike. In most, if not all, phases of Western Civilization, this type of restriction has been placed upon only the women of the society.

# Self-Fulfillment for Women and Men in Sparta

Arthur Weigall

Lycurgus had evidently realized that the small ruling class would have no chance of maintaining itself in power, or, indeed, of protecting itself from annihilation at the hands of a rebellious helotry, except by the practice of some kind of code of strict discipline which would prevent its falling into slack or luxury-loving ways in the lazy air of this beautiful valley. He saw, no doubt, that the only hope of preserving the existence of this upper class at all lay in its whole-hearted adoption of a system of military training and an ideal of service to the state which should override all personal or family considerations and should convert the entire body of the Spartiates into a kind of machine, the sole purpose of which should be the maintenance of its own iron authority. The code which he forced upon them, however, was so severe that existence at such a price must sometimes hardly have seemed worth while; and, indeed, a story is told of a certain man of Sybaris who, having visited Sparta, declared that the Spartans' readiness to face death in battle was not to be wondered at, since it would be preferable to die a thousand deaths than to endure such a life as theirs.[1] The marvel is that the system was maintained for so many centuries; but if this fact says much for human endurance it also demonstates the tremendous resistance to change in the minds of any governing body of old men.[2] Lycurgus, however, took the precaution of refusing to allow his Spartans to go abroad except on the most urgent business, and he did what he could to prevent foreigners from coming to Sparta; and thus he put a considerable check on criticism.

When a baby was born, whether boy or girl, the law enjoined that it was to be taken before a committee appointed by the Ephors; and if it was a good and healthy specimen it was allowed to live, but if it was puny or unhealthy it was carried off to a certain chasm at the foot of the Taygetus mountains and there left to die or to be devoured. At the age of seven a boy was taken from his home, and was sent to live with other boys in one of the institutions established by the state for the training of the young in courage, endurance, and discipline. Here he was placed in a group under the captaincy of some one particularly promising boy, whose orders he had to obey, the frequent punishments inflicted by him having to be endured without complaint. Reading, writing, and music were taught; but apart from this the training was almost entirely physical.

The boys were constantly under the eye of elderly inspectors, who would often encourage them to fight with one another, so that an opinion might be formed thus early in life as to their military potentialities. The minimum of clothing was allowed them, and in all their games and exercises they were made to strip quite naked; while at nights they had to sleep on wooden boards covered with dry reeds which they were made to gather with their bare hands without the use of a knife. Affectionate friendships between elder and younger boys were encouraged, so that every younger boy should have somebody to regard as his hero, and every elder boy somebody weaker than himself to train in adventure and bravery. Thus, as Plutarch says, "there was not any one of the more promising boys who had not a 'lover' to bear him company"—a statement, however, which does not necessarily imply any impropriety, though the point is hard to determine, owing to the absence of direct evidence, the Greeks not regarding even the extremes of emotional attachment between two males as anything remarkable, unusual, or offensive.

At the age of twelve the boys' clothing was still further cut down; they were forbidden to wear shoes; and they were not allowed to have baths except on certain days in the year. Their food supplies were now diminished in order that they might be encouraged to forage for themselves; and raids by bands of boys upon people's orchards or vegetable-gardens were winked at by the authorities, and even thefts of meat from the shops were regarded as healthy indications of youthful enterprise. All kinds of tests of endurance and the silent bearing of pain were imposed; and when they were more or less fully grown the youths had to submit to a terrible flogging at the altar of the goddess Artemis—a barbarous custom which had its origin in a half-forgotten religious rite,[3] the practice of scourging the victim of a human sacrifice being very widespread in primitive times.[4] These boys were flogged until their blood streamed over the altar, while their parents stood amongst the crowd of spectators, complacently watching the ordeal. "I myself," writes Plutarch, "have seen several boys flogged to death at the altar of Artemis"; and, in fact, death during the *diamastigosis,* as the disgusting business was called, was considered as honorable as death in battle.

At the age of twenty the Spartan youth was considered ready for military service, and was sent to live in barracks, where he became a member of a mess which generally consisted of about fifteen young men. A piece of land was assigned to each individual; and he was expected to contribute to the common table whatever produce it afforded him. The fare was simple, the basis of every meal being the celebrated black-broth of Sparta, which was so unpalatable that it was said in jest to require no less a seasoning than that of sheer hunger and fatigue. Confectionery and sweetmeats were considered injurious to health;[5] and even banquets on great occasions consisted chiefly of bread, meat, beans and other vegetables, salads, and dried figs.[6]

No Spartan was allowed to engage in any trade, and money-making was forbidden. All gold and silver was called in, and heavy bars of iron were used as a medium of exchange.[7] The land was worked by the helots, and its produce shared; and the houses were all of more or less one pattern, devoid of ornamentation, nor were any lights allowed to be used at night. Music was the single art which was encouraged, and this only for military or patriotic purposes. There was no literature, and even speech at any length was discouraged, the short, pithy remarks of the Spartans being so notorious that we still speak of that style of address as "laconic," that is to say, pertaining to Laconica, the Spartan country. Mirth, however, was compulsory, and Lycurgus himself dedicated a little statue to Laughter. Modern excavations have shown that in the time of Sappho, and earlier, Spartan artists were turning out a certain number of statuettes; but this art presently died out.

At the age of thirty a man was allowed to marry; but love and romance were discouraged, and, in fact, Athenaeus states[8] that the choice of a bride was often left to chance, several men at night-time being pushed into an unlit room with an equal number of girls, and left to grope in the darkness for a mate. This marriage-lottery, however, was no great hazard, for Spartan women were largely of one pattern—robust, healthy-looking, athletic creatures, whose sole purpose in life was the production of healthy children for the future service of the state. Girls were trained like the men in athletics and gymnastics; they wrestled, threw the discus and the javelin, and performed various feats of strength; they were often present at the men's sports and sometimes even ran races with them; and in all such exercises they were expected to go naked or else to wear but a short *chiton,* or tunic. Modesty was deprecated as tending, I suppose, toward love's romance, the partial concealment of the feminine form being in all ages largely erotic; and, in fact, Euripides[9] tells us that no Spartan girl had a chance of being modest, even if she wished to be. "In order to do away with all acquired womanishness," writes Plutarch, "Lycurgus directed, also, that the young women should walk naked in the public processions, as did the young men, and should dance, too, in that condition, and sing their songs, whilst the men stood around watching and listening to them. . . . Nor was there anything shameful in this nakedness of the women, for all wantonness was excluded."

Girls were not married until they were about twenty years of age. On a bride's wedding-day her hair was cut short and she was dressed in a man's clothes; after which she was taken into a dark room, and placed upon a hard straw-mattress. The bridegroom then groped his way in, wearing his working-clothes, having come straight from the military mess, and to the mess he returned an hour or two later. Subsequently they met in secret and as best they could manage, having as yet no house of their own; and it is said that often the wife bore children to her husband without ever having seen him by the light of day, though it is not easy to reconcile this assertion with the statement that men and unmarried girls met together with such entire freedom on the athletic field. Later the couple was assigned a house, and of this the wife was absolute mistress; and whereas in many parts of Greece the wife addressed her husband as "lord" or "master," in Sparta it was the man who called his wife *despoina*, "lady" or "mistress." Women, rather than men, were considered as the natural holders of property, the men being too busy with military affairs; and certainly in the fourth century B.C., if not in Sappho's time, nearly half the lands of Laconica were actually owned by women. Married women were not supposed to frequent the playing fields as they had done when they were girls; but their general movements were not much restricted, and, on the whole, they were a good deal freer than the men, although the need for conforming to the Spartan code enslaved their minds completely enough.

As has been said, a Spartan woman's main object in life was the production of healthy children, and for this purpose she was permitted on occasion to select a man, other than her husband, to be the father of her child. Sometimes two women, who were not satisfied with their offspring, would exchange husbands; sometimes an elderly or ailing husband would, with his wife's consent, hand her over temporarily to a fitter man; and sometimes a woman would keep two or three men for the purpose of her experiments in eugenics. If she did not like the man to whom she was married, moreover, she was entitled to leave him and to take her belongings with her, a divorce being then arranged. Plutarch states that Lycurgus was definitely of the opinion that just as dogs and horses were bred with care from selected couples, so human offspring should be produced by scientific breeding, and should be reared and trained, when infancy was past, by professionals, the idea of family life and the home being foolishly sentimental. At the same time, Plutarch adds, married women were permitted to make professions to young girls of that kind of love in which both parties are of the same sex.

In spite of all this the ladies of Sparta were generally considered to be moral and chaste; and the statements of Aristotle and Plato[10] that these licenses legalized the most unrestrained immorality were not subscribed to by foreign critics, who usually gaped at Spartan customs in respectful astonishment, though they sometimes admitted that Spartan husbands were inclined to be henpecked. Personally, I am of opinion that the study of Lycurgus is one which belongs to the province of the pathologist, for his code, in its sexual aspect, has too close an affinity with certain well-known perversions of the human mind to be regarded as the creation of pure idealism. The youths with their male "lovers," the girls forced to walk naked in the public processions, the brides dressed as men, the wives with their right to make trial of the qualities of different men, the parents obliged to witness the flogging of their sons, and so forth, are matters which point to something very like sexual lunacy in the author of the system; and one reads with sympathy of the man—a certain Alkander by name—who went after Lycurgus with a stick and nearly beat the life out of him. It is true that this personage was chiefly incensed at the ordinance which obliged him to eat at a communal table and to make a show of enjoying the disgusting black-broth there set before him; but one may well imagine him to have been in revolt against the whole code.

Spartan women, I may add, were taught to regard their sons as the absolute property of the state, and we read of a mother saying to her soldier-son as he set out for the wars, "Come back either *with* your shield, or *upon* it"; and these mothers were wont to declare that they were more fortunate when their boys died in battle than when they returned unhurt. A certain Spartan woman was much commended for having killed her son because he had saved his life in battle by running away; and another is stated to have shouted the equivalent of "Hurrah!" when she heard that her eight sons had all been killed. It was not until the age of sixty that men were allowed to retire from their military and communal duties, and take up their residence at home; and if by this time they were widowers they were expected to marry again. Men without wives were regarded as miscreants; and it is said that they were liable to be set upon and roughly handled by groups of angry women, nor was it any joking matter to be mauled by the powerful ladies of Sparta.

The position of women in Sparta is of particular interest to us in connection with Sappho; for in this regard the Aeolian civilization of Lesbos had more in common with Dorian institutions than with those of the other Greek races. The code of Lycurgus in its relation to women presupposes a considerable freedom of the sex amongst his people; and there is plenty of evidence to show, in fact, that in all the Doric states the standing of women was very much higher than it was in, say, Ionia or Attica. Some of these Doric states were situated on the coast of Asia Minor and the neighboring islands, and must have been in constant touch with Lesbos. On the mainland of Caria, a hundred and fifty miles south of Mitylene, stood the important Dorian city of Halicarnassus, and on the promontory south of it was Knidos (Cnidus). Between these two cities lay the island of Kos, where there was a mixed population of Dorians and Aeolians; and to the south again was the island of Rhodes, with its three Dorian cities, Lindos, Ialysos, and Kameiros. But between this Dorian region and the Aeolian lands lay the territory of the Ionians, where women were regarded in the Oriental manner as very inferior to men. Thus Lesbos was as likely to be influenced by the one as by the other; and it would therefore seem that there was a basic similarity between the Aeolians and the Dorians in their treatment of women, and that the code of Lycurgus simply pushed to extremes an attitude with which the Lesbians were familiar.

There is not much direct evidence, other than that supplied by the life of Sappho herself, as to the position of women in Lesbos; but the general inference, as I have already said, is that they were almost as free as the western women of today. When Lesbos was visited by Tournefort[11] about two hundred years ago, the Lesbian women were noted for their lack of feminine bashfulness, and the fact that, in spite of the island being under the rule of Islam, they then often went naked to the waist, and that their ordinary dresses did not cover the breast, indicates that there was still a very strong tradition of freedom from that kind of male dictation which demands the veiling and the seclusion of their womenkind. A century later the traveler Skene[12] describes the Lesbian women as being extremely masculine, as inheriting all landed property, and as being the managers of all family affairs. In fact, he says that they used to go out to work, or to hunt on horseback, while the men sat at home to spin. I do not wish to suggest that the men of Lesbos in Sappho's time were henpecked by their wives, as the Spartan men were said to be; but it seems that we are to picture Lesbian women as then being particularly free—as free in some aspects as the Spartans, and, indeed, freer, since they were not called upon to conform to a soulless system which developed the body and stultified the brains.

## Notes

1 Athenaeus, xii, 15; iv, 15.

2 Most of the following details will be found in Plutarch's *Life of Lycurgus*. See also Xenophon: *Respublica Lacedaemoniorum*; and Aristotle: *Politics*.

3 Pausanias, iii, 16, 6.

4 Lycurgus is said to have *substituted* the scourging for the sacrifice; but it is probably more correct to say that he *retained* the scourging and abolished the actual killing.

5 Athenaeus, xiv, 74.

6 Athenaeus, iv, 15 ff.

7 Chapter Eighteen.

8 Athenaeus, xiii, 2.

9 Euripides: *Andromache*, 595.

10 Aristotle: *Politics*, ii, 9; Plato: *Laws*, 780.

11 Tournefort: *Voyage into the Levant*.

12 Skene: *Wayfaring Sketches*, 1847.

## Questions

1 How does the opening essay define the terms **hubris**, **nemesis**, and **polis**? Have Americans ever suffered from hubris? If so, has nemesis followed?

2 What hypocrisy does Meldon Levine describe? Why do students, almost everywhere a privileged group, criticize the system? Has the student consciousness of the 1960s died?

3 Why does Solon believe that the rich are less well off than those of modest means? Do you agree with him that true happiness can come only with death? Does this idea render Jefferson's "pursuit of happiness" invalid?

4 Does any part of the contemporary world meet the standards for the state as described in Plato's **Republic**?

5 Do you see any parallels between the life in Sparta or Athens and contemporary life? To which model are you attracted, Sparta or Athens? Why?

# 5

# Law and Order, Protest and Violence, Roman Style

R. Bausch

We have heard much of the protest and violence in America and little of
the protest and violence in ancient Rome. But Rome's problems were in
many ways similar to our own. Both republics offered hope for liberty and
justice for all; both even offered hope for political and economic equality,
so far as humanly possible. Rome's Republic, 509–27 B.C., failed to
live up to its promises. America, despite its problems, still offers hope for
all mankind, for there is the hope that America, with its many races,
religions, and nationalities, can demonstrate to a divided world
that peoples of diverse backgrounds can live in relative harmony with
progress toward liberty and justice for all. This is the promise of America.
Some myths, canons, and hangups will be factors in determining
the answer to the promise.

# With Liberty and Justice for Some

Frederick Gentles

There were fires in the sky . . . there was a violent earthquake
and a cow talked—there was a rumor that a cow talked the
previous year, but nobody believed it: this year they did. Nor
was that all: it rained lumps of meat. Thousands of birds (we
are told) seized and devoured the pieces in mid-air, while what
fell to the ground lay scattered about for several days without
going putrid. The Sybilline Books were consulted by two officials, who found in them the prediction that danger threatened
from a "concourse of alien men," who might attack "the high
places of the City, with the shedding of blood." There was also
found, amongst other things, a warning to avoid factious politics. This annoyed the tribunes, who swore the prophecies were
a fake, deliberately invented to stop the passage of the proposed
law. A dangerous clash was imminent, and only avoided by—
would you believe it?—a report from the Hernici that the
Volscians and the Aequians, in spite of their recent losses, were
on the warpath again. The old cycle was being repeated.[1]

The year was just the other side of 450 B.C. and the place was
Rome, where the Establishment, represented by the Patricians, was
being challenged—challenged by the Plebeians, whose tribunes were
demanding changes. According to the Roman historian Livy, the
tribunes of the Plebeians had suggested that the laws be codified to
curb the powers of tyrannical consuls. The suggestion was really a
demand, and the Patricians were so disturbed at this threat to their
power that they declared war on the nearby tribes to distract the
people from domestic troubles. The Plebeians rioted. They actually

protested the war—a war, they said, that was not necessary. As violence took hold in the Forum and on the streets, uncompromising partisans arose on both sides. One young conservative, the champion of the Patrician cause, hounded the tribunes out of the Forum and scattered the mob by threats and beatings. An equally uncompromising liberal tribune brought this young nobleman to trial for intemperate, lawless, and violent acts, and thereby succeeded in paving the way for the passage of the famous Twelve Tables, Rome's first written law.

This is the story of the Roman Republic. It is the story of the haves being challenged with protest and violence by the have-nots. It is a story remarkably like that of nineteenth and twentieth-century Europe and America, where laboring men, farmers, immigrants, and women struggled for political and economic rights against those with business and property interests. In Rome and America an establishment class creates the myths, and makes the canons—or laws—which become settled in the minds of many as the way of life. But the Roman and American establishments were unique. They were usually willing to compromise, especially if there were threats to the general welfare.

The willingness of conservative and liberal factions to compromise their differences in a republican form of government breathed life into both Roman and Western civilizations for many generations. The American Republic, not yet two hundred years old, is one of the oldest in the Western world, and, except for four years of the Civil War, change has been made within the framework of constitutional government. The Roman Republic, 509–27 B.C., lived nearly four hundred years before crumbling into civil strife, civil war, and Julius Caesar. This is not to say, however, that during that four centuries of prevailing law and order there was peace and harmony in the Roman world. The evolution of liberty and justice for all was often mutated by protest, agitation, and even violence.

After their success in codifying the law, the Plebeians next agitated for the right to intermarry with the Patrician class. Livy tells of the bitterness of the common people and of the violence of the Establishment. The tribune Canuleius, addressing the Assembly of citizens, declared:

> Men of Rome, the violence with which the Senate has been opposing our programme of reform has made me realize more vividly than ever before the depth of the contempt in which you are held by the aristocracy. I have often suspected it, but now I know; they think you are unworthy of living with them

within the walls of the same town. Yet what is the object of our proposals? It is merely to point out that we are their fellow-citizens—that we have the same country as they, even though we have less money. We seek the right of intermarriage, a right commonly granted to other nations on our borders—indeed, before now Rome has granted citizenship, which is more than intermarriage, even to a defeated enemy. We propose that a man of the people may have the right to be elected to the consulship: is that the same as saying some rogue who was, or is, a slave? Such is their contempt for you that they would rob you, if they could, of the very light you see by; they grudge you the air you breathe, the words you speak, the very fact that you have the shape of men.[2]

Indeed, the Romans too had their ghettos, their upper-crust society with uncontaminated blood living in uncontaminated neighborhoods, and violent methods to keep people in their place.

But the Plebs persisted. Canuleius continued:

One could hardly offer a more signal insult to one section of the community than to consider it unfit to marry with, as if it were too dirty to touch: it is like condemning it to exile and banishment within the city walls. They take every precaution against the dreadful risk of becoming related by blood to us poor scum. We expect to gain nothing from marrying into your class except to be considered as human beings and citizens of Rome; and your opposition is wholly unreasonable—unless you take pleasure merely in humiliating and insulting us.[3]

Any parallels in twentieth-century Europe and America?

But the Plebs continued their fight to become part of the Haves. One exasperated Patrician consul finally called a meeting to protest to the people their constant demands. His heart-rending appeal is an exhibit of sheer frustration over the continuing ferment. He emphasizes the extreme flexibility and generosity of the conservatives in granting one reform after another, though he does admit, indirectly, that the lower class does not have full civil liberty:

The truth is that our communal life is poisoned by political discord and party strife, and it was that which raised his [the enemy] hopes of destroying us, seeing as he did, your lust for liberty in perpetual conflict with our lust for power, and each party's loathing of the representative magistracies of the other. What, in God's name, do you want now? Once it was tribunes, and to preserve the peace we let you have them; then it was *decemvirs,* and we permitted their appointment. Soon you were sick of them; we forced them to resign. . . . Again you wanted tribunes—and got them. . . . You have your tribunes to protect you, your right of appeal to the people, your popular decrees made binding on the Senate, while in the empty name of justice all our privileges are trampled under foot: all this we have borne, and are still bearing. How is it all to end? Will the time ever come when we can have a united city, a united country? You have beaten us, and we accept our defeat with more equanimity than you your victory.[4]

The consul seems to be asking, what more do you Plebeians want, blood? And that was it. The Plebs wanted blood, and they eventually got the right to intermarry into Patrician families.

In forcing the Patricians to share their power, the Plebs at one time threatened to bring the economy to a halt by walking out of the city and letting the Patricians do the dirty work; this early example of the general strike was effective, though the Plebs resorted to such extreme measures only on occasion. The Plebeians continued to gain more rights as the Republic continued on down through the years, because the system was flexible enough. But at last a new aristocracy of leading Patrician and Plebeian families came to rule Rome, and the earlier promise of the Republic to provide a legislature responsive to the needs of the people gave way to the tyranny of the new elite and a legislature and executive responsive to its special needs. There was to be liberty and justice only for those who had made it, not for all.

Two major factors that led to the tragedy of the Roman Republic were the acquisition of an empire, starting with the Punic wars, and the creation of a military-commercial complex, which resulted from conquest and trade. The idea of a federal republic, which at its beginnings gave citizens of the Italian states rights equal to or nearly equal to the rights of the citizens of Rome, was not extended to the Greek, Spanish, and African colonies the Republic had taken. Rather, the colonies were treated as sources of loot, slaves, and tribute by the proconsuls and by the carpetbaggers who followed them south— and east and west. The colonies were exploited, as colonies were to be exploited on into the twentieth century. The wealth and slaves flowing back to Rome on all the roads leading to that great city undermined the morals and the simple life-style of a predominantly agricultural community. Old ways were changed as farming became commercial and absentee landlords bought up huge estates to be worked by slaves. Leases on the public lands were acquired by the wealthy. The small farmer was frequently in trouble with Rome's stringent debtor laws passed by the Establishment and finally he found himself in Rome to compete with other farmers and the multiplying slave population for jobs. He became one of the motley mob of the idle, the hungry, the illiterate, and the unwashed. As part of the mob, he became fair game for ambitious politicians and military men who needed popular support as consuls and generals.

As wealthy Patrician and Plebeian families turned to commerce, and as a new middle class of prosperous businessmen, contractors, bankers, and government bureaucrats rose to political influence, great tenement blocks were constructed to house the poor in ghettos described by one historian as no better than rabbit warrens. The rich became richer, the poor became poorer, and urban conditions deteriorated to a point that threatened all, though not all could see the threat. However, Tiberius Gracchus, tribune for the year 133 B.C., saw the need for resettling the surplus population on the land. He proposed that leases on the public lands be limited in size and that the landless be given government subsidies to start private enterprises. This was a program of poor-relief, and, as usual, there was opposition from the wealthy, especially from those who had leases on thousands of acres of the public lands that had been acquired as Rome conquered Italy.

Tiberius pushed his law through despite political maneuvers by the Senate, and he appointed a land commission composed of himself, his brother, and his father-in-law to carry out the reform. However, when he ran for an unprecedented second term as tribune to carry out this and other reforms, the conservative extremists took the law into their own hands, gathered a force, and made for the Forum, where some three hundred fell, including Tiberius, who was clubbed to death with a footstool. This date, 133 B.C., is taken as the beginning of the breakdown of law and order in the Republic: compromise and reform gave way to a century of bloody battles between gangs of liberal and conservative hoodlums and, finally, to civil war and dictatorship.

Ten years later, the brother of Tiberius, Gaius Gracchus, became tribune and introduced a new deal that provided for resumption of the land commission, a dole of wheat to every resident citizen who applied in person, road and bridge building for commercial purposes, and the settlement of the surplus population in colonies favorably placed for trade. Gracchus planned to reform the government entirely by taking ultimate power from the Senate and giving it to the tribunes, who would have sole executive power, and to the Assembly of people. But when he planned to extend Roman citizenship with its many fringe benefits to several other Italian communities, the mob, upon whom he depended for votes in the Assembly, reacted against this measure that would have brought greater peace and unity to Italy. Romans were jealous of their material privileges as citizens, and they were not about to share the wheat dole, the special accommodation at spectacles, and the bribes they received for votes at election time. There was a backlash, a Roman citizens' backlash. The Senate feared Gracchus, too, and declared a state of emergency when mobs gathered. In the melee, Gracchus, surrounded by his enemies, had his slave run him through. People in the streets had seen him running from his pursuers but did nothing to help him—they did not want to get involved. His head was cut off and taken to the consul Opimius, who then ordered the slaying of three thousand of Gaius' followers without trial.

The next hundred years were the years of the professional soldier, although the Republic continued on in name. With the acquisition of empire and the commercial spirit, Rome was unable to keep the military subordinate to civilian control. The consul as chief executive was also a general. Marius, Sulla, Pompey, Caesar, Crassus, Antony, and Augustus were generals who dominated the political scene after the time of the Gracchi. They were all connected, directly and indirectly, with banking, commercial, and huge property interests. And it is fatal for a country with democratic aspirations to place its military men in a position to exercise primary political power. The army is not a democratic institution, and generals, when given political power, are inclined to direct civilians as they direct soldiers—which means giving orders and no back-talk allowed.

The historian Sallust, who lived during these shaky times, says that Marius was consumed by ambition to become consul and was qualified in every way except by his red blood and his country-style grammar. He curried the favor of the people, however, won success as a general against Jugurtha in Africa, and through sheer doggedness was elected consul an unprecedented six times between 107 and 100 B.C. By recruiting soldiers from the common people of Rome, Marius made them more loyal to him than to Rome. (Some twenty-one centuries later, Mussolini and Hitler made new use of this old idea.) Democracy was as good as dead when left to generals of the army such as Sulla, Marius, and their successors. The first century before Christ was a witches' Sabbath of rival military and commercial factions conspiring and murdering for political control of the wealthy city, its Italian colonies, and its Mediterranean empire. The people were pawns in the struggle, used by politician-generals to further their selfish ambitions. (The idea of a military state is well known to people living in twentieth-century Czechoslovakia, Russia, Spain, Greece, Paraguay, Portugal, to mention only a few.)

Tacitus, another historian, who lived a century after Sallust, blamed the decline and fall of the Republic on man's love of wealth and power, and he found this behavior instinctive in all men:

> From time immemorial, man has had an instinctive love of power. With the growth of our empire, this instinct has become a dominant and uncontrollable force. It was easy to maintain equality when Rome was weak. World-wide conquest and the destruction of all rival communities or potentates opened the way to the secure enjoyment of wealth and an overriding appetite for it. This was how the smouldering rivalry between senate and people was first fanned into a blaze. Unruly tribunes alternated with powerful consuls. Rome and the Roman forum had a foretaste of what civil war means. Then Gaius Marius, whose origin was of the humblest, and Lucius Sulla, who outdid his fellow nobles in ruthlessness, destroyed the republican constitution by force of arms. In its place they put despotism. After them came Gnaeus Pompey, who, though more secretive, was not better, and from then on the one and only aim was autocracy. Roman legions did not shrink from civil war at Pharsalia or Philippi. . . .[5]

Did Tacitus have the clue to the causes of man's problems down through the ages? Or is his observation too simple? He called the age degenerate.

Janus (now January), was an ancient Italian deity who presided over doors and gates and over beginnings and endings and was usually represented with two faces turned in opposite directions. Closed doors symbolized peace. Open doors symbolized war.

But the gates of the temple of Janus were closed for the first time in two hundred years in January of 29 B.C. This meant the end of civil strife and foreign war and a time of universal peace. The gates were not to be opened again for two hundred years, when the *Pax Romana* came to an end and Rome once again, this time the Empire, started on a long period of decline and decay.

Rome fell; will we?

In Rome, as in America, there was excessive spending on the military establishment. There was the philosophy among many of eat, drink, and be merry for tomorrow we die. Rome became, at least in part, a hedonistic society. Law and order broke down and violence took over as the selfish undermined both government and culture. The quality of life deteriorated, and one can only guess what the violence and trivia might have been had the Romans invented TV. President Nixon is concerned with the quality of life in America. What is quality?

Dante pointed out that Augustus Caesar and Jesus Christ were contemporaries. Both were princes of peace, one for the universal state and the other for the universal brotherhood of man. Neither prevailed. Christ did not even prevail among Christians, in Ireland or in many other places in the Christian world. Tacitus suggests the fault is in the instinctive behavior of man; Ashley Montagu would disagree, believing man to be a product of his environment, conditioned to behave in certain ways. Based on what you have read in this essay, with which man do you agree?

## Notes

1 Livy, *The Early History of Rome*, translated by Aubrey de Selincourt (London: Penguin, 1960), p. 178.
2 *Ibid.*, pp. 255–256.
3 *Ibid.*, p. 258.
4 *Ibid.*, p. 243.
5 Tacitus, *The Histories*, translated by Kenneth Wellesley (London: Penguin, 1964), pp. 103–104.

**The Roman upper class was hung up on the fear of their pure and superior
blood being contaminated by lower-class blood. The myth was not a
new one, for the Egyptians and Mesopotamians of a much earlier day had
their lines of "pure" blood also. This myth was not to die but rather
to continue into Europe and the two Americas, where Hitler, the Spanish
aristocrats in the new world, and the KKK, along with many other groups,
seized on to the idea of racial supremacy. In the selection that follows,
the Tribune Canuleius protests vigorously the discrimination against common
citizens and makes a strong case for an integrated society with liberty
and justice for all. Livy, a contemporary of Angustus and of Christ, lived
from 59 B.C. to 17 A.D. The reading is from his Book Four, "War and Politics."**

# The Civil Rights Problem, 450 B.C.

Livy

The next consuls were Marcus Genucius and Caius Curtius. War
and political dissension made the year a difficult one. Hardly had it
begun, when the tribune Canuleius introduced a bill for legalizing
intermarriage between the nobility and the commons. The senatorial
party objected strongly on the grounds not only that the patrician
blood would thereby be contaminated but also that the hereditary
rights and privileges of the *gentes,* or families, would be lost. Further,
a suggestion, at first cautiously advanced by the tribunes, that a law
should be passed enabling one of the two consuls to be a plebeian, subsequently hardened into the promulgation, by nine tribunes, of a bill
by which the people should be empowered to elect to the consulship
such men as they thought fit, from either of the two parties. The
senatorial party felt that if such a bill were to become law, it would
mean not only that the highest office of state would have to be shared
with the dregs of society but that it would, in effect, be lost to the
nobility and transferred to the commons. It was with great satisfaction,
therefore, that the Senate received a report, first that Ardea had
thrown off her allegiance to Rome in resentment at the crooked practice which had deprived her of her territory; secondly, that troops from
Veii had raided the Roman frontier, and, thirdly, that the Volscians
and Aequians were showing uneasiness at the fortification of Verrugo.
In the circumstances it was good news, for the nobility could look forward even to an unsuccessful war with greater complacency than to
an ignominious peace. Accordingly they made the most of the situation; the Senate ordered an immediate raising of troops and a general

169

mobilization on the largest possible scale and with even greater urgency than in the previous year, in the hope that the revolutionary proposals which the tribunes were bringing forward might be forgotten in the bustle and excitement of three imminent campaigns. Canuleius replied with a brief but forceful statement in the Senate to the effect that it was useless for the consuls to try to scare the commons from taking an interest in the new proposals, and, declaring that they should never, while he lived, hold a levy until the commons had voted on the reforms which he and his colleagues had introduced, immediately convened an assembly. The battle was on: the consuls and the Senate on the one side, Canuleius and the populace on the other, were in the full flood of mutual recriminations. The consuls swore that the lunatic excesses of the tribunes were past endurance, that it was the end of all things, that war was being deliberately provoked far more deadly than any with a foreign enemy. "The present situation," they said, "is not, we admit, the fault of one party only: the senate is not less guilty than the people, or the consuls than the tribunes. In all communities the qualities or tendencies which carry the highest reward are bound to be most in evidence and to be most industriously cultivated—indeed it is precisely that which produces good statesmen and good soldiers; unhappily here in Rome the greatest rewards come from political upheavals and revolt against the government, which have always, in consequence, won applause from all and sundry. Only recall the aura of majesty which surrounded the Senate in our father's day, and then think what it will be like when we bequeath it to our children! Think how the laboring class will be able to brag of the increase in its power and influence! There can never be an end to this unhappy process so long as the promoters of sedition against the government are honored in proportion to their success. Do you realize, gentlemen, the appalling consequences of what Canuleius is trying to do? If he succeeds, bent, as he is, upon leaving nothing in its original soundness and purity, he will contaminate the blood of our ancient and noble families and make chaos of the hereditary patrician privilege of taking the auspices to determine, in the public or private interest, what Heaven may will—and with what result? that, when all distinctions are obliterated, no one will know who he is or where he came from! Mixed-marriages forsooth! What do they mean but that men and women from all ranks of society will be permitted to start copulating like animals? A child of such intercourse will never know what blood runs in his veins or what form of worship he is entitled to practice; he will be nothing—or six of one and half a dozen of the other, a very monster!

"But even this is not enough: having made hay of the dictates of religion and the traditions of our country, these revolutionary fire-eaters are now out for the consulship. They began merely by suggesting that one of the two consuls might be a plebeian, but now they have brought in a bill which would enable the people to elect consuls as it pleased, from either party—plebeian or patrician. And whom are they likely to elect? Obviously, men of their own class, and the most turbulent demagogues at that. We shall have men like Canuleius and Icilius in the highest office of state. God forbid that an office invested with an almost kingly majesty should fall so low! We should rather die a thousand times than allow such a shameful thing to happen. We are very sure that our forefathers too, had they guessed that by wholesale concessions they would exacerbate, rather than appease, the hostility of the commons and lead them to make further demands each more exaggerated than the last, would have faced at the outset any struggle, however fierce and embittered, rather than permit such laws to be imposed upon them. The concession in the matter of tribunes only led to another, and so it goes on. It is impossible to have tribunes side by side with a governing class in the same community; either the nobility or the tribunate must go. Now—better late than never—we must make a firm stand against their reckless and unprincipled conduct. Are we to take no action when they first deliberately embroil us, thus inviting a foreign invasion, and then prevent us from arming for defense against the danger for which they were themselves responsible? Or when, having more or less invited an enemy to attack us, they refuse to allow us to raise troops—nay, worse, when Canuleius has the audacity to declare in the Senate that unless the members of the House permit his proposals to be accepted as law, as if he were a conquering hero, he will rescind the order for mobilization? What is such a statement but a threat to betray his country, to submit passively to the storming and capture of Rome? It is indeed a timely word of encouragement to the Volscians, to the Aequians, to the men of Veii—but hardly to the common people of Rome. The enemy may well be confident in their ability to climb, with Canuleius in command, to the Citadel on the heights of the Capitol! Gentlemen, unless the tribunes, when they robbed you of your dignity and privileges, robbed you of your courage too, we are ready to put first things first: we will lead you against criminal citizens of Rome before we lead you against an enemy in arms."

While opinions of this sort were being vented in the Senate, Canuleius was defending his proposed reforms and attacking the consuls elsewhere. "Men of Rome," he said, "the violence with which the

Senate has been opposing our program of reform has made me realize more vividly than ever before the depth of the contempt in which you are held by the aristocracy. I have often suspected it, but now I know: they think you are unworthy of living with them within the walls of the same town. Yet what is the object of our proposals? It is merely to point out that we are their fellow-citizens—that we have the same country as they, even though we have less money. We seek the right of intermarriage, a right commonly granted to other nations on our borders—indeed, before now Rome has granted citizenship, which is more than intermarriage, even to a defeated enemy. By our other proposal we intend no innovation, but merely seek the recovery and enjoyment of the popular right to elect whom we will to positions of authority. What is there in this to make them think that chaos is come again? Is this enough to justify what came near to being a personal assault upon me in the Senate, or their threat to use violence against the sacrosanct office of the tribunes? If the people of Rome are allowed to vote freely for the election to the consulship of whom they please—if even a man of their own class, provided that he is worthy of it, may hope to rise to this high honor—does that mean that our country's stability and power are necessarily done for? We propose that a man of the people may have the right to be elected to the consulship: is that the same as saying some rogue who was, or is, a slave? Such is their contempt for you that they would rob you, if they could, of the very light you see by; they grudge you the air you breathe, the words you speak, the very fact that you have the shape of men. They declare—if I may say so without irreverence—that a plebeian consul would be a sin in the sight of heaven. . . .

" . . . One could hardly offer a more signal insult to one section of the community than to consider it unfit to marry with, as if it were too dirty to touch: it is like condemning it to exile and banishment within the city walls. They take every precaution against the dreadful risk of becoming related by blood to us poor scum. Come, come, my noble lords—if such a connection is a blot on your fine escutcheon—though I would mention that many of you were originally Albans or Sabines, not of noble birth at all, and got your present rank as a reward for services either at the hands of the kings or, later, of the people—could you not keep your precious blood pure simply by determining, on your own initiative, not to marry plebeian wives and not to let your sisters and daughters marry out of the patricate? No patrician girl need, I assure you, fear for her virtue so far as any of us are concerned: rape is a patrician habit. No one would have forced a marriage contract upon an unwilling party—but to set up a legal ban upon the right of intermarriage, *that*, I repeat, is the final insult to the commons. Why not go further and propose a ban on marriages between rich and poor? Marriages have always been a matter of private arrangement between families, and now you propose to subject them to the restraint of a law which is the very reflection of your own arrogant conceit, for the purpose, I presume, of splitting society in two and of turning united Rome into two separate communities. I wonder you do not pass a law to stop a plebeian living next door to a nobleman, or walking in the same street, or going to the same party, or standing by his side in the Forum. What difference does it make if a patrician marries a plebeian wife, or a plebeian a patrician one? There is no loss of privilege whatever, as children admittedly take the rank of the father; we expect to gain nothing from marrying into your class except to be considered as human beings and citizens of Rome; and your opposition is wholly unreasonable—unless you take pleasure merely in humiliating and insulting us.

"Finally tell me this: does the ultimate power in the state belong to you or to the Roman people? When we finished with the monarchy, was it to put supreme authority into your hands or to bring political liberty to all alike? Have the people, or have they not, the right to enact a law, if such is their will? Or are you to quash every proposal of ours by proclaiming a levy of troops immediately it is brought up, and as soon as I, in my capacity as tribune, begin to call upon the tribes to vote, is the consul to reply by administering the military oath and ordering mobilization, with threats against me and my office and the commons in general? Do not forget that twice already you have learned by experience the value of your threats in face of our united resolution—do you wish to pretend that on those occasions you abstained from actual physical conflict purely out of tender feelings toward us? or was the reason, perhaps that the stronger party happened to be the one to exercise restraint?"

Sallust (86–35 B.C.) became a tribune of the Plebeians in 52 B.C.,
after serving Caesar as an officer in the campaigns of the Civil War.
His histories of the Jugurthine War and the Catiline Conspiracy show his
bias against the arrogance of the Roman aristocracy. In this preface
to his "Catiline," he relates the sordid side of Roman politics and gives
several reasons for the decline and fall of the Republic. According to Sallust,
what is the nature of politics and what is the nature of a Catiline?

# Growing Love of Money and Lust for Power

Sallust

Every man who wishes to rise superior to the lower animals should strive his hardest to avoid living all his days in silent obscurity, like the beasts of the field, creatures which go with their faces to the ground and are the slaves of their bellies. We human beings have mental as well as physical powers; the mind, which we share with gods, is the ruling element in us, while the chief function of the body, which we have in common with the beasts, is to obey. Surely, therefore, it is our intellectual rather than our physical powers that we should use in the pursuit of fame. Since only a short span of life has been vouchsafed us, we must make ourselves remembered as long as may be by those who come after us. Wealth and beauty can give only a fleeting and perishable fame, but intellectual excellence is a glorious and everlasting possession.

Yet it was long a subject of hot dispute among men whether physical strength or mental ability was the more important requirement for success in war. Before you start on anything, you must plan; when you have made your plans, prompt action is needed. Thus neither is sufficient without the aid of the other.

Accordingly the world's first rulers, who were called kings, adopted one or other of two different policies, seeking either to make the most of their intellectual endowment or to develop their bodily strength. In those days men had not yet learnt to be covetous: each was content with what he had. It was only when Cyrus[1] in Asia and the Spartans and Athenians in Greece began to bring cities and nations into subjection, and to engage in wars because they thirsted for power and thought their glory was to be measured by the extent of their dominions, that the test of experience decided the ancient controversy: brains were shown to be more important than brawn. It is a pity that kings and rulers do not apply their mental powers as

From *The Conspiracy of Catiline* by Sallust, translated by S. A. Handford
(Penguin Classics, 1965), pp. 175–179, 181–183. Copyright © S. A. Handford, 1965.

effectively to the preservation of peace as to the prosecution of war. If they did, human life would be less chequered and unstable than it is: we should not see everything drifting to and fro in change and confusion. Sovereignty can easily be maintained by the same qualities as enable a man to acquire it. But when idleness replaces industry, when self-restraint and justice give place to lust and arrogance, the moral deterioration brings loss of station in its train. A degenerate ruler is always supplanted by a better man than himself.

Success in agriculture, seafaring, or building always depends on human excellence. But many are the men who, slaves of gluttony and sloth, have gone through life ignorant and uncivilized, as if they were mere sojourners in a foreign land, reversing, surely, the order of nature by treating their bodies as means of gratification and their souls as mere encumbrances. It makes no odds, to my mind, whether such men live or die; alive or dead, no one ever hears of them. The truth is that no man really lives or gets any satisfaction out of life, unless he devotes all his energies to some task and seeks fame by some notable achievement or by the cultivation of some admirable gift.

The field is wide, and men follow their natural bent in choosing this path or that. It is noble to serve the state by action, and even to use a gift of eloquence on its behalf is no mean thing. Peace, no less than war, offers men a chance of fame: they can win praise by describing exploits as well as by achieving them. And although the narrator earns much less renown than the doer, the writing of history is, in my opinion, a peculiarly difficult task. You must work hard to find words worthy of your subject. And if you censure misdeeds, most people will accuse you of envy and malice. When you write of the outstanding merit and glory of good men, people are quite ready to accept what they think they could easily do themselves; but anything beyond that is dismissed as an improbable fiction.

My earliest inclinations led me, like many other young men, to throw myself wholeheartedly into politics. There I found many things against me. Self-restraint, integrity, and virtue were disregarded; unscrupulous conduct, bribery, and profit-seeking were rife. And although, being a stranger to the vices that I saw practiced on every hand, I looked on them with scorn, I was led astray by ambition and, with a young man's weakness, could not tear myself away. However much I tried to dissociate myself from the prevailing corruption, my craving for advancement exposed me to the same odium and slander as all my rivals.

After suffering manifold perils and hardships, peace of mind at last returned to me, and I decided that I must bid farewell to politics for good. But I had no intention of wasting my precious leisure in idleness and sloth, or of devoting my time to agriculture or hunting—tasks fit only for slaves. I had formerly been interested in history, and some work which I began in that field had been interrupted by my misguided political ambitions. I therefore took this up again, and decided to write accounts of some episodes in Roman history that seemed particularly worthy of record—a task for which I felt myself the better qualified inasmuch as I was unprejudiced by the hopes and fears of the party man.

It is my intention to give a brief account, as accurate as I can make it, of the conspiracy of Catiline, a criminal enterprise which I consider specially memorable as being unprecedented in itself and fraught with unprecedented dangers to Rome. I must preface my narrative by a short description of Catiline's character.

Lucius Catiline was of noble birth. He had a powerful intellect and great physical strength, but a vicious and depraved nature. From his youth he had delighted in civil war, bloodshed, robbery, and political strife, and it was in such occupations that he spent his early manhood. He could endure hunger, cold, and want of sleep to an incredible extent. His mind was daring, crafty, and versatile, capable of any pretense and dissimulation. A man of flaming passions, he was as covetous of other men's possessions as he was prodigal of his own; an eloquent speaker, but lacking in wisdom. His monstrous ambition hankered continually after things extravagant, impossible, beyond his reach. After the dictatorship of Lucius Sulla, Catiline had been possessed by an overmastering desire for despotic power, to gratify which he was prepared to use any and every means. His headstrong spirit was tormented more and more every day by poverty and a guilty conscience, both of which were aggravated by the evil practices I have referred to. He was incited also by the corruption of a society plagued by two opposite but equally disastrous vices—love of luxury and love of money.

Since I have had occasion to mention public morality, it seems appropriate to go back further and briefly describe the principles by which our ancestors guided their conduct in peace and war, their method of governing the state which they made so great before bequeathing it to their successors, and the gradual degeneration of its noble character into vice and corruption.

The city of Rome, as far as I can make out, was founded and first inhabited by Trojan exiles who, led by Aeneas, were wandering without a settled home, and by rustic natives who lived in a state of anarchy uncontrolled by laws or government. When once they had come to live together in a walled town, despite different origins, languages, and habits of life, they coalesced with amazing ease, and before long what had been a heterogeneous mob of migrants was welded into a united nation.

When, however, with the growth of their population, civilization, and territory, it was seen that they had become powerful and prosperous, they had the same experience as most people have who are possessors of this world's goods: their wealth aroused envy. Neighboring kings and peoples attacked them, and but few of their friends aided them; the rest were scared at the prospect of danger and held aloof. The Romans, however, were alert both at home and abroad. They girded themselves in haste and with mutual encouragement marched forth to meet their foes, protecting by force of arms their liberty, country, and parents. Then, after bravely warding off the dangers that beset them, they lent aid to their allies and friends, and made new friends by a greater readiness to render services than to accept help from others. . . .

Thus by hard work and just dealing the power of the state increased. Mighty kings were vanquished, savage tribes and huge nations were brought to their knees; and when Carthage, Rome's rival in her quest for empire, had been annihilated,[2] every land and sea lay open to her. It was then that fortune turned unkind and confounded all her enterprises. To the men who had so easily endured toil and peril, anxiety and adversity, the leisure and riches which are generally regarded as so desirable proved a burden and a curse. Growing love of money, and the lust for power which followed it, engendered every kind of evil. Avarice destroyed honor, integrity, and every other virtue, and instead taught men to be proud and cruel, to neglect religion, and to hold nothing too sacred to sell. Ambition tempted many to be false, to have one thought hidden in their hearts, another ready on their tongues, to become a man's friend or enemy not because they judged him worthy or unworthy but because they thought it would pay them, and to put on the semblance of virtues that they had not. At first these vices grew slowly and sometimes met with punishment; later on, when disease had spread like a plague, Rome changed: her government, once so just and admirable, became harsh and unendurable. . . .

As soon as wealth came to be a mark of distinction and an easy way to renown, military commands, and political power, virtue began to decline. Poverty was now looked on as a disgrace and a blameless life as a sign of ill nature. Riches made the younger generation a prey to luxury, avarice, and pride. Squandering with one hand what they grabbed with the other, they set small value on their own property while they coveted that of others. Honor and modesty, all laws divine and human, were alike disregarded in a spirit of recklessness and intemperance. To one familiar with mansions and villas reared aloft on such a scale that they look like so many towns, it is instructive to visit the temples built by our godfearing ancestors. In those days piety was the ornament of shrines; glory, of men's dwellings. When they conquered a foe, they took nothing from him save his power to harm. But their base successors stuck at no crime to rob subject peoples of all that those brave conquerors had left them, as though oppression were the only possible method of ruling an empire. I need not remind you of some enterprises that no one but an eyewitness will believe —how private citizens have often levelled mountains and paved seas for their building operations. Such men, it seems to me, have treated their wealth as a mere plaything: instead of making honorable use of it, they have shamefully misused it on the first wasteful project that occurred to them. Equally strong was their passion for fornication, guzzling, and other forms of sensuality. Men prostituted themselves like women, and women sold their chastity to every comer. To please their palates they ransacked land and sea. They went to bed before they needed sleep, and instead of waiting until they felt hungry, thirsty, cold, or tired, they forestalled their bodies' needs by self-indulgence. Such practices incited young men who had run through their property to have recourse to crime. Because their vicious natures found it hard to forgo sensual pleasures, they resorted more and more recklessly to every means of getting and spending.

## Notes

1 King of Persia 559–529 B.C.
2 In 146 B.C.

Law and order, protest and violence were also issues in the Roman Empire. Christians had persistently defied Roman law, and by the fourth century A.D., the Romans, under the Emperor Diocletian, were persecuting them at a wholesale rate. But beginning in 311, the emperors Galerius, Constantine, and Licinius issued edicts of toleration for Christians in the Empire. Constantine even called a council at Nicaea in 325 to settle the Arian controversy on the nature of Christ, and he himself had become a Christian. Near the end of the century, Theodosius issued an edict declaring that all his subjects must become Christians or suffer punishment. Thus, in just a few years, Christians had moved a long way. But the controversy over poverty and purity versus riches and ruination continued, with many Christians living in caves, sitting on pillars, and otherwise torturing their bodies to show their contempt for the material and their love of the spiritual.

# Christians and Romans

Glanville Downey

Constantine had observed the official attempts to deal with the problem of the Christians, and the constancy of these people to their religious ideas impressed him, as it did other pagan officials. When Diocletian's program of the reconstruction of the state was still going forward, any element of disloyalty among the citizens was dangerous, and Roman law had always prescribed some of the most painful penalties for treason. Intelligent officials had observed that in the face of these terrible threats some Christians were willing to renounce their subversive religion and make the required profession of loyalty. But there were many who could not be induced by the most severe torture or the threat of the most painful death to change. These people's spectacular constancy actually made converts to their religion. In the eastern half of the empire, the domain of the fiercely anti-Christian Galerius, persecution had been most intense. Here the presence of a body of obstinate Christians, attracting popular attention, constituted a political factor in the plans of both Galerius and his rivals.

Early in 311 there was in fact a remarkable change in the persecution. Galerius had contracted a painful disease, which he believed was the vengeance of the god of the Christians. On April 30 he issued an edict of toleration which accorded legal recognition to Christians. They now had the right to individual freedom of conscience and the right to assemble for worship, so long as they did "nothing contrary to good order." Galerius died painfully a few days after the publication of the decree,

From *The Late Roman Empire* by Glanville Downey. Copyright © 1969 by Holt, Rinehart and Winston, Inc. Reprinted by permission of Holt, Rinehart and Winston, Inc.

and the Christians greeted his suffering and death as a sign of the power of God.

It was in the following year, according to a tradition which was unclear in antiquity and has been a subject for debate among modern scholars, that the Christian deity was supposed to have actually intervened in the affairs of Constantine. In his official capacity, Constantine had had Apollo as his divine companion and protector. According to the tradition, however, in 312, at a critical point in his struggle for power, Constantine actually turned to Christianity, reportedly as a result of a direct communication from the deity. In a traditional Roman empire, this was surely one of the most surprising things that an emporer could do.

Constantine's act—one of the most celebrated conversions in the history of the Church—was a turning point in the history of Europe. The consequences, in the establishment of the Christian Roman Empire and the tradition of Christian monarchy, are evident; but the surviving ancient records of Constantine's own experience are sparse and enigmatic. It has been impossible to determine the emperor's motives and the real nature of his conversion, in the religious sense. Much of the evidence reflects the sudden joy of the triumphant Church. However, the circumstances of the time make it seem possible that Constantine's action was a political expedient, designed to gain the support of the Christians. It is also possible to believe on the basis of Constantine's later history that the conversion was the result of a real religious experience.

An account of the episode has been preserved which is supposed to have been written by Constantine's friend and adviser, Eusebius, the scholarly bishop of Caesarea in Palestine, to whom Constantine, many years later, was supposed to have related his experience. The account presents difficulties and its authorship by Eusebius has been questioned, but whether it is an official account or a legend, it has became famous.

In 312, the contest for power had reached a point at which there had to be an encounter between Constantine and his rival Maxentius, who held the city of Rome. This might be a decisive battle. Constantine, in Gaul, set out with his army for Rome. According to the tradition, as the crisis approached Constantine began to understand that events had shown that the pagan gods had failed to support their worshipers in the struggle for power. Constantine knew of the Christian god, and knew that his father had been sufficiently interested in this god to be lenient to the Christians. This thought brought hope, and Constantine prayed to his father's god. The supernatural help was ready and Constantine was granted a vision, at noon, as the army was on the march. The vision— stated to have been seen by the soldiers as well as by Constantine—was a cross of light in the sky, above the sun, accompanied by an inscription,

BY THIS CONQUER. While Constantine was still pondering the meaning of this sign, Christ appeared to him in a dream and instructed him to place on the shields of his soldiers the monogram *chi rho*, ☧, the initial letters of the name of Christ in Greek, and in this way to go into battle. Constantine obeyed and defeated Maxentius in the battle of the Milvian Bridge outside Rome (October, 312). Maxentius was killed in the battle and Constantine was proclaimed Augustus by the Senate. The Milvian Bridge was a spectacular victory, won against heavy odds, and it put Constantine far along in his climb to power.

Constantine joined forces with Licinius, the heir of Galerius, who was seeking to make himself master of the East. Each issued an edict of toleration (Constantine in 312, Licinius in 313) which granted complete freedom to Christianity as well as to all other religions. Confiscated property was restored to the churches.

. . .

### The Church and the Bright New Era

St. Jerome, who was accustomed to speaking his mind, once wrote that the Church by its emancipation under Constantine had gained in material position and wealth, but had lost its true spiritual life. Changes of many kinds inevitably followed when the Church was suddenly transformed into a public institution. From being an illicit and persecuted cult, it found itself in a position of prestige which brought a sudden increase in membership, new wealth, and political influence. Now that the Church was secure in its ownership of real estate, people gave or bequeathed property, often as a token of thanksgiving, sometimes in hope that such gifts would benefit their souls. Unavoidably the clergy found themselves increasingly preoccupied with such mundane matters.

On a higher level the Church could look to the government for material benefits—church buildings, endowments, privileges for the clergy, political support. There came into being a class of worldly prelates who found it to the advantage of their dioceses, and to their own benefit, to spend their time at the imperial court, where competition for imperial favor might call for worldly talents.

Perils such as these do not seem to have been foreseen by the churchmen of the period before Constantine's reign. The records of the Church councils under Constantine show that the bishops had to spend time on mundane matters and on new questions such as whether the clergy might be married, or, if already married, must separate from their wives.

But not only mundane matters became acute. There were basic points of belief that had been debated before the time of Constantine but had not been satisfactorily settled. The most important of these problems, which was also going to prove the most difficult to resolve, was how to formulate a satisfactory statement of the nature of Christ and his relationship to God the Father and to the Holy Spirit. The whole doctrine of the Trinity was proving to be one of the most difficult teachings of the Church to explain to inquirers and converts; indeed not all Christians found the doctrine easy to understand. But within the problem of the Trinity, the question of the nature of the divinity of Christ took priority, for this concerned the nature and indeed the validity of the salvation that the Church offered.

The New Testament depicted a Christ who was both divine and human, and it was difficult for the uninstructed to understand how both a divine and a human nature could have been united in a body that was visibly physical. The problem was crucial, for redemption and salvation offered by a truly divine person were quite different from redemption and salvation offered by a person who was not fully divine, or perhaps indeed had no divine character. If Christ were the Son of God, and were fully divine, did this mean that there were two Gods? Was the Son as fully God as the Father? Did this mean that in Christianity, as in the pagan cults, there was a plurality of gods? On the other hand, if the Son were less fully divine than the Father, he would, as a less divine person, be subordinate to the Father. In this case there would seem to be something like a hierarchy of gods such as pagans were familiar with in their pantheon. In fact the notion of a subordinate Christ, divine but less fully divine than the Father, might make it easier for some pagans to accept Christianity.

This Christological problem had begun to be a matter of concern among scholars of the Church in the middle and latter part of the third century. The problem was important enough to lead to the development of rival systems of theological thought in the schools at Antioch and Alexandria. In the reign of Constantine the problem became acute as a consequence of the success of the teaching of Arius, a priest in Alexandria. Arius asserted that the Son was in some sense later in existence than the Father because there must have been a time when the Son did not yet exist, and that the Father must have created the Son out of nothing because the substance of the Father, by its nature, must be indivisible.

Arius' teaching seemed logical to many people, and it spread sufficiently to call for investigation by Arius' superior, the bishop of Alexandria. The teaching was condemned by a council of Egyptian bishops and Arius was excommunicated. But the doctrine had sufficient appeal to enable Arius to gain support outside of Egypt, and the controversy grew until there was a major split in the eastern part of the Church. There was a war of pamphlets. The laity of all ranks took sides passionately, disputing the theological issues among themselves and supporting their local bishops in their contests with bishops of opposing views. It was typical of the major theological controversies of the Late Empire that they were not confined to internal clerical struggles within the Church but involved the whole Christian population.

. . .

The Council of Nicaea, summoned in 325 to deal with the Arian controversy, was a milestone in the history of Christianity in its new status as an institution within the state. The epoch-making aspects of the council were that it was an ecumenical gathering of bishops summoned by the emperor in his capacity as head of the state; that it formulated an official creed that was to serve not only as a declaration of faith but as a test of orthodoxy; and that its decrees were enforced by the police of the state.

The creed adopted at Nicaea was an attempt to devise a statement concerning the nature of Christ which would provide a proper basis for worship that would also be acceptable to Christians who were attracted by Arius' ideas. The creed stated that Christians believed in Christ who was begotten of the Father, only-begotten, that is, begotten of the same substance as the Father; that he was God out of God, Light out of Light, true God out of true God, of the same substance with the Father.

. . .

## The Ascetic Movement

While the Church had been creating the new Christian community in the cities, towns, and villages, another branch of the Christian community was coming into being on another plane. The ascetic calling, a characteristic phenomenon of the Late Roman Empire, was not new with Christianity. There had been ascetics in the classical world, such as Diogenes the Cynic, a philosopher who lived in a barrel, and Indian fakirs had visited Athens and Rome. What was new in Christian asceticism was the source of the motivation.

Renunciation of the world by the solitary ascetic and by the monk living in a religious community might represent several different impulses. To some Christians, from the Church's earliest days, the flesh, with its frailty and temptations, became abhorrent; lust had to be overcome before man could partake fully of the joys of Christianity. This impulse might lead to excessive mortification of the flesh—even to eccentricities such as living on the tops of pillars or in trees, which the

Church disapproved but could not very well stop completely. In many cases, denial of self and mortification of the body represented the same passionate desire to give one's life for the sake of the Lord that in the early days of the Church had compelled many Christians to welcome martyrdom. With persecution ended after the emancipation of the Church, a man who earlier might have been a martyr became a monk.

Other Christians, especially in the early period of the Church's freedom, withdrew into solitude because they disapproved of the way in which the Church was acquiring worldly interests and material wealth, to the detriment, they considered, of its spiritual life. Still others withdrew from the distractions of the world to free themselves for contemplation and prayer. This was the most constructive form of the ascetic life. Some young men, for example John Chrysostom, retired for some years to the desert or to a mountain cave in order to achieve self-denial in preparation for the active ministry. Others attempted to use the ascetic life as a refuge from the burdens of taxation, compulsory public service, and military obligations.

In the early fourth century the monastic communities were founded which became so influential in the life of the Church and of Christian society. The monks, spending their time in prayer and labor, sought a spiritual perfection which they believed was not possible for persons living in the world. Christianity, like Platonism, taught that there were two worlds, the visible world of material things and the invisible world of the spirit, which was in fact the true world. The lives of the ascetics represented, for them, not an escape from reality but an escape into reality. Often these holy men became spiritual advisers to lay people who came to consult them. Their life constituted prayer for the whole Christian community. The celebrated desert solitary St. Anthony became the champion of the faith in Egypt and the national hero. Many monasteries rescued orphans and conducted schools and hospitals. Monks served as physicians and nurses in the army.

In any such system there could be abuses. Wandering monks, not living under discipline, roamed the countryside begging for food or, as nonbelievers said, stealing. Groups of monks not attached to regular establishments lived in cities and made a pleasant vocation of ministering to fashionable ladies. Some monks were illiterate or had only the lowest level of education, but this was true also of many people in the world. What was regarded as the idleness of the monks, and the eccentricities of some, brought the ascetic life into disrepute. But the ascetic movement was a natural development of the times, sociologically as well as religiously, and in spite of abuse it maintained a tradition of otherworldliness that lent strength to the Church.

. . .

## Theodosius, the State Church, and Pagan Society

Theodosius' reign (379–395) opened a major epoch in the history of the Late Roman Empire. He had as colleagues in the West the youthful Gratian, and after his death Gratian's half-brother Valentinian II (383–392), but Theodosius was always the dominant figure and operated both in West and East as occasion demanded.

Theodosius was a competent ruler, a serious person, and a deeply religious Christian. He was the first emperor who did not take the traditional title *pontifex maximus*. From the beginning of his reign he was determined to make Christianity a state religion in more specific terms than Constantine and his successors had been able to achieve. In February 380, he issued the famous edict in which he declared that all his subjects must adhere to the orthodox Christian faith, that is, they were to recognize the nature of the Trinity as composed of Father, Son, and Holy Spirit. All who did not were heretics and were to incur the severe legal disabilities appropriate to their crime. Their places of meeting were not entitled to the legal status of churches. They were subject to punishment on two levels. God would take vengeance on them, and the government would follow with its own means of punishment.

The terms of this edict were reinforced by another decree the following January. The faith of Nicaea was to be respected everywhere. To make the meaning of this plain, the edict summarized the articles of the Nicene Creed. Heretics were not to be allowed to call themselves Christians; their churches were to be given to the Nicene orthodox; and they were to be driven out of the cities.

These edicts represented, first, a new attempt to settle the Arian controversy and its ramifications, and second, a step forward in the legal status of the Church, in that orthodoxy was now defined and protected by law and heresy became a crime against the state—that is, a crime against the Roman people. Theodosius' religious policy was a counterpart to that of Diocletian a century earlier. Theodosius considered the persecution of heretics to be necessary to the security of the state for the same reason that Diocletian had persecuted Christians. It is difficult to decide whether Theodosius' religious zeal was a reflection of his Spanish origin or whether he was acting under the forceful guidance of Bishop Ambrose of Milan.

Paganism was Theodosius' next target. Not only private worship of the gods, but astrology, magic, divination, and the oriental cults were still active. Each of these varieties of belief offered special dangers to Christianity. Especially in the West, the worship of the oriental god Mithra was a vital force, its teaching and rites able to win from its initiates a moral exaltation and spiritual devotion equal in intensity to the spirituality of Christianity.

It was astrology and the other occult arts that called forth Theodosius' first edict against paganism, in December 381. This law forbade pagan rites intended to foretell the future and prohibited visits to temples for the consultation of oracles. The law was an acknowledgment of the influence that the occult had always possessed in the Greco-Roman world, among persons of all degrees of education and in every level of society. The masters of the occult arts were often invited to practice their skill in the great houses of the nobility. Legislation against astrologers and religious quacks had appeared regularly, but it was impossible to root out the fascination of their lore.

. . .

Bishop Ambrose in reply called for freedom of conscience, asserting that it was unfair to compel Christian senators to meet in the presence of a pagan altar. He threatened the emperor with excommunication if he granted the petition, and the petition was rejected. The whole transaction, beginning with a demonstration of the strength that paganism still possessed among the members of the Roman aristocracy, showed what power the Church could exhibit in the person of an energetic bishop such as Ambrose.

Indeed a famous clash between the bishop and the emperor a few years later again illustrated the difficult position of the sovereign, personally and officially, in respect to the authority of the Church. Bishop Ambrose took every occasion to uphold the Church against the civil power. In 388, Christian monks at Callinicum in Mesopotamia incited a mob of Christians to burn a synagogue and a chapel of Christian heretics. Since the Jewish religion was officially protected, the mob's violence must be punished. When Theodosius ordered the bishop of Callinicum to rebuild the syangogue, Bishop Ambrose delivered a sermon in the presence of the emperor in which he criticized Theodosius' order and attacked the Jews. The emperor pointed out that this was not the only occasion on which monks had committed civil crimes; but when the bishop threatened him with excommunication, he gave way and promised amnesty to the rioters.

Two years later the famous episode of the massacre at Thessalonica occurred. A law issued in the spring of 390 prescribed the death penalty for men guilty of unnatural vice. Under this law, the military commander at Thessalonica imprisoned a popular charioteer who had seduced a handsome boy. A mob, indignant at this treatment of their favorite chariot racer, murdered the military commander and some members of his staff. Since imperial officials were considered to be personal representatives of the emperor, the murder of a high officer by a city mob was a serious crime amounting to treason.

It was customary on such occasions for a whole city to be punished. Theodosius issued an order to assemble the people of Thessalonica in the circus, where they were systematically slaughtered. In a massacre which lasted seven hours, it is recorded that three thousand people were killed. Theodosius, realizing that his order was excessive, revoked it, but not in time to prevent the killing. Bishop Ambrose wrote Theodosius with his own hand a private letter informing him that he could not be admitted to Holy Communion until he had done penance in the form prescribed by the Church for those guilty of a sin of this kind. Though precisely what followed is not recorded, the emperor must have done penance in satisfactory fashion, as he was admitted to communion the following Christmas.

The celebrated story of the bishop shutting the door of the church in the emperor's face is an apocryphal embellishment which rests on no good evidence. The emperor would not have attempted to enter the church while not authorized to do so, and the bishop would not have shut him out in the manner alleged. The consequences of such action on the part of either would have been incalculable. Ambrose in his funeral sermon on Theodosius' death praised the emperor's high qualities and his services to the Church. But Ambrose had established the principle that (as he expressed it in a letter to the emperor Valentinian II) "the emperor is in the church, not above the church, and the good emperor does not spurn the assistance of the church; he seeks it." Was there any greater honor, the bishop asked, than for the emperor to be called a son of the Church? The bishop's success in his dealings with the emperor set an example that later prelates remembered with good effect.

Though some scholars have questioned whether he is entitled to the epithet "the Great," Theodosius I left his mark on church and state. He finished work that Constantine had set on foot but had not been able to complete. The Church was now definitely established as a state church, and the emperor had declared the state's role in his legislation concerning the Church. With these milestones established, it remained for Justinian to complete the process out of which the Christian Roman Empire emerged in its final form. But in the interval between the reigns of Theodosius I and Justinian the state suffered some profound changes.

## Questions

1 This chapter's essay compares the United States to the Roman Republic, with the obvious question: Rome declined and was overrun; will we suffer the same fate? Is the comparison of the two republics accurate? Do you

     see differences between the two states that could also be stressed?

2 Can you make any comparisons between the Kennedy brothers and the Gracchi? Do you think Professor Gentles intends you to do so?

3 Livy's discussion of the civil rights problem in 450 B.C. could almost have been a discussion in the U.S. in the 1960s. However, do you see any differences between the two societies?

4 When Christianity was accepted by Constantine as the official state religion, did the Church lose its true spiritual life, as St. Jerome contended? Do opposition and unpopularity foster stronger belief in a religion's followers than do acceptance and popularity?

5 Constantine's era also saw the beginning of the Christian ascetic movement. Is it easier to live a spiritual life "in a vacuum"? Did the ascetics fulfill the purpose of religion, or does the Church have social obligations?

6 Since Rome there have been church-state conflicts in many countries. Did the U.S. solve all such conflicts by its policy statement in the first amendment to the Constitution?

7 Do you agree with Santayana's dictum that nations which do not learn from the past are doomed to repeat the mistakes of the past? Do you think we are doomed, or can we learn the lessons of history?

# 6

# Women in the Ancient World

R. Bausch

**CHORUS OF MEN:** There is nothing so resistless as a woman in her ire,
   She is wilder than a leopard, she is fiercer than a fire.
**CHORUS OF WOMEN:** And yet you're so daft as with women to contend,
   When 'tis in your power to win me and have me as a friend.
**CHORUS OF MEN:** I'll never, never cease all women to detest.

Aristophanes in his Lysistrata described the battle of the sexes as it might
have been during the destructive Peloponnesian Wars in the fifth century B.C.
The battle is an old one, with some vigorous women fighting what is to
date, at any rate, a long-lost cause to gain equal rights with men. Why has
the male generally been dominant in so many different societies, both
uncivilized and so-called civilized, and why have women been so unsuccessful
in their efforts to gain equality? Some male chauvinists, ancient and modern,
would have you believe that it is because of the natural superiority of men
over the weaker, the gentle, the cursed, the second sex.

# They Had a Word for Male Chauvinists— ΣΤΥΡΙΔ

Frederick Gentles

Of course, man is superior to woman. Is not God a man and is there
not a Father Sun and a weaker Sister Moon? The generic term of human
beings is mankind, not womankind, and the land of your birth is your
fatherland. (Though how mother came to be applied to earth, Asia,
India, and Russia is somewhat of a puzzle to male chauvinists.) The
world's leaders in politics, science, invention, literature, and the engi-
neering of great structures have been men, and the head of the family
most everywhere is the father. Father knows best. For further proof that
men are naturally superior to women, you need only consult your nearest
history book. It is mostly about men and their wars, and chances are
better than a hundred to one it was written by a man.

But the eminent anthropologist Ashley Montagu explains that recent
scientific studies show that physically, psychologically, and socially women
are superior to men.[1] Physically, women live an average of five to six
years longer than men. Psychologically, they are more stable, with fewer
of them alcoholics, suicides, or prison inmates, and socially, they have a
more fundamental understanding and need of love—something the male-
dominated world has long been in need of. The female, says Montagu, is
"more considerate, more self-sacrificing, more cooperative, and more
altruistic than usually falls to the lot of the male."[2] This is the genius
of the woman, he says; this is the genius and intelligence of humanity.

It is a fact, however, that though the woman may have a superior
body and greater emotional stability to survive longer in life, she is

weaker in the use of physical power. Hence, the male has often used his strength to dominate the female, even resorting to brutality when he thought necessary. We may think only of one so crude as the caveman beating his wife, but we have records of an English law prohibiting wife beating after 9 P.M. and news accounts in our own newspapers of wife beaters before and after 9 P.M. There are records, ancient and modern, not only of man's brutality to man but man's brutality to woman. It is not a very pleasant subject, and we shall not linger here except to emphasize that man's muscular will has been an important factor in his dominating woman. His ego must be satisfied in some way, and if he cannot obtain power by some other means, he uses force. Ismene, in Sophocles' play *Antigone*, says it well, at least for many women down through history:

Remind ourselves that we

Are women, and as such not made to fight

With men. For might unfortunately is right

And makes us bow to things like this and worse.

Other means than force were used to cow the female. In his *Politics*, Aristotle states that "as between male and female the former is by nature superior and ruler, the latter inferior and subject. And this must hold good of mankind in general." And who is going to argue with one of the most remarkable minds in all of history? Certainly not the antique male chauvinists. Indeed, in one place Aristotle seems to wonder whether to classify women with humans or with animals. In searching the records for Attica's population during the Golden Age, one finds estimates of 40,000 adult male citizens, 20,000 mine slaves, 70,000 other slaves, 24,000 outlanders, but no accounting of women. They were not even second-class citizens. No wonder: the historian Thucydides said that any decent women should be shut up in the house. During the Golden Age, wives of citizens were, indeed, shut up, and they left the house only when chaperoned by a servant or a slave. When the master entertained guests, women were expected to retreat to the upstairs rooms with the children.

Women in the glorious days of Rome were better off in that they did go out with their husbands, they owned property, supervised the household and the slaves, and had the right of divorce. They even drove the burros to town, though there was a report they were not very good drivers. As in Greece, however, the father, the *paterfamilias*, was the head of the household, and unwanted infants, particularly girl infants, were often exposed to the elements to catch their death of cold or to meet some more horrible end. Edith Hamilton, in *The Roman Way*,[3] says that one of the Roman male's greatest achievements was in inculcating the idea that woman's supreme duty is to be chaste. Hence, she says, the world's standard for centuries, the double standard, was formalized. It was cleverly done, says Miss Hamilton, and naïve or prudent women seldom if ever questioned the extramarital habits of their men. Julius Caesar was quite the playboy, but when there was some question about the fidelity of his wife, he divorced her, saying "Caesar's wife must be above suspicion." And so has it ever been with the little Caesars in their little homes. There were many women of easy virtue in all societies, and they were typically exploited by the male chauvinists of Mesopotamia, Egypt, Persia, Greece, and Rome, and by those in the Middle Ages—or anywhere else in place and time.

The ancient Christians took their cue from the Hebrews of the Old Testament, fellow Romans, and history about where women should be placed in society. Over one-half of the Bible's sixty-six books are named after men, two after women, and the Apostle Paul's sentiments on women only reflected earlier Hebrew sentiments:

"To the unmarried and the widows I say that it is well for them to remain single as I do."—I Cor. 7:8.

"The unmarried man is anxious about the affairs of the Lord, how to please the Lord; but the married man is anxious about worldly affairs, how to please his wife."—I Cor. 7:32.

"So that he who marries his betrothed does well; and he who refrains from marriage will do better. A wife is bound to her husband as long as he lives."—I Cor. 7:38, 39.

"As in all the churches of the saints, the women should keep silence in the churches. . . . If there is anything they desire to know, let them ask their husbands at home."—I Cor. 14:34, 35.

"Wives, be subject to your husbands, as to the Lord. For the husband is the head of the wife as Christ is head of the church, his body, and is himself its Savior. As the church is subject to Christ, so let wives also be subject in everything to their husbands."—Eph. 5:22–24.

It is said in defense of Paul that he was only reflecting the life and times of the first Christian century. But the attitudes have persisted through twenty centuries, and the Christian Church has perpetuated the myth of feminine inferiority. The medieval world is largely a man's world. The big names are men: Augustine, Jerome, Gregory Magnus, Charlemagne, Benedict, Henry II, Francis, Dominic, and so on. An Eleanor of Aquitaine, a Joan of Arc, or even the Virgin Mary stand out only to emphasize the inferiority of the female to a superior male figurehead. The recent motion picture on the life of St. Francis of Assisi and his devoted follower Clare, founder of the Second Order of St. Francis, the *Poor Clares*, was titled *Father Sun, Sister Moon*. Despite efforts at modernization by Christian churches today, women are still not equal in many respects, and the counsel of St. Paul prevails to some degree. Of course, women in the Christian world have been freer than their Moslem sisters, who are just now, in most countries at least, beginning to shed the veil after centuries of submission not only to Allah but to the male. All things, said the Greek sophists, are relative, but many women throughout the world are getting tired of relativity.

According to news reports and letters to various editors, other women are quite satisfied. Their history has not been all that bad. They have been supported, pampered, honored, titled, respected, revered, anointed, adored, and deified in all ages, and they have enjoyed and profited from the attentions of their slaves—men. But they have not been content to remain mere objects while civilization passed them by. They have made important contributions. Historian V. Gordon Childe[4] suggests that the great turning point away from barbarism and toward civilization occurred when women discovered the use of seeds and thus started the science of agriculture. While their men were away hunting and fishing, women were the first cultivators. He says that ethnographic evidence points to women discovering or inventing the following: threshing and grinding grain into flour, baking of bread and cakes, brewing of beer and fermentation of other liquor, spinning and weaving of cotton and flax into fabrics for clothing and home use, making of pottery for household uses, and fertilization of the land. These accomplishments stand up well with any accomplishments made by men.

The Sumerians had a priestess, Bau, in Lagash who managed a huge temple industry that processed beer, baked bread, and manufactured cloth, metal, tools, ploughs, wagons, and other sundry goods. Ancient Egypt produced a number of remarkable women, one of the greatest being Queen Hatshepsut, who reigned 1500 years before Christ and left one of the largest and most unique temples, which still stands beneath great cliffs at the edge of the desert and is admired for its great steps, columns, light, and gracefulness. She gave Egypt twenty years of peace in an age of nearly constant warfare. It is abundantly clear from the paintings, statues, beautiful jewelry, cosmetic paints and jars, hair curlers, combs, and mirrors that women played a most important part in Egyptian civilization. .

Although the Athenian citizen of the Golden Age kept his wife pretty much secluded, some women chose to lead a freer life. The Hetairae—companions—were professional women, somewhat on the order of the geishas of Japan, who entertained men with their artistic and intellectual talents. The most famous of these was Aspasia, the mistress of Pericles and later his wife, who, according to Plato, was the true author of Pericles' famous Funeral Oration. She established a school of rhetoric and philosophy at Athens, and among the great names who sat in on her lectures were Euripides, Alcibiades, and Socrates. Philosopher historian Will Durant says that her home was like a French Enlightenment salon, where art, science, literature, and philosophy were discussed. Aspasia, he says, "became the uncrowned queen of Athens, setting fashion's tone, and giving to the women of the city an exciting example of mental and moral freedom."[5] However, the conservatives were shocked, Aspasia was brought to trial for indecent behavior, and only Pericles' eloquence got her case dismissed (and caused the demise of his own political fortunes).

The Greek woman was center stage in many of the great dramas, though parts were all played by men, owing in good part to the discriminating union of actors. The strong characters of Antigone, Medea, Phaedra, Hecuba, Helen are well known. At least two plays were directed at the stupidity of the male chauvinists. In *The Trojan Women*, Euripides makes a pacifist's plea for peace by showing the pitiful plight of the women of Troy after the great war, and in *Lysistrata* Aristophanes shows how women might use their talents to rid the world of war.

Though Aristotle often denigrated women, his great teacher Plato, elevated them to an equal station in his ideal state, *The Republic*. They were to be admitted to all occupations, including the bearing of arms, and to the top rank of philosopher-rulers. After all, he reasoned, why waste the talents of half the population? Natural gifts are to be found in both sexes, and they should be permitted to be developed. "Can anything be better for a commonwealth than to produce in it men and women of the best possible type?" The answer is obvious, and, though Plato did not say it directly, anyone who thinks otherwise is ΣTUPIΔ. (Of course, he also said wives should be shared—as should husbands—and that children should be held in common. Though the Chinese in the Great Leap Forward in 1958 tried something like this in their communes, it was not successful, and the idea is too liberal for most of us today.)

*La dolce vita*, the sweet life, represented in ancient Rome a swinging, liberated set somewhat comparable to the increased freedom for women today. Though the ancient Roman woman did not have political rights, she associated freely with men and might be found talking with them in parks, baths, streets, and public festivals. She might be discovered as a poetress, athlete, lawyer, doctor, actress, artisan, or even as a gladiator fighting lions in the arena. "It was a gay, colorful, multisexual society that would have astonished the Periclean Greeks," says Will Durant. "In the spring fashionable women filled the boats, shores, and villas of Baiae and other resorts with their laughter, their proud beauty, their amorous audacities, and political intrigue. Old men denounced them longingly."[6]

The genius of the female was apparent in the strength of the Roman family, however. Her organization, administration, cooperation, and self-lessness assured the success of one of Rome's strongest institutions. Pliny the Younger in one of his letters describes the love, affection, devotion, and gracious way of living in the family of a friend whose young daughter suffered a fatal illness:

To Aefulanus Marcellinus:

I am writing to you in great distress: our friend Fundanus has lost his younger daughter. I never saw a girl so gay and lovable, so deserving of a longer life or even a life to last forever. She had not yet reached the age of fourteen, and yet she combined the wisdom of age and dignity of womanhood with the sweetness and modesty of youth and innocence. She would cling to her father's neck, and embrace us, his friends, with modest affection; she loved her nurses, her attendants, and her teachers, each one for the service given her; she applied herself intelligently to her books and was moderate and restrained in her play. She bore her last illness with patient resignation and, indeed, with courage; she obeyed her doctors' orders, cheered her sister and father, and by sheer force of will carried on after her physical strength had failed her. This will power remained with her to the end, and neither the length of her illness nor the fear of death could break it. So she has left us all the more sad reasons for lamenting our loss. Hers is a truly tragic and untimely end—death itself was not so cruel as the moment of its coming. She was already engaged to marry a distinguished young man, the day for the wedding was fixed, and we had received our invitations. Such joy, and now such sorrow![7]

But with the ease of divorce for both women and men in the first century A.D., and with the hedonistic philosophy of "eat, drink, and be merry, for tomorrow we die" among greater numbers of people, many of the ruling class families began to break up. The swinging, sweet life lacked the foundations for a continuation of civilization as earlier republican Rome knew it. Christian values eventually undermined the Roman, and the Middle Ages set in. Women had a place in that new world, but, as we have seen, it was in a secondary role. The ancient myths were propagated and entrenched as tradition. The determined movement toward liberation was to await the suffragettes of the late nineteenth century and, again, the women's liberation movement of the late twentieth.

Are women ever going to win their battle for equality? As late as 1974 there was no woman among 100 United States Senators or 50 state governors, although Margaret Chase Smith was recently Senator from Maine and Mrs. George Wallace was governor of Alabama. Only a few women were in the House of Representatives, none were in the President's cabinet, and none among mayors of large cities. There are few women executives in business or labor unions and relatively few in medical, legal, scientific, and other professions except for nursing and teaching. Why? Is it the result of a division of labor, with women handling the time-consuming responsibilities of the home while the man operates in the wider world of economics, political, and cultural affairs? Or is it because of male chauvinism, with its fears of competition, its prejudices, and reluctance to break with tradition?

History has progressed naturally, says the Hegelian school of philosophers of history. Every group needs a leader to make the important decisions from family to state to nation. The male, for many reasons, has dominated in all societies in place and time. Why change, ask members of this school. Change is necessary, say many women, because male leaders have been participants in the great tyranny of discrimination and subjection of women. Ashley Montagu wrote his 1968 book *The Natural Superiority of Women* because he recognized the time was overdue to destroy the old myths of male superiority, which supported an unfair and unenlightened way of life. He wrote the book, he says, not to separate the sexes into warring factions, but to bring them together by recognizing the need for love, understanding, and equality.

## Notes

1 Ashley Montagu, *The Natural Superiority of Women* (New York: Macmillan, 1968).

2 *Ibid.*, p. 158.

3 Edith Hamilton, *The Roman Way* (New York: Norton, 1960), p. 33.

4 V. Gordon Childe, *What Happened in History* (Baltimore, Md.: Penguin, 1954), pp. 58, 59.

5 Will Durant, *The Life of Greece* (New York: Simon and Schuster, 1939), p. 253.

6 Will Durant, *Caesar and Christ* (New York: Simon and Schuster, 1944), p. 370.

7 *The Letters of the Young Pliny*, translated by Betty Radice (Baltimore, Md.: Penguin, 1963), p. 152.

That women played a significant role in ancient Mesopotamia is demonstrated in the Code of Hammurabi, of about 1700 B.C., in which a number of articles referred to their rights and privileges. In many respects, women were treated equally with men, though the father was head of the family. The articles recognize the importance of the marriage contract and provide for the settlement of a variety of marital problems. What age-old woman-man problems are revealed in these laws?

# Women in Ancient Mesopotamia

Code of Hammurabi

108. If the mistress of a beer-shop has not received corn as the price of beer or has demanded silver on an excessive scale, and has made the measure of beer less than the measure of corn, that beer seller shall be prosecuted and drowned.

109. If the mistress of a beer-shop has assembled seditious slanderers in her house and those seditious persons have not been captured and have not been haled to the palace, that beer-seller shall be put to death.

110. If a votary, who is not living in the convent, open a beer-shop, or enter a beer-shop for drink, that woman shall be put to death. . . .

117. If a man owes a debt, and he has given his wife, his son, or his daughter [as hostage] for the money, or has handed someone over to work it off, the hostage shall do the work of the creditor's house; but in the fourth year he shall set them free.

118. If a debtor has handed over a male or female slave to work off a debt, and the creditor proceeds to sell same, no one can complain.

119. If a man owes a debt, and he has assigned a maid who has borne him children for the money, the owner of the maid shall repay the money which the merchant gave him and shall ransom his maid. . . .

127. If a man has caused the finger to be pointed at a votary, or a man's wife, and has not justified himself, that man shall be brought before the judges, and have his forehead branded.

128. If a man has taken a wife and has not executed a marriage-contract, that woman is not a wife.

129. If a man's wife be caught lying with another, they shall be strangled and cast into the water. If the wife's husband would save his wife, the king can save his servant.

130. If a man has ravished another's bethrothed wife, who is a virgin, while still living in her father's house, and has been caught in the act, that man shall be put to death; the woman shall go free.

From *Babylonian and Assyrian Laws, Contracts and Letters*, edited by C. H. W. Johns (New York: Scribner's, 1904), pp. 44–67 *passim*.

131. If a man's wife has been accused by her husband, and has not been caught lying with another, she shall swear her innocence, and return to her house.

132. If a man's wife has the finger pointed at her on account of another, but has not been caught lying with him, for her husband's sake she shall plunge into the sacred river.

133. If a man has been taken captive, and there was maintenance in his house, but his wife has left her house and entered into another man's house; because that woman has not preserved her body, and has entered into the house of another, that woman shall be prosecuted and shall be drowned.

134. If a man has been taken captive, but there was not maintenance in his house, and his wife has entered into the house of another, that woman has no blame.

135. If a man has been taken captive, but there was no maintenance in his house for his wife, and she has entered into the house of another, and has borne him children, if in the future her [first] husband shall return and regain his city, that woman shall return to her first husband, but the children shall follow their own father.

136. If a man has left his city and fled, and, after he has gone, his wife has entered into the house of another; if the man return and seize his wife, the wife of the fugitive shall not return to her husband, because he hated his city and fled.

137. If a man has determined to divorce a concubine who has borne him children, or a votary who has granted him children, he shall return to that woman her marriage-portion, and shall give her the usufruct of field, garden, and goods, to bring up her children. After her children have grown up, out of whatever is given to her children, they shall give her one son's share, and the husband of her choice shall marry her.

138. If a man has divorced his wife, who has not borne him children, he shall pay over to her as much money as was given for her bride-price and the marriage-portion which she brought from her father's house, and so shall divorce her.

139. If there was no bride-price, he shall give her one mina of silver, as a price of divorce.

140. If he be a plebeian, he shall give her one-third of a mina of silver.

141. If a man's wife, living in her husband's house, has persisted in going out, has acted the fool, has wasted her house, has belittled her husband, he shall prosecute her. If her husband has said, "I divorce her," she shall go her way; he shall give her nothing as her price of divorce. If her husband has said, "I will not divorce her," he may take another woman to wife; the wife shall live as a slave in her husband's house.

**Sigmund Freud's famous theory of the Oedipus complex stated that the son is so attracted to his mother that he hates his father. But as Erich Fromm views Sophocles' Oedipus plays, the issue is between those representing contrary matriarchal and patriarchal attitudes—that is, those favoring equality and democracy against those upholding authority and obedience. Incest, Fromm says, is only a minor factor—not a major one, as Freud believed. Are we to believe, then, that if matriarchal attitudes had triumphed over patriarchal, the world would have been spared much blood and conflict over the centuries? Would peace, equality, and justice have prevailed?**

# The Oedipus Complex

Erich Fromm

Bachofen* showed that the difference between the patriarchal and the matriarchal order went far beyond the social supremacy of men and women, respectively, but was one of social and moral principles. Matriarchal culture is characterized by an emphasis on ties of blood, ties to the soil, and a passive acceptance of all natural phenomena. Patriarchal society, in contrast, is characterized by respect for man-made law, by a predominance of rational thought, and by man's effort to change natural phenomena. In so far as these principles are concerned, the patriarchal culture constitutes a definite progress over the matriarchal world. In other respects, however, the matriarchal principles were superior to the victorious patriarchal ones. In the matriarchal concept all men are equal, since they are all the children of mothers and each one a child of Mother Earth. A mother loves all her children alike and without conditions, since her love is based on the fact that they are her children and not on any particular merit or achievement; the aim of life is the happiness of men, and there is nothing more important or dignified than human existence and life. The patriarchal system, on the other hand, considers obedience to authority to be the main virtue. Instead of the principle of equality, we find the concept of the favorite son and a hierarchical order in society.

The relationship (Bachofen says) through which mankind has first grown into civilization which is the beginning of the development of every virtue and of the formation of the nobler aspects of human existence is the matriarchal principle, which becomes effective as the principle of love, unity, and peace. The woman sooner than the man learns in caring for the infant to extend her love beyond her own self to other human beings and to direct all her

---

*Editor's note:* In 1861 Johann Jakob Bachofen published *Mother Right* in which he analyzed Greek mythology. Fromm's interpretation is based on Bachofen's theory.

From *The Forgotten Language* by Erich Fromm. Reprinted by permission of Grove Press, Inc. Copyright © 1951 by Erich Fromm.

gifts and imagination to the aim of preserving and beautifying the existence of another being. All development of civilization, devotion, care, and the mourning for the dead are rooted in her[1]

The motherly love is not only more tender but also more general and universal. . . . Its principle is that of universality, whereas the patriarchal principle is that of restrictions . . . The idea of the universal brotherhood of man is rooted in the principle of motherhood, and this very idea vanishes with the development of patriarchal society. The patriarchal family is a closed and restricted organism. The matriarchal family, on the other hand, has that universal character with which all evolution begins and which is characteristic of maternal life in contrast to the spiritual, the image of Mother Earth, Demeter. Each woman's womb will give brothers and sisters to every human being until, with the development of the patriarchal principle, this unity is dissolved and superseded by the principle of hierarchy. In matriarchal societies, this principle has found frequent and even legally formulated expressions. It is the basis of the principle of universal freedom and equality which we find as one of the basic traits in matriarchal cultures. . . . Absence of inner disharmony, a longing for peace . . . a tender humaneness which one can still see in the facial expression of Egyptian statues penetrates the matriarchal world. . . .[2]

Bachofen's discovery found confirmation by an American scholar, L. H. Morgan, who entirely independently came to the conclusion[3] that the kinship system of the American Indians—similar to that found in Asia, Africa, and Australia—was based on the matriarchal principle and that the most significant institution in such cultures, the gens, was organized in conformity with the matriarchal principle. Morgan's conclusion about principles of value in a matriarchal society were quite similar to Bachofen's. He proposed that the higher form of civilization "will be a repetition—but on a higher level—of the principles of liberty, equality, and fraternity which characterized the ancient gens." Both Bachofen's and Morgan's theories of matriarchy were, if not entirely ignored, disputed by most anthropologists. This was also the case in the work of Robert Briffault, who in *The Mothers*[4] continued Bachofen's research and confirmed it by a brilliant analysis of new anthropological data. The violence of the antagonism against the theory of matriarchy arouses the suspicion that the criticism was not entirely free from an emotionally founded prejudice against an assumption so foreign to the thinking and feeling of our patriarchal culture. There is little doubt that many single objections to the matriarchal theory are justified. Nevertheless, Bachofen's main thesis, that we find an older layer of matriarchal religion underneath the more recent patriarchal religion of Greece, seems to me to be established by him beyond any doubt.

. . .

How different is the end of *Oedipus at Colonus* from that of *King Oedipus*. In the latter, his fate seemed to be sealed as that of the tragic criminal whose crime removes him forever from his family and from his fellow men, destined to be an outcast, abhorred though perhaps pitied by everyone. In the former he dies as a man surrounded by two loving daughters and by new friends whose benefactor he has become, not with a feeling of guilt but with a conviction of his right, not as an outcast but as one who has eventually found his home—with the earth and the goddesses who rule there. The tragic guilt that had pervaded *King Oedipus* has now been removed, and only one conflict has remained as bitter and unsolved as ever—that between father and son.

The conflict between the patriarchal and matriarchal principles is the theme of the third part of the trilogy, *Antigone*. Here the figure of Creon, which has been somewhat indistinct in the two former tragedies, becomes colorful and definite. He has become the tyrant of Thebes after Oedipus's two sons have been killed—one by attacking the city in order to gain power, the other defending his throne. Creon has ordered that the legitimate king should be buried and that the challenger's body should be left unburied—the greatest humiliation and dishonor to be done to a man, according to Greek custom. The principle that Creon represents is that of the supremacy of the law of the state over ties of blood, of obedience to authority over allegiance to the natural law of humanity. Antigone refuses to violate the laws of blood and of the solidarity of all human beings for the sake of an authoritarian, hierarchical principle.

The two principles for which Creon and Antigone stand are those which Bachofen characterized as the patriarchal as against the matriarchal principle, respectively. The matriarchal principle is that of blood relationship as the fundamental and indestructible tie, of the equality of all men, of the respect for human life and of love. The patriarchal principle is that the ties between man and wife, between ruler and ruled, take precedence over ties of blood. It is the principle of order and authority, of obedience and hierarchy.

Antigone represents the matriarchal principle and thus is the uncompromising adversary of the representative of patriarchal authority, Creon. Ismene, in contrast, has accepted the defeat and given in to the victorious patriarchal order; she is a symbol of women under patriarchal domination.

## Notes

1 J. J. Bachofen, *Der Mythus von Orient und Okzident*, edited by Manfred Schroeder (Munich: Ch. Becksche Buchhandlung, 1926), pp. 14 f.

2 *Ibid.*, pp. 15, 16.

3 Tentatively in his *Systems of Consanguinity and Affinity*, 1871, and more definitely in *Ancient Society* (Chicago: Charles H. Kerr & Co., 1877).

4 New York: The Macmillan Company, 1927.

Solon was archon of Athens in 594 B.C. and is noted for his reforms
benefiting the people at large. In this selection, Plutarch, writing around
A.D. 100, describes some of Solon's unique reforms for women. Following is
Plutarch's description of Aspasia, the mistress and later the wife of
Pericles. In what ways can you detect that these two worlds, about 150 years
apart, are men's worlds?

# Greek Women

Plutarch

In all other marriages he forbade dowries to be given; the wife was to
have three suits of clothes, a little inconsiderable household stuff, and
that was all; for he would not have marriages contracted for gain or an
estate, but for pure love, kind affection, and birth of children. When the
mother of Dionysius desired him to marry her to one of his citizens,
"Indeed," said he, "by my tyranny I have broken my country's laws, but
cannot put a violence upon those of nature by an unseasonable marriage."
Such disorder is never to be suffered in a commonwealth, nor such unseasonable and unloving and unperforming marriages, which attain no
due end or fruit; any provident governor or lawgiver might say to an old
man that takes a young wife what is said to Philoctetes in the tragedy—
     "Truly, in a fit state thou to marry!"
and if he find a young man, with a rich and elderly wife, growing fat in
his place, like the partridges, remove him to a young woman of proper
age. And of this enough.

Another commendable law of Solon's is that which forbids men to
speak evil of the dead; for it is pious to think the deceased sacred, and
just, not to meddle with those that are gone, and politic, to prevent the
perpetuity of discord. He likewise forbade them to speak evil of the
living in the temples, the courts of justice, the public offices, or at the
games, or else to pay three drachmas to the person, and two to the public.
For never to be able to control passion shows a weak nature and ill-
breeding; and always to moderate it is very hard, and to some impossible.
And laws must look to possibilities, if the maker designs to punish few
in order to their amendment, and not many to no purpose.

He is likewise much commended for his law concerning wills; for
before him none could be made, but all the wealth and estate of the
deceased belonged to his family; but he by permitting them, if they had

From *Plutarch, The Lives of the Noble Grecians and Romans* (New York:
Modern Library, n.d.), pp. 108–111, 200, 201.

no children, to bestow it on whom they pleased, showed that he esteemed friendship a stronger tie than kindred, and affection than necessity; and made every man's estate truly his own. Yet he allowed not all sorts of legacies, but those only which were not extorted by the frenzy of a disease, charms, imprisonment, force, or the persuasions of a wife; with good reason thinking that being seduced into wrong was as bad as being forced, and that between deceit and necessity, flattery and compulsion, there was little difference, since both may equally suspend the exercise of reason.

He regulated the walks, feasts, and mourning of the women, and took away everything that was either unbecoming or immodest; when they walked abroad, no more than three articles of dress were allowed them; an obol's worth of meat and drink; and no basket above a cubit high; and at night they were not to go about unless in a chariot with a torch before them. Mourners tearing themselves to raise pity, and set wailings, and at one man's funeral to lament for another, he forbade. To offer an ox at the grave was not permitted, nor to bury above three pieces of dress with the body, or visit the tombs of any besides their own family, unless at the very funeral; most of which are likewise forbidden by our laws, but this is further added in ours, that those that are convicted of extravagance in their mournings are to be punished as soft and effeminate by the censors of women.

. . .

Solon's laws in general about women are his strangest; for he permitted any one to kill an adulterer that found him in the act; but if any one forced a free woman, a hundred drachmas was the fine; if he enticed her, twenty; except those that sell themselves openly, that is, harlots, who go openly to those that hire them. He made it unlawful to sell a daughter or a sister, unless, being yet unmarried, she was found wanton. Now it is irrational to punish the same crime sometimes very severely and without remorse, and sometimes very lightly, and as it were in sport, with a trivial fine; unless there being little money then in Athens, scarcity made those mulcts the more grievous punishment. In the valuation for sacrifices, a sheep and a bushel were both estimated at a drachma; the victor in the Isthmian games was to have for reward an hundred drachmas; the conqueror in the Olympian, five hundred; he that brought a wolf, five drachmas; for a whelp, one; the former sum, as Demetrius the Phalerian asserts, was the value of an ox, the latter, of a sheep. The prices which Solon, in his sixteenth table, sets on choice victims, were naturally far greater; yet they, too, are very low in comparison of the present. The Athenians were, from the beginning, great enemies to wolves, their fields being better for pasture than corn. Some affirm their tribes did not take their names from the sons of Ion, but from the different sorts of occupation that they followed; the soldiers were called Hoplitae, the craftsmen Ergades, and, of the remaining two, the farmers Gedeontes, and the shepherds and graziers Aegicores.

. . .

After this, having made a truce between the Athenians and Lacedaemonians for thirty years, he ordered, by public decree, the expedition against the isle of Samos, on the ground, that, when they were bid to leave off their war with the Milesians they had not complied. And as these measures against the Samians are thought to have been taken to please Aspasia, this may be a fit point for inquiry about the woman, what art or charming faculty she had that enabled her to captivate, as she did, the greatest statesmen, and to give the philosophers occasion to speak so much about her, and that, too, not to her disparagement. That she was a Milesian by birth, the daughter of Axiochus, is a thing acknowledged. And they say it was in emulation of Thargelia, a courtesan of the old Ionian times, that she made her addresses to men of great power. Thargelia was a great beauty, extremely charming, and at the same time sagacious; she had numerous suitors among the Greeks, and brought all who had to do with her over to the Persian interest, and by their means, being men of the greatest power and station, sowed the seeds of the Median faction up and down in several cities. Aspasia, some say, was courted and caressed by Pericles upon account of her knowledge and skill in politics. Socrates himself would sometimes go to visit her, and some of his acquaintance with him; and those who frequented her company would carry their wives with them to listen to her. Her occupation was anything but creditable, her house being a home for young courtesans. Aeschines tell us, also, that Lysicles, a sheep-dealer, a man of low birth and character, by keeping Aspasia company after Pericles's death, came to be a chief man in Athens. And in Plato's Menexenus, though we do not take the introduction as quite serious, still thus much seems to be historical, that she had the repute of being resorted to by many of the Athenians for instruction in the art of speaking. Pericles's inclination for her seems, however, to have rather proceeded from the passion of love. He had a wife that was near of kin to him, who had been married first to Hipponicus, by whom she had Callias, surnamed the Rich; and also she brought Pericles, while she lived with him, two sons, Xanthippus and Paralus. Afterwards, when they did not well agree, nor like to live together, he parted with her, with her own consent, to another man, and himself took Aspasia, and loved her with wonderful affection; every day, both as he went out and as he came in from the market-place, he saluted and kissed her.

In the comedies she goes by the nicknames of the new Omphale and Deianira, and again is styled Juno. Cratinus, in downright terms, calls her a harlot.

"To find him a Juno the goddess of lust
Bore that harlot past shame,
Aspasia by name."

It should seem also that he had a son by her; Eupolis, in his Demi, introduced Pericles asking after his safety, and Myronides replying—

"My son?" "He lives: a man he had been long,
But that the harlot-mother did him wrong."

Aspasia, they say, became so celebrated and renowned, that Cyrus, also who made war against Artaxerxes for the Persian monarchy, gave her whom he loved the best of all his concubines the name of Aspasia, who before that was called Milto. She was a Phocaean by birth, the daughter of one Hermotimus, and, when Cyrus fell in battle, was carried to the king, and had great influence at court. These things coming into my memory as I am writing this story, it would be unnatural for me to omit them.

During one of the darkest periods of the Peloponnesian War, the women of
Athens, led by Lysistrata, seized the Acropolis with its sacred buildings and
determined not to go home until their men terminated the war. Aristophanes'
comedy highlights the divergent points of view between women and men
in wartime and at the same time shows the need of one for the other. Since
women are as much, if not more, affected by war as are men, should they not
have a say in the determination of war and peace? And political and economic
problems? Aristophanes put these questions to his Greek audiences.

# Lysistrata

Aristophanes

(*At this juncture the* WOMEN *wheel round the corner of the Acropolis,
and the two Choruses suddenly meet face to face.*)

Stop! easy all! what have we here? (*To the* MEN.) You vile, abandoned
  crew,

No good and virtuous men, I'm sure, would act in the way you do.

CHORUS OF MEN: Hey, here's an unexpected sight! hey, here's a demonstration!

A swarm of women issuing out with warlike preparation!

CHORUS OF WOMEN: Hallo, you seem a little moved! does this one troop
  affright you?

You see not yet the myriadth part of those prepared to fight you.

CHORUS OF MEN: Now, really, Phaedrias, shall we stop to hear such
  odious treason?

Let's break our sticks about their backs, let's beat the jades to reason.

CHORUS OF WOMEN: Hi, sisters, set the pitchers down, and then they
  won't embarrass

Our nimble fingers, if the rogues attempt our ranks to harass.

CHORUS OF MEN: I warrant, now, if twice or thrice we slap their faces
  neatly,

That they will learn, like Bupalus, to hold their tongues discretely.[1]

CHORUS OF WOMEN: Well, here's my face: I won't draw back: now slap
  it if you dare,

And I won't leave one ounce of you for other dogs to tear.

CHORUS OF MEN: Keep still, or else your musty Age to very shreds I'll
  batter.

From *Five Comedies of Aristophanes*, translated by Bickley Rogers (London:
G. Bell & Sons, Ltd.). Notes renumbered.

CHORUS OF WOMEN: Now only touch Stratyllis, sir; just lift one finger at her!

CHORUS OF MEN: And what if with these fists, my love, I pound the wench to shivers?

CHORUS OF WOMEN: By Heaven, we'll gnaw your entrails out, and rip away your livers.

CHORUS OF MEN: There is not than Euripides a bard more wise and knowing.

For women *are* a shameless set, the vilest creatures going.

CHORUS OF WOMEN: Pick up again, Rhodippe dear, your jug with water brimming.

CHORUS OF MEN: What made you bring that water here, you God-detested women?

CHORUS OF WOMEN: What made you bring that light, old Tomb? to set *yourselves* afire?

CHORUS OF MEN: No, but to kindle for your friends a mighty funeral pyre.

CHORUS OF WOMEN: Well, then, we brought this water here to put your bonfire out, sirs.

CHORUS OF MEN: *You* put our bonfire out, indeed!

CHORUS OF WOMEN:                               You'll see, beyond a doubt, sirs.

CHORUS OF MEN: I swear that with this torch, offhand, I've half a mind to fry you.

CHORUS OF WOMEN: Got any soap, my lad? If so, a bath I'll soon supply you.

CHORUS OF MEN: A bath for *me*, you mouldy hag!

CHORUS OF WOMEN:                               And that a bride-bath, too.

CHORUS OF MEN: Zounds, did you hear her impudence?

CHORUS OF WOMEN:                               Ain't I freeborn as you?

CHORUS OF MEN: I'll quickly put a stop to this.

CHORUS OF WOMEN:                               You'll judge no more, I vow!

CHORUS OF MEN: Hi! set the vixen's hair on fire.

CHORUS OF WOMEN:                               Now, Achelous, now![2]

CHORUS OF MEN: Good gracious!

CHORUS OF WOMEN:                               What! you find it hot?

CHORUS OF MEN: Hot? murder! stop! be quiet!

CHORUS OF WOMEN: I'm watering you, to make you grow.

CHORUS OF MEN: I wither up from shivering so.

CHORUS OF WOMEN: I tell you what: a fire you've got,
　So warm your members by it.

*(At this crisis the tumult is stayed for an instant by the appearance on the stage of a venerable official personage, one of the Magistrates who, after the Sicilian catastrophe, were appointed, under the name of Probuli, to form a Directory or Committee of Public Safety. He is attended by four SCYTHIAN ARCHERS, part of the ordinary police of the Athenian Republic. The WOMEN retire into the background.)*

MAGISTRATE: Has then the women's wantonness blazed out,
　Their constant timbrels and Sabaziuses,
　And that Adonis-dirge upon the roof[3]
　Which once I heard in full Assembly-time.
　'Twas when Demostratus (beshrew him) moved
　To sail to Sicily: and from the roof
　A woman, dancing, shrieked *Woe, woe, Adonis!*
　And *he* proposed to enrol Zacynthian hoplites;
　And *she* upon the roof, the maudlin woman,
　Cried *Wail Adonis!* yet he forced it through,
　That God-detested, vile Ill-temprian.
　Such are the wanton follies of the sex.

CHORUS OF MEN: What if you heard their insolence today,
　Their vile, outrageous goings on? And look,
　See how they've drenched and soused us from their pitchers,
　Till we can wring out water from our clothes.

MAGISTRATE: Ay, by Poseidon, and it serves us right.
　'Tis all our fault: they'll never know their place,
　These pampered women, whilst we spoil them so.
　Hear how we talk in every workman's shop.
　*Goldsmith,* says one, *this necklace that you made,*
　*My gay young wife was dancing yester-eve,*
　*And lost, sweet soul, the fastening of the clasp;*
　*Do please reset it, Goldsmith.* Or, again,
　*O Shoemaker, my wife's new sandal pinches*
　*Her little toe, the tender, delicate child,*
　*Make it fit easier, please.*—Hence all this nonsense!
　Yea, things have reached a pretty pass, indeed,
　When I, the State's Director, wanting money
　To purchase oar-blades, find the Treasury gates
　Shut in my face by these preposterous women.

Nay, but no dallying now: bring up the crowbars,
And I'll soon stop *your* insolence, my dears.

(*He turns to the* SCYTHIANS, *who, instead of setting to work, are looking idly around them.*)

What! gaping, fool? and *you*, can *you* do nothing
But stare about with tavern-squinting eye?
Push in the crowbars underneath the gates,
You, stand that side and heave them: I'll stop here
And heave them here.

(*The gates are thrown open, and* LYSISTRATA *comes out.*)

LYSISTRATA:                O let your crowbars be.
Lo, I come out unfetched! What need of crowbars?
'Tis wits, not crowbars, that ye need today.

MAGISTRATE: Ay, truly, traitress, say you so? Here, Archer!
Arrest her, tie her hands behind her back.

LYSISTRATA: And if he touch me with his finger-tip,
The public scum! 'fore Artemis, he'll rue it.

MAGISTRATE: What, man, afeared? why, catch her round the waist.
And *you* go with him, quick, and bind her fast.

CALONICE (*coming out*): And if you do but lay one hand upon her,
'Fore Pandrosus, I'll stamp your vitals out.[4]

MAGISTRATE: Vitals, ye hag? Another Archer, ho!
Seize this one first, because she chatters so.

MYRRHINA (*coming out*): And if you touch her with your finger-tip,
'Fore Phosphorus, you'll need a cupping shortly.

MAGISTRATE: Tcha! what's all this? lay hold of this one, Archer!
I'll stop this sallying out, depend upon it.

STRATYLLIS: And if he touch her, 'fore the Queen of Tauris,[5]
I'll pull his squealing hairs out, one by one.

MAGISTRATE: O dear! all's up! I've never an archer left.
Nay, but I swear we won't be done by women.
Come, Scythians, close your ranks, and all together
Charge!

LYSISTRATA: Charge away, my hearties, and you'll soon
Know that we've here, impatient for the fight,
Four woman-squadrons, armed from top to toe.

MAGISTRATE: Attach them, Scythians, twist their hands behind them.

LYSISTRATA: Forth to the fray, dear sisters, bold allies!
O egg-and-seed-and-potherb-market-girls,

O garlic-selling-barmaid-baking-girls,
Charge to the rescue, smack and whack, and thwack them,
Slang them, I say: show them what jades ye be.

(*The* WOMEN *come forward. After a short struggle the* ARCHERS *are routed.*)

. . .

LYSISTRATA: I will.
Think of our old moderation and gentleness,
    think how we bore with your pranks, and were still,
All through the days of your former pugnacity,
    all through the war that is over and spent:
Not that (be sure) we approved of your policy;
    never our griefs you allowed us to vent.
Well we perceived your mistakes and mismanagement.
    Often at home on our housekeeping cares,
Often we heard of some foolish proposal you
    made for conducting the public affairs.
Then would we question you mildly and pleasantly,
    inwardly grieving, but outwardly gay;
*Husband, how goes it abroad?* we would ask of him;
    *what have ye done in Assembly today?*
*What would ye write on the side of the Treaty stone?*[6]
    Husband says angrily, *What's that to you?*
*You, hold your tongue!* And I held it accordingly.

STRATYLLIS: That is a thing which I *never* would do!

MAGISTRATE: Ma'am, if you hadn't, you'd soon repented it.

LYSISTRATA: Therefore I held it, and spake not a word.
Soon of another tremendous absurdity,
    wilder and worse than the former we heard.
*Husband,* I say, with a tender solicitude,
    *Why have ye passed such a foolish decree?*
Vicious, moodily, glaring askance at me,
    *Stick to your spinning, my mistress,* says he,
*Else you will speedily find it the worse for you,*
    *War is the care and the business of men!*[7]

MAGISTRATE: Zeus! 'twas a worthy reply, and an excellent!

LYSISTRATA: What! you unfortunate, shall we not then,
Then, when we see you perplexed and incompetent,
    shall we not tender advice to the State?

So when aloud in the streets and the thoroughfares
      sadly we heard you bewailing of late,
*Is there a Man to defend and deliver us?*
        *No,* says another, *there's none in the land;*
Then by the Women assembled in conference
      jointly a great Revolution was planned,
Hellas to save from her grief and perplexity.
        Where is the use of a longer delay?
Shift for the future our parts and our characters;
      you, as the women, in silence obey;
We, as the men, will harangue and provide for you;
      then shall the State be triumphant again,
Then shall we do what is best for the citizens.

MAGISTRATE: Women to do what is best for the men!
That were a shameful reproach and unbearable!

LYSISTRATA: Silence, old gentleman.[8]

MAGISTRATE:                                   Silence for *you?*
Stop for a wench with a wimple enfolding her?
      No, by the Powers, may I *die* if I do!

LYSISTRATA: Do not, my pretty one, do not, I pray,
      Suffer my wimple to stand in the way.
      Here, take it, and wear it, and gracefully tie it,
      Enfolding it over your head, and be quiet.
      Now to your task.

CALONICE: Here is an excellent spindle to pull.

MYRRHINA: Here is a basket for carding the wool.

LYSISTRATA: Now to your task.
      Haricots chawing up, petticoats drawing up,[9]
      Off to your carding, your combing, your trimming,
      *War is the care and the business of women.*

## Notes

1 *Bupalus.* If we smite them on the cheek, as Hipponax the poet threatened in his lampoons to smite his unhappy antagonist, Bupalus.

2 *Achelous.* The largest Hellenic river. The name Achelous was used to denote water generally. The Women are deluging their opponents.

3 *Adonis-dirge.* Plutarch, in his *Life of Nicias* (chapter 13), describes these and similar omens of ill which preceded the Athenian expedition to Sicily. And he also (chapter 12) tells us that the orator Demostratus took a leading part in recommending that fatal measure.

4 *Pandrosus.* Since in every other speech throughout this short altercation the Women invoke Artemis in one or other of her characters, I cannot but believe that in this invocation also the name of Pandrosus, the All-bedewer, is intended to apply to Artemis as identical with Hecate or the Moon.

5 *Queen of Tauris.* Artemis.

6 *The Treaty stone.* Treaties were inscribed on pillars. In the present passage we are dealing with the pillar containing the Peace of Nicias. Some three years later Alcibiades persuaded the Athenians to write on this pillar, underneath the Treaty, that the Lacedaemonians had failed to abide by their oaths. This is no doubt the transaction to which Lysistrata is alluding.

7 *War is the care and the business of men!* From the speech of Hector to Andromache, in the sixth book of the *Iliad.*

8 *Silence, old gentleman.* Lysistrata is putting her system into immediate practice, and therefore addresses the same language and assigns the same duties to the Magistrate, as the Men had been accustomed aforetime to address and assign to the Women.

9 *Haricots chawing up.* Women were in the habit of chewing some eatable as they wove or spun.

In these selections from Janine Assa's book, The Great Roman Ladies, one sees not only the upper crust but also glimpses of the general populace. Life was gay, life was full for the sensuous Romans. In many ways, one can see miniatures of ourselves in the lives of these people.

# The Great Roman Ladies

Janine Assa

## The Family

"Drinking, eating, sleeping together—this is marriage, so I gather." The three ancient forms of marriage, *usus, confarreatio,* and *coemptio*—or cohabitation, ritual repast, and symbolic sale—combined to place a woman in marital tutelage, or rather to transfer her from the guardianship of the paterfamilias to that of the husband. Certain traditionalist families continued to remain attached to them for several generations, but in general practice all that fell into disuse.

Under the empire the marriage ceremony already resembled ours: it consisted of an exchange of consent. But it was not a public function. Neither the state nor the religion of the city intervened. Though the ceremony was purely private, some enjoyed embellishing it with intricacies: a religious ritual or an official escorting of the young bride to her husband's house had no other function than to make a matter-of-fact situation more solemn.

In such a marriage, as we shall see, the woman did not completely come under her husband's control, but sometimes remained legally in the bosom of her original family. It became necessary for legislation to establish the existence of reciprocal obligations between married people, and between a mother and her children.

In other cases too, the state concerned itself with marital relations: Augustus promulgated a law concerning adultery. For sixty days the father or the husband enjoyed the exclusive right to punish the guilty wife, but after this interval the right belonged to anyone. What was more, the husband could not pardon; he was bound to repudiate the adulterous wife.

Marriage was preceded by betrothal. The age varied a great deal, and sentiment was very often excluded. The custom scarcely differed from the practice dear to the *ancien régime* or to Oriental peoples: agreement between the two families constituted all that was essential; young girls were

219

betrothed while they were still children. Tiberius' first wife, Vipsania Agrippina, one of Agrippa's daughters, was engaged at the age of one year; Octavia, the daughter of Claudius and Messalina, was seven years old when she was betrothed to Nero.

The betrothal ceremony was not so solemn as that of marriage. It consisted basically of a banquet where relatives and friends gathered as witnesses to the concluded agreement. The young man had to offer the girl gifts, of which the principal one was a symbolic ring, a simple iron band sometimes encircled with gold, the pledge of fidelity which the future wife had to wear on the finger we now call the ring finger. The Romans had chosen this finger in preference to others because ancient science believed to have discovered in it a nerve communicating directly with the heart.

After the young girl had reached the legal marriageable age, in her twelfth year, the marriage ceremony took place. A girl was married between the ages of twelve and nineteen, the optimal age being between fourteen and sixteen. Agrippina the Younger married Domitius Ahenobarbus, her first husband, quite early, at the age of twelve; Livia was first married at sixteen; Julia began her series of marriages at fourteen . . . At twenty a single Roman lady was already an old maid, subject to the penalty of the law against celibacy.

With the approach of the wedding, everyone was occupied exclusively in making up the young bride's trousseau, buying her jewels and finery, choosing the servants destined to follow her to her new home. When the great day arrived, the two dwellings of the engaged couple, resplendently draped with tapestries and garlands, were filled from daybreak on with relatives, friends, and hangers-on. The bride wore a tunic without a hem, drawn in with a woolen girdle and covered with a saffron-yellow mantle. A flame-colored veil covered her head, surmounted by a simple crown of field flowers. In her father's house, surrounded by her kin, she received her fiancé who was accompanied by his family and friends. A sacrifice, usually performed in the brilliantly lit and decorated atrium in the presence of ten witnesses, preceded the exchange of vows: *ubi tu Gaius ego Gaia* (where and when you will be Gaius, I shall be Gaia). The cheers and good wishes of the guests punctuated the ceremony, which became a prolonged and luxurious feast, the excess of which Augustus attempted to moderate by law. The total expense of a nuptial feast was not to exceed a thousand sesterces. This provision shared the fate of all overly ambitious laws: a thousand sesterces for the expenses of a festival plus gifts to the crowd and hangers-on! The extreme modesty of the legal maximum condemned this law to such rapid disuse that one wonders if it was ever applied at all.

When evening came, the newly married girl was conducted to her husband's house: a noisy procession, preceded by flute-players and torch-bearers whose liveliness gave pleasure to neighbors and passers-by.

By the light of the nuptial torch held aloft by the *pronubus,* two other "ushers" lifted the bride and carried her, her feet never touching the ground, across the threshold of her married home, which was decked with white draperies and garlands. The first "bridesmaid" then led her to the nuptial chamber to which her husband came, while the guests retired.

On leaving her father's household for her husband's, the young married woman was furnished with an imposing trousseau, accompanied by plenty of servants, and became the possessor of various property both personal and real, besides her dowry. In the marriage of consent which became the ordinary form of conjugal union, only the dowry became part of the husband's fortune; already the latter's rights had become severely restricted. This sheds light on the reaction Horace ascribes to the woman surprised *in flagrante delicto:* she fears for her dowry. All the wife's own property remained in her sole possession; the husband did not even have a life interest in it. This property was inalienable and not distrainable even in the event of fraudulent bankruptcy. When the marriage was sincere and close, a husband might place the remainder of his own fortune in his wife's name before being declared insolvent, suspending his payments, and thus rendering himself inaccessible to the demands of his creditors. The edicts of Augustus and Claudius even forbade the wife to put up bail for her husband, so careful always was the law to protect feminine weakness which, for all it was affirmed, was not actually a reality.

The woman endowed with a judicious mind who had freed herself from paternal control, perhaps by means of emancipation, and whom marriage had not subjected to a husband's mastery, was then the administrator of all her possessions. She might manage them, draw up contracts, acquire and dispose of property, all with the cooperation of a guardian; but in practice this guardianship was not a burden, and she was easily free of it.

The unrestricted handling of her property gave her considerable independence, and among writers the rich woman was an ideal subject for satire. "A woman thinks that everything is permitted her, she blushes at nothing any more, once she wears an emerald necklace and great pearls hang from her ears. Nothing is more intolerable than a rich woman." In many cases the husband himself had nothing to say. . . .

In her monumental history of women, The Second Sex, Simone de Beauvoir describes the lot of women in Moslem, Mesopotamian, Egyptian, Hebrew, and Christian cultures. She quarrels with what she sees as inconsistencies of Christians, among them their view of abortion, the killing of the unborn, as a sin against God and man, but the killing of men, women, and children in wartime as not so. Does Mlle de Beauvoir give the impression that the triumph of the male and the humiliation of the female was a male chauvinist conspiracy?

# The Second Sex

Simone de Beauvoir

## Patriarchal Times and Classical Antiquity

Woman was dethroned by the advent of private property, and her lot through the centuries has been bound up with private property: her history in large part is involved with that of the patrimony. It is easy to grasp the fundamental importance of this institution if one keeps in mind the fact that the owner transfers, alienates, his existence into his property; he cares more for it than for his very life; it overflows the narrow limits of this mortal lifetime, and continues to exist beyond the body's dissolution—the earthly and material incorporation of the immortal soul. But this survival can only come about if the property remains in the hands of its owner: it can be his beyond death only if it belongs to individuals in whom he sees himself projected, who are *his*. To cultivate the paternal domain, to render worship to the manes of the father—these together constitute one and the same obligation for the heir: he assures ancestral survival on earth and in the underworld. Man will not agree, therefore, to share with woman either his gods or his children. He will not succeed in making good his claims wholly and forever. But at the time of patriarchal power, man wrested from woman all her rights to possess and bequeath property.

For that matter, it seemed logical to do so. When it is admitted that a woman's children are no longer hers, by the same token they have no tie with the group from whence the woman has come. Through marriage woman is now no longer lent from one clan to another: she is torn up by the roots from the group into which she was born, and annexed by her husband's group; he buys her as one buys a farm animal or a slave; he imposes his domestic divinities upon her; and the children born to her belong to the husband's family. If she were an inheritor, she would to an exessive degree transmit the wealth of her father's family to that of her husband; so she is carefully excluded from the succession. But inversely, because she owns nothing, woman does not enjoy the dignity of being a person; she herself forms a part of the patrimony of a man: first of her father, then of her husband. Under the strictly patriarchal regime, the father can, from their birth on, condemn to death both male and female children; but in the case of the former, society usually limits his power: every normal newborn male is allowed to live, whereas the custom of exposing girl infants is widespread. Among the Arabs there was much infanticide: girls were thrown into ditches as soon as born. It is an act of free generosity on the part of the father to accept the female child; woman gains entrance into such societies only through a kind of grace bestowed upon her, not legitimately like the male. In any case the defilement of childbirth appears to be much worse for the mother when the baby is a girl: among the Hebrews, Leviticus requires in this case a purification two months longer than when a boy is brought into the world. In societies having the custom of the "blood price," only a small sum is demanded when the victim is of female sex: her value compared to the male's is like the slave's compared with the free man's.

When she becomes a young girl, the father has all power over her; when she marries he transfers it *in toto* to the husband. Since a wife is his property like a slave, a beast of burden, or a chattel, a man can naturally have as many wives as he pleases; polygamy is limited only by economic considerations. The husband can put away his wives at his caprice, society according them almost no security. On the other hand, woman is subjected to a rigorously strict chastity. In spite of taboos, matrilineal societies permit great freedom of behavior; prenuptial chastity is rarely required, and adultery is viewed without much severity. On the contrary, when woman becomes man's property, he wants her to be virgin and he requires complete fidelity under threats of extreme penalties. It would be the worst of crimes to risk giving inheritance rights to offspring begotten by some stranger; hence it is that the paterfamilias has the right to put the guilty spouse to death. As long as private property lasts, so long will marital infidelity on the part of the wife be regarded like the crime of high treason. All codes of law, which to this day have upheld inequality in the matter of adultery, base their argument upon the gravity of the fault of the wife who brings a bastard into the family. And if the right to take the law into his own hands has been abolished since Augustus, the Napoleonic Code still promises the indulgence of the jury to the husband who has himself executed justice.

When the wife belonged at once to the paternal clan and to the con-jugal family, she managed to retain a considerable freedom between the two series of bonds, which were confused and even in opposition, each serving to support her against the other: for example, she could often choose her husband according to her fancy, because marriage was only a secular event, not affecting the fundamental structure of society. But in the patriarchal regime she is the property of her father, who marries her off to suit himself. Attached thereafter to her husband's hearth, she is no more than his chattel and the chattel of the clan into which she has been put.

When the family and the private patrimony remain beyond question the bases of society, then woman remains totally submerged. This occurs in the Moslem world. Its structure is feudal; that is, no state has appeared strong enough to unify and rule the different tribes: there is no power to check that of the patriarchal chief. The religion created when the Arab people were warlike and triumphant professed for woman the utmost scorn. The Koran proclaims: "Men are superior to women on account of the qualities in which God has given them pre-eminence and also because they furnish dowry for women"; woman never had either real power nor mystic prestige. The Bedouin woman works hard, she plows and carries burdens: thus she sets up with her spouse a bond of reciprocal dependence; she walks abroad freely with uncovered face. The veiled and sequestered Moslem woman is still today in most social strata a kind of slave.

I recall seeing in a primitive village of Tunisia a subterranean cavern in which four women were squatting: the old one-eyed and toothless wife, her face horribly devastated, was cooking dough on a small brazier in the midst of an acrid smoke; two wives somewhat younger, but almost as disfigured, were lulling children in their arms—one was giving suck; seated before a loom, a young idol magnificently decked out in silk, gold, and silver was knotting threads of wool. As I left this gloomy cave—kingdom of immanence, womb, and tomb—in the corridor leading upward toward the light of day I passed the male, dressed in white, well groomed, smiling, sunny. He was returning from the marketplace, where he had discussed world affairs with other men; he would pass some hours in this retreat of his at the heart of the vast universe to which he belonged, from which he was not separated. For the withered old women, for the young wife doomed to the same rapid decay, there was no universe other than the smoky cave, whence they emerged only at night, silent and veiled.

The Jews of Biblical times had much the same customs as the Arabs. The patriarchs were polygamous, and they could put away their wives almost at will; it was required under severe penalties that the young wife be turned over to her husband a virgin; in case of adultery, the wife was stoned; she was kept in the confinement of domestic duties, as the Biblical portrait of the virtuous woman proves: "She seeketh wool, and flax . . . she riseth also while it is yet night . . . her candle goeth not out by night . . . she eateth not the bread of idleness." Though chaste and industrious, she is ceremonially unclean, surrounded with taboos; her testimony is not acceptable in court. Ecclesiastes speaks of her with the most profound disgust: "And I find more bitter than death the woman, whose heart is snares and nets, and her hands as bands . . . one man among a thousand have I found; but a woman among all those have I not found." Custom, if not the law, required that at the death of her husband the widow should marry a brother of the departed.

This custom, called the *levirate*, is found among many Oriental peoples. In all regimes where woman is under guardianship, one of the problems that must be faced is what to do with widows. The most extreme solution is to sacrifice them on the tomb of the husband. But it is not true that even in India the law has ever required such holocausts; the Laws of Manu permit wife to survive husband. The spectacular suicides were never more than an aristocratic fashion. Much more frequently the widow is handed over to the heirs of the husband. The levirate sometimes takes the form of polyandry; to forestall the uncertainties of widowhood, all the brothers in a family are given as husbands to one woman, a custom that serves also to protect the tribe against the possible infertility of the husband. According to a passage in Caesar, it appears that in Brittany all the men of a family had thus in common a certain number of women.

The patriarchate was not established everywhere in this radical form. In Babylon the laws of Hammurabi acknowledged certain rights of woman; she receives a part of the paternal estate, and when she marries, her father provides a dowry. In Persia polygamy was customary; the wife was required to be absolutely obedient to her husband, chosen for her by her father when she was of marriageable age; but she was held in honor more than among most Oriental peoples. Incest was not forbidden, and marriage was frequent between brother and sister. The wife was responsible for the education of children—boys up to the age of seven and girls up to marriage. She could receive a part of her husband's estate if the son showed himself unworthy; if she was a "privileged spouse" she was entrusted with the guardianship of minor children and the management of business matters if the husband died without having an adult son. The marriage regulations show clearly the importance that the existence of a posterity had for the head of a family. It appears that there were five forms of marriage:[1] (1) When the woman married with her parents' consent, she was called a "privileged spouse"; her children belonged to her husband. (2) When a woman was an only child, the first of her children was sent back to her parents to take the place of their daughter; after this the wife became a "privileged spouse." (3) If a man died unmarried, his family dowered and received in marriage some woman from outside, called an adopted wife; half of her children belonged to the deceased, the other half to her living husband. (4) A widow without children when remarried was called a servant wife; she was bound to assign half of the children of her second marriage to the dead husband. (5) The woman who married without the consent of her parents could not inherit from them before her oldest son, become of age, had given her as "privileged spouse" to his own father; if her husband died before this, she was regarded as a minor and put under guardianship. The institution of the adopted wife and the servant wife enabled every man to be survived by descendants, to whom he was not necessarily connected by a blood relationship. This confirms what I was saying above; for this relationship was in a way invented by man in the wish to acquire beyond his own death an immortality on earth and in the underworld.

It was in Egypt that woman enjoyed most favorable conditions. The goddess mothers retained their prestige in becoming wives; the couple was the religious and social unit; woman seemed to be allied with and complementary to man. Her magic was so slightly hostile that even the fear of incest was overcome and sister and wife were combined without hesitation.[2] Woman had the same rights as man, the same powers in court; she inherited, she owned property. This remarkable fortunate situation was by no means due to chance: it came from the fact that in ancient Egypt the land belonged to the king and to the higher castes of priests and soldiers; private individuals could have only the use and produce of landed property—the usufruct—the land itself remained inalienable. Inherited property had little value, and apportioning it caused no difficulty. Because of the absence of private patrimony, woman retained the dignity of a person. She married without compulsion and if widowed she could remarry at her pleasure. The male practiced polygamy; but though all the children were legitimate, there was only one real wife, the one who alone was associated in religion and bound to him legally; the others were only slaves without any rights at all. The main wife did not change status in marrying: she remained mistress of her property and free to do business. When Pharaoh Bochoris established private property, woman occupied so strong a position that she could not be dislodged; Bochoris opened the era of contracts, and marriage itself became contractual.

. . .

## Myths, Dreams, Fears, Idols

It was Christianity, paradoxically, that was to proclaim, on a certain plane, the equality of man and woman. In her, Christianity hates the flesh; if she renounces the flesh, she is God's creature, redeemed by the Saviour, no less than is man: she takes her place beside the men, among the souls assured of the joys of heaven. Men and women are both servants of God, almost as asexual as the angels and together, through grace, resistant to earthly temptations. If she agrees to deny her animality, woman—from the very fact that she is the incarnation of sin—will be also the most radiant incarnation of the triumph of the elect who have conquered sin.[3] Of course, the divine Saviour who effects the redemption of men is male; but mankind must cooperate in its own salvation, and it will be called upon to manifest its submissive good will in its most humiliated and perverse aspect. Christ is God; but it is a woman, the Virgin Mary, who reigns over all humankind. Yet only the marginal sects revive in woman the ancient privileges and powers of the great goddesses—the Church expresses and serves a patriarchal civilization in which it is meet and proper for woman to remain appended to man. It is through being his docile servant that she will be also a blessed saint. And thus at the heart of the Middle Ages arises the most highly perfected image of woman propitious to man: the countenance of the Mother of Christ is framed in glory. She is the inverse aspect of Eve the sinner; she crushes the serpent underfoot; she is the mediatrix of salvation, as Eve was of damnation.

It was as Mother that woman was fearsome; it is in maternity that she must be transfigured and enslaved. The virginity of Mary has above all a negative value: that through which the flesh has been redeemed is not carnal; it has not been touched or possessed. Similarly the Asiatic Great Mother was not supposed to have a husband: she has engendered the world and reigned over it in solitary state; she could be wanton at her caprice, but her grandeur as Mother was not diminished by any wifely servitude. In the same way Mary knew not the stain of sexuality. Like the warlike Minerva, she is ivory tower, citadel, impregnable donjon. The priestesses of antiquity, like most Christian saints, were also virgin: woman consecrated to the good should be dedicated in the splendor of her intact strength; she should conserve in its unconquered integrity the essence of her femininity. If Mary's status as spouse be denied her, it is for the purpose of exalting the Woman Mother more purely in her. But she will be glorified only in accepting the subordinate role assigned to her. "I am the servant of the Lord." For the first time in human history the mother kneels before her son; she freely accepts her inferiority. This is the supreme masculine victory, consummated in the cult of the Virgin—it is the rehabilitation of woman through the accomplishment of her defeat. Ishtar, Astarte, Cybele were cruel, capricious, lustful; they were powerful. As much the source of death as of life, in giving birth to men they made men their slaves. Under Christianity life and death depend only upon God, and man, once out of the maternal body, has escaped that body forever; the earth now awaits his bones only. For the destiny of his soul is played out in regions where the mother's powers are abolished; the sacrament of baptism makes ridiculous those ceremonies in which the placenta was burned or drowned. There is no longer any place on earth for magic: God alone is king.

## Notes

1 This outline follows C. Huart. *Perse antique et la civilization iranienne*, pp. 195–6.

2 In certain cases, at least, the brother was bound to marry his sister.

3 This explains the privileged place she occupies, for example, in Claudel's work.

## Questions

1 Compare Ashley Montagu's thesis about women with the views of Aristotle, Caesar, and St. Paul. With whom do you agree? Why do women occupy so few positions of importance in contemporary America? Will or should this situation change?

2 What was apparently the position of women in ancient Mesopotamia, as indicated by the Code of Hammurabi?

3 Would Western civilization be different if it had developed from matriarchal societies rather than from patriarchal societies? Explain.

4 Is the problem of overpopulation today a help or a hindrance to the struggle for women's rights? Why?

5 Explain Simone de Beauvoir's view of the link between private property and the status of women. Is there any way to change the situation of women without restructuring the system of private ownership?

# 7

# Spiritual Light From the East

We see ourselves through seeing others; it is a means of gaining perspective and understanding. By taking a brief look at Eastern civilization— best seen not through stories of rulers, dates, and events but through its philosophies and religions—we hope to gain new insights into our Western civilization. The myths, the canons, and the hangups are quite different from the West. It is the venerable Asia that down through the ages has advised law and order and the leading of the good and moral life. The Eastern philosophies have an important message for the West in today's hectic world. The message is peace and quiet. The message is love and understanding of life. (The Christian message is similar, of course, but unfortunately the practice has often been otherwise in both East and West.)

# From Asia With Love

Frederick Gentles

> The student learns by daily increment.
> The Way is gained by daily loss,
> Loss upon loss until
> At last comes rest.
>
> By letting go, it all gets done;
> The world is won by those who let it go!
> But when you try and try,
> The world is then beyond the winning.*

You students of life and history, don't be blind! Find the way through the Tao; the Tao is the way. Learn and you cannot succeed; unlearn until you have emptied your heads of everything—then you have learned. Become a born loser, and after you have lost everything, you cannot lose. Then you will be a success.

Lao Tzu, a contemporary of Confucius, developed this philosophy of life—a philosophy that was to guide and influence the lives of millions of Chinese. One must be content with nothing. This is the Way. Only stupid men laugh at the Tao. If they did not laugh, it would not be the Tao.

The good ruler undoes everything, and then there will be nothing to do. Good. Discard profit and there will be no thieves. Nothing is preferable to Something. Desire only leads to trouble and failure. Get rid of Desire. This is the Way. This is the Tao, the uncarved block. But once you carve the block with writing, the block is no longer the

*From *The Way of Life*, Leo Te Ching, a new translation by R. B. Blakney. Copyright © 1955 by Raymond B. Blakney. By arrangement with The New American Library, Inc., New York.

Tao. Words only confuse; they do not convey one's thoughts accurately. Better to not say anything.

Every society has a particular world view, and Chinese cosmology, based on the *I Ching,* or *Book of Changes,* considers the universe as one great unified mechanism. Within this view, the Tao makes use of the ancient idea of Yin and Yang—the duality of life. Unity is represented by a circle that is divided in two by an S-line: one side of the circle is the Yin, the Female principle in the universe, representing the negative side of life—darkness (the dark earth), cold, weakness, evil, error; the other side of the circle is the Yang, the Male principle in the universe, representing the positive side of life—light (the red sun), warmth, strength, good, truth. The constant interaction between the Yin and the Yang produces universal or cosmic harmony. One complements the other, and, indeed, they may even transform into each other. Contrary to the belief of many people, the two sides are not mutually exclusive; that is, within the black Yin side is a red circle representing the Yang, and within the red Yang is a black circle representing the Yin. Thus there is no purity in life; there is no absolute. In weakness there is strength, and in strength there is weakness; in all evil there is good and in all good there is evil; in all truth there is error and in all error there is truth.

In life and in Oriental and Occidental history one finds duality, paradoxes, contradictions, call them what you will. Mao Tse-tung has an essay on contradiction in which he says that every society, every mode of thought has its own contradictions and quality. There is nothing that does not contain contradiction, he says. There would be no world without plus and minus factors in things and in each of us, contradictory factors. The law of the unity of opposites, as Mao terms the phenomenon in life, is basic to Marx's dialectical materialism of thesis, antithesis, synthesis, though he admits that tracing contradictions can get exceedingly complex. He admits contradictions in Chinese Communism, and he sees contradictions in American life. There are contradictions in the Christian Church, liberty, equality, war, peace, victory, and defeat. Mao's victory was a defeat. In victory there is defeat.

We have heard of Oriental despotism and tortures, the Black Hole of Calcutta, the Huns, Genghiz Khan, the Mongols, and to the Westerner these things conjure up images of a mysterious and dangerous East. And it is true that there have been great wars—civil, racial, and national—and cruelty and bloodshed in the East, very largely for the same reasons as in the West: that is, to gain power and wealth. Statistics for the number killed must run into the hundreds of millions for both civilizations, East and West, and a historian studying the enormous slaughter on the two sides of the planet would be hard put to determine which was the more bloodstained. E is E and W is W, and on this particular trait of killing their fellow man, the two meet.

But there has been love, a lot of it, in Oriental civilization. The emphasis is on love in Hindu, Buddhist, Confucianist, and Mohist (not Maoist) institutions, and, according to one historian of Far Eastern civilization, love has been practiced to a high degree among the faithful hundreds of millions. The East can learn production methods from the West to increase the standard of living for its hungry masses, and the West can learn from the East, if it will, the great philosophy of love and wisdom.

> The sage must distinguish between knowledge and wisdom. Knowledge is of things, acts, and relations. But wisdom is of Brahman alone; and, beyond all things, acts, and relations, he abides forever. To become one with him is the only wisdom.[1]

Two great faiths began in India. Hinduism remained; Buddhism spread. Hinduism is the most complex and diverse of faiths with its uncounted gods and tolerance of all sorts of beliefs, including the Christian. There is no one church, there are no aggressive missionaries, and there is no compulsion to follow one form of worship, because all is divine, even the Creator's mountains, streams, trees, stones, insects, and animals of all kinds, especially the holy cow, which symbolizes the whole dumb creation of God. Yet within this diversity is unity; all mankind is in that great sea of the cosmic soul. This is the unity that only some are able to realize.

In Hinduism, the individual is immersed in God, who is everywhere and in all things. The roots of this belief are in the animism of simple people everywhere who wonder about the miracle of earth and life and who believe God or gods are responsible for all creation and everything that happens. (There is something of animism in the Holy Spirit of the Trinity.) In the Hindu, the individual soul or Atman must yoke itself, through meditation and concentration, to the universal soul or Brahma. When this yoke (yoga) is made, one realizes he is part of the great unending universe or cosmos and that there is no death, there is only a changing and a returning. There is an everlasting becoming until one reaches Nirvana, a blissful state that cannot be explained in words or by human experience, except to say that in it one is reunited with Brahma. If one has lived the good life, his karma (or fate) is to be reincarnated into a better life next time around, and if one lives a life of sin, he has suffered illusion and his karma is to be reincarnated in a lower form. When one finally reaches Nirvana, he is no longer chained to the wheel of life, he need not be reincarnated again; he has reached eternal bliss.

According to the *Upanishads,* one of the great scriptural books of the Hindu faith, the divine is in each of us, in each of us there is a breath of the eternal. "As a lump of salt when thrown into water melts away and the lump cannot be taken out, but wherever we taste the water it is salty, even so, O Maitreyi, the individual self, dissolved, is the Eternal."[2] Man suffers only because of his unwillingness to realize his ties to the divine:

> The Self, Maitreyi, is to be known. Hear about it, meditate upon it. By knowing Self, my beloved, through hearing, reflection, and meditation, one comes to know all things. . . .
>
> Let the gods ignore him who thinks that the gods are different from the Self.[3]

Another of the Hindu scriptures, the *Bhagavad-Gita,* emphasizes a positive morality of doing good unto others since others are a part of Self. By injuring others one injures Self. Due to the ignorance of the wicked, there is bloodshed and terror in the world. The wicked take pride in themselves and in the goods they possess. The wise man, the man of knowledge and wisdom, avoids violence, pride, hate, and anger; the wise man is patient and generous and has control of himself at all times.

The tradition of nonviolence, being harmless to others, has probably played a larger part in Indian culture than in any other major civilization. This tradition appealed to Henry David Thoreau, whose nineteenth-century transcendentalism was greatly influenced by Eastern thought and religion. It inspired him to protest the tyranny of the United States' government in starting the Mexican War and recognizing the institution of slavery. In the twentieth century, Mahatma Gandhi inherited the tradition of nonviolence and passive resistance, which he used with such phenomenal success to free India from its status as an English colony. The Reverend Martin Luther King, Jr. was also inspired by the tradition of love and nonviolence of the Hindus. And although he was hated by many, he did not reciprocate the hate, nor did Gandhi in his time. They suffered, as Christ suffered, because of the ignorance of the wicked. It takes a very strong and a very lovely person not to hate.

One who is nonviolent in thought and in deed is close to the world spirit, which is far along the road from matter. An Indian scholar has suggested that matter may be thought of as a block at the lower left corner of a page—this one, for instance—and the world spirit as a block in the upper right corner. It is the purpose of the individual to move from matter toward spirit. Plants, such as trees and flowers, are a step up from matter, exhibiting what is termed life. Animals are farther along and exhibit consciousness, while man is farther along still and shows intelligence. The more intelligent persons will be heading up toward the world spirit while those of lesser intelligence will be closer to the material block. Most Indians consider themselves somewhere between the saintly men on the way up and the evil men on the way down. They have been a practical people, say the historians, interested in their daily rice; they have deplored evil ways and revered virtue and virtuous men.

For several centuries prior to 1857, much of Hindu India was dominated by Muslims, whose faith was in many ways opposite to the Hindu. The Muslim believed in one god and only one; the Hindu had countless deities. The Muslim forbade images; the Hindu had hundreds of them. The Muslim believed in the brotherhood of man while the Hindu had a caste system in which some men were considered untouchable. The Muslim was somewhat intolerant of other faiths and spread across whole continents on missions to convert the heathen; the Hindu had the most tolerant of religious faiths and was not aggressively missionary. Yet the two faiths managed to exist for centuries side by side, until the modern spirit of nationalism produced such lingering distrust and lack of understanding that in 1947 the Muslim country of Pakistan was born out of India by way of civil war. The bitterness, hatred, and distrust linger on.

Siddhartha Gautama, the Buddha, the Enlightened One, shows the way, shows the light. The eternal law is love. Buddha (563?–?483 B.C.), born a prince and possessing all the good things of this earth, in his early manhood left his family and his kingdom to search for enlightenment. After many years of poverty and struggle, he found what he was looking for, while sitting under the famous Bo (fig) tree. What he discovered there are the Four Noble Truths:

1. All life is filled with suffering.
2. Suffering is caused by a desire for impermanent things.
3. Suffering can be ended by ending the desire for impermanent things.
4. The Eightfold Path that ends suffering is: right view, right thought, right speech, right action, right livelihood, right effort, right mindfulness, and right concentration.

Through correct mind-control and correct meditation or serenity, love is gained by turning away every selfish thought. These are the last two steps of Buddha's Eightfold Path to eliminate suffering in this world.

Buddha's own life exemplified his teaching of the Golden Mean—
a middle road between the extremes of asceticism (where one may
not be of use to others) and self-indulgence (where one may do injury to others as well as to self). Buddhism has succeeded so well as
a practical day-to-day religion that today, 2500 years after its found-
ing, about twenty percent of the world's population has been directly
influenced by the faith.

In his book on Buddhism, Christmas Humphries suggests that
civilization and progress, if carried too far, may be antagonistic to
love:

> Civilization is inseparable from competition, which produces
> and implies antagonism. Man against man, business firm against
> business firm, nation against nation and race against race, such
> is the ceaseless cry. Competition has its uses, but when its use-
> fulness is past it becomes a fetter in the path of progress, and
> must give way in time to cooperation based on mutual under-
> standing and respect. One of the greatest pronouncements ever
> made in the field of morality is contained in the Dhammapada:
> "Hatred ceaseth but by love. This is the eternal law."[4]

As Christianity, five hundred years later, was to move westward
from the land of its birth, Buddhism began to move eastward from
India. In time and place the faith fragmented into many interpretations of the mind of Buddha. To the southeast in Asia, Ceylon, Burma,
Thailand, Cambodia, and, to a lesser extent, in Vietnam, the Lesser
Vehicle of Buddhism, the Hinayana or Thervada school, predominates
with its simple and single emphasis on the sending out of loving-
kindness to all mankind. In the *Discourse on Universal Love,* the
Buddha said:

> As a mother, even at the risk of her own life, protects and
> loves her child, her only child, so let a man cultivate love with-
> out measure toward the whole world, above, below, and around,
> unstinted, unmixed with any feeling of differing or opposing
> interests. Let a man remain steadfastly in this state of mind all
> the while he is awake, whether he be standing, walking, sitting,
> or lying down. This state of mind is the best in the world.[5]

The Thervada school has been described by Christmas Humphries as
the finest moral philosophy in the world today:

> It is reasonable, making no appeal to dogmatic assumption;
> it is objective, and will stand the criticism of logic and science.
> It is self-reliant, claiming assistance from neither God nor gods,
> saviours or priestly men; it is the most tolerant creed on earth
> and expresses compassion not only for all men, but for all ani-
> mals and the least living thing. By the ignorant it is described

as pessimistic. If this were true, and it is quite untrue, it is strange that its adherents today, the Sinhalese, Burmese, Siamese and Cambodians, are among the merriest, happiest people on earth.[6]

North in Asia is the Greater Vehicle, the Mahayana, which is practiced in many forms in the Himalayas, Tibet, China, Japan, and Korea.

One of the most significant types of behavior, and explanations of behavior, coming out of Asia belongs to the Zen school of Buddhism, which flowered first in China as Ch'an and developed later in Japan in several forms. Zen has its background in the paradoxes of the Tao and in the void of Nirvana, in the nonconceptual world of the Hindu and of Mahayana Buddhism. There is duality and conflict in the world because there is language, and language is not of the real world. Language and thought are invented, and we think and speak with these symbols. The nonverbal world of no-thought does not have symbols and classes; hence, there can be no conflict, no duality. The direct way to truth is not through symbols but through getting rid of symbols.

The Tao of Lao Tzu and the *Book of Changes* describe the Yin and Yang, the diversity within the unity, and the interaction between good and evil, truth and error, and so forth. Zen recognizes conflict in the world of words; indeed, so often it is a war of words. It is as impossible for man to achieve harmony in this world as it is for a thermostat to maintain a constant seventy degrees, says Alan W. Watts in his thoughtful little book *The Way of Zen*. There must be variation for the man to operate, and there must be variation for the thermostat to operate. Where there is love, there must also be hate. Where there is evil, there must also be good. Of course, the degree of variation is important. There are dangers inherent in any body of ideas if they are used in the extreme.

> Since the world points up beauty as such,
> There is ugliness too.
> If goodness is taken as goodness,
> Wickedness enters as well.
>
> For is and is-not come together;
> Hard and easy are complementary;
> Long and short are relative;
> High and low are comparative;
> Pitch and sound make harmony;
> Before and after are a sequence.[7]

This is life. Accept it. Calmly.

However, Dr. Watts reports that one San Francisco politician hates the left wing so much he will not, when driving, make a left turn. Though he must go 'round in circles, the left is still there. And so is the right for those on the left. The mind is bound in this dualistic pattern, and it is difficult to think in any other terms or in a mixture of the two, says Dr. Watts.

> Yet Zen is a liberation from this pattern, and its apparently dismal starting point is to understand the absurdity of choosing, of the whole feeling that life may be significantly improved by a constant selection of the "good." One must start by "getting the feel" of relativity, and by knowing that life is not a situation from which there is anything to be grasped or gained—as if it were something which one approaches from outside, like a pie or a barrel of beer. To succeed is always to fail—in the sense that the more one succeeds in anything, the greater is the need to go on succeeding. To eat is to survive to be hungry.[8]

One does not have a choice. There is a well-known saying by Ch'ing-yuan:

> Before I had studied Zen for thirty years, I saw mountains as mountains, and waters as waters. When I arrived at a more intimate knowledge, I came to the point where I saw that mountains are not mountains, and waters are not waters. But now that I have got its very substance, I am at rest. For it's just that I see mountains once again as mountains, and waters once again as waters.[9]

Aristotle perpetuated a lot of trouble by classifying things. Man is proud to be of this or that classification, and he is now numbered, stamped, labeled, communized, propagandized, capitalized, sterilized, Anglicized, homogenized, and bamboozled by government, company, school, church, club, newspaper, and TV. Forever, and words, words, words. All is artificial, because words are artificial, says the Zen Buddhist. Zen is meditation and a release from duality and conflict. Zen cannot be explained in words. Zen is an experience.

Zen is the quiet life. One does not necessarily improve the world by doing something. One may do his part in improving the world by doing nothing. If more people did nothing there wouldn't be so much conflict. Cats, dogs, tigers, and pigs do a lot of lying around; people lie about also—on the beach, in the mountains, and at bars, where only a minimum amount of conflict takes place. The United States is making a start on a guaranteed annual income for everyone. With increasing automation and cybernation (computers giving birth to more computers), we are heading toward a civilization based on use of leisure time. How will man behave when he has more leisure? Perhaps it will be a more peaceful world.

But Zen Buddhists do not withdraw from the world. They eat, breathe, sleep, defecate, walk, jog, and even love. They also work, and they believe in work:

> The insight which lies at the root of Far Eastern culture is that opposites are relational and so fundamentally harmonious. Conflict is always comparatively superficial, for there can be no ultimate conflict when the pairs of opposites are mutually interdependent. Thus our stark divisions of spirit and nature, subject and object, good and evil, artist and medium are quite foreign to this culture.[10]

Zen and Confucianism complemented one another in both China and Japan. They were both oriented on man rather than on god, on love rather than hate, on things being relative rather than on things being absolute. Confucius, who lived in the sixth century B.C., was a this-worldly man who believed in law and order from the nation down through the feudal domains to family and individual.

But Confucius' world was out of order. The Chou-dynasty emperors had been losing power to those who feared a big and centralized government. Rather than big-government tyranny, there was local-government tyranny, with large provinces conquering small provinces, feudal lords conquering and losing territory, armies marching up and down and across China fighting, fighting, fighting. Taxes were high to support the growing armies, crops were destroyed, peasants were poor, and there was graft and corruption at all levels. What to do about this chaos and anarchy?

Confucius was really a behavioral scientist. He said that man has seven natural instincts of joy, anger, sorrow, fear, love, hate, and desire. One must bring these natural emotions under control and see that they work for the common good. Let us have "correct thoughts" appears time and again in the works of Confucius. "Correct thoughts" is the "Know thyself" of Socrates, the "Do unto others" of Christians, the "love" of Buddha, and the "peace" of the hippies.

Correct thinking means bringing the world into harmony by having humility, being loyal to family, obeying the law, worshipping whatever gods have to be worshipped, respecting knowledge, and being patient, gentle, and kind. Patience is particularly important. Patience is basic to the conservatism of the Chinese in the 2500 years since Confucius. But patience finally led to exasperation as the Chinese saw British, French, Russians, Germans, Portuguese, and Japanese overrunning their land in the nineteenth and twentieth centuries. Confucius and the conservative spirit of believing in the past were blamed for the backwardness of China in the new world. Mao Tse-tung has his "Mao-think" as the new correct thinking, and Confucius is dead. After more than 2500 years of guiding Chinese morality and Chinese history, Confucius is dead.

His was a discriminating love. It was a love of family. The Chinese family historically has been closely knit, highly disciplined, and traditionally loyal. There has been little juvenile delinquency because of family pride and training, and old people have been well cared for by respectful relatives. Cousins, uncles, aunts, and others of the immediate family have been favored over outsiders. This was at once a strength and a weakness in Chinese civilization. The strengths are obvious and beautiful. But the weaknesses led to nepotism, with jobs and favors going to family members rather than to more qualified or deserving people. The weaknesses led to the idea that what was good enough for my fathers is good enough for me and thus to the failure of China to keep pace with a changing world. The weaknesses led, at least in part, to catastrophes for China in the twentieth century.

Actually, the weaknesses were apparent much earlier than the twentieth century. Mo Tzu, who lived only a short time after Confucius and who was considered a leading rival to Confucian thought, believed that discriminating love was narrow-minded. Why discriminate? Why not love all men equally? Only all-encompassing love can bring about harmony in the world. With discriminating love there will always be continuous and bitter conflict.

People being people, individuals being individuals, how can this all-encompassing love be accomplished? Through a ruler who will be an example to the people, said Mo-Tzu; he will persuade and even compel people to love one another. But this compulsion to love, this Mohism, sounds like totalitarianism. It sounds like Karl Marx and Mao Tse-tung—and it is. However, Oriental peoples have never really been oriented to the idea of individualism as it appears in Western civilization—in ancient Greece, in Renaissance Europe, or in modern America—loss of individualism in a totalitarian system doesn't hold the same terrors for them as for us. Chiang Kai-shek once said that China could never operate with the degree of individualism found in the West. There are just too many people for a high degree of individualism to exist. Mao-think virtually compels respect and love for the poor peasant population of China today. Mao is a modern Mo-Tzu, but he has not been successful either. China under Mao has had a riot of conflict.

Ideas and institutions change, but for all the change in time and place, there has remained a central unity in spite of the diversity in world religions. This unity is love. The Christian faith has encompassed such diverse elements as the ascetic pillar saints, rich Calvinists, pacifist Quakers, infallible popes, Christ-like figures such as St. Francis, Italian Communist, and medieval knights marching as to war, fighting and slaughtering one another, each side carrying the Cross and images of the Virgin Mary. The Buddhist faith has encompassed such diverse elements as the sacred Dalai Lama in Tibet, the monastery saints in Cambodia, the warlike and highly nationalistic *bushido* knights in Japan, mean monks in Zen schools, and the faithful marching as to war in China. The manyfold ways in which man behaves is fantastic.

Then, what about love? Should it be self, filial, or all-encompassing? Freud said that man is so much in love with himself that he will destroy himself along with others. Confucius opted for filial love. Mohists, Hindus, Buddhists, and Christians emphasize universal love. Edwin Aldrin said that during the flag ceremony on the moon he and Neil Armstrong sensed "an almost mystical unification of all the people in the world at that moment."[11] Devout Hindus and Buddhists have this feeling all the time.

Then why all the bitterness and conflict these many centuries? What is the real hangup? We can learn to love others. We do learn to love others. But not all others. Unless we land on the moon.

### Notes

1 Swami Prabhavananda and Frederick Manchester, translators, *The Upanishads, Breath of the Eternal* (New York: New American Library, 1957), p. 42. By permission of the copyright holder, the Vedanta Society of Southern California.

2 *Ibid.*, p. 88.

3 *Ibid.*, p. 87.

4 Christmas Humphries, *Buddhism* (London: Penguin, 1951), p. 121.

5 *Ibid.*, p. 124.

6 *Ibid.*, p. 79.

7 R. B. Blakney, translator, *The Way of Life, Lao Tzu* (New York: New American Library, 1955, p. 54.

8 Alan W. Watts, *The Way of Zen* (New York: Vintage, 1957), p. 116. By permission of Pantheon Books, a division of Random House, Inc.

9 *Ibid.*, p. 126.

10 *Ibid.*, p. 175.

11 *Life,* August 22, 1969.

Our prisons are filled with people who have permitted desire to rule their lives. They have believed objects of sense—money, for instance—are theirs for the taking and are worth risking their lives to obtain. But not only prisoners have lost sight of reality, according to Indian teaching. Others who believe that earthly possessions and joys constitute reality are equally mistaken about the meaning of life. The Bhagavad Gita, one of the great Hindu scriptures, along with the Vedas and Upanishads, insists that the mentally stabilized person is without desire, fear, anger, self-interest, egotism. He is tranquil. He is not confused.

# Disciplining the Mind

**The Bhagavad Gita**

49. For action is far inferior
       To discipline of mental attitude, Dhanamjaya.
    In the mental attitude seek thy (religious) refuge;
       Wretched are those whose motive is the fruit (of action).
50. The disciplined in mental attitude leaves behind in this world
       Both good and evil deeds.
    Therefore discipline thyself unto discipline;
       Discipline in actions is weal.
51. For the disciplined in mental attitude, action-produced
       Fruit abandoning, the intelligent ones,
    Freed from the bondage of rebirth,
       Go to the place that is free from illness.
52. When the jungle of delusion
       Thy mentality shall get across,
    Then thou shalt come to aversion
       Towards what is to be heard and has been heard (in the Veda).
53. Averse to traditional lore ("heard" in the Veda)
       When shall stand motionless
    Thy mentality, immovable in concentration,
       Then thou shalt attain discipline.
           Arjuna said:
54. What is the description of the man of stabilized mentality,
       That is fixed in concentration, Késava?
    How might the man of stabilized mentality speak,
       How might he sit, how walk?
           The Blessed One said:

Reprinted by permission of the publishers from *The Bhagavad Gita*, translated and interpreted by Franklin Edgerton, Cambridge, Mass.: Harvard University Press, Copyright, 1944, by the President and Fellows of Harvard College; renewed 1972 by Eleanor H. Edgerton. Notes renumbered.

55. When he abandons desires,
     All that are in the mind, son of Prtha,
   Finding contentment by himself in the self alone,
     Then he is called of stabilized mentality.
56. When his mind is not perturbed in sorrows,
     And he has lost desire for joys,
   His longing, fear, and wrath departed,
     He is called a stable-minded holy man.
57. Who has no desire towards any thing,
     And getting this or that good or evil
   Neither delights in it nor loathes it,
     His mentality is stabilized.
58. And when he withdraws,
     As a tortoise his limbs from all sides,
   His senses from the objects of sense,
     His mentality is stabilized.
59. The objects of sense turn away
     From the embodied one that abstains from food,
   Except flavor,[1] flavor also from him
     Turns away when he has seen the highest.
60. For even of one who strives, son of Kunti,
     Of the man of discernment,
   The impetuous senses
     Carry away the mind of violence.
61. Them all restraining,
     Let him sit disciplined, intent on Me;
   For whose senses are under control,
     His mentality is stabilized.
62. When a man meditates on the objects of sense,
     Attachment to them is produced.
   From attachment springs desire,
     From desire wrath arises;
63. From wrath comes infatuation,
     From infatuation loss of memory;
   From loss of memory, loss of mind;
     From loss of mind he perishes.
64. But with desire-and-loathing-severed
     Senses acting on the objects of sense,
   With (senses) self-controlled, he, governing his self,
     Goes unto tranquillity.
65. In tranquillity, of all griefs
     Riddance is engendered for him;

> For the tranquil-minded quickly
>> The mentality becomes stable.
66. The undisciplined has no (right) mentality,
>> And the undisciplined has no efficient-force;[2]
> Who has no efficient-force has no peace;
>> For him that has no peace how can there be bliss?
67. For the senses are roving,
>> And when the thought-organ is directed after them,
> It carries away his mentality,
>> As wind a ship on the water.
68. Therefore whosoever, great-armed one,
>> Has withdrawn on all sides
> The senses from the objects of sense,
>> His mentality is stabilized.
69. What is night for all beings,
>> Therein the man of restraint is awake;
> Wherein (other) beings are awake,
>> That is night for the sage of vision.
70. It is ever being filled, and (yet) its foundation[3] remains unmoved—
>> The sea: just as waters enter it,
> Whom all desires enter in that same way
>> He attains peace; not the man who lusts after desires.
71. Abandoning all desires, what
>> Man moves free from longing,
> Without self-interest and egotism,
>> He goes to peace.
72. This is the fixation that is Brahmanic[4] son of Prtha;
>> Having attained it he is not (again) confused.
> Abiding in it even at the time of death,
>> He goes to Brahman-nirvana.[5]

Here ends the Second Chapter called Discipline of Reason-method.

## Notes

1 (Vs 59) *Visaya vinivartante / niraharasya dehinah / rasavarjam raso 'py asya / param drstva nivartate*: The fasting man, until he "sees the highest," cannot help feeling longing for food, i.e., for "flavor," the object of the sense of taste, though he feels no longing for the objects of the other senses. After a sufficiently long fast (interpreted as a sign that he "sees the highest"), a man ceases even to feel hungry. Hindu commentators and modern interpreters have a different interpretation, abandoning the simple and familiar meaning of the word *rasa* (which

can hardly mean anything but "flavor" in the above sense, coming immediately after *visayah* and clearly meant as one of the "objects of sense"), for a more forced one.

2 (Vs 66) *Bhavana*: here, "effective religious impulse"; the word *bhavana* means "bringing to be, tendency to produce something (here, religious effort)." It is a technical word of the Mimamsa system. See Edgerton, *The Mimamsa Nyaya Prakasa*, Glossarial Index s.v., and p. 5 ff.

3 (Vs 70) Or, "stability."

4 (Vs 72) I.e., fixation in or of Brahman, or resulting in the attainment of Brahman. S, *brahmani bhava*; R, *brahmaprapika*.

5 (Vs 72) I.e., *nirvana* in, or that is, Brahman; R, *nirvanamayam brahma*.

To a degree, Buddhism requires that a person detach himself from his own problems and see his life in the perspective of the universe. This, together with a reverence for all life and meditation, leads to enlightenment. It is often said that we in the West should slow our swift pace after the almighty dollar, recognize other than material values of life, and learn to relax. Buddhism is available as a form of mental therapy. But so is Christianity, which in its early form emphasized sharing, brotherly love, and the spiritual life.

# Buddhism

Nancy Wilson Ross

The Buddha, in spite of his profound mind, tended in general to keep his teachings within the bounds of simple human understanding, holding fast to the necessity for acquiring that nonegocentric nonpersonal viewpoint which alone, in his opinion, could mitigate life's inevitable suffering and widen the individual perspective. There is one story among many that particularly well illustrates the Buddha's doctrinal emphasis on overcoming the astigmatism of a too personal viewpoint. A distraught mother came to the Buddha carrying a dead child in her arms. She had been unable to accept its death and, almost insane with grief, had traveled a long distance to speak to the Great Teacher of whom she had heard. When, hoping for a miracle, she appeared before the Buddha with the little corpse in her arms, he did not say to her that he could or could not bring back the dead, nor did he deliver any sermon on the universality of her experience. Instead, he suggested very quietly that she go forth and find for him a single mustard seed—but one of a very special kind; it must come from a household in which there had never been a death. During the mother's fruitless search for a household that had never known death, she was able at last to relate her own loss to that of others and therein to find eventual cure for her grief.

The Buddha had an astute way of cutting the cloth of his teaching according to his followers' needs. For aspirant monks, who had difficulty in removing their thoughts from the world's distractions and attractions, he did not hesitate to prescribe meditations on dead bodies, decaying corpses, piles of human bones or the least pleasant of the body's processes. But uncompromising as was his stand about the way to truth, he was never unaware of individual needs. There is a story of a monk, dying of dysentery, who lay neglected in one of the resting places of the

Buddha's disciples. When the Buddha discovered the sufferer, he him-
self took over his care, bathing and tending him as if he were his child.
In chiding the neglectful fellow monks, he spoke words that have a
Biblical ring: "He who would wait on me let him wait on the sick."

Buddhism, though often described as a religion for rationalists and
intellectuals, plainly developed not along the line of wisdom, *prajna*,
but also along that of compassion, *karuna*. In the type of Buddhism
followed in the southern countries of Ceylon, Thailand and Burma, a
meditation on *metta*, or the sending forth of loving-kindness to the whole
world, is practiced daily by the monks. This practice has its origin in an
early scripture known as *The Discourse on Universal Love* in which
the Buddha is quoted as saying:

> As a mother, even at the risk of her own life, protects and loves her
> child, her only child, so let a man cultivate love without measure
> toward the whole world, above, below, and around, unstinted, un-
> mixed with any feeling of differing or opposing interests. Let a man
> remain steadfastly in this state of mind all the while he is awake,
> whether he be standing, walking, sitting or lying down. This state
> of mind is the best in the world.

Among the most significant and, to some people, most appealing of
various Buddhist doctrines that appeared after the Master's death is that
of the *bodhisattva*, a Mahayana development. Bodhisattvas are highly
evolved beings, on their way to Buddhahood, who have voluntarily
chosen to lend their special powers to help mankind achieve illumina-
tion. The difference between a Buddha and a bodhisattva might be said
to be that the former is truly "awake," often, indeed, referred to as "the
Awakened One," whereas the latter is a being of a "wakeful nature" or
one who is "awakening." These sublimely compassionate beings, destined
to become future Buddhas, are a natural mythological outgrowth of the
teaching of universal loving-kindness. The distinguishing traits—known
as the Ten Perfections—characteristic of bodhisattvas vary in some es-
sentials from sect to sect, but the following list may be taken as representative: liberality, morality, renunciation, wisdom, energy, forebear-
ance, truthfulness, resolution, good will and equanimity. Bodhisattvas
have inspired some of the most distinctive creations in the entire field of
Asian art. Sometimes these Buddhas-to-be are presented with feminine
countenances, as in the Chinese Kuan Yin (Kwannon in Japan)—an
appearance considered suitable for the conveyance of an impression of
boundless compassion. Frequently, their entire aspect is androgynous.

The bodhisattva ideal exemplifies another of the differences between
the two chief branches of world Buddhism, Hinayana and Mahayana.
Hinayana or Theravada Buddhism, the conservative Buddhism of coun-

tries like Ceylon, Burma and Thailand, tends to emphasize the ideal of the *arhat*, an individual who through unremitting meditative effort attains release from the "round of becoming" for himself alone. The Mahayana branch, which belongs to Tibet, China, Korea and Japan, places stronger emphasis on all creation's sharing a common karma to which every individual contributes either for good or ill. To the Mahayanists the Buddha's own decision to go forth into the world and share his enlightenment was the highest proof of his spiritual attainment.

If, as the Buddha taught, the universe is "mind only," it would follow in Mahayana doctrine that whoever does a good deed or a bad one unavoidably affects all life. This theory of universal, indissoluble interdependence is taught today in the Japanese Kegon School of Buddhism in the image of a great web which is to be pictured, during meditation, as extending throughout the whole universe, its vertical lines representing time, its horizontal ones space. Wherever the threads of this vast imaginary net cross one another, there should be imagined a crystal bead symbolizing a single existence. Each of these crystal beads reflect on its bright surface not only every other bead in the vast net but also every reflection of every other reflection—countless, endless reflections, each in a sense independent, and yet all bound together in a single related totality.

As Buddhism was, down the years, inevitably influenced by Hinduism, there developed concepts of the Buddha himself as a cosmic deity, one in a long line of spiritual beings who appear on earth in successive eons to serve as man's guides and helpers. (Hinduism, it will be remembered, finally accepted the Buddha as merely another appearance of its often incarnated god Vishnu.) In other parts of Asia where Buddhism penetrated, the concept of Buddhist incarnations led to further elaborations which specifically claim Siddhartha Gautama as the seventh in a line of past and future Buddhas of which Maitreya, now waiting as a bodhisattva somewhere outside the earth's space-time, will be the next. That the Buddha, who was born in the sixth century B.C., may have accepted the Indian theory of avatars is suggested in one of the sayings attributed to him:

"I have seen the Ancient Way, the old Road that was taken by the formerly All-Awakened, and that is the path I follow."

. . .

In referring to Buddhism's growing Western influence, Dr. Graham Howe has said in his *Invisible Anatomy*: "In the course of their work, many psychologists have found, as the pioneer work of C. G. Jung has shown, that we are all near-Buddhists on our hidden side. . . . To read a little Buddhism is to realize that the Buddhists knew, two thousand five hundred years ago, far more about modern psychology than they have yet been given credit for. . . . We are now rediscovering the Ancient Wisdom of the East."

India, the land of the Buddha's birth, is today showing an unquestioned revival of Buddhist influence, largely because of the rising strength of the Untouchables. Like the original Buddha, no true Buddhist could respect the strictures of caste, and therefore Buddhists from earliest days accepted Untouchables in their midst. Today, an Indian Untouchable who becomes a Buddhist tacitly steps outside the ancient, still slowly changing forms of the Hindu caste system.

In bringing to a close this necessarily brief account of Buddhism it might be added that in place of the moral imperative "Thou shalt not"— so much a part of Judeo-Christian precepts—Buddhism in general offers a perhaps sounder psychological counsel, "It would be better if you refrained from." This attitude is basic to both Mahayana and Theravada, much as they may differ in other matters—like Mahayana's use of intercessory rites versus the almost puritanic self-reliance of the Theravada, or the former's belief in the efficacy of prayers versus the stress on "works" in the latter, and other significant differences on which there has not been space to dwell at any length.

But although interpretations of Buddhist doctrine may vary, the teaching that life is One is emphasized by all sects and branches of this vital religious philosophy, followed by so many hundreds of millions of people. The Oneness of all life is a truth, Buddhism asserts, that can be fully realized only when false notions of a separate self—whose destiny can be considered apart from the whole—are forever annihilated. When the individual seeker has finally acquired this supreme sense of the Oneness of all life, he has, indeed, reached the bliss of Nirvana. Freed completely of the limiting conditions connected with the sense of a personal ego, he has come to "the end of separateness."

Confucian doctrines guided Chinese culture for over 2500 years, and even today Confucius is not dead in China. Confucius counseled moderation in all things, harmonious living, honesty in government, reverence for ancestors, and a looking backward for guidance. "Forever occupy your thoughts with education," he said.

# Confucius

Lin Yutang

### First Discourse

Confucius said:[1] When I enter a country, I can easily tell its type of culture. When the people are gentle and kind and simple-hearted, that shows the teaching of poetry. When people are broad-minded and acquainted with the past, that shows the teaching of history. When the people are generous and show a good disposition, that shows the teaching of music. When the people are quiet and thoughtful, and show a sharp power of observation, that shows the teaching of the philosophy of mutations (*Book of Changes*). When the people are humble and respectful and frugal in their habits, that shows the teaching of *li* (the principle of social order). When the people are cultivated in their speech, ready with expressions and analogies, that shows the teaching of prose, or *Spring and Autumn*.[2] The danger in the teaching of poetry is that people remain ignorant, or too simple-hearted. The danger in the teaching of history is that people may be filled with incorrect legends and stories of events. The danger in the teaching of music is that the people grow extravagant. The danger in the teaching of philosophy is that the people become crooked. The danger in the teaching of *li* is that the rituals become too elaborate. And the danger in the teaching of *Spring and Autumn*, is that the people get a sense of the prevailing moral chaos. When a man is kind and gentle and simple-hearted, and yet not ignorant, we may be sure he is deep in the study of poetry. When a man is broad-minded and acquainted with the past, and yet not filled with incorrect legends or stories of events, we may be sure he is deep in the study of history. When a man is generous and shows a good disposition and yet not extravagant in his personal habits, we may be sure he is deep in the study of music. When a man is quiet and thoughtful and shows a sharp power of observation, and yet is not crooked, we may be sure that he is

From *The Wisdom of Confucius,* edited and translated by Lin Yutang. Copyright 1938 and renewed 1966 by Random House, Inc. Reprinted by permission of the publisher. Notes renumbered.

deep in the study of philosophy. When a man is humble and polite and frugal in his personal habits and yet not full of elaborate ceremonies, we may be sure he is deep in the study of *li*. When a man is cultivated in his speech, ready with expressions and analogies and yet is not influenced by the picture of the prevailing moral chaos, we may be sure that he is deep in the study of *Spring and Autumn*.[3]

. . .

**Third Discourse**

*Li Based on Human Nature.* The reason the Sage is able to regard the world as one family and China as one man (what is true of human nature in one man is true for all), is that he does not make arbitrary rules, but on the other hand tries to understand human nature,[4] define the human duties and come to a clear realization of what is good and what is bad for mankind. It is through this that he is able to do so. What is human nature? It consists of the seven things, joy, anger, sorrow, fear, love, hatred and desire, all of which do not have to be learned (i.e., they are natural instincts). What are the human duties? Kindness in the father, filial piety in the son, gentility in the elder brother, humility and respect in the younger brother, good behavior in the husband, obedience in the wife, benevolence in the elders, and obedience in the juniors, benevolence in the ruler and loyalty in the ministers—these ten are the human duties. What is good for mankind means general confidence and peace, and what is bad for mankind means struggle for profit, robbery and murder. Therefore how can the Sage, or ideal ruler, dispense with *li* in his efforts to cultivate the seven emotions and the ten duties, and to promote mutual confidence and peace and courtesy and discourage the struggle for profit and robbery? Food and drink and sex are the great desires of mankind, and death and poverty and suffering are the great fears or aversions of mankind. Therefore desires and fear (or greed and hatred) are the great motive forces of the human heart. These, however, are concealed in the heart and are not usually shown, and the human heart is unfathomable. What other principle is there besides *li* which can serve as the one all-sufficient principle to explore the human heart?

Therefore man is the product of the forces of heaven and earth, of the union of the *yin* and the *yang* principles, the incarnation of spirits and the essence of the five elements (metal, wood, water, fire and earth). Therefore man is the heart of the universe, the upshot of the five elements, born to enjoy food and color and noise. . . .

## On Education

*The Need for Education.* To desire to do right and to seek what is good would give a person a little reputation but would not enable him to influence the masses. To associate with the wise and able men and to welcome those who come from a distant country would enable a person to influence the masses, but would not enable him to civilize the people. The only way for the superior man to civilize the people and establish good social customs is through education. A piece of jade cannot become an object of art without chiselling, and a man cannot come to know the moral law without education. Therefore the ancient kings regarded education as the first important factor in their efforts to establish order in a country. That is the meaning of the passage in the *Advice to Fu Yueh* (by King Kaotsung of the Hsia Dynasty, now a chapter of *Shuking*) which says, "Forever occupy your thoughts with education." Just as one cannot know the taste of food without eating it, however excellent it may be, so without education one cannot come to know the excellence of a great body of knowledge, although it may be there.

Therefore only through education does one come to be dissatisfied with his own knowledge, and only through teaching others does one come to realize the uncomfortable inadequacy of his knowledge. Being dissatisfied with his own knowledge, one then realizes that the trouble lies with himself, and realizing the uncomfortable inadequacy of his knowledge, one then feels stimulated to improve himself. Therefore it is said, "The processes of teaching and learning stimulate one another." That is the meaning of the passage in the *Advice to Fu Yueh* which says, "Teaching is the half of learning."

*The Ancient Educational System.* The ancient educational system was as follows: There was a primary school in every hamlet of 25 families, a secondary school in every town of 500 families, an academy in every county of 2500 families, and a college in the capital of every state (for the education of the princes and sons of nobles and the best pupils from the lower schools.) Every year new students were admitted, and every other year there was an examination.[5] At the end of the first year, an effort was made to see how the pupils were able to punctuate their sentences and to find out their natural inclinations. At the end of three years, an effort was made to find out their habits of study and their group life. At the end of five years, they would try to see how well read in general the pupils were and how closely they had followed their teachers. At the end of seven years, they would try to find out how their ideas had developed and what kind of friends they had selected for themselves. This is called the Minor Graduation (*hsiaoch'eng*—from the lower grades). At the end of nine years, they were expected to know the various subjects and have a general understanding of life and to have laid a firm foundation for their character from which they could not go back. This was called the Major Graduation (*tach'eng*—from the higher grades).[6]

By such an educational system only is it possible to civilize the people and reform the morals of the country, so that the local inhabitants will be happy and those in distant lands will love to come to the country. This is the principle of *tahsueh,* or higher education. That is the meaning of the passage in the *Ancient Records* which says, "The ants are busy all the time" (*the importance of continuous study*).

## Notes

1 Without quotation marks in the original, it is impossible to decide where the exact words of Confucius end. See the appearance of a quotation from Confucius at the end of the third paragraph.

2 These constituted the *Six Classics* of Confucius' days.

3 The *Spring and Autumn* as we have it today is a chronicle of political events in the centuries preceding Confucius, written by the Sage himself. But the name *Spring and Autumn*, or *Ch'unCh'iu*, was a general name for chronicles of the different countries in Confucius' time. Several such *Ch'unCh'iu* were known to exist. The moral chaos in Confucius' time and the centuries preceding was unbelievable. Kings were murdered by their princes, and princes married their father's concubines, and there was a great variety of incestual relationships. . . .

4 The Chinese terms for "nature," "emotions," "heart," "mind," "will," etc., overlap in their meaning, as compared with the corresponding English words. *Hsin* means "the heart" and "the mind." *Hsing* means "original nature," "instinct." *Ch'ing* means (in the above passage) "nature," "natural feelings," "emotions." *Chih* means the "will," "direction of the mind," "hope," "ambition," "aspirations." *Yi* means "idea," "intention." *Yu* means "desires." *Jen* means "moral character," "true manhood." *Chih* (another word) means "wisdom," "the intellect."

5 "Every other year" is the regular interpretation. The phrase *chung nien*, however, can mean "in the middle of the year" as well as "in the in-between year" (or alternate years). According to *Chouli*, however, there was said to be a grand examination every three years.

6 According to *Neitseh* (Chapter XII, *Liki*), the age of entering school is given as ten. The studies of music, poetry, dancing, and archery begin at the age of thirteen. This seems to indicate a nine-year program from ten to nineteen, the last two years between the Minor and Major Graduations probably considered the "secondary education." At twenty, the college education begins. Men were supposed to marry at thirty and women at twenty, and at the latest twenty-three, "for special reasons."

Confucian love started with the family and ancestor worship and worked outward to village, city, province, and nation. Mo Tzu, who was born about the time Confucius died, 480 B.C., objected to this rather narrow and discriminating form of love. He advocated that we should love all men equally. Is this comparable to the Christian concept of love? How is Mohism, as it is called, related to the Maoism in China today?

# Universal Love of Mo Tzu

Fung Yu-lan

### Mo Tzu's Criticism of Confucianism

According to Mo Tzu, "the principles of the Confucianists ruin the whole world in four ways": (1) The Confucianists do not believe in the existence of God or of spirits, "with the result that God and the spirits are displeased." (2) The Confucianists insist on elaborate funerals and the practice of three years of mourning on the death of a parent, so that the wealth and energy of the people are thereby wasted. (3) The Confucianists lay stress on the practice of music, leading to an identical result. (4) The Confucianists believe in a predetermined fate, causing the people to be lazy and to resign themselves to this fate. (The *Mo-tzu*, ch. 48.) In another chapter entitled "Anti-Confucianism," the *Mo-tzu* also says: "Even those with long life cannot exhaust the learning required for their [Confucianist] studies. Even people with the vigor of youth cannot perform all the ceremonial duties. And even those who have amassed wealth cannot afford music. They [the Confucianists] enhance the beauty of wicked arts and lead their sovereign astray. Their doctrine cannot meet the needs of the age, nor can their learning educate the people." (Ch. 39.)

These criticisms reveal the differing social backgrounds of the Confucianists and Mohists. Already before Confucius, persons who were better educated and more sophisticated had been abandoning the belief in the existence of a personal God and of divine spirits. People of the lower classes, however, had, as always in such matters, lagged behind in this rise of skepticism, and Mo Tzu held the point of view of the lower classes. This is the significance of his first point of criticism against the Confucianists. The second and third points, too, were made from the same basis. The fourth point, however, was really irrelevant, because, though the Confucianists often spoke about *Ming* (Fate, Decree), what they meant by it was not the predetermined fate attacked by Mo Tzu. This has been pointed out in the last chapter, where we have seen that *Ming*, for the Confucianists, signified something that is beyond human control. But there are other things that remain within man's power to control if he will exert himself. Only after man has done everything he can himself, therefore, should he accept with calm and resignation what comes thereafter as inevitable. Such is what the Confucianists meant when they spoke of "knowing *Ming*."

## All-Embracing Love

Mo Tzu makes no criticism of the Confucianists' central idea of *jen* (human-heartedness) and *yi* (righteousness); in the *Mo-tzu*, indeed, he speaks often of these two qualities and of the man of *jen* and man of *yi*. What he means by these terms, however, differs somewhat from the concept of them held by the Confucianists. For Mo Tzu, *jen* and *yi* signify an all-embracing love, and the man of *jen* and man of *yi* are persons who practice this all-embracing love. This concept is a central one in Mo Tzu's philosophy, and represents a logical extension of the professional ethics of the class of *hsieh* (knights-errant) from which Mo Tzu sprang. This ethics was, namely, that within their group the *hsieh* "enjoy equally and suffer equally." (This was a common saying of the *hsieh* of later times.) Taking this group concept as a basis, Mo Tzu tried to broaden it by preaching the doctrine that everyone in the world should love everyone else equally and without discrimination.

In the *Mo-tzu*, there are three chapters devoted to the subject of all-embracing love. In them, Mo Tzu first makes a distinction between what he calls the principles of "discrimination" and "all-embracingness." The man who holds to the principle of discrimination says: It is absurd for me to care for friends as much as I would for myself, and to look after their parents as I would my own. As a result, such a man does not do very much for his friends. But the man who holds to the principle of all-embracingness says, on the contrary: I must care for my friends as much as I do for myself, and for their parents as I would my own. As a result, he does everything he can for his friends. Having made this distinction, Mo Tzu then asks the question: Which of these two principles is the right one?

Mo Tzu thereupon uses his "tests of judgment" to determine the right and wrong of these principles. According to him, every principle must be examined by three tests, namely: "Its basis, its verifiability, and its applicability." A sound and right principle "should be based on the Will

of Heaven and of the spirits and on the deeds of the ancient sage-kings."
Then "it is to be verified by the senses of hearing and sight of the common people." And finally, "it is to be applied by adopting it in government and observing whether it is beneficial to the country and the
people." (*Mo-tzu*, ch. 35.) Of these three tests, the last is the most important. "Being beneficial to the country and the people" is the standard
by which Mo Tzu determines all values.

This same standard is the chief one used by Mo Tzu to prove the
desirability of all-embracing love. In the third of three chapters, all of
which are titled "All-embracing Love," he argues:

> The task of the human-hearted man is to procure benefits for the
> world and to eliminate its calamities. Now among all the current
> calamities of the world, which are the greatest? I say that attacks on
> small states by large ones, disturbances of small houses by large ones,
> oppression of the weak by the strong, misuse of the few by the
> many, deception of the simple by the cunning, and disdain toward
> the humble by the honored: these are the misfortunes of the world.
> . . . When we come to think about the causes of all these calamities,
> how have they arisen? Have they arisen out of love of others and
> benefiting others? We must reply that it is not so. Rather we should
> say that they have arisen out of hate of others and injuring others.
> If we classify those in the world who hate others and injure others,
> shall we call them "discriminating" or "all-embracing"? We must
> say that they are "discriminating." So, then, is not "mutual dis-
> crimination" the cause of the major calamities of the world? There-
> fore the principle of "discrimination" is wrong.
>
> Whoever criticizes others must have something to substitute for
> what he criticizes. Therefore I say: "Substitute all-embracingness
> for discrimination." What is the reason why all-embracingness can
> be substituted for discrimination? The answer is that when every-
> one regards the states of others as he regards his own, who will
> attack these other states? Others will be regarded like the self. When
> everyone regards the cities of others as he regards his own, who will
> seize these other cities. Others will be regarded like the self. When
> everyone regards the houses of others as he regards his own, who
> will disturb these other houses? Others will be regarded like the self.
>
> Now, when states and cities do not attack and seize one another,
> and when clans and individuals do not disturb and harm one an-
> other, is this a calamity or a benefit to the world? We must say it is
> a benefit. When we come to consider the origin of the various
> benefits, how have they arisen? Have they arisen out of hate of
> others and injuring others? We must say not so. We should say

that they have arisen out of love of others and benefiting others. If we classify those in the world who love others and benefit others, shall we call them "discriminating" or "all-embracing"? We must say that they are "all-embracing." Then is it not the case that "mutual all-embracingness" is the cause of the major benefit of the world? Therefore I say that the principle of "all-embracingness" is right. (*Mo-tzu*, ch. 16.)

Thus, using a utilitarianistic argument, Mo Tzu proves the principle of all-embracing love to be absolutely right. The human-hearted man whose task it is to procure benefits for the world and eliminate its calamities, must establish all-embracing love as the standard of action both for himself and for all others in the world. When everyone in the world acts according to this standard, "then attentive ears and keen eyes will respond to serve one another, limbs will be strengthened to work for one another, and those who know the proper principle will untiringly instruct others. Thus the aged and widowers will have support and nourishment with which to round out their old age, and the young and weak and orphans will have a place of support in which to grow up. When all-embracing love is adopted as the standard, such are the consequent benefits." (*Ibid.*) This, then, is Mo Tzu's ideal world, which can be created only through the practice of all-embracing love.

Oriental religions have had a great affinity with nature and an appreciation of the beauties of life. Though the Japanese world view has been influenced by Chinese and Indian ideas, the people have synthesized foreign views with their own. In this selection, Professor Earhart of Western Michigan University describes six themes of Japanese religion.

# Themes in Japanese Religion

H. Byron Earhart

The general unity of Japanese religion is evidenced by a nexus of persistent themes in Japanese religious history. Six themes are suggested here as representative, but of course not exhaustive, of the unity of Japanese religion.

One theme which runs through Japanese religious history is the closeness of man, gods, and nature. In this context "gods" can be understood as either the kami of Shinto or the Buddhas and bodhisattvas (Buddhist divinities) of Buddhism. (Because there is no exact English equivalent for the word kami, it will be used throughout the text without translation. The important thing to remember is that kami is much more inclusive than the English word "god.")[1] Man is closely related to both kami and Buddhas. In fact, he can even rise to the status of a kami or Buddha. The emperor was considered to be a living kami, since he was a direct descendant of the kami. Other human beings can attain divinity, too. For example, the military ruler (*shogun*) Ieyasu Tokugawa was venerated as divine or semi-divine even during his lifetime (late sixteenth and early seventeenth centuries). The founders of Buddhist sects and especially the founders of the New Religions during the last two centuries also attained more or less divine status. In contrast with monotheistic religions such as Judaism and Christianity, Japanese religion emphasizes neither one sovereign God nor a sharp distinction between the several gods and man. Man and gods alike share in the beauty of nature. The Judaeo-Christian theological tendency is to think of a hierarchy with God first, man second, and nature a poor third. In Japanese religion the three are more on equal terms. Man, gods, and nature form a triangle of harmonious interrelationships. Agriculture and fishing are closely related to the rituals and festivals of Shinto shrines and Buddhist temples. Zen Buddhism in particular, together with Shinto, express a love of nature that makes them akin to the Taoist sentiments of China. The harmony between man, the gods, and nature is a cornerstone of Japanese religion.

A second theme of Japanese religious history is the crucial function of the family system, including both living and dead members. The dead are so important in Japanese religion that the label of ancestor worship has been applied to Japanese as well as to Chinese religion. Family unity and continuity are essential for carrying out the important rituals honoring the dead ancestors. Even beyond the family system, there is great religious significance in the dead, their burial (or cremation), and periodic memorials. In fact, the dead can rise to the status of "gods." A dead person is referred to euphemistically as a Buddha (hotoke), and the tacit understanding is that after a fixed number of periodic memorials the dead person joins the company of ancestors as a kind of kami. Some shrines are dedicated to the spirits of famous men, such as the great Tokugawa ruler Ieyasu. At present, the religious function of most Buddhist priests and temples is to perform masses and memorials.

The family is important not only for revering ancestors but also for providing cohesion for religious activities. The home was formerly the center of religious devotion. Traditionally, every home featured a miniature shrine (sometimes called "god-shelf" or kamidana) for daily prayers. There was also a Buddhist altar (butsudan) for offerings to the family ancestors and periodic memorials. The kamidana are still found in many homes, especially in rural areas, but also are retained in such places as small shops and even in ocean-going ships. The butsudan are found in almost every home, even in the modern apartments where the kamidana are often missing. These family altars are not so ancient, representing an economic prosperity of later times, but they indicate the central religious function of the home. Other semi-religious seasonal activities (notably at New Year's) take place at the home. In ancient times the head of the clan was also a priest; in later times many shrines and temples were closely linked to specific families. It is not surprising that as Shinto and Buddhism became more highly organized they assumed the form of a hereditary priesthood. Japanese social as well as religious organization emphasizes a hierarchical ordering based on respect for elders.

A third theme found in Japanese religious history is the significance of purification, rituals, and charms. In front of every Shinto shrine, water is provided for washing the hands and rinsing the mouth before approaching the shrine. The insistence on purification—both physical and spiritual—is still basic to Japanese religion. Formerly there were many prohibitions and purifications connected with such matters as death and menstruation. This emphasis on purity carries over into such contemporary customs as the hot baths, and the damp face cloth provided for guests. Purification rituals using salt, water, and fire—all considered to be purifying agents—are found in Buddhist, Shinto, and folk traditions. Other rituals take care of every conceivable human and spiritual need. Many rituals are connected with agriculture and fishing, in order to relate man, gods, and nature in a beneficial manner. Some rituals meet personal crises, such as sickness. The paper charms distributed by shrines and temples include a number of specific boons, like warding off fire, preventing or curing sickness, and other "practical" benefits. Even Buddhist scriptures (in Chinese translation) were recited as blessings, and phrases from the scriptures were memorized as semi-magical formulas. Taoistic charms and formulas crept into both Shinto and Buddhism, but Buddhism was the major source of popular prayers and magical formulas.

A fourth theme of Japanese religious history is the prominence of local festivals and individual cults. Buddhist temples and Shinto shrines are not the site of weekly services, as is the case with Christian churches, but this does not diminish their importance. Because periodic festivals are the expression of the whole village, or section of a large city, they are unifying forces which link the individual homes into a larger religious group. Often social and economic activities of small villages center around the Shinto shrine. The local festival with its carnival atmosphere is quite typical of Japanese religiosity. In this light we can understand the fact that in Japan the celebration of Christmas has become popular, even though Christianity in general has not prospered.

Individual cults, though not organized on a national scale, play a crucial role in religious devotion. The bodhisattvas of Buddhism, especially Jizo and Kannon, have claimed probably the largest following. Statues of these bodhisattvas are found in the villages or along the roadside as well as in temples, and they receive the devotion of all those who look to them for spiritual help. Usually priests play little or no role in these devotional cults. Ordinarily a small group of people will form a voluntary association (called *ko*) which meets regularly in the members' homes for devotion to one bodhisattva. Various kami (including gods of Indian and Chinese origin) are revered by groups of fishermen or other tradesmen. Often the existence of a flourishing cult of this kind at a shrine or temple accounts for most of its visitors and financial income.

A fifth theme within Japanese religious history is the way in which religion is woven into everyday life. This theme is simply another aspect of the previous four themes. The Japanese identification with gods and nature, the importance of the family, the significance of rituals and charms, and the prominence of individual cults—all lead religion into a natural and close relationship to everyday life. For example, even if there is no regular weekly attendance at Shinto shrines and Buddhist temples corresponding to the Judaeo-Christian sabbath, there are regular stages in an individual's life which take him to shrines and temples. Traditionally, the young infant was carried to the local Shinto shrine and presented to the guardian deity. In case of sickness or special need, one usually visited the shrine or temple which granted that specific blessing. Likewise, in recent times the traditional wedding often takes place in a Shinto shrine, and the funeral mass is performed (like the subsequent memorial celebrations) in a Buddhist temple.

Through both formal and informal means, religion has been specifically related to concrete economic activities. Some temples and shrines, for example, are oriented to the fishing communities in which they are found; they pray for large catches, safety on the sea, and repose for the drowned. Some saints are formally considered the patron figures of certain crafts. In an informal sense, many folk practices are inseparable from the various stages of rice cultivation. Religion even pervades the Japanese sense of humor. For example, the great Zen saint of China, Bodhidharma (who sat in meditation until his legs fell off), is remembered in Japan as the legless doll called Daruma who, as many times as he falls, always rights himself.

A sixth theme of Japanese religious history is the natural bond between Japanese religion and the Japanese nation. It is true that from the Meiji Restoration of 1868 until 1945 Japanese religion took on a nationalistic character which supported the state in its military campaigns. However, the close tie between Japanese religion and the nation at large is an indelible feature of Japanese history. It is as true of Buddhism as of Shinto, because Buddhism lent a hand in unifying and supporting the government. All the formative elements of Japanese religion have blended with and supported the national heritage. Indeed, this is partly what wove Buddhism, Confucianism (Neo-Confucianism), and religious Taoism into the warp and woof of Japanese religion.

### Note

1 See Daniel C. Holtom, "The Meaning of Kami," *Monumenta Nipponica,* III (1940), 7–27, 32–53; IV (1941), 25–68. Holtom tried to interpret kami through the Melanesian term *mana,* which is suggestive, even though not quite the same as kami.

### Questions

1 After reading this chapter, how would you compare the status of women in Asia with women in the West?

2  Many Westerners currently seem to be very interested in Eastern religions. Does this interest appear to you to be a genuine search for new values or a superficial fad?

3  Do you think that Eastern ideas can be adopted by the West without radical changes in Western society? Could we combine the best of both worlds?

4  Which religion, Buddhism or Hinduism, would be more acceptable to Americans as a way of life? Why? Which might be better for contemporary India?

5  How do you account for the difference between the way older persons are regarded in the East and in the West?

6  Does Japanese religious practice coincide with Judaeo-Christian theology?

# 8

# The Changing Face
# of Heresy

The dictionary defines heresy as: "A doctrinal view or belief at variance with the recognized standards or tenets of any established religious, philosophical, political, or other system, school, or party; an opinion or doctrine subversive of settled beliefs or accepted principles." Heresy, like beauty, is in the eye of the beholder. People make their own judgments about who is a heretic and then use great pressure to compel them to conform. The nonconforming Frenchmen around the little town of Albi during the late Middle Ages were persecuted for their unusual religious beliefs by a stronger majority long before the Church was persuaded to start a holy crusade against them. America has had its witch hunts from the time of the Salem trials to the era of Senator Joseph McCarthy in the 1950s, and later. The compulsion to conform is great, even in a rather free and permissive society such as ours. Those who do not conform are considered heretics. Would you say that both conformity and heresy are important in any viable, that is, vital, society?

# The Cycle of Conformity and Heresy

Frederick Gentles

> They see but do not say. You have them cowed.
> —ANTIGONE

Antigone was a heretic in ancient Greece. She spoke out and acted against the king of Thebes. Her sister, Ismene, would not join her in burying their dead brother because Creon the king had decreed the young traitor was not to be given an honorable burial. Ismene conformed. She saw the injustice of the law, but she was not about to speak out or take action against it. It does not do to meddle, she said. Conform.

Every age is an age of conformity, but some ages seem to have more nonconformists than others. In conformity there is the safety and comfort of numbers of people doing just the right thing in just the right way to insure the carrying on of traditions. And, of course, this is necessary to provide stability in any society, because law and order are usually logical alternatives to lawlessness and disorder. Those who go along with the masses, in the Soviet Union, in Nazi Germany, or in any other society, are good citizens, and those who object to established ways are heretics and may be hounded out of town or otherwise persecuted. Be a good citizen. Don't rock the boat. America: Love It or Leave It.

America: Change It or Lose It! Heresy! Though the late Middle Ages was an age that insisted on conformity to a high degree, it produced many heretics who became famous martyrs and whose followers lived after them to change the world. The modern age is more sophisticated and in many ways more tolerant than that of seven hundred years ago, but there are nevertheless huge numbers of people, especially among senior citizens, who seem to be rabidly intolerant of new styles of dress, hair, beards, religion, politics, sideburns, and so on. The Kennedys and Martin Luther King, not loved by most traditional types, are only some of the modern martyrs who have inspired their followers to bring about great social and economic changes in a world that is still strongly attached to the old ways. Like Antigone, they spoke out against what they considered to be the tyranny of the majority in compelling conformity to unjust laws. They were not cowed.

The Christian Church was the dominant institution in the Middle Ages, but the conformity it sought was constantly challenged by kings, princes, and poor souls who did not believe in everything the Church stood for. These people spoke out vociferously and put conscience—and often times self-interest—above loyalties to what they considered to be a man-made institution. The Church fathers put up a strong fight against heresies by using such weapons as sermons, excommunications, inquisitions, interdicts, and even war to perpetuate conformity in a world that was pulling in other directions with new ideas, new cities, new nations, and new money enterprises. Power and wealth corrupted individuals within the Church, and this made it easier for heretics to attract followers—just as Christianity had attracted followers from a corrupt Roman Empire a thousand years before.

The man and woman who are now the patron saints of San Francisco and of France refused to submit to those who would force them to conform to traditional ways of behaving. One would today still be a heretic because of his eccentric ways, while the other would be accepted, except, possibly, her bizarre appearance, because she helped change the direction of men's thoughts from Church to nation. John Wycliffe and John Hus were two other heretics whose influence is felt in many places today, particularly in divided Ireland and in nationalist Czechoslovakia. There is a changing face of heresy, and there is also an unchanging face of tradition, from the Middle Ages to modern times.

Both Protestants and Catholics pay homage to the beautiful Christlike figure of St. Francis, with his love for all mankind and all creation. Though the older generation told him he never had it so good, he gave up a rich family inheritance to devote his life to the poor. He kicked off his fine clothes, took to sackcloth or any other covering he could beg, and began a great movement of purity and poverty that had particular appeal to the youth of the time. His example inspired thousands to reject traditional society for a life devoted to helping others instead of just helping themselves. But a Christ-like figure in any age is considered to be crazy by those whose lives are dedicated to getting ahead.

"Everybody knew, of course, that Franciscans were communists; but this was not so much being a communist as being an anarchist," writes G. K. Chesterton in his biography *St. Francis of Assisi*.[1] Although St. Francis, because of his nonconformity, narrowly escaped being officially declared a heretic, many of his followers received the official seal. Chesterton says:

> If the Franciscan movement had turned into a new religion, it would after all have been a narrow religion. In so far as it did turn here and there into a heresy, it was a narrow heresy. . . . And St. Francis, however wild and romantic his gyrations might appear to many, always hung on to reason by one invisible and indestructible hair.[2]

St. Francis was married to Lady Poverty. Members of his order, called mendicant, begged for food, clothing, and shelter, not to save their own souls so much as to save others'. As someone like St. Dominic was needed to convert the heathen to Christianity, says Chesterton, someone like St. Francis was needed to convert the Christians to Christianity. He lived with lepers, he lived in caves, and he replied to the curses of his father by saying that his Father in Heaven blessed his poverty. Though Franciscans did not conform as so many friends and relatives expected, they themselves demanded conformity in realizing a life of purity. In 1322, nearly one hundred years after the death of Francis, Pope John XXII, from his rich palace at Avignon, condemned as heresy the doctrine of the poverty of Christ. Franciscan extremists, the Spirituals, were branded as heretics, and many were burned at the stake. Both Christ and Francis were heretics because they denied Establishment values of material success and traditional ways.[3]

St. Francis of Assisi was an Italian, an imitator of Christ, dedicated to Poverty. St. Joan of Arc was a Frenchwoman, a teenager extraordinary, dedicated to Frenchmen. She was patriot, nationalist, Protestant, Catholic, individualist, heretic, and saint. She cut her hair short, wore men's clothing, defied Church authority, and thereby irritated to distraction those who were offended by such nonconformist actions. Especially were her critics concerned with her short hair and men's clothing. An old archdeacon said that her dress was scandalous, indecent, and against all custom; she was ridiculed about it throughout her trial for heresy. But she had a mind of her own. As a soldier for France directing men and armies, a leader must not appear to be too feminine. As a young woman of nineteen on trial for her life, she was still not going to let others tell her how she should appear. Joan was Joan and that was that.

She was one of the first apostles of nationalism, says Bernard Shaw, and as such she fell afoul the power of the Church. She placed ultimate faith in her God instead of in her Church and thereby became a Protestant one hundred years before Martin Luther. She was a woman at war with foreigners in her country. George Bernard Shaw, Dublin Protestant, but sympathetic biographer of St. Joan, describes the trial and the indictment against her. Warwick, an English nobleman during the Hundred Years' War, and Cauchon, the Bishop of Beauvais, who had brought Joan to trial with the help of the English, are speaking:

> WARWICK [*playing the pink of courtesy*]   I think you are not entirely void of sympathy with The Maid's secular heresy, my lord. I leave you to find a name for it.
>
> CAUCHON   You mistake me, my lord. I have no sympathy with her political presumptions. But as a priest I have gained a knowledge of the minds of the common people; and there you will find yet another most dangerous idea. I can express it only by such phrases as France for the French, England for the English, Italy for the Italians, Spain for the Spanish, and so forth. It is sometimes so narrow and bitter in country folk that it surprises me that this country girl can rise above the idea of her village for its villagers. But she can. She does. When she threatens to drive the English from the soil of France she is undoubtedly thinking of the whole extent of country in which French is spoken. To her the French-speaking people are what the Holy Scriptures describe as a nation. Call this side of her heresy Nationalism if you will: I can find you no better name for it. I can only tell you that it is essentially anti-Catholic and anti-Christian; for the Catholic Church knows only one realm, and that is the realm of Christ's kingdom. Divide that kingdom into nations, and you dethrone Christ. Dethrone Christ, and who will stand between our throats and the sword? The world will perish in a welter of war.
>
> WARWICK   Well, if you will burn the Protestant, I will burn the Nationalist, though perhaps I shall not carry Messire John with me there. England for the English will appeal to him.[4]

Scene IV of the play concludes with a statement by the chaplain that England for the English is natural but that Joan's wearing men's clothing and fighting is not; she has rebelled against the Church, against God, and against England. "Let her perish. Let her burn." In 1431, at the age of nineteen, she was burned at the stake. In 1920, nearly five hundred years later, she was canonized as a saint. Which of today's heretics will be tomorrow's heroes?

The nationalism kindled at this time burns fiercely today in the hearts of men around the world, although the highly romantic kind of nationalism Joan may have held in her heart did not take immediately since monarchy was at that time the only political vehicle available to bring about national unity. It remained for the American and French revolutions and Napoleon to germinate a new peoples' nationalism, which took root in the nineteenth century and blossomed with great vigor in the twentieth with Hitler, de Gaulle, Ho Chi-minh, and everywhere flags, flags, flags. Joan was a warrior saint. She, together with the royal imperative toward territorial conquest, projected a new and unique institution in human history. She could neither read nor write but she was a patriot, and that is what counts under the king or under the national flag.

As the Middle Ages moved toward the Renaissance, the idea of a nation began to eat away at the idea of a universal Church. The Great Schism, 1378–1417, divided loyalties along national lines, with some new nations loyal to a pope at Rome and some to another at Avignon. At one time there were three popes claiming the chair. The great Schism gave the Englishman John Wycliffe more reason to continue his attack on the established Church and on the papacy, which he saw as a tyranny over the minds of men. He agreed with the radical element of the Franciscans who believed the holding of property by the clergy was against the teachings of Christ, and he agreed with other Franciscans, such as Roger Bacon, Duns Scotus, and William of Ockham, who contested some of the beliefs of Thomas Aquinas of the rival Dominican order. Heresy was in the air at this time—a time of challenge to the old guard. Even Aquinas was considered a heretic by some for bringing Aristotle and other pagan philosophers into Christian dogma. Roger Bacon and other Oxford University Franciscans encouraged scientific experimentation and questioned papal authority. Although Bacon was imprisoned at one time for the novelties of his teaching, he escaped the official tag of heretic.

Wycliffe exhibited something of the rising national feeling by objecting to English moneys being sent to the Roman pontiff, and then he went on to demonstrate Protestant beliefs some one hundred and fifty years before Martin Luther nailed the ninety-five Theses to the church door at Wittenberg: like Luther, he objected to the sale of indulgences used as pardons for sins, he rejected six of the seven sacraments, and he said that the worship of saints and veneration of their relics was false because these and other practices of the Church were man-made. He declared that all necessary religious truth can be learned from the Bible, which he and other Oxford scholars, contrary to Church authority, translated into English. Of course, he was tried as a heretic, but the trial in London was broken up by mob violence. Six years later, in 1383, he was called to Rome for another trial, but he refused to go and thus escaped the official tag of heretic while he lived. However, the Council of Constance declared him a heretic long after he was dead and ordered his remains dug up to be scattered on unhallowed ground.

Wycliffe's ideas caught on among the Czechs in Bohemia, where John Hus and students of the new University of Prague took up the cry of independence from Rome and independence from the German influence that was quite strong in that land. As rector of the University, he wrote and preached that many of the Church doctrines were simply human invention, and especially he protested the idea of indulgences. He was excommunicated by the pope but secured from the Emperor Sigismund a guarantee of safe passage to and from the Council of Constance to present his case.

Hus refused to recant, and in July of 1415 he was burned at the stake. Instead of purifying the air by burning out heresy, the martyrdom of Hus made heresy catch on. A holy crusade had to be organized against the rebellious Husites in Bohemia. The bloodletting lasted about twenty years, the crusade failed, and the heresy persisted on to the time of the Reformation.

The Age of Intolerance, with its Inquisition, its religious persecution, and its religious wars, was to last until the time of the English civil wars and the Thirty Years' War (1618–1648), when Cardinal Richelieu of France aligned his Catholic country with some Protestant countries to kill other Catholics and Protestants of enemy countries; the war that started as a religious war ended as a national war. The process that had begun in the late Middle Ages was now complete—nationalism had replaced Catholicism in demanding the ultimate loyalties of men. What had begun as heresy had ended in conformity.

European man has successively extended his identity, starting with family, then clan, then from clan to tribe, from tribe to feudal principality, and, aside from religious loyalty to the Church universal, from feudal principality to nation. Of the heretics we have discussed, only one was not wrapped up in the national institution. He extended his identity as far as all mankind.

But all mankind is too large a thought for many, who are tied up in the smaller dimensions of identifying with nation, state, tribe, clan, family, and self. It would be heresy today to extend one's identity by flying the United Nations flag over the national flag. One would surely be persecuted by conformists, just as the Romans persecuted the Christian minorities and the Christians later persecuted the heretics. Some would even consider flying the United Nations flag a Communist conspiracy.

Actually, it is a Christian conspiracy. And it is a Buddhist, Jewish, Bahai, and Muslim conspiracy that someday might actually succeed. That is, if one is an optimist about man's behavior and his potentialities and thinks man will succeed as Christ and Francis hoped he would. On the other hand, if one is a pessimist about man's behavior and his limitations, and points to the Berlin Wall separating communists and capitalists and the more recent Belfast Wall separating Catholics and Protestants, then man will not succeed in creating One World. One World is impossible, just as over 200 million people of diverse natures living peacefully in the United States is impossible . . . It is a heresy.

### Notes

1 G. K. Chesterton, *St. Francis of Assisi* (London: Hodder and Stoughton, 1964), p. 178.

2 *Ibid.*, pp. 184–185.

3 A cartoon in the *Wall Street Journal* pictured a Christ-like figure with robe, long hair, beard, and bare feet walking the streets of Manhattan carrying a sign: YOU WOULDN'T BELIEVE ME IF I TOLD YOU.

4 Bernard Shaw, *Saint Joan* (Baltimore, Md.: Penguin, 1952), p. 99.

Hippies and yippies, beatniks and bohemians, have disgusted many
members of the current Establishment. Each is a bit different from the
other, but there are similarities in their rejection of traditional society—
their unusual appearance, their communal living, their heretical ideas.
Traditional types of any age would make life difficult for the bizarre
young man discussed in this article.

# A Bizarre Young Man

Jeffery and Elizabeth Smith

This is the true story of a young man who grew up with all the
advantages of a well-to-do family, a devoted mother, and a stern but
just father, a prominent businessman respected throughout the community.

As a teen-ager he seemed a normal young man, gifted and promising, with a successful career before him in the family business.
Though quite a party goer, and not adverse to a little hard drinking,
he was active in church work, and served a brief hitch as an officer
in the army.

Then suddenly a change came over him. Within a year he had
broken with his family, and, without visible means of support, was
drifting from one leaky pad to another, bearded, barefoot, dirty, and
in rags. The change came about in a strange way.

Though his case history shows no sign of drug addition, he began
to act, much of the time, as though he were on a "trip," withdrawn
and experiencing visions and hallucinations. These triggered a series
of violent and criminal acts, directed, significantly, against his own
family.

He was caught robbing his father's warehouse, selling the goods at
a fraction of their value, and squandering the money on strange
whims. His father in desperation took him to court.

This led to a terrible scene. Judicial proceedings had just got under
way, when suddenly the youth became very violent, stripped off all
his expensive clothes, threw them at his father's feet, and stormed
naked into the street.

From "A Bizarre Young Man" by Jeffery and Elizabeth Smith, *This World
Magazine, San Francisco Chronicle*, May 28, 1967.

From this time on his actions and way of life became increasingly bizarre. He insisted nothing mattered but the practice of "love" and "brotherhood." He took up with peace, and advocated integration, not just racial but a kind of total integration.

He turned against education and urged the runaways and dropouts who flocked to share his pads to stay away from books. Often he would block traffic by dancing wildly in the streets. He and his friends spent their days looking for handouts and standing on street corners shouting their "love" and "brotherhood" harangues at passing crowds.

Teen-age girls, many of them beautiful, talented and of good family, left home under his influence. They cut their hair as short as possible, dressed in odd clothes, and refused to have anything to do with marriage. Instead they engaged in all sorts of pacifistic acts and extreme do-gooderism.

The young man claimed he was trying to "live like Jesus," all the while growing dirtier and more ragged, begging, mumbling to sticks and stones, "communicating" with anything that happened along. He dragged more and more fine young people away from their homes, schools, careers, into this squalid and appalling way of life, all of them, like him, hipped on "Love, Love, Love."

Although his address was not Haight-Ashbury, but Assisi, he belongs, in a way, to San Francisco. It was named for him.

The Middle Ages was a time of extreme religious fervor, with inquisitions, official and unofficial, to ferret out religious heresy and new ideas. Our contemporary world is experiencing a time of extreme "political" fervor, with similar inquisitions to root out political heresy and new ideas. Some people are afraid of ideas, and political prisoners, both communist and capitalist, are found on both sides of the Iron Curtain. Pope Innocent III ordered a crusade against the heretical Albigensians of southern France, who were crushed after great violence and bloodshed. About the same time, the Dominican order was formed to try to convert the Albigensians and eventually to assist the Office of the Holy Inquisition to fight heresy. Bernard Gui (1261–1331) was an ardent Dominican from Spain who presided over hundreds of trials for heresy. The Waldenses, of whom he speaks, were victims of another bloody crusade.

# The Manual of the Inquisitor

Bernard Gui

### Of the Sect of the Waldenses and First of Its Origins and Beginnings

The sect or heresy of the Waldenses or the Poor of Lyon came into being about the year of our Lord 1170. The man responsible for its creation was an inhabitant of Lyon, Waldes or Waldo, whence the name of its devotees. He was wealthy, but, after giving up all his property, determined to practice poverty and evangelic perfection in the manner of the apostles. He had had the Gospels and several other books of the Bible translated into vulgar tongue for his use, as well as several maxims of Saints Augustine, Jerome, Ambrose and Gregory, grouped under titles, which he and his followers called sentences. They read them very often, although they hardly understood them; nevertheless, infatuated with themselves, although they had little learning, they usurped the role of the apostles and dared to preach the Gospel in the streets and public squares. The said Waldes or Waldo drew into this presumption numerous accomplices of both sexes whom he sent out preaching as disciples.

These people, although stupid and unlearned, traveled through the villages, men and women, and entered homes, and, preaching in the squares and even in the churches, the men especially, spread about them a mass of errors.

Summoned by the Archbishop of Lyon, the lord Jean aux Blanches-

From "The Manual of the Inquisitor" by Bernard Gui, from staff, Columbia College, *Introduction to Contemporary Civilization in the West* (New York: Columbia University Press, 1960), pp. 258–259. Copyright © 1946, 1954, 1960 Columbia University Press.

Mains, who forbade them such a presumption, they refused obedience, declaring, in order to excuse their madness, that one should obey God rather than man. God ordered the apostles to preach the Gospel to all beings, they said, applying to themselves that which had been said of the apostles, whose followers and successors they boldly declared themselves to be, by a false profession of poverty and by masquerading under an appearance of holiness. Indeed they despised the prelates and clergy because, they said, they owned great wealth and lived in pleasures.

Owing to this arrogant usurpation of the function of preaching, they became teachers of error. Summoned to renounce preaching, they disobeyed and were declared in contempt, and consequently excommunicated and banished from their town and country. Finally, as they persisted, a council held at Rome before the Lateran Council [reference is to fourth Lateran Council, 1215] declared them schismatic and condemned them as heretics. Thus multiplied upon the earth they scattered through the provinces, into neighboring regions and unto the borders of Lombardy. Separated and cut off from the Church, and joining, on the other hand, with other heretics and drinking in their errors, they blended with their own concoctions the errors and heresies of earlier heretics.

## The Errors of the Present Waldenses (They Previously Held Several Others)

Disdain for ecclesiastical authority was and still is the prime heresy of the Waldenses. Excommunicated for this reason and delivered over to Satan, they have fallen into innumerable errors, and have blended the errors of earlier heretics with their own concoctions.

The misled believers and sacrilegious masters of this sect hold and teach that they are in no way subject to the lord Pope or Roman Pontiff, or to the other prelates of the Roman Church, and that the latter persecute and condemn them unjustly and improperly. Moreover, they declare that they cannot be excommunicated by this Roman Pontiff and these prelates, and that obedience is owed to none of them when they order and summon the followers and masters of the said sect to abandon or abjure this sect, although this sect be condemned as heretical by the Roman Church.

Miss Lela Kahl wrote this take-home essay, while a freshman student at San Diego Mesa College, in response to the Ismene quotation from Sophocles' "Antigone" below. The paper was written during the week in October 1969 that Vice-President Spiro Agnew (drawing cheers from his partisan audience) called the Vietnam-war protest organizers "merchants of hate" and "parasites of passion" and said the nation can "afford to separate them from our society—with no more regret than we should feel over discarding rotten apples from a barrel." Mr. Agnew and Miss Kahl may be in disagreement over what is positive rebellion and creative protest. Were Antigone and St. Francis "rotten apples"?

# Let Us Defend Authority?

Lela Kahl

ISMENE    And, now, we two are left.
Think how much worse our end will be than all
The rest, if we defy our sovereign's edict
And his power. Remind ourselves that we
Are women, and as such are not made to fight
With men. For might unfortunately is right
And makes us bow to things like this and worse.
Therefore shall I beg the saints below
To judge me leniently as one who kneeled
To force. I bend before authority.
It does not do to meddle.

Conformity to society and to the laws of the land has been inherent in every civilization since the dawn of culture on this earth. Since the emergence of the primitive societies consisting of the family unit, the clan, the tribe and eventually the villages and towns, conformity and adaptation have been essential. Most people in the past were forced to adjust. The powers which ruled them tolerated only one way of life—that of mandatory conformity. The process of social indoctrination, the platicizing of the individual (adaptation), begins at birth. Even in the most primitive tribal society, the child was molded and trained to the job he would perform in the future. The young male was taught fighting, self-defense, courage, hunting techniques and leadership ability. He was prepared by a series of rigorous tests until he was fully initiated as a grown male member of the tribe. Likewise,

From "Let Us Defend Authority?" by Lela Kahl. By permission of Lela Kahl and Eric and Eva Kahl.

the female child was prepared throughout her life for maternal duties which included cooking, cleaning, childcare and subservience to her husband. Children were considered outcasts of society if they displayed "abnormal" characteristics such as rebellious individuality or excessive questioning of traditional social myths. This is true even today (the "angry young man" in Britain, the beatnik, hippie, etc.).

Adaptation has been the theme of every church, club, fraternity and party. Conformity has been the requirement of all associations, especially religious, for it is vital for the individual to be accepted by the group and by himself. Primitive man revered the spirits of the animals he hunted for food, in order to be assured of a good hunt and harvest. This led to totemism and the worship of the fertility goddess. In order to be assured of a happy afterlife, primitive man revered his own spirit as well as his ancestors' and made sacrifices to the gods, as well as placing food and implements alongside his carefully buried dead. Religion's seductive promises of eternal paradise strengthened the "virtue" of acceptance.

Adaptation has been the code of every written and understood law. In primitive societies, the chief, the council of elders and the jury of adult males were the lawgivers and enforcers. In the civilizations of Mesopotamia, the "lugals," kings and priests dictated the law and they were obeyed (Hammurabi's code). In Egypt, the pharoahs were the lawmakers. The archons in Greece prescribed the law and, for the most part, it was followed. Pericles describes this in his Funeral Oration (by Thucydides):

> . . . in our public acts we are prevented by doing wrong by fear; we respect the authorities and the laws, especially those which are ordained for the protection of the injured as well as those unwritten laws which bring upon the transgressor admitted dishonor.

Laws have been at work as long as man has been here. All laws have been recognized, observed and broken, but traditionally, it has been the "good" man who has acted according to the law (such as Ismene). But what about those people who break the law (Antigone) or stray away from the norms in areas such as religion, politics and society in general? Do they have any effect on history—are they important? The answer is an emphatic "yes!", for it is these individuals who prove a basic truth in human behavior—we cannot conform. There seems to be a pattern in man's behavior such that he can submit only up to a certain point and then he must rebel. Because of man's instinct of rebellion, he has never been satisfied with the limits of his body. Even in primordial times, he investigated the world about him and harnessed energy to help do his work. The discovery of fire, the wheel, the domestication of animals, methods of scientific agriculture—all these are basic examples of rebellion against nature.

From ancient Egypt comes an example of nonconformity in terms of religion. During the reign of Amenhotep IV (1375–1358 B.C.) the traditional God Amon-Re was rejected. Amenhotep adopted as his religion (and his peoples') the worship of Aton in the place of Amon-Re. The pharoah changed his name to Akhentaton ("He who is devoted to Aton"), left Amon-Re's city to found a new capital (Akhetaton) and passed the rest of his life in worshipping Aton and in composing hymns and prayers. After his death, his weak successor, Tutankhamen, returned to the ancient capital of Thebes and the worship of Amon-Re.

In the field of politics and social dissension, Thucydides (460–400 B.C.) was certainly a pace-setter. In his account of the Peloponnesian Wars, he fixes the blame on his home city-state of Athens. He declares that it was due to Athens' imperialistic attitude and "territorial imperative" that she fought Sparta and eventually caused her own decadence and decline. Even in the free thinking and open society which Athens enjoyed, Thucydides' direct attack on his homeland (in the form of a written account) was unheard-of and certainly a display of a rebellious, nonconforming attitude.

In the play *Antigone,* Sophocles gives a prime example of conformity and rebellion in the area of law and order. A perfect excerpt from the play:

CREON    And art thou not ashamed to act apart from the rest of them . . .?

ANTIGONE    No; there is nothing shameful in piety to a brother.

In the same sense, there is nothing shameful in following one's own principles when one is willing to accept the consequences, even death.

These examples from ancient history all have one thing in common—they are constructive rebellions, not minor ones concerning dress, manners and tastes (in today's society these are expressed by long hair, hippie movements, etc.). But most important is the fact that there are so few of them, a major concept in understanding the theories of this paper. Constructive rebellion is the productive way toward nonconformity, involving positive criticism in the fields of basic human values, such as religion, politics and morality. In American history, examples of constructive rebellion can be found in the Declaration of Independence, the Bill of Rights, the abolition movement, women's suffrage, labor strikes and, recently, the October 1969

Moratorium Day protests against our involvement in the war in Vietnam.

Constructive rebellion, protest, and revolt are *vital* to every society, for without them the society becomes stagnant and most assuredly deteriorates. Perhaps because there was not enough constructive rebellion in the ancient civilizations (probably because the masses were not given the opportunity to protest), those societies did not have the chance to change and better themselves. The examples which I *have* cited are so prominent in history because they are the rarities of their societies. If the United States today attempts to learn anything from past history to insure the continuence of its progressive culture, it must recognize the mistakes past civilizations made in quenching forms of constructive protest. Positive revolt is natural to man and beneficial to society, and by using it to better his world, the man of today can be assured of an improved environment tomorrow.

The appeal of the Christian faith is its emphasis on love, but during the Middle Ages this love was threatened, subverted, or somewhat modified by differences in interpretation of scripture, church rituals, and the activities of the clergy. Elements of the Reformation are apparent centuries prior to Martin Luther's nailing of his Ninety-five Theses to the church door in Wittenberg, Germany. How did heretics differ from those who merely criticized the Church? What was the danger of heresy? How effective was the Inquisition in curbing heresy?

# Medieval Heresy

Joseph Ward Swain

The medieval church was usually successful in its efforts to control and direct the religious life of western Europe. When critics complained of abuses, or inspired preachers proclaimed new ideas, the church found ways to turn them to its advantage, as with Peter Damiani and Bernard of Cluny on the one hand or Joachim of Floris and Francis of Assisi on the other. But sometimes the church could not absorb the new ideas, or else its slowness caused the reformers to lose patience. This was especially the case in the twelfth century. The rise of towns and the revival of trade had brought far-reaching social changes that touched almost every aspect of medieval life and raised grave problems for the church. Sometimes these problems were primarily social, especially those concerning the poor in the towns, but sometimes they dealt with new ideas. In each case the church was slow to act, partly perhaps because nearly all its high officials, being men drawn from the feudal aristocracy, looked at the world through feudal spectacles and were not well informed as to what was happening in the new world of the communes. At any rate, others saw more quickly than they that something was wrong. At first the church officials would not listen to such warnings, and sometimes innovators were condemned as heretics.

The church had always been distressed by heretics who, for one reason or another, refused to accept its teachings on some seemingly important matter. In the century after Constantine, when Christians controlled the government of the Roman Empire, many harsh laws were enacted and people were occasionally executed for heresy. Sometimes their heresies concerned practices, more frequently they centered around theological doctrines, but all the important heresies eventually included more funda-

From pp. 523–530 in *The Harper History of Civilization*, Vol. I by Joseph Ward Swain. Copyright © 1958 by Joseph Ward Swain. By permission of Harper & Row, Publishers, Inc.

mental matters as well. Thus, in the fourth century, Donatism was originally a question of practice (strictness or leniency in forgiving persons who had denied Christ in time of persecution) while Arianism concerned theology. . . . Before long, however, it appeared that in the main the Donatists of Africa sprang from the lower classes, being largely of Punic or African descent and speaking Punic, while the orthodox were the Romanized Latin-speaking upper classes; in the East, the Arians were recruited largely among the Greek upper classes while the followers of Athanasius were Orientals, but in the West the old Romans were orthodox while the barbarian Goths were Arian. These quarrels therefore covered more than mere theology. Rival social groups were engaged in a mighty struggle for power within the church.

The medieval church usually laid even greater stress upon its unity than it did upon the accuracy of its theology. A heretic, in its eyes, was not primarily a man whose theology was mistaken, for many points in theology were not yet clearly defined. The dangerous heretic was one who made his erroneous ideas an excuse for attacking the church. Thus St. Bernard of Clairvaux, who always was quick to brand his opponents as heretics, went wrong himself on more than one point in theology, and even the mighty St. Thomas Aquinas erred on occasion. Likewise, mere criticism of the church organization did not make a man a heretic. A St. Peter Damiani might castigate the clergy in unmeasured language, or an emperor might wage war upon the pope and set up an antipope of his own, but such persons acted as members of the church which they wished to reform or dominate. If, as we say, a man "had his heart in the right place"—in other words, if he was conspicuously loyal to the church—he could permit himself wide freedom in his criticisms and intellectual speculations. But if he broke away from the church, defied its authorities, and attacked it from the outside, and if he then used new and strange theological doctrines to justify his attacks—as such persons usually did—he became a heretic and his doctrines were quickly condemned as heretical. But it was only in time of crisis, when the position of their church seemed endangered, that medieval churchmen engaged in hysterical heresy hunts. Mention of a few heresies famous in the Middle Ages will be enough to show how they developed and how they were combated.

## Waldensians and Albigensians

It is a mistake to assume that everyone—or nearly everyone—in the Middle Ages was a devout and pious person. There were always many people who took their religion very lightly and many who made jest of holy things. The popular poetry and songs of the age were filled with ridicule of the clergy and parodies of church ritual. This anticlerical feeling was strongest in towns, where it was intensified by the fact that the communes had frequently been forced to fight bishops, or even the pope himself, to maintain their liberties. In a larger way, it may be said that the whole spirit and temper of town life differed as widely from that of a monastery as it did from that of a village. As the towns were filled with beggars on the verge of starvation, it was not surprising that some should cast envious eyes upon the wealth of churches and monasteries, and that anticlerical political leaders, such as Arnold of Brescia, . . . should talk of forcibly purifying the church and bringing her back to the glorious days of her "apostolic poverty" by distributing her wealth among the poor. It was by remarks such as this that Arnold became a heretic.

Peter Waldo was a rich merchant of Lyons, France, who about 1170 underwent conversion, distributed his property to the poor, and began preaching. As he was not an ordained priest, the bishop and even the pope ordered him to desist, But Waldo ignored the order, continued his preaching, and organized his followers as the "Poor Men of Lyons"—a group not unlike the early Franciscans, who came half a century later. This organization spread rapidly through southern France and northern Italy. At first Waldo entertained no heretical doctrines, but persecution drove his followers into strong anticlerical positions, and they developed radical views regarding the church, the clergy, and the Christian life. They insisted that everyone—men and women alike—had the right to preach, and they sought to make men independent of the clergy by denying Catholic doctrines regarding transubstantiation, penance, and purgatory. They became careful students of the Gospels, from which they learned pacifism and other extreme doctrines. They have been called the first Protestants, but in an even truer sense they may be called precursors of St. Francis, for the line separating heretics from saints is sometimes very narrow. On several occasions the popes launched crusades against these Waldensians—one such massacre, in 1654, inspired Milton's powerful sonnet beginning, "Avenge, O Lord, Thy slaughtered saints"—but in Italy the heretics persevered and a few thousand Waldensians still dwell in Alpine valleys near the French frontier.

Another group of heretics were called "Albigensians." The name is derived from the town of Albi, in southern France, where heretics of this school were particularly strong, but they called themselves "Cathari," meaning the "Pure Ones." They resembled the Waldensians in many respects, but they also showed wide differences. The origins of Albigensianism are still shrouded in mystery. There can be little doubt that they were deeply influenced by the ideas of the Manicheans of the late Roman Empire—in whose errors even the great St. Augustine was entangled for a while—but the continuity of the sect in the West from ancient times cannot be proved. Perhaps small groups of Manicheans survived the Dark Ages in out-of-the-way corners, but modern scholars usually prefer to believe that the heresy was reintroduced into Europe from the East by traders and pilgrims in the eleventh century. In any case, it spread rapidly through southern France in the twelfth century. In Languedoc it was protected by the powerful counts of Toulouse, and there it apparently won a majority of the population.

The complicated oriental theology of the Albigensians postulated two supreme powers, one good and one evil, God and Satan. The latter was identified with the Jehovah of the Old Testament, and the pope and the Catholic clergy were declared to be his worshipers. The Albigensians claimed that they, and they alone, worshiped the one true God. The manner of life prescribed for the faithful was so austere that few could attain it. Albigensians were therefore divided into two groups, a few *perfecti*, who led this higher life, and a multitude of *credentes* ("believers"), who were not yet ready to assume so difficult a burden. Like many other medieval heretics, the Cathari attributed the scandalous corruption of the Catholic clergy to excessive wealth; and the heresy appealed strongly to the nobility of southern France when it encouraged them to purify the church by relieving it of this wealth. The men who seized the wealth need not distribute it among the poor, as Arnold of Brescia and the Waldensians had taught, but might keep it for themselves—provided of course that they felt morally strong enough to resist the temptations it would undoubtedly bring. A surprisingly large number of Cathari were willing to assume this risk, and the church trembled for her possessions. Neverthless, the rank and file of the Albigensians were serious and sober folk whose austere morality was frequently superior to that of their orthodox opponents.

The church found it very difficult to stamp out this nefarious heresy. When preaching proved powerless against it, and when excommunication and interdicts were found equally ineffective, Innocent III decided to launch a general crusade against the Albigensians (1208). As Philip Augustus, king of France, refused to have any share in the enterprise, leadership fell to a French knight—Simon de Montfort, father of the man who later helped found the English parliament. Simon was a high-minded though fanatical idealist, but the pope helped him raise an army by turning the tables on the Albigensians and promising the crusaders that they might keep whatever lands they seized. A wild horde of pious and avaricious warriors swooped down upon unhappy Languedoc, and as the Cathari did not share the evangelical pacifism of the Waldensians, years of bitter fighting ensued. Eventually the heretics were defeated, and in 1229 Languedoc was annexed to France. . . .

St. Francis certainly gave little thought to the suppression of heresy, yet he and his Franciscans were a major factor in checking the spread of Waldensian and similar troubles. They appealed to the same class of persons as the Waldensians, and their appeals were more effective. Countless persons who might otherwise have strayed into heresy now became Franciscans, or at least found satisfaction as members of the "third order," and therefore remained loyal Catholics. Yet even the Franciscans sometimes fell under suspicion. St. Francis managed to remain in the good graces of the church, and the Conventuals caused little trouble, but the Spirituals embarrassed the church greatly by preaching that Christ and his apostles had lived in complete poverty. Within a hundred years of their founder's death, Spiritual Franciscans were being burned at the stake as heretics.

The case was different with St. Dominic (1170–1221), the Spanish founder of the Dominican order. Having received a good education, Dominic was sent in 1205 to preach among the Albigensians of Languedoc. He became convinced that this heresy could best be checked by raising intellectual standards among the Catholic clergy, and to this end he founded the Dominican order in 1215. Like Francis, he insisted that his followers live in poverty, begging their way, but unlike Francis—who held book learning in low esteem—Dominic laid great emphasis upon education. He and his followers probably led few Albigensians back into the Catholic fold, and the heresy was liquidated by the crusaders rather than by the friars. Nevertheless, Dominic and the Dominicans, like Francis and the Franciscans, undoubtedly prevented many Catholics from falling into heresy. In later years the Dominicans became great champions of orthodoxy, often calling themselves *Domini canes*—"watchdogs of the Lord." They even became prominent professors of theology in the universities, the great St. Thomas Aquinas being one of their number.

## The Inquisition

The various heresies prevalent early in the thirteenth century caused the church to standardize its methods of discovering and punishing heretics, which in turn led to the establishment of the Inquisition. Various Roman emperors, especially Theodosius I, had declared heresy to be a capital crime, but the more intelligent Christians of antiquity, such as St. Augustine, preferred that heretics be argued with and, if obdurate, be given spiritual penances or perhaps be fined, but nothing more. In the early Middle Ages the higher clergy usually took the same attitude, and even so redoubtable a foe of heresy as St. Bernard went no further. In their sermons, however, these men inveighed so bitterly against heretics that their more bloodthirsty hearers, whose love of theological truth was emotional rather than rational, sometimes invoked violent measures to rid the world of these pestilential fellows. When heretics were few in number and unpopular, they frequently suffered from lynch law. The secular governments then intervened with severe laws against heresy, partly to preserve the peace, partly to prevent dissensions among the people, partly to pay off old debts to the church. The Emperor Frederick II, who was himself often accused of "atheism" by clerical critics, was one of the first to make heresy a capital offense, but other Christian sovereigns quickly followed his example.

Meantime the church was developing its machinery for deciding whether or not a man was a heretic. At first this duty had fallen to the bishops, but as these officials frequently had neither the skill nor the means nor even the desire to judge carefully (several bishops in Languedoc had become Albigensians), the popes began sending out men of their own, known as "inquisitors," to perform the task. In 1233 Gregory IX announced that thereafter the inquisitors would be chosen from the Dominican order, and during the next few years elaborate rules were issued for their guidance.

These rules have often been criticized as making trials under the Inquisition a travesty of justice. The proceedings were secret, with the judge also serving as accuser; the accused man was never confronted with the witnesses against him, or with their testimony; he was not allowed counsel, and witnesses who defended him were themselves suspected of heresy; and the testimony of two witnesses—even heretics, criminals, or young children—was enough to convict. In 1252 Innocent IV approved the use of torture to procure confessions from suspected heretics. A confession wrung from the accused in the torture chamber had to be repeated "freely" the next day, but the unfortunate man knew that if he failed to repeat it, he would be sent back to the torturers. If the accused confessed at once, and especially if he implicated several other persons, he might get off with a long period of penance and the confiscation of his property, but extreme cases were punished with death by burning at the stake. As church officials might not shed blood, the convicted heretic was handed over to the "secular arm"—the officials of the state—for execution. In characteristic style the inquisitors always urged mercy, though everyone knew that, should a secular judge actually show mercy, he would be excommunicated at once and might even be accused of heresy himself.

Such being the nature of the Inquisition, we are not greatly surprised to find that grave abuses soon appeared. Even in the thirteenth century popes sometimes used the Inquisition to rid themselves of political enemies. Thus one pope accused Manfred of heresy and, when that emperor failed to appear for trial, had him condemned as a contumacious heretic (1266), thereby making the papal crusade against him appear somewhat more respectable. . . . Several years later Boniface VIII excommunicated the whole Colonna family as heretics, but the sentence was reversed when the head of that great family vindicated his orthodoxy by arresting the pope. In the frequent wars that disturbed Italy during the next two centuries, the popes used the Inquisition frequently to advance their personal or family interests, while antipapal writers sometimes charged the pope with being a heretic himself. Kings were equally quick to invoke so valuable an aid. When Philip IV of France decided to despoil the Templars, he first had them convicted of heresy, as well as of other crimes, after using extreme torture to secure confessions. More than a hundred years later the English used the same device to rid themselves of Joan of Arc—now St. Joan. Even private individuals found the Inquisition helpful, not only in liquidating enemies and rivals, but even in escaping from unprofitable contracts, for the church then taught that a Catholic need not keep faith with a heretic. A peculiarly gruesome aspect of the work of the Inquisition was its trial of persons already dead. Thus we have the record of one man who successfully broke a contract by inducing the Inquisition to convict the other party of heresy a full fifteen years after his death. It must be added, however, that the worst of the abuses which have given the Inquisition so bad a name became common only in the fourteenth and fifteenth centuries, when the Middle Ages were tottering to an end and everything essentially medieval was falling into decay.

In the first essay in this volume, we spoke of different societies programming
their people in diverse ways to fit into their particular pattern of culture—
all through history and all over the world. In some cases, deprogramming
and reprogramming have been thought necessary. Indeed, some of the
so-called Jesus freaks have been captured by their concerned parents in
order to bring them back into the particular faith they rejected.

# De-programming Jesus Groups

Marguerite Sullivan

In a San Diego hotel room, a teenage girl sits on the floor, eyes closed,
rocking back and forth:

"Praise you, Jesus. Praise you, Jesus," she murmurs.

Around the hotel room, eight teenagers and adults watch.

"Patty, what is your relationship to Jesus?" one asks.

The girl tosses out a Bible quotation. The other teenagers answer with
another and the debate begins.

It's not Bible study.

The scene is the "de-programming" of what the "de-programmers" call
the "cultists of the Jesus movement," many of whom are brought to San
Diego forcibly by their parents to be de-programmed.

De-programming, essentially, is a parental backlash to youths they
feel have been captivated and "hypnotized" by religious brainwashing.

The de-programming was started more than a year ago by parents in
Parents to Free Our Sons and Daughters from Children of God (COG),
a youth Jesus movement. De-programming is now targeted at other
"cultist" youth groups, they said.

Participants in the de-programming are mainly fundamentalist Christians and youths, who themselves have been de-programmed.

"We're just a group of Christians that share with people who have
been deceived," said Mrs. George Meese of San Diego, one of the de-
programming leaders.

She says de-programming is slated "at where Satan has entered into
the Jesus movement." The youths are released only after they realize
they were "tricked" by "cultist" leaders into false beliefs, she said.

Leaders of the groups affected by de-programming counter that it is
contrary to religious freedom, is illegal and immoral.

From " 'De-programming': Parents Seek to Counter Jesus Groups" by Marguerite Sullivan, *San Diego* (California) *Union*, December 18, 1972, pp. B–1,
B–5. Reprinted by permission of the San Diego Union.

San Diego has become a center for the de-programming with youths being spirited away from the religious communes by their parents to San Diego. They come from all over the nation.

De-programming begins when parents contact one of the de-programming leaders, Mrs. Meese or Ted Patrick, also of San Diego.

Parents often must "kidnap" their youths from the communes, says Patrick, and bring them to an area hotel where they are locked into a room with their parents and five to 10 de-programmers for a day to two weeks "treatment."

Parents often sleep in front of the door to make sure their youngsters don't flee.

The technique in de-programming, said Mrs. Meese, "is to make the youngsters recognize they haven't been using their brains," in questioning the beliefs they were taught in the religious "cults."

De-programming is done, she said, through "positive" interpretation of the Bible, "counter brainwashing" and through an intense question-and-answer marathon.

The "deceptive" views they try to break down, said Mrs. Meese and Patrick are: that God is one of hate and not love; that youths will lose salvation if they leave the movement; that youths must hate their parents "because the Bible says you can't serve two masters"; and other misinterpretations of the Bible.

Many of the youths, said Mrs. Meese, have been told by "cultist" elders that work and school are evil and that all money must be given to the religious movement.

Besides COG, in the last year, youths have been de-programmed from such groups as the Tony and Susan Alamo Christian Foundation in Saugus, the Love-In of New York, Love of Seattle, Love Israel in Seattle, Truth and Light from Colorado, Scientology, and Hare Krishna, said Patrick.

In 90 percent of the cases, said Mrs. Meese, the youngsters (whose ages average from 18 to 23) must be taken forcibly by their parents to San Diego for treatment.

First the youths are asked by de-programmers to explain their relationship to Christ and if they are sure they worship God and not their elders.

As the youths talk about their beliefs, the de-programming team members counter with theirs.

At first, said Mrs. Meese, the youngsters are hostile, then they fast, then become passive and sometimes violent, attempting to escape.

"And then they begin to see we do love them because we keep coming back. They start listening. When they start asking questions, that's the sign they are beginning to use their heads."

"Finally we study the scriptures together and they repent to ask God's forgiveness for being deceived."

After the de-programming, she said, many of the youth feel dependent on the de-programmers. "They want to live in San Diego because they feel secure with the fellows," said Mrs. Meese.

"But our goal is to get them back into society and into Bible-believing churches where you can serve the Lord and go to school and be employed and love your parents."

De-programmers are of several denominations. Mrs. Meese is a member of the Skyline Wesleyan Church and Patrick is active in the Bethel American Methodist Episcopal Church.

Both got into de-programming when their youths flirted briefly with the Children of God group. They started speaking publicly against the movement. When other parents called them to ask advice when their children joined COG, de-programming began.

Patrick, who also does on-site de-programming around the country, said the work is done at no fee. Parents pay only their expenses, usually the hotel room and transportation, he said.

If the youths remain in de-programming long enough, he said, there's a 100 percent success rate.

But there have been some failures. There was the boy who jumped from a second-story San Diego motel room and returned to his New Mexico commune. And Arlene, 23, a divorcee with a 3-year-old daughter returned to the Alamo Foundation after she was brought here by her Los Angeles parents.

After 10-days of de-programming, Arlene convinced an older brother to take her to his home in Los Angeles, where she took a taxi back to the Alamo Foundation. She filed a report with the Los Angeles County Sheriff's deputies complaining her parents had held her against her will. She later dropped the complaint.

Two other recent de-programming subjects have been from the Alamo Foundation, a tax-exempt group, which Mrs. Alamo calls a "basic fundamental Christian evangelistic church." More than 300 members—mostly young people—live at the foundation.

Mrs. Alamo decried de-programming: "The things they are putting people through are a nightmare. They are absolutely held prisoners, subjected to brainwashing 24-hours a day."

She said the de-programmers were not religious leaders and were unqualified "to even discuss the Bible. Who are they to say one is not teaching the Bible?

"There are a lot of churches that one doesn't understand but that doesn't give someone the right to do something like this de-programming."

Many of the Alamo followers, she said, were ex-drug users, whom the foundation had rehabilitated. "Many of the kids' parents are as active in our church as the kids are. Members range from age one to 80."

But the parents who have "kidnaped" their youths from religious communes see de-programming differently.

"De-programming really starts kids to thinking again. It shows them where they were wrong and stimulates their interest again," said Dr. Earl G. Blackburn, of Quakertown, Pa., whose daughter went through de-programming after seven months in COG.

But "recovery," the parents claim, isn't simply a week of de-programming. "It is very deep and long drawn out," said Dr. Blackburn. "They can revert back if you are not careful. Follow-up is essential."

It took him only an hour to give up COG beliefs, he said.

Mrs. Lillian Judd of Hawthorne, N.Y., whose 18-year-old daughter went through de-programming last February, says the "whole experience was the will of God."

When she called her daughter, Susan, from New York at her religious commune, Mrs. Judd said Susan "said God came in vengeance and stressed the idea 'if you hate not your mother and father you cannot be my disciples.'"

"But this was out of context. It means only that you love God before you love other things," said Mrs. Judd.

She said she came across the country to get her daughter out of the commune. "I had to deceive her to get her out by telling her I was taking her to dinner."

Instead they came down to San Diego where Susan was in de-programming for a week.

At first, said Mrs. Judd, Susan "just sat on the floor and rocked back and forth," in what appeared to be a hypnotic state. De-programmers "spoke to her in a calm way" and showed her what had been misinterpreted from the Bible—"and that God was a God of love and not vengeance," said Mrs. Judd.

"It took 24 hours before we could talk to her," she said. Susan said she had been told the government was evil and the church was evil, she said.

Today Susan is working as a waitress and, her mother said, "working to help de-program others."

## Questions

1 The followers of the very unorthodox St. Francis of Assisi demanded conformity to their established pattern. Do nonconformists generally breed conformists? Why or why not?

2 Are there any modern Waldensians? If so, what is the Establishment's reaction to them? If you conclude there are none, why aren't there?

3 Former vice-president Spiro Agnew and Antigone both broke the law. Do you see any differences in their actions or motivations?

4 Do any contemporary American historians blame their own country for negative actions, such as imperialism or waging unjust war, like Thucydides did in his own time?

5 How would you define "constructive rebellion"?

6 What is the difference between the innovator and the critic? What do you think prompts the passive critic to become the radical revolutionary?

7 Does the Inquisition have a contemporary counterpart? Have crimes been committed in the name of a new orthodoxy, "national security"?

8 Is de-programming a teenager against his wishes an infringement of his legal or moral rights? Would you consent to de-programming? Why or why not?

# 9

# Medieval Universities
# Then and Now

Resemblances between certain aspects of university life in the Middle Ages
and the present are remarkable. Then, as now, administrators grappled
with the challenges of university governance and finance, faculties sought
protection for prerogatives such as academic freedom, and students
sought release from the pent-up pressures of pedagogical routines.
The striking similarities, and some of the differences, are shown in the
essay below.

# Campus Capers From Manuscript to Microfilm

Melvin Steinfield

From ornate Carolingian manuscripts to soaring Gothic cathedrals,
from stirring poetry to speculative philosophy, from beautiful tapestries to haunting melodies, from art to science, the contributions of
medieval civilization to the Western heritage are rich and colorful.
Many of these achievements have become a vital part of modern life.

Yet the generalization we stubbornly cling to, in the face of considerable evidence to the contrary, is that the Middle Ages deserves
to be characterized as the "Dark Ages." Both the "Dark Ages" label
and the picture of the Middle Ages as a thousand-year period of
mostly wasted time is an indictment that was handed to us by a biased
little group of Renaissance historians who were so proud of their way
of life that they could not acknowledge objectively their debts to their
medieval forerunners.

Nor could they recognize the worth of the medieval values that
their own age was rejecting with vehement denunciations. Limited by
the perspective of their own historical period, the Renaissance historians created a distorted image which disparaged and minimized the
actual accomplishments of the Middle Ages. Like other writers before
and after, they could not seem to break out of the narrow box of their
own time and place.

Recently, historians began to take a fresh look at some of the neglected aspects of the medieval past. They started their probing research without the Renaissance hangups that have encouraged most
people to frown upon the Middle Ages. This contemporary re-evalua-
tion has produced a more favorable verdict on the nature of the
medieval achievements and shortcomings. It has certainly shed new
light on perhaps the most significant legacy of the Middle Ages: the
University. It has not been adequately stressed that the university is
a creation of the Middle Ages. And that it was surprisingly modern in
many ways.

"The university is a medieval contribution to civilization, and more specifically, a contribution of the twelfth century,"[1] writes one authority, Charles Homer Haskins. Another author notes the connection between the modern university and the medieval university:

> The first debt which the modern university owes to its medieval predecessor is one of existence. Great as were the other civilizations of the past, none of them produced universities as we understand the term today. There is nothing like the continuity of preserving, teaching and finding knowledge that is the glorious history of the medieval universities. Their primary contribution is themselves. Although we have changed some of the methods, added new studies, and multiplied buildings, resources, and faculties, basically the essential idea of the medieval university as a place where an apprentice to learning could become a master of it has remained the same. Our modern universities are perhaps our most medieval organizations.[2]

Thus one must be cautious when confronted with condemnations of the "medieval" elements in the modern university.

The university then, as now, provided the "degree." This degree was the "union card" or ticket to Establishment success; with it one's credentials were sound. Then, as now, the chief motivation for many students was not learning for its own sake, nor the pursuit of truth unto its innermost parts; then, as now, the chief motivation for many students appears to have been the practical one of securing a better job. Another incentive was that students who attended medieval universities were generally exempted from military service.

The facts attest that whether we are talking about superficial matters such as academic dress, or more substantive matters such as approach and organization, the modern university resembles its medieval counterpart quite closely in many ways. The concepts of bachelor's, master's, and doctor's degrees, faculty organizations, lecture methods, and examinations originated in the medieval university. Students wrestled with financial problems and administrators wrestled with the problems of unruly students.

Student recreational activities were well-developed arts and included, but were not limited to, drinking, gambling, loving, and rioting. They were as energetic in the pursuit of fun as today's students. Perhaps even more so:

> The students of the medieval universities were, on the whole, rowdier and more exuberant than students of American universities today, more imaginative in their pranks, and more hostile toward the surrounding towns. Thus the history of medieval

universities is punctuated by frequent town-gown riots. New students were hazed unmercifully; unpopular professors were hissed, shouted down, and even pelted with stones.[3]

Girl-watching was a favorite form of eye-exercise for students who felt they had been hitting the books too much. There were students who ". . . affect rooms overlooking the street to see the girls across the way or those who pass by, or who often appear in church principally on this account, that you may see the ladies!"[4] (At first the universities did not own any buildings; they rented facilities from the townspeople. Students had to arrange their own dormitory deals. Presumably the prices for rooms with a "view" were higher.)

In surveying the varieties of student life on the university campus in the Middle Ages, one soon discovers that girl-watching was often merely a mild prelude to other forms of student affairs:

> Jacob Butrigarius and Baldus write that it is enough to prove a woman a prostitute if students visit her by day and night, without proving the commission of any sexual act, since, when a student talks with such a one, it is not to be presumed that he is repeating the Lord's prayer. And the same Baldus says that the leaser of a house to a student cannot evict him because he has brought prostitutes there and therefore injured the property, since this should have been presumed as a common occurrence.[5]

Another diversion was scribbling sexual epithets on the walls. Heidelberg University still has graffitti from the Middle Ages.

If there was lots of sex on campus, there was also lots of liquor, especially during exam periods. In the medieval university, beer gushed into steins and students poured into town. When both occurred simultaneously townspeople questioned the value of living near a university. Groups of restless students with beer on their breaths roamed the streets in search of excitement. More than once they found it. The rival gangs of students threw rocks, made noise, and in general carried on. Student rampages developed into a major problem:

> Various forms of practical joking of the more violent order enjoyed a high degree of popularity. Among the archives of the University of Leipzig is a "libellus formularis" or collection of forms for rectorial proclamations against the various kinds of disorder which were wont to break out periodically in a medieval university like the recurrent epidemics of pea-shooting, catapulting, and the like at a modern school. Among these is a form of proclamation against destroying trees and crops in the ad-

joining country, against "wandering with arms after the town-hall bell," against throwing water out of the window upon passers-by, against wandering at night and beating the watch . . . against interfering with the hangman . . . in the performance of his duty . . .[6]

It seems that nearly everywhere in medieval European universities students were involved in vigorous releases of surplus calories. When students at Leipzig made throwing stones at professors a regular activity, it became necessary for the administration to devise a scale of ascending punishments for "hitting without wounding" and "wounding without mutilation."

"Oxford students went through the streets with swords and bows and arrows shortly before the hour of curfew and assaulted all who passed by." Students at Rome went "wandering armed from tavern to tavern and other unhonest places. . . ." "The student is much more familiar," says Robert de Sorbon [a founder of the University of Paris], "with the text of the dice, which he recognizes at once, no matter how rapidly they are thrown, than with the text of the old logic." Students at Paris even had to be warned to stop playing dice on the altar of Notre Dame after one of their festival processions.[7]

Thus it can be seen that Medieval students were no less rambunctious than modern students.

Besides the similarity of student recreational activities, there are other ways in which the medieval university was remarkably modern. Competition among universities to attract students is not limited to the twentieth century Big Ten and Ivy League. Charles of Anjou informed the teachers and students of the University of Paris in 1272 that the University of Naples ". . . has just been opened with modern improvements, with assurance of suitable protection, and appropriate favors to help its development." He continued in a modern vein when he cited the attractions of the setting of the university: "This very city . . . is praised for the purity of its air, its comparable and healthful location, its richness in all products of the soil, its convenience for communication by sea with other parts of Italy." His conclusion was a perfect Madison Avenue punchline: "Wherefore [to all beginners and graduates] let them come, in so far as they are able, to this University, as to a great feast which is adorned by the presence of illustrious guests and which overflows with an abundance and variety of refreshing food."[8]

The concept of learning by osmosis was not confined to the modern university student: "And the spoken word of the professor has some occult virtue that penetrates deeper into the mind of the hearer and makes a greater impression upon the memory than private reading. . . ."[9]

The notion of group instruction was unknown in antiquity—it was a contribution of the medieval university. Another concept that originated in the Middle Ages was the formal teaching license. The idea of a general liberal arts curriculum also originated at this time.

In addition to the many similarities between medieval and modern universities, there were several instances in which the medieval university actually outshone the modern one. For example, academic freedom was protected in the thirteenth century more than it has been at times in the twentieth. In the thirteenth century, the Papacy failed on several occasions to prevent the study of Aristotelian philosophy at Paris. It met with less success in thwarting the study of a radical doctrine then than Senator Joseph McCarthy did in the early 1950's. (However, Peter Abelard was driven out of Paris by St. Bernard.)

On the other hand, professors were in a poorer position with respect to their students than has thus far been the case in twentieth-century America. Some student guilds were so powerful that the authority of the faculty looked quite small by contrast. The students at Bologna directly paid and controlled their professors' salaries. According to the 1317 statutes of the University of Bologna, a professor desiring a leave of absence even for a single day had to obtain permission from his own students. That did not leave much time for honeymoon or bereavement unless the students approved.

Whenever faculty, students, and administration acted in unison, they were a formidable force. The mere threat of moving to another town would invariably gain concessions or price reductions from the town merchants who catered to the university food, clothing, and lodging trade. As universities acquired their own buildings, this threat lost its effectiveness. Thus, ironically, greater wealth brought a partial reduction of university power in the community, because the more it gained in material resources, the more intertwined it became in the power structure of the town and the less likely it would be to move to another town.

There were, of course, significant differences between medieval and modern universities. Students and professors could not enjoy the advantages of large modern libraries since, for all practical purposes, they simply did not exist. Emphasis in courses was on learning to master specific authoritative texts. Course selection was much more limited than today. College-sponsored extracurricular events were unheard of. Lectures could not be varied with electronic audio-visual aids, and the general physical comforts of modern technological society were not available in the cold, damp lecture halls. Taken together, these differences meant that the medieval student would have to overcome more severe obstacles to learning than the modern student. But happiness and contentment are relative states of mind. Students through the ages tend to adjust to the conditions of learning.

On the whole, then, the modern university is not as different from the medieval university as is sometimes supposed. "Medieval," therefore, need not be a pejorative term. For it must be remembered that the university as we know it today was essentially a medieval creation. While witch trials were being conducted in Salem, Massachusetts, in the late seventeenth century, the University of Bologna in Italy and the University of Paris in France could point to a history that at that time was already more than five centuries long. And when Harvard College was founded in Cambridge, Massachusetts, in the seventeenth century, it could draw from the rich record of experiences that had been accumulating at Oxford University in England and at Valencia in Spain since the early 1200's.

From the panty raids of the 1950's to the more politically motivated sit-ins and demonstrations of the 1960's, American students (whose oldest university goes back a mere three hundred and fifty years) have been behaving in a manner little different from their counterparts in the Middle Ages—where it all began.

There is no doubt, however, that the radical protests by students and professors during the past decade have seemed to escalate in both intensity and frequency as the issues magnified from mild personal concerns to broad human concerns. Extending dorm privileges provided the issue for some militancy. But the most fervent passions were released over such questions as ROTC and Dow Chemical recruiters on campus and the role of the university in the war machine. Vietnam continued to supply a steady stream of volatility, especially the American and South Vietnamese invasion of Cambodia in the spring of 1970, which led to the Kent State and Jackson State murders, and also the American resumption of bombing during the winter of 1972, just before final peace negotiations were concluded.

While it is difficult to foresee precisely which issues will occupy campus activists during the post-Vietnam period, the history of campuses from Abelard to Ellsberg does not justify any expectation of a quieter atmosphere. From the Gothic to the Atomic Age, one thing has stayed the same: ivy does not grow in silence.

## Notes

1 Charles Homer Haskins, *The Renaissance of the Twelfth Century* (Cambridge, Mass.: Harvard University Press, 1927). Quoted in Brisson D. Gooch, *Interpreting Western Civilization,* Vol. I (Homewood, Ill.: Dorsey, 1969), p. 167.

2 L. J. Daly, *The Medieval University* (New York: Sheed & Ward, 1961), p. 213.

3 C. Warren Hollister, *Medieval Europe—A Short History,* second edition (New York: Wiley, 1968), p. 261–262.

4 Gerald M. Straka, *The Medieval World and Its Transformations,* Vol. II of *Western Society: Institutions and Ideals* (New York: McGraw-Hill, 1967), p. 255.

5 *Ibid.*

6 Hastings Rashdall, *The Universities in the Middle Ages,* F. M. Powicke and A. B. Emden, eds. (London: Oxford University Press, 1958), Vol. 3, p. 426. Quoted in Norman F. Cantor and Michael S. Werthman, *The History of Popular Culture to 1815* (New York: Macmillan, 1968), p. 170.

7 James Westfall Thompson and Edgar Nathaniel Johnson, *An Introduction to Medieval Europe* (New York: Norton, 1937), pp. 735–736. These were quotes by much earlier sources which Thompson and Johnson were reprinting. The last sentence is Thompson and Johnson's own words.

8 *Ibid.*

9 Straka, *op. cit.,* p. 256.

Peter Abelard (1079–1142) was the bold thinker whom students flocked to hear in the formative days of the University of Paris. The introduction to his famous book "Sic et Non" outlines an approach to authority that is distinctively modern in its outlook. Can you see a relationship between Abelard's ideas and the radical protests described in the several articles that follow?

# The Modern Outlook

Peter Abelard

There are many seeming contradictions and even obscurities in the innumerable writings of the church fathers. Our respect for their authority should not stand in the way of an effort on our part to come at the truth. The obscurity and contradictions in ancient writings may be explained upon many grounds, and may be discussed without impugning the good faith and insight of the fathers. A writer may use different terms to mean the same thing, in order to avoid a monotonous repetition of the same word. Common, vague words may be employed in order that the common people may understand; and sometimes a writer sacrifices perfect accuracy in the interest of a clear general statement. Poetical, figurative language is often obscure and vague.

Not infrequently, apocryphal works are attributed to the saints. Then, even the best authors often introduce the erroneous views of others and leave the reader to distinguish between the true and the false. Sometimes, as Augustine confesses in his own case, the fathers ventured to rely upon the opinions of others.

Doubtless the fathers might err; even Peter, the prince of the apostles, fell into error; what wonder that the saints do not always show themselves inspired? The fathers did not themselves believe that they, or their companions, were always right. Augustine found himself mistaken in some cases and did not hesitate to retract his errors. He warns his admirers not to look upon his letters as they would upon the Scriptures, but to accept only those things which, upon examination, they find to be true.

All writings belonging to this class are to be read with full freedom to criticize, and with no obligation to accept unquestioningly; otherwise the way would be blocked to all discussion, and posterity be deprived of the excellent intellectual exercise of debating difficult questions of language and presentation. But an explicit exception must be

From *Sic et Non* by Peter Abelard, from James Harvey Robinson, *Readings in European History,* Vol. I (Boston: Ginn, 1904), pp. 450–451.

made in the case of the Old and New Testaments. In the Scriptures, when anything strikes us as absurd, we may not say that the writer erred, but that the scribe made a blunder in copying the manuscripts, or that there is an error in interpretation, or that the passage is not understood. The fathers make a very careful distinction between the Scriptures and later works. They advocate a discriminating, not to say suspicious, use of the writings of their own contemporaries.

In view of these considerations, I have ventured to bring together various dicta of the holy fathers, as they came to mind, and to formulate certain questions which were suggested by the seeming contradictions in the statements. These questions ought to serve to excite tender readers to a zealous inquiry into truth and so sharpen their wits. The master key of knowledge is, indeed, a persistent and frequent questioning. Aristotle, the most clear-sighted of all the philosophers, was desirious above all things else to arouse this questioning spirit, for in his *Categories* he exhorts a student as follows: "It may well be difficult to reach a positive conclusion in these matters unless they be frequently discussed. It is by no means fruitless to be doubtful on particular points." By doubting we come to examine, and by examining we reach the truth.

"The history of Paris," writes Paul Lacroix, "teems with episodes, some curious, and only too many tragic, which denote the turbulent and seditious tendencies of the University students." In Lacroix's selection below he makes some mention of student militancy but also refers to milder forms of amusement. The games and rampages at the University of Paris were typical of activities engaged in by medieval students at other universities.

# Student Anarchy

Paul Lacroix

But if the books of study used in the ancient schools are now out of date and long since forgotten, such is not the case with the different kinds of recreation in which boys and young men used to indulge as a relaxation from a course of study often abstract and always severe. The *Gargantua* of Rabelais, and the familiar dialogues of Mathurin Cordier, enable us to frame a list of games which are still played, though in some cases under slightly different names; as, for instance, the ball, prisoner's-base, leap-frog, quoits, *clicquette* (pieces of wood, or shords, which were beaten one against another to make them ring), ninepins, bat and trap, spinning-tops and whipping-tops, the *fossette,* or pitch-farthing (which was formerly played with nuts), odd or even, cards, draughts, tennis, heads or tails, tip-cat, etc.

These were the peaceable games of children and scholars, but they were too tame for the turbulent tastes of the older students, whose bad reputation is still proverbial. From all time, grave magistrates, illustrious writers, famous citizens, and even saintly personages have prefaced their career of labor, study, and virtue by a more or less prolonged sowing of wild oats. At all times, moreover, Paris offered only too many temptations to vice and dissipation. It is easy, therefore, to understand what must have been the condition, in the twelfth and thirteenth centuries, when the police as an institution, were hardly known, and when public morality still felt the effects of long years of decadence, of a population of students penned up in a territory which they looked upon as a freehold, consisting, as they did, of youths on the verge of manhood and of full-grown men, belonging to various nationalities, and left to their own passions. When it is further remembered that a degree of arts could not be obtained before the age of one-and-twenty, and one of theology till the age of thirty-five

From *Science and Literature in the Middle Ages and the Renaissance* by Paul Lacroix (New York: Frederick Ungar, 1964), pp. 30–33.

(after eight years' study in the latter case), no wonder that this turbulent quarter was a nuisance, and even a danger for the honest and peaceful inhabitants of Paris.

The whole city was more than once disturbed, and public safety endangered, by the aggressive and disorderly habits of the students. Not a day passed without quarrels and fights, arising out of the most futile causes. The insulting epithets which the students applied to each other show, moreover, the antipathies which prevailed amongst them, and the coarseness which was common to them all. The English had the reputation of being cowards and drunkards; the French were proud and effeminate; the Germans dirty, gluttonous, and ill-tempered; the Normans boastful and deceitful; the Burgundians brutal and stupid; the Flemish bloodthirsty, vagabond, and house-burners; and so forth for the rest.

With all this, the person of a *clerk* (a title appertaining to every student who had obtained his license) was, according to the canons of the Church, inviolable; to lay hands upon a student was to commit a crime which entailed excommunication, and which the Pope alone could absolve. This will explain the audacity and arrogance of the students, and it is no wonder that the civil authorities were, for all the most minute precautions, continually at a loss how to repress the excesses of these riotous youths, who, going about day and night in armed bands, indulged in every kind of disorder, and did not stop at any crime.

The establishment of the colleges led to a decided change for the better. Previously to this happy innovation the students took advantage of the most trifling religious or literary occurrence to increase the number of festivals, which were celebrated with no lack of dancing, masquerades, banquets, etc. All these scholastic rejoicings were afterwards reduced to two *refreshments* (days intended for a carousal), one at the beginning, the other at the end of the public examinations, a period at which the candidates elected a captain from amongst themselves, and to a fête in honor of the patron saint of each nation. This was exclusive of the great festivals celebrated in honor of such and such a *patron* of the University corporation.

Some fascinating questions about the variations in student militancy are raised by one of today's most famous observers of the university scene. In what ways do Barzun's views of campus protest differ from those of Pusey and Hitchcock, authors of the two articles that follow?

# A History of Student Protest

Jacques Barzun

Now that the open season on college presidents has come around again, appointed bodies and self-appointed seers are busy defining the right way to govern academic places. I hope they hit upon useful ideas. But if its primary aim is *study*, there are not sixteen ways of running a college or university. Except for interesting but inessential variations, there are only three, and not all three yield to the same extent the conditions favorable to study.

Let us look at the earliest—student power. We've had it, quite literally: It marked the very beginnings of universities. Since it is returning, full- or half-strength, into the American system, it deserves attention in some detail. The typical precedents are Bologna and Paris. Bologna shows the internal relationships; Paris the day-to-day workings.

In both universities the idea was participation. Authority lay with the general assembly. There was no distinct central organization, but a loose collection of units. The *universitas* or corporation was the name of this grouping, which implied nothing academic. At Bologna, the students soon seized control, thereby expressing the burghers' control of the city. The sons dictated to the professors, and the city fathers backed up the youthful will by law.

For example, professors and doctors could not leave the university, under penalty of death, or even go out of town without permission. They had to swear absolute obedience to the student-elected student rector, who at the behest of the general assembly could pass or change any rule. The students collected the fees, paid the salaries, and issued the working rules: If the teacher cut a class, he was fined; likewise, if he could not draw five students, if he skipped a chapter or a difficulty, or if he kept on talking after the ringing of the bell. At any time the lecturer could be interrupted by a beadle summoning him to appear before the rector and learn of his misdeeds.

As the great historian of universities, Rashdall, puts it—and notice in passing that boycott is the true name for student strike or sit-in: "By means of the terrible power of boycotting which they could bring into play against an offending professor, the student clubs were masters of the situation." Not until Bonaparte conquered Italy five centuries later was a professor again considered fit to be rector of a university.

Rashdall's reference to student clubs brings us to the situation at Paris. Medieval students were divided into "nations," just as the teachers were divided into subject-matter faculties. But the nation soon ceased to denote birthplace and became an arbitrary aggregate. The French nation at Paris included Spaniards, Italians, Greeks, and Levantines; the English took in Flemings, Scandinavians, Finns, Hungarians, Dutch, and Slavs— no British insularity then! These clubs were further divided into cliques, usually based on parish allegiance. Here was no compact group of bourgeois fathers' sons, but an international and vagrant crowd of large proportions. The results for university governance were to be expected— incessant quarrels, shaky alliances, jealous betrayals.

For each nation had to vote as one unit in the assembly and elect a new rector *each month*. They voted also on proctors, beadles, financial officers, examiners, and deans. They also had to choose one ad hoc committee after another to look into endless charges and abuses. In the great year 1266, the papal legate Simon de Brie tried in vain to get the recor's term extended to six weeks, in hopes of reducing the number of contested elections and student defiance of the rectors and the rules. At one time two rectors claimed authority. Simon finally got them both to resign in exchange for a statute permitting a nation to secede and thus escape disputer rules. This feud of 1266 lasted a good fifteen years.

The suggestive point in this truly flexible system is that it went on all fours with the prevailing theory of government—"what affects all must be by the consent of all." It was democracy to the full. A representative body was not supposed to express the collective will of its constituents but to give every individual will a chance. Three students (out of several thousand) could ask for a change of statutes, and officers were elected who specialized in statute-changing.

The frequent elections fitted in with the reigning philosophy. Aristotle had said that no one should be entrusted with any but the briefest tenure of office and that the whole assembly must not only legislate but administer. And student control obviously meant a deal of administering— collecting fees, paying salaries, renting or buying school buildings, watching the financial officers, approving student lodgings, supervising book publishers (copyists), issuing summonses, levying fines, and seeing to the taking of oaths on an unprecedented scale.

All this plus the fights of town and gown and the internal feuds that, according to one authority, were "akin to later international wars in their ferocity and destructiveness," must have made the student life rich and exciting. Everything was an issue, including the hiring of messengers, of which the several nations had from twelve to 160 each. A touching detail of organization was that the rector might bring to the meetings of the assembly his bosom friend as bodyguard.

This elaborate structure so far was all for administration. Not a word yet about the *studium*, the classwork. The rector, students, and (elected) deans looked after it very much as was done at Bologna, that is, by supervising the professors. This arrangement called for certain abilities in the rector, and since the freshmen, who were eligible, often were under the entrance age of fourteen, the Paris rules came to stipulate that the rector must be at least twenty years old.

With these provisions in mind and knowing the ways of youth, one can get a sense of the student-run university of the middle ages. One sees these eager, free-lance, turn-and-turn-about administrators as belonging to the somewhat older group of students and apprentice teachers, the bold and daring, handsome and articulate—those who, like M. Cohn-Bendit [a French revolutionary student organizer in the 1960s] in our day, glory in the feeling of "we do what we like."

One can imagine them angry at the previous administration, impatient with the snarls of bureaucracy that they could so quickly fix by some further rules, exhilarated at the thought of the coming meeting with a good fight in prospect, and ready always for the actual bloodshed on the narrow winding street, if townsmen or a gang from the wrong parish or nation should debouch from the next corner.

And as one describes the scene, one is suddenly hushed at the thought of François Villon [a fifteenth-century French poet] gathering up his genius amid the confusion and surviving as the symbol of an emancipated day. Was he perhaps one of those excluded as "vagabond scholars" from taking part in the making of the curriculum, the degree requirements, the class schedules and examinations, and the plan of festivities? Or was he one of the many non-scholars, those hangers-on mysteriously called "martinets"? No one knows, but some of his brilliance and energy must have existed elsewhere in the mass, or there would have been no medieval university, no medieval mind to write about.

University administration by student groups is not to be sneezed at. It is cheap and never monotonous. By controlling the faculty it certainly prevents the flight from teaching, and it affords the young the pleasure of making their elders hop, skip, and perform. In fighting all of society and themselves, too, the medieval students preserved minority rights to a degree otherwise unexampled. That is, such rights were freely enjoyed by the victors and survivors of the scrimmage. The rest—well, there is a price to pay for every good thing, and the good achieved was the very appealing, youthful kind of life: the free-for-all.

Besides, student power need not be as perpetually violent as it was in the glorious thirteenth century. It can be had at the somewhat lower price of a lack of continuity and a repetition of hopeful errors, for in one student generation experience hardly has a chance to accumulate and make a difference; and who cares in youth about the confusion that comes of injecting practical and political action into the rather different atmosphere of study? So let's gaze fondly back at the happy days of student power.

The second mode of managing universities is illustrated by what happened when the confusion became too great—or at least when it seemed to the neighbors to have got out of hand. A historian of the time who, as legal representative of the university, cannot have been prejudiced against it says: "Studies were in chaos . . . the rooms on one side were rented to students and on the other to whores. Under the same roof was a house of learning and of whoring." There was no reason in the nature of youth itself why this boisterous exercise of self-government and self-indulgence should stop. But by 1500 the scheme was swept away in the collapse of the medieval theory and practice of government. In one short generation—by 1530—a new University of Paris was in being.

The force at work was the rise of the nation state, the movement that gave "nation" its modern meaning. The One Hundred Years' War had shown the country's need for an effective central power to put down disorders and stop the waste. That power was the king, and it was the king who put an end to student power within the university. In 1450, he restrained their excessive feasting. He then ordered the papal legate to reform the university from top to bottom. By 1475 he was imposing a loyalty oath and, soon after, threatening students with a kind of draft. Finally, in 1499, he prohibited their boycotts and strikes.

From then on, whether under king or revolutionary government, dictator or Parliament, continental universities have been ruled by the central authority. The degree of control has varied widely with time and place. Still, out of ancestral respect for learning, the European university has always enjoyed certain privileges. For example, even under the Russian czars the police were forbidden to enter the university, a tradition that curiously persisted through the Russian repression at Prague in the summer of 1968.

No one needs to be told that in times of trouble since 1500 universities under central control have been threatened, dictated to, or shut down;

professors suspended for sedition, exiled for refusing to take oaths, prose-cuted and shot for political crimes, and, from the beginning of the twentieth century, periodically heckled, insulted, or physically attacked by their own students. These appear to be inevitable by-products of making the university political through its link with the state.

Central control is, of course, the opposite of student power, but they have one feature in common—the multiplicity of rules. When codes and tribunals regulate university affairs, the legalistic outlook and the con-tentious temper prevail and warp the emotions appropriate to study. And contrary to expectations, even the management of the university's ma-terial concerns is not thereby improved but worsened. The reason is plain. Both these styles of administration—the anarchical and the auto-cratic—bring to the fore people whose temperaments are the reverse of systematic and studious.

Imagine the American university going down the road it has lately chosen and becoming thoroughly reactionary, which is to say, going back to either of these earlier modes of governance. In the one case, that of student power, we should see the emergence of a new type of academic man, wanting and achieving power at a much younger age than his predecessors—in fact, a graduate student or beginning teacher. He would be a man of strong feelings, caught by some sort of doctrine, ready to drop his work at any time for the turbulence of mass meetings and the stress of political strategy, and not averse to exchanging blows when denunciation, blackmail, and obscenity fail—a man, in short, prepared to strike in all senses of the word; a man given to the life of impulse and self-will, like the old-fashioned duelist, and also given to the heady pleasure of moral indignation; a man ever suspicious—and with good reason; a partisan, but restless, dissatisfied with all arrangements includ-ing his own, because his idealism and his strength alike drive him to find a life totally free of *conditions*.

We need not ask whether men such as this in a reactionary university would wield their power in behalf of an outside political party, as in the Japanese university, and use professors as indentured servants closely supervised. The texture of the straitjacket might be looser owing to the presence of diverse student leaders similarly moved to have their way.

But we cannot doubt that an opposite reaction to central control would bring with it the enforcement of a political orthodoxy. The type of man who would rise in such a system is quickly described: the commissar with a Ph.D. And he too would be a poor provider of the complex physical arrangements prerequisite to study: His mind would be incessantly on things so much higher. Indeed, if one absolutely must have rule from on top, it would be better to put there a retired member of the Mafia seeking to make his peace with God by good works. For he would have no doctrine but order, and after a few faculty-club shootings, seminars would meet on time.

The third mode of university administration is the one we have so rashly abandoned over the space of a few months. The American university was a characteristic creation. Drawing on the old English collegiate model for its best habits, it assumed that the faculty *was* the university, and as such the protector of two great treasures—students and learning. Learning was something to be transmitted to the young and added to when possible. Study was thus the single aim for both faculty and students.

The running of academic affairs by a faculty through a mixture of convention and consensus was, of course, easier when the faculty was small and its members lived so close together. But the triumph of the American universities is that between 1890 and 1950 many of them grew to the size of a town yet kept the spirit and action of the original free university, the university governed not by the one or the many, but by principles.

These principles were simple enough: influence and deference; rationality and civility; above all, reciprocity.

Most people, including some academic men, had, of course, no idea how American or any other universities were run and could discern no principles whatever in the day-to-day operations. So when the cry of tyranny and revolt was raised, they rushed to pull down the fabric, on the assumption that where there's a complaint there must be an evil. The questions of what evil and where it lay precisely were never thought of. Indignation in some, passivity in others conspired to establish as a universal truth that the American university was an engine of oppression, rotten to the core, a stinking anachronism. So down it came.

That it must stay down for a good while appears inevitable from the nature of its former freedom. How was it free? Not because its members were angels and its statutes copied from Utopia but because its concentration on study had brought the world at large to respect its autonomy—hence, no interference from the state—while freedom of thought and speech, academic freedom, had generated within the walls the principles listed above. The free university is that in which the scholar and teacher is free to learn and to teach. He is free because society values and keeps its hands off the double product—the educated student on one side, new knowledge on the other.

Principles, of course, need devices for their application and protection. The American university had evolved some fairly good ones for the purpose:

1) The trustees (or regents or legislative committees), whose defined role showed that they did not own the university, nor were employers of employees: they bestowed tenure as a guaranty against themselves.

2) The administration, conceived again not as bosses but as servants; easily removed if unsatisfactory; in practice, a body that worked like slaves to suit faculty wishes and that protected scholars against trustees as well as against parents and alumni.

3) The professional associations—learned, accrediting, or self-serving like the American Association of University Professors—all upholders of academic freedom.

4) Public opinion and notably the press, which until very recent years could be counted on to respect and defend the individual scholar, researcher, discoverer, expert.

At each level, the attitude of the imperfect beings entrusted with administrative responsibilities was that they could only influence the action of others, not command it; that decisions must be rational and discussions civil; that any signs of strong reluctance after discussion must be deferred to, and that rights and duties, like concessions, must be reciprocal.

This is not to say that the institution always worked like a dream. Friction, abuses, injustice beset all human undertakings. But no one can deny that compared with other institutions, universities enjoyed a government in keeping with their high purpose—government by separation of powers, by consent through committees, and by extensive self-restraint. Within the best universities and colleges there was continuous consultation, a wide tolerance of eccentricity and free-wheeling, a maximum of exceptions and special attention—and these had long since been extended to the students.

In recalling this fast-waning institution, one may indeed think of occasions when the principles were violated. But one should also think of the great diversity of opinion and of purpose that was permitted to flourish, even when challenged. For example: boards of trustees, generally Republican and conservative, allowing leaves to professors working in Washington for the New Deal or for John Kennedy; or in the Thirties ignoring the Communist affiliation even of junior officers without tenure. Go back fifty years and you will think of the protectors of Veblen and his work, of defiant instruction in Marxism, of research and indoctrination in contraception. You will think of President Lowell [of Harvard] saying: "If the Overseers ask for Laski's resignation, they will get mine." Lowell was not exactly a socialist defending a fellow member of his party.

Nor should we forget the common realities of the last half century— the open campus, receptive to all the shocking modern literature and subversive speakers; the college newspapers receiving subsidies from administrations they denounce and insult by name; the frequent public championing of dissent, as when President Brewster of Yale stood between angry alumni and Professor Staughton Lynd.

Fifteen years ago, Walter P. Metzger, the leading authority on academic freedom, summed up the extraordinary character of the American university: "No one can follow the history of academic freedom without wondering at the fact that any society, interested in the immediate goals of solidarity and self-preservation, should possess the vision to subsidize free criticism and inquiry, and without feeling that the academic freedom we still possess is one of the remarkable achievements of man. At the same time, one cannot but be appalled at the slender thread by which it hangs."

When certain students, with encouragement from many sides, cut the thread, they did it (as they thought) in the name of still greater freedom. They wanted a "voice," and, with a trifle of self-contradiction, a "dialogue" on "non-negotiable demands." Sentimentalists believed that the university "bulldozed the student," carried on "a war against the young." The truth is that for years student opinion had been exerting an influence on curriculum and campus rules and habits, not only through free expression in the sacrosanct student paper, but, more importantly, through free access to faculty members and ease of deportment with them. Go to Europe and Asia and see how they "interact" there. Here student reports of bad teachers have affected promotions and choice of men—a force acting from day to day and not only in annually published evaluations.

The common faith in education as an individual right had also made the student's free choice among programs and courses the accepted thing, while the combining of programs, the multiplicity of certificates and degrees, the preservation of credits through all changes of mind—all these practices encouraged the development of the untrammeled self.

To be sure, this student freedom was only freedom to be a student. As long as parents believed in certain mores, there were parietal rules and library fines and some fuss made over cheating at examinations or stealing books from the bookstore. But that was not because the university was tyrannical; it was because, rightly or wrongly, students were thought young and inexperienced and in need of guidance.

Before 1900 and the free elective system, the ancient discipline and professorial control had made students rebellious. From Jefferson's University of Virginia to Charles W. Eliot's Harvard, student hostility and violence were a recurrent problem. It seemed to be resolved by letting the student choose his courses and preparing him for them sooner. He became docile, which means teachable, and he was believed to acquiesce in the fact that he knew less than his teachers, did not own the university, and benefited from what it stood for.

Such was the institution that a couple of years' violence have made into a historical memory. True, the American university had begun to lose its soul through misguided public service, and students had grievances they should have analyzed and publicized. But by organizing hatred instead, by assaulting and imprisoning their teachers, dividing faculties into factions, turning weak heads into cowards and demagogues, ignoring the grave and legitimate causes for reform, advocating the bearing of arms on campus, and preferring "confrontation" to getting their own way, hostile students have ushered in the reactionary university of the future, medieval model.

For it is clear that once the traditions of deference and civility are broken they cannot be knit up again at will. No one can be sure of the future, but the past is not dumb. Medieval student power met its quietus when the aggressive traits of its leaders were, so to speak, taken over by the state. The students, losing their privilege, became subjects like any other and were put down. For the American university there is no telling whether the return to the Middle Ages will not be halted at the phase of royal repression. Already more than half the states have passed acts of control, mild yet menacing by simply being there.

Nobody with a heart and a mind can look forward to the fulfillment of either reactionary hope—it took so long to develop the republic of learning in which *study* was the sole aim and test of the institution! Who can bear to think of reliving 1266 and All That? Still, it will be interesting to watch what happens to the university during the next seven hundred years.

Harvard University, one of the Western world's most renowned and prestigious institutions of higher learning, was like a fortress besieged during the turbulent year of 1969–70. Here its president, in his annual report, assesses the nature of the turmoil that was weathered after great discomfort.

# Earthquake on Olympus

Nathan Pusey

To the members of the Board of Overseers:

Gentlemen: I have the honor to present an eighteenth annual report.

The academic year 1969–70 was filled with anxiety during its passage. Yet now in retrospect it appears to have been a constructive period when attitudes began to alter, and restorative forces reasserted themselves.

There was much to worry about. Fiscally it was the first year during the Pusey administration when the University did not operate safely in the black. But a greater immediate source of apprehension was an almost unbroken series of efforts by various dissident groups to create campus disturbances. These began with a violent attack on the Center for International Affairs shortly after college opened in September. The inciters were a group of fifteen or more men and women few if any of whom appear to have been Harvard students. Two weeks later a group calling itself the November Action Committee (Harvard students were clearly involved this time) staged a noisy "mill-through" in the same Center. In October occurred the Vietnam Moratorium, happily without serious incident here. In November SDS [Students for a Democratic Society] held a "meeting" in the office of the Dean of the College presided over by a former student who had remained in the area to work as an organizer for the Progressive Labor Party after his official separation from the College. A week later occurred another invasion of University Hall and the detention of a dean. Members of the African and Afro-American Association of Students liberated the Dean from the white students restraining him, but then he was subjected to further harassment in the streets. In early December the Organization for Black Unity occupied University Hall. Six days later members of this group demonstrated at the construction site of Gund Hall, following which they invaded the Faculty Club and then again occupied University Hall. They agreed to depart several hours later when Harvard obtained a temporary restraining order.

From the President's Report, Harvard University, 1970, by Nathan Pusey.

323

In February, early in the new semester, SDS held a rally outside University Hall and marched to the Office of Graduate and Career Plans on Dunster Street to confront individuals recruiting for Officers Candidate School. Some seventy to eighty individuals pushed into the building, interfered with interviewing and left after much talk. In March SDS led a sit-in of about ninety people in Pierce Hall to protest recruitment for the Institute of Defense Analysis. There was a further invasion of the Center for International Affairs the following month to affront members of the committee appointed by the Overseers to visit this branch of the University. Some Overseers had personal experience of this unhappy event and of the subsequent harassment which continued in the streets all the way to Harvard Square. In mid-April, as a planned sequel to a much publicized "peace rally" in Boston, young radicals perpetrated a shocking "trashing" in Harvard Square, the first revelation of this hideously destructive tactic in our neighborhood. This time it was unmistakably clear that the offenders included few Harvard participants, and it may be that, except for a scattering of incorrigibles, our students began to be "turned off" from violent tactics by this inexcusable event.

In May, however, there was understandable unrest here and elsewhere following the invasion of Cambodia and the tragic student deaths at Kent State and Jackson State. These events led to a mass rally at Soldiers Field, much animated talk of a strike, two unsuccessful attempts to burn the ROTC building, Shannon Hall, and, following one of these, one poorly attended, half-hearted march on the President's House. At about this time a "free university" set up an unauthorized 24-hour operation in empty Lawrence Hall, which was scheduled shortly to be demolished. During one of the nights of its "liberation" this building caught fire (apparently accidentally) and was almost totally destroyed at the cost of injury to several Cambridge firemen. On the eleventh of May a "militant" picket line again prevented faculty officers and staff from entering University Hall. Three days later there occurred a demonstration outside Massachusetts Hall, in the course of which the Administrative Vice President of the University was roughly handled. Two days after this other officers of the University were prevented from entering Holyoke Center. Further disturbances took place in and around Harvard Square during the summer, including two additional senseless "trashings" in July and August. As if to complete the cycle the academic year 1970–71 began, as had its predecessor, with an attack on the Center for International Affairs, this time with the explosion of a bomb apparently set off by non-Harvard people. Fortunately there was no personal injury and relatively little damage to property.

It is a disgraceful story insofar as it is owed to members of a generation professing superior insight, heightened sensitivity and lively human concern; but there it is, for the record. It is worth observing, however, that with the exception of the tumultuous period in May the numbers involved were never large. Furthermore the more reprehensible acts, the "trashings" and the bombing, appear to have been, if not entirely, at least very largely non-Harvard. Even more heartening is the fact that the marches on Shannon Hall were turned back, not by the few University police on hand at the time, but rather by other aroused students—a very large number of them freshmen—who were resolved to prevent such senseless activity discreditable to all young. I do not know how this change in attitude came about, but it was certainly welcome. In view of the way standards of acceptable behavior in academic communities had been declining for several years there was no reason to expect it. But there, all of a sudden, it appeared on a May evening. One of the small number of police officers, fully resigned to being trampled on as the mob surged toward Shannon Hall, told me later that he and his associates were simply astounded to find students standing *with* them to oppose the rush—astounded and I am sure also immensely pleased. As were all of us who had for so long watched these discouraging developments—the seemingly endless series of affronts to reason and fairness and decency, shameful events which have been perpetrated and even vociferously defended for so long here and on other campuses by "angry" young men and women professing to speak in the name of virtue, as if there could be any virtue in pushing people around and in using force to compel assent.

It must also be recorded that during the past year, in contrast to the previous one, there was a machinery available in the Faculty of Arts and Sciences deliberately designed to deal with cases of discipline resulting from the use of disruptive tactics or force. This Faculty had adopted a statement on rights and responsibilities for members of its academic community in June 1969, and a committee had been designated to succeed the Committee of Fifteen (which had been elected the preceding year to deal with cases arising from the first forcible occupation of University Hall). This committee, made up of faculty and students and charged with responsibility to hear and decide cases of student infringement of articles in the Resolution on Rights and Responsibilities, functioned courageously, discerningly, and effectively through the year. Nearly 100 cases came before this group. Twenty-two students were asked to leave the University for varying periods of time; 28 others were required to withdraw but had their punishment suspended. In the preceding year (following the occupation of University Hall) the connection of 16 students with the University was severed by the Committee of Fifteen. Twenty-five others, required to withdraw, had their penalties suspended. The University is much in debt to those faculty and students who consented to perform this distasteful but very necessary chore. If they had not done so—and exercised their judgment with fairness and firmness, the University could hardly have avoided crippling anarchy. For this they deserve community approbation.

Socrates a long time ago urged that terms not be bandied about loosely, but rather used with precision. Clarity of thought is sharpened in proportion to the clarity of language. Thus far in this chapter there has been the frequent use of the term "radical," as if it includes a single type. In the following 1971 article by this history professor at St. Louis University, distinctions are made between educational, cultural, and political radicals, and some discussion of ideological versus methodological radicalism also is included. It should go a long way toward sharpening the clarity of discussions about campus activism. Can you think of any types of radicalism not included in the article?

# Profile of the Noisemakers

James Hitchcock

The predicament of the radical professor is essentially the same as the predicament of all intellectuals in American society—uncertainty over his own usefulness. In normal times Americans tend to ignore ideas and denigrate their importance; the cliché image of the professor is the absent-minded fuss-budget fiddling harmlessly with esoteric interests, fit to be patronized or ignored. In times of crisis, however, even Philistines lunge at metaphysical explanations of threatening events, and ideas and idea-makers suddenly appear as strong, sinister and highly effective manipulators of reality.

For professors this attitude is usually reversed. In normal times, stung by charges of effete irrelevance, they are likely to insist rather solemnly that "ideas have consequences" and to make sometimes excessive claims on behalf of formal education and its relation to life. In crisis times, however, as citizens in the mainstream angrily accuse them of fomenting rebellion and immorality, they are just as likely to deny all responsibility for student actions and to disclaim all connection between what is taught in the classroom and what occurs on the barricades.

Any attempt to assess the influence of "radical" professors obviously depends on an understanding of the term, and as on most questions the academy's definition is considerably to the left of society's. A radical professor is not, for example, someone who makes speeches against the Vietnam war, votes to sever ties with ROTC, cancels classes in sympathy with an occasional student strike called over a major issue like Kent State, or favors the Princeton Plan whereby students take a vacation from

From "A Short Course in the Three Types of Radical Professors," by James Hitchcock, *The New York Times Magazine*, February 21, 1971. © 1971 by The New York Times Company.|Reprinted by permission. Notes renumbered.

school to campaign for peace candidates. Neither is he someone who would abolish all attempts to regulate student morals or who favors giving students a voice in university affairs. All these positions are generally recognized as "liberal," although on many campuses they are still major issues capable of polarizing the faculty.

It is much more difficult to define what a radical professor is than what he is not, and many who call themselves radicals or who would welcome the epithet are regularly told by other self-styled radicals that in fact they are not radicals at all. Some of the confusion is due to political sectarianism, the claim of various groups on the left that they alone are authentic revolutionaries. But much of it is also due to the fact that there are at least three distinct types of professional (and student) radicalism—educational, cultural and political.

Educational radicals are generally people who look upon the university as a community of primary concern and who see their own task as one of making this community a livelier, richer and more attractive place. Generally, although not always, they favor giving students an equal voice in running the institution. Beyond that they want largely unstructured learning situations, without course requirements, grades, lectures, etc. All learning is to be spontaneous and self-directed. No defined curriculum should exist, and any conceivable subject is open to investigation if students are interested in it. Modes of learning generally considered nonacademic should be utilized, like encounter groups, living in the city, film-making, etc. (Two New York professors, Neil Postman and Charles Weingartner, have developed these ideas in their book, *Teaching as a Subversive Activity*.)

Cultural radicals often have the same concerns as educational radicals, but their focus is beyond the campus. They are indifferent or opposed to all "learning situations," no matter how innovative, since life itself is the great teacher. In this conception the university is merely a youth ghetto where young people forge new life-styles and develop new consciousness through experiments with drugs, sex, communal living, rock music, astrology, etc.

Political radicals are the most familiar type and in certain ways the most old-fashioned, in their acceptance, at least to a degree, of the ideals of disciplined work and abstract rationality (as in Marxian or Marcusean dialectics). Like the cultural radicals they are not primarily concerned with the universities as such and chiefly regard them as convenient bases of operation for effecting social change. They are interested in "democratizing" the schools through open admissions and "politicizing" them through frequent strikes and in the recruitment of students for the propagation of activist causes. Political radicals are innumerable in the professorial ranks. Some of the better-known include Douglas Dowd, a Cornell economist; Howard Zinn, a Boston University political scientist; and John Froines, a University of Oregon chemist who was a defendant in the Chicago Seven conspiracy trial.

There are inevitably some people who are radical in all three senses and many others who, while closely identified with one position, are sympathetic to the others. (Edgar Z. Friedenberg, a University of Buffalo professor of education now on leave teaching in Canada, is notable as an individual associated with all three forms of radicalism.) Frequently, however, there is also antagonism among the various factions. Cultural and political radicals tend to see the educational radicals as provincial in their concern with the university, and hence as trivial. Some educational radicals genuinely fear that the other groups will destroy the universities. Political radicals often accuse cultural radicals of being on "ego trips," turned in on themselves and their own fulfillment, luxuriating in bourgeois gratifications while injustices cry out for action. Cultural radicals in turn see political radicals as uptight, overly intellectual, dictatorial and enslaved to a public role. (The politically radical M.I.T. professor Louis Kampf reports being visited in his class by a squad of cultural radicals exhorting the class to "straighten out your heads." They ended by shooting Kampf with water pistols.)

Professors are abundantly associated with educational and political radicalism but less commonly with cultural radicalism, probably because the latter in effect requires that a man abandon any defined social role. (Timothy Leary, once a Harvard lecturer, took this route; a more recent example is Yale Law professor Charles Reich, author of *The Greening of America*, or Theodore Roszak, the California history professor who wrote *The Making of a Counter Culture*. Professors can, however, continue to teach (and draw their salaries) while promoting educational or political change, and can even look upon their teaching as an instrument to these ends.

In America the professional academic is almost by definition at least mildly alienated from his society, however much a part of the Establishment he may appear to students. Although radicals emphasize the professor's role as a servant of the state and the corporation, until recently most professors tended to choose their vocations almost like monks—they rejected potentially lucrative careers like law and medicine to undertake poorly paid, misunderstood and unappreciated pursuits redeemed by intangibles like good students, leisure and the joys of research. In the nineteen-fifties particularly, a bright young man's choice of an academic career was often a conscious rejection of the allurements which "the world" held out.

Professors, when they think about their situation, are often troubled by their social role, or lack of one. Most reject the idea that a social role is unnecessary. Many are satisfied that they affect society through their students, but this formulation still leaves open the nature of their influence. Some search for a more direct link with society. By temperament they are often observers —contemplative, quizzical, uncommitted. Inevitably the logic of their position leads to social criticism.

The radicalism of the past decade, in which some professors appear to have lost all commitment to an academic discipline or to teaching in the ordinary sense, is related to an earlier phenomenon—the fact that until the Kennedy Administration there were few occupations which a liberal, critical-minded young man could enter without suppressing his beliefs and his hopes for meaningful activity. Many individuals entered academic life because of the freedom and the congenial environment it provided. Living in a society they could not fully accept, many dissatisfied young men could think of nothing better to do than study it.

The emergence of academic radicalism in the nineteen-sixties was thus for some professors a liberation and a delayed fulfillment of youthful dreams—they would have liked to have been political men, but their times prevented them. After a new taste of the world the monk discovered that the cloister could no longer hold him.

Although like most professors radicals do not generally believe that the rewards of their calling are adequate, they also feel a certain guilt at the privileges of their status—leisure, the right to think and speak critically, freedom from the constant need to "produce" on the job. (The accounting demanded in promotion and tenure reviews comes only at infrequent intervals.) They feel compelled, in some way, to justify their special existence. Professorial compulsion to speak out on virtually every public issue is often not arrogance or vanity but the simple belief that if the intellectual will not speak no one else can be expected to.

Nonetheless an obvious gulf separates the genuine radical professor, who approves and engages in direct action, disruption and confrontation, and the academic who, however strong his opinions, is prevented by principle or temperament from going beyond legally tolerated channels of dissent. Many rather crude motives have been advanced to explain professorial radicalism—lust for power, simple arrogance, desire for popularity, search for a lost youth, etc. Many equally simple complimentary motives have been advanced—fierce moral sense, total dedication to truth or teaching by example. No doubt this whole range of motives has its place in the complex of academic radicalism. But for many professors the ultimate root of their radical commitment is a more subtle thing—their uncertain relationship with "the world" and the recurring fear that "reality" is eluding them.

By definition the professor is an élite personage—by education, by status and function, by values and beliefs. The essence of his calling is insubstantial and ethereal—words printed and spoken and those allegedly potent but unseen weapons, ideas. In the beginning these attract the radical with compelling and hypnotic beauty. In an ugly and dishonest world the pure word seems more real than anything else.

But in the end this seduction begins to seem an illusion, especially when others who never chose the academy and the realm of thought— militant blacks, grape-strikers, Latin-American guerrillas, student activists —begin to demonstrate that reality is not as obdurate as the professor had supposed and is far more tractable to their needs than to his words. What was once a phenomenon of paradise—the world of leisured thought and spacious judgment—is revealed as a trap which has destroyed the manhood of the unsuspecting professor.

Academic radicalism is therefore perhaps most often a search to rediscover the "reality" from which the professor now feels profoundly estranged, and his participation is often aimed less at real changes in the world (although in a vague way he does want "the Revolution") than at his own spiritual transformation.

A San Francisco State professor tells how "I was a good boy in the academy. . . . I even wrote three books. . . . One day . . . two big black kids hoisted me up on their shoulders, and I spoke . . . the adrenalin pours into you, the beautiful feeling [that] . . . those of us who were on strike were on the side of life. I say those who did not join . . . actually chose a kind of death."[1]

At every point the professor's radicalism is likely to be a reversal of the values he formerly lived by. Once committed to rationality and balance (especially during the hysteria of the McCarthy era), he now regards these as rather pale and cowardly. He is enormously taken with the student use of invective, slogan and obscenity, and quite envious because of his own clumsiness in these genres. Once preoccupied with high culture and "the best that has been thought and said," he now realizes that truth is most accessible in revolutionary tracts, rock music and the "spontaneous" doings of blacks, students and selected "workers." Formerly a believer in transtemporal ideas and ideals, spirit and values, he now realizes the truth in the Marxist contention that all reality is an expression of class structure and material interests. (Professor Kampf, who is president-elect of the Modern Language Association, reveals how he was deluded in his youthful obsession with 18th-century English literature because, "Neither Swift nor Pope would have received me into his home. Kampf, the Jewish socialist from Washington Heights. . . ." Trying to introduce working-class students to "culture" is a form of oppression, he insists, "a weapon in the hands of those who rule."[2]

The radical metaphor of reality is a simple spatial figure, roughly divided into higher and lower realms. Everything emanating from the "higher"—authority, high culture, tradition, rationality, balance, gentility —is at best suspect and usually pernicious. Everything originating in the "lower"—equality, folk culture, iconoclasm, strong passion, violence, raw experience—holds promise of life and truth. Here educational, cultural and political radicals are momentarily at one, joined at their common source by the educational radical's insistence on democracy and spontaneous learning, the cultural radical's lust after experience and elemental life, and the political radical's faith in "the people."

The fanaticism and unhappiness of the radical professor is necessarily related to his loss of faith in his chosen vocation, a loss of faith rendered inevitable by his new vision of reality, in which books, ideas and discourse, even of a quite radical kind, cannot possibly be genuine or in the last analysis important. For various reasons both selfish and idealistic the professor does not abandon his post, but increasingly he tends to use it as a convenient base of operation for other pursuits. (Thus some professors see prolonged academic strikes not as an interruption in education but the very essence of the process.)

The radical professor is necessarily involved in the continuously troubling struggle to give meaning and relevance (a word now seldom used) to activities he scarcely any longer believes in. Professor Kampf describes how, teaching a seminar on Proust, he was unable to make it real until the meetings were transferred to a room which was serving as a sanctuary for draft-resisters, and Proust could be related directly to what was occurring there. (He does not describe exactly how he related Proust to the sanctuary, but does observe that he will probably not teach Proust again.) When the cultural radicals visited his class, one of the students stripped naked in a successful attempt to nonplus the invaders, and the class became meaningful because the students spent two hours discussing the significance of this action.

This continuous welling up of "life" from the lower half of society— the young and powerless—effectively precludes even the possibility of education in the traditional sense. Professor Kampf rejects the validity of esthetic judgments about literature, because they are demanded by a society which thrives on competition and consumption, and they make real experience of the literature impossible. Each man's perceptions, especially if they are untutored, are correct in themselves. The teaching of literature in the normal way is oppressive, according to Kampf, because students are ashamed when told that their feelings about a particular work are invalid. The prominence of social scientists in the New Left is not accidental, since ultimately this radicalism sees no reality beyond a set of social relationships—a variety of groups and classes all struggling against one another, each of whose claims can only be judged on the basis of how disadvantaged it is with respect to the other groups. There are no values transcending class lines which need to be respected, and thus Professor Kampf maintains that there can be no educational reform outside the context of "specific social objectives."

However, the democratic vision of the professors, like that of the students, tends to founder on the shores of the white working class, since if working-class attitudes are accepted as valid, and if the professor forswears all ambition of imposing his own ideas, the university will have to find a place for the hardhat mentality which seems to flourish amid the working-class young even more than amid their parents. Few radicals seem to be interested in the proposal of Gus Tyler of the International Ladies Garment Workers Union that the campuses should be populated with older people, white- and blue-collar workers on temporary leave from their jobs, to pursue continuing education. Most radicals prefer to see the universities remain ghettos of young people, who are more readily amenable to radical movements of all kinds. (A sincere acceptance of older workers on the campus might entail, for example, serious, appreciative studies of the music of Lawrence Welk, a prospect even the most "democratic" radicals are not prepared for.)

The accusation by conservatives like Spiro Agnew that radical professors are ultimately the cause of student radicalism is therefore an error made by applying a traditional point of view to a wholly new situation. The "democratic" ideology of radical professors prevents them from aspiring to teach students in the ordinary sense, and one useful index of a professor's radicalism is precisely the extent to which he claims to learn more from the students than he teaches them (a claim that is usually not exaggerated). Student radicals are by definition young people who question all values bequeathed from above, and who necessarily mistrust everyone in authority. A professor, even of proven radical credentials, can never be wholly trusted by radical students so long as he continues to hold a job and draw a salary from the university.

Paradoxically "radical" professors may actually have less real influence on most campuses than "liberal" professors. Radical students often enter marriages of convenience with radical teachers, but such students insist on retaining control of their own movements and readily sever all ties with faculty when it suits their purposes. (Radical faculty sometimes do the same.) The most extreme radical young people, like the Weathermen, appear to have almost no sustained and meaningful contact with adults of any kind, and the dynamics of their deepening extremism seem to develop almost entirely within the tight confines of isolated youth ghettos that reject virtually all of the adult world.

By contrast, students who are conservative, moderate, liberal, or merely uncertain often look for faculty leadership. A respected professor known to be "balanced" in his opinions can sometimes have great effect when he takes a stand for a strike or condemns a particular policy of the government or the university. Such faculty not infrequently hold positions of actual leadership in liberal student movements. Faculty thus involved define their roles in various ways, but sometimes they see themselves as conservatives demonstrating that the older generation, and older institutions, can be responsible.

Student radicals are drawn inexorably leftward, finally to the point of desperate acts, by a self-created trap—the expectation of immediate and tangible success in the struggle, which logically requires the continuous rejection of tactics which "don't work" and the adoption of more extreme and risky methods. Professors are often radicalized by a similar self-created trap, albeit a much more complex one. By assuming that the underclasses (especially the young) are more in touch with reality than he is, the professor effectively precludes any criticism of their actions. Indeed the more extreme and irrational their acts, the more "real" they appear and the more ashamed the professor is of his own effeteness. (A Cornell professor is quoted as saying about student terrorists, "God bless them! I will not join them, but God bless them!")

The professorial self-image, formed perhaps in the quiescent Eisenhower years, is part of the same trap. He has justified his life by defining himself as an outsider and a critic of society, and no matter how radical his students become he cannot make the emotional transition to the role of moderator or conservator of traditional values. Thus although prior to about 1964 he may have loved the university and the life of scholarship, he is quite prepared to countenance the destruction of both if the Revolution requires it. To do anything else would be to admit that he is in fact a part of the Establishment, and that he has always deluded himself as to the nature of his true role. The modern intellectual's general commitment to the avant-garde, to innovation, obviously works to the same end, preventing real scepticism with respect to what appears to be the inevitable direction of history.

Most radical professors have probably been surprised and disturbed by outbreaks of systematic violence perpetrated by radical students and the National Guard, and they seek to cope with it through various rationalizations which hint at suppressed guilt feelings. A group of Boston professors is circulating a national letter suggesting that most terrorist acts have been the work of police spies in the student ranks. A few theorists, like the late German radical Theodor W. Adorno, have denied any connection between their ideas and students' actions. Some radical mentors insist that they have been misunderstood. Most adopt the position of not "approving" violence but "understanding" it in the light of unalleviated evils and provocations. But if radical professors are more accurately seen as followers of their students than leaders, they still have some indirect responsibility for their students' beliefs.

Adults who suspect professorial influence behind student actions are commonly misled by the students' penchant for quoting Herbert Marcuse and other older intellectuals, without realizing that only a small fraction of those who quote Marcuse are likely ever to have read him with any care or understanding. Student radicals tend to be quintessentially American in their basic indifference to theory, which sometimes becomes a fierce anti-intellectualism. (Marcuse himself does not approve the students' attacks on the universities, and some young radicals despise him as a cloistered theorizer.) Nonetheless the ideas of the professors are important to the New Left. Ideas are important to action in two ways—they serve to justify it to the world, and they explain it to the person who himself performs the act.

Student radicalism includes levels of articulateness ranging from almost total incoherence to great subtlety and power; some students are masters of intricate theory. But behind even the best articulated radical grievances there are evident deep and inchoate rage, despair and disenchantment which seem to lack an "objective correlative," in T. S. Eliot's phrase. (These feelings are directed, for example, not only at the obvious gross evils in society but also at most of the people who are trying to alleviate these evils, and even at other radicals.) Without the presence of radical professors systematically exposing the "oppressive character" of the entire culture there would undoubtedly still be youthful rebellion, even of the most extreme kind. But it would be a rebellion quite blatantly irrational and nihilistic. The older intellectual performs for the adolescent rebel the service of systematizing his often incoherent feelings, channeling them in specific directions and justifying them under a moral and political rubric. (Nihilistic instincts are validated, for example, by ingenious explanations of how even the smallest facet of American society serves oppressive purposes.) He also gives them a certain respectability by demonstrating that they are actually more rational than the beliefs of apparently "sane" liberals and moderates. (This is done by ignoring the often random character of social reality and postulating a gigantic and highly coordinated "system" in which everything fits, from the Vietnam war to the teaching of poetry.)

Sometimes the radical professor also affects the radicalization of his students in another, generally unintended, more profound way—by the negative example of his own life. The students' deep and perhaps ineradicable cynicism about the entire culture (not only of America but of the whole West), and about institutions like the university, is continually fed by their awareness that so many of the most attractive people of the older generation—intelligent, sympathetic, morally concerned parents, professors, and clergy—are ridden with self-doubt often bordering on contempt and have ceased to believe in the vocation they follow. Kate Haracz, a Michigan State student, describes one of her professors:

> Monday—M.'s travesty. He keeps talking about how the technology of the kindergarten and the technology of the college classroom are essentially the same. It's a recent point, but he ruins it, so I bought a coloring book and crayons. . . . He started out . . . by reading from *Functionaries* . . . suddenly slammed the book on the table, and yelled "Julius Hoffman is a functionary." . . . this is just another stunning example of the simplistic, repeat-the-cool-thing-which-those-in-sociology-circles-say-you-should-say analysis. . . . The man simply repeats blindly the last thing he's heard. . . . today, as he sauntered into the room, you could tell he's made up his mind to be cool. He sat in the back of the room and waited. About 20 minutes after class was supposed to start, he said, "What do you want to do today?" . . . It soon degenerated into another session of liberal breast-beating about values in education and how rotten the System is. I walked out. I've got better things to do than listen to this crap which they all take so seriously like they have just discovered the secret of the universe. They actually think it is daring (and consequently cool) to say that the System reeks. . . . I'm sick of all that tearful, Monday-morning, gutless-wonder soul-searching. . . ."[3]

Young people who regularly encounter adults of this kind would be hard pressed to believe anything good about the "system" even if they are not inclined, and if they are not radicalized by this repeated experience they are at least led to assume that most radical condemnations are justified, since the most apparently concerned people of the older generation are more than eager to confess to any charge leveled at them, and individuals like M. demonstrate the hollowness of the university by their very mode of rebelling against it.

The future of the radical professor is at present an uncertain one, since a wave of reaction seems to be building up which may lead to campus purges. There is some support for this even within the academic community, although the majority of teachers and students in most institutions are probably determined that this shall not happen. The situation is crucially different from the McCarthy era in that it is unlikely that very many people will be prosecuted now solely for their ideas. Professors who formed their principles of academic freedom on the experiences of the nineteen-fifties are now confused by the fact that so many academics have advanced beyond verbal dissent. Some professors have participated in illegal acts like seizing buildings or "unprofessional" acts like disrupting other teachers' classes or refusing to meet their own. Even if the academic community closes ranks around the accused it is not clear that existing laws and customs regarding tenure really protect such persons. In effect the limits of acceptable professorial conduct have broadened enormously in the last five years, but it is not clear whether this is a permanent or an emergency condition, nor is it embodied in law.

By instinct most professors are strongly opposed to outside interference in university affairs and are highly uncomfortable at the thought of any kind of political purge. But the campus battles of the last six years have opened many deep and unhealable wounds, especially in older professors who feel that either in themselves or through their institutions they have been systematically humiliated and repudiated by radical students abetted by radical colleagues. Some radicals also serve fair warning that they will never leave the campuses in peace until they have destroyed them or transformed them totally, and some professors have concluded rather reluctantly that a purge is necessary for the universities' very survival. In most universities the senior faculty still has paramount power, although it is now diluted by student power and other kinds democratization. It is likely that within the next year there will be crucial test cases regarding tenure and promotion which will do much to determine the tolerable limits of dissent in the academy.

Like society, most universities have their silent majorities of both faculty and students, whose sentiments are presumed to be conservative but who generally remain inactive and inarticulate. This academic silent majority, however, is probably a good deal more ambivalent and confused than its political counterpart. Most professors and students are repelled by many features of campus radicalism, but the moral passion and ideological coherence of the radicals continuously forces the intellectual to question to what degree his feelings are prejudiced and self-serving, a defense against unpleasant realities. Typically many academics feel guilty about supporting the radicals, guilty about not supporting them and guilty about doing nothing. They have thus been inordinately affected by events from the outside like police raids, because these momentarily tip the precarious balance in the radicals' favor. By now, how-ever, the campus communities have become sophisticated about the dy-namics of confrontation, and this fact plus recent acts of leftist terrorism has probably led to a determination by most faculty to be open to reform while remaining in active opposition to disruptive methods. It is not clear if this strategy will prove workable.

To a surprising degree normal education seems to have continued at the most agonized institutions during the nineteen-sixties, judging by such external criteria as dissertations completed, books and articles pub-lished, faculty and students recruited, football games played, even classes successfully held. But no one would say that the universities have not changed, or that they will ever again be the same. Beyond the obvious and important changes—student power, intensive recruitment of blacks, more "relevant" curriculums and political awareness—one radical thought has sunk deep into the universities' bones, leaving few people untouched. This is the simple question whether the life of the mind is any longer a legitimate way of existence, and whether the search for truth is not a self-indulgent evasion of the searing demands for active life in society. Whether these questions are seen as the product of a new and penetrating moral vision, or as the incessant beating of a fanatic rhetoric on tender consciences, they persist, and there are few professors now prepared to answer them with total confidence.

## Notes

1 Quoted from *Commentary*, August, 1969, p. 8.

2 This and other mentions of Professor Kampf refer to his article in *Change*, May-June, 1970, pp. 27–34.

3 Quoted from *Change*, May-June, 1970, pp. 20, 24, 25.

## Questions

1 Is Peter Abelard's route to learning effective? Have you been encouraged to use this method in any of your classes?

2 Is the function of the university to teach knowledge for its own sake or to prepare students for jobs?

3 What were the advantages and disadvantages of the stu-dent-controlled medieval universities? If you were given more power in your institution, what would be your goals?

4 Does Barzun appear unduly pessimistic about the future of American higher education?

5 Did the violence at Harvard University effect any changes? If violence does produce changes, is the violence then justified?

6 Should professors who join radical students to demand immediate solutions be punished? Is dismissal appropriate punishment?

7 Describe the ideal teacher (professor).

# 10

# Art and Life

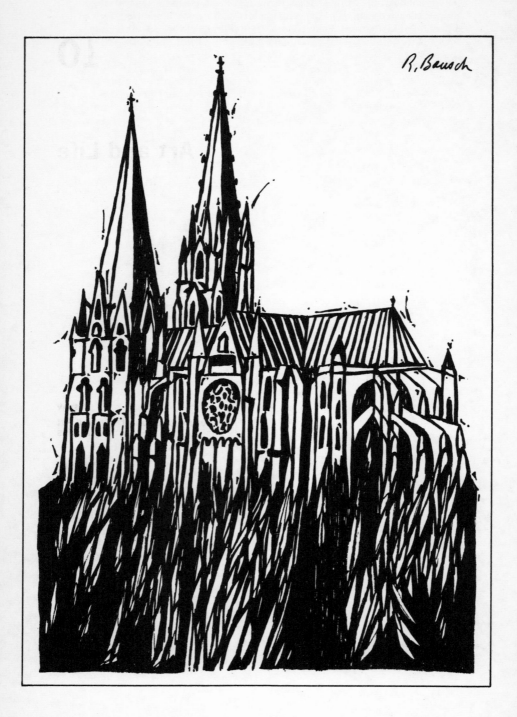

Because imaginative individuals have been involved in art throughout history and prehistory, the world is much the richer. Products of these gifts range from the cave paintings of Cro-Magnon Man to the contents of New York's Museum of Modern Art. Each culture, from primitive to so-called civilized, has had its unique style in painting, sculpture, architecture, dress, and music; art is as varied as the imaginations of the peoples who have inhabited the planet. It has been said that Richard Wagner, with his stirring nationalistic musical compositions, made art a serious social concern for the modern age. But art was a serious social concern long before—in the Middle Ages, for instance. What was there about art that made it so important to medieval peoples? Was it art for art's sake as such or was art used as a crutch to support other needs in life?

# The Imagination of Life and Art

Frederick Gentles

Art has served man as a means to decorate and beautify his temples, public buildings, homes, dinner tables, wagons, boats, snowmobiles, and dune buggies. It has given pleasure to eye, ear, nose, and tongue, and it has pleased the mind as poetry, drama, and literature. Art may be intellectualized, as when one interprets the mystic smile of the Mona Lisa or the philosophy of Pope's *Essay on Man*, but more often it is just to be experienced as symbolic of something that stirs the senses or the spiritual emotions. Everywhere, there has been art for useful purposes and also art for art's sake. Imagination and a little knowledge have been keys to getting involved.

Imagination stems from the word image—to picture or to create an impression in the mind's eye. There is something intellectual about the process of imagining, of course, but there is something sensual at the same time. One might marvel at the intellectual ingenuity of building skyscrapers in the Middle Ages, admiring the skill of the architects, stone-cutters, masons, glaziers, sculptors, carpenters, aerialists, and theologians in creating a great cathedral of towering walls, colorful stained-glass windows, ornate portals, soaring pillars, and intricate rose windows. On the other hand, Henry Adams, in his rhapsodic description of Notre Dame de Chartres, favors the sensual values when he suggests returning to playing dolls again in order to appreciate this great medieval cathedral. "If you can go back to them, and get rid for one small hour of the weight of custom, you shall see Chartres in glory." We do not come to this marvelous building for instruction, he says, but only for "a sense of what those centuries had to say, and a sympathy with their ways of saying it." This is imagination, and without it there is little or no appreciation of a work of art. One gives life to stone, paint, and sound by intelligently interpreting a work or just letting the experience of the eye, ear, and mind soak into the body—something like playing dolls again.

Arnold Hauser in his *Social History of Art* contrasts the sensuality of the classical art of Greece and Rome with the spirituality of the Middle Ages, when Christian art did not serve aesthetic or sensual purposes so much as spiritual or godly purposes. This dimension of art was so powerful that by the seventh and eighth centuries people were alleged to be worshipping statues and paintings as magic, protective, and sacred objects, and sometimes taking an image itself for the incarnation of a saint or Christ as God. In the Eastern Roman (or Byzantine) Empire, a campaign was directed against the worship of icons (religious paintings) as a form of idolatry. The worship of images was considered to be dangerous and subversive of religion. After a struggle lasting about 100 years, the iconoclasts, or image breakers, were defeated; icons were then restored in homes and churches. Many of the iconoclasts joined the Islamic faith, in which images were not permitted to interfere with a person's concentration upon the one God, Allah. However, the mosques of the followers of the prophet Muhammad were elaborately decorated with colorful geometric figures and mosaics, and the architecture of some mosques was as inspirational as the contemporary Romanesque and Gothic churches in Christian Europe.

Religion and art were intertwined with everyday living, from the baptismal font at birth to the Gregorian chants and illuminated scriptural pages highlighting confirmation, marriage, communion, and burial rituals in parish churches. The most beautiful of these churches in the later Middle Ages were often dedicated to the most revered figure in Christianity, the Virgin Mary, or Our Lady (Notre Dame) of this city or that —Laon, Soissons, Chartres, Paris, Amiens, Reims, and so on. She watched over the city from her queenly palace, usually in the center city, and people from all walks of life, burghers, knights, kings, and peasants competed for her favor—and not just on Sunday at 11 A.M.

But art was more than a spiritual experience to medieval people. Art was life in many other forms. To the kings and princes, art was a display of wealth and beauty in the form of stylized crowns, necklaces, bracelets, medals, tapestries, oak furniture, or whatever else the commissioned artists and artisans were instructed to create. To the nobility of lords, knights, and ladies, art was fine dress in many colors, expensive armored suits, lances, swords, tables set with flowers and a variety of foods, and troubadors, minnesingers, and clowns to entertain. Royalty and nobility often collected works of art purely for avarice and pride and as a means of concentrating their wealth in tangible goods, much as today collectors are buying Picassos and Rembrandts not so much for their beauty but as a hedge against inflation.

The burgher, though busy earning his daily bread, found time to enjoy contests of song to determine the meistersinger of the town, poetry competitions, wandering minstrels, mimes, and magicians, in addition to working on and worshipping in the town church. If the lowly peasants were too far away from town, at least they had the sunsets, bird song and bird flight, wild flowers, gurgling brooks, and the sound of rain on the roof; that is, if they had the imagination to bring beauty and awe to these natural phenomena. Life with its art escaped no one with some imagination because it served practical purposes in providing pleasures to the senses, solace to the spirit, and security to the collecting impulse.

Professor Huizinga, author of the third reading in this chapter, suggests that medieval art was principally *applied* art. It had meaning that people could easily understand, experience, and apply directly to their lives. Beauty enhanced a work, of course, but it was not necessary to it. The symbol created by the imagination was more important. A rough wooden cross might inspire as much piety as a decorative gold one, a simple church as much devotion as a Gothic masterpiece. Imagination might be brought as easily to one as to the other, depending on the fancy of the individual. Art was part of the reality of life. It was real.

But it might be unreal at the same time. It might act as a narcotic to transfer a person into another world, emotionally or spiritually. The avidity with which a person uses the imagination, or plays dolls again, determines the degree to which he may move into another world. A Wagnerian opera, *Siegfried*, for instance, may send a modern listener directly back into the medieval forest. An illuminated manuscript might transport a busy but imaginative New Yorker back to a monastery near Augsburg, Germany, in the year 1075. Jacques Barzun, in writing of the medieval love story, "Tristan," says that "Art as the embodiment of feeling was a surcease from the pain of reality, a narcotic, like love." It was, then, a means of escape from reality. At times, the reality of life in the Middle Ages was pretty grim, and escape was necessary.

Unreality must be a part of life, too, especially for the very imaginative person. But what is reality and unreality? Who were the realists—those who revered the icons or those who destroyed them, the iconoclasts? Who were the realists—those who collected art for security or those who used art to fortify their religious spirits? Who were closer to reality—the kings with their precious jewels or the peasants who were next to the soil and nature? Could there be an immaterial reality? In any case, art was useful, and whether it was real or unreal does not really matter. As long as it can be enjoyed, who cares?

What is art? Here anthropology professor Adamson Hoebel of the University of Minnesota gives his definition. He also discusses art among primitive peoples and decorative art from that on simple tools to the façade hiding the internal combustion engine.

# What Is Art?

Adamson Hoebel

The urge to beautify is one of the most interesting and unique, certainly one of the most remarkable, characteristics of the human being. It is, as seen by Justice Oliver Wendell Holmes, "one of the glories of man that he does not sow seed and weave cloth, and produce all the other economic means simply to sustain and multiply other sowers and weavers. . . . After the production of food and cloth has gone on a certain time, he stops producing and goes to the play, or he paints a picture or asks unanswerable questions about the universe, and thus delightfully consumes a part of the world's food and clothing."[1] Unlike so many of the basic drives that may be more or less directly linked to the imperatives of biological survival, the aesthetic and artistic drives are much more obscure in their origins and functions. Man could survive without art, yet man and art are inseparable. To be artless is to be dehumanized. Not without reason are the arts and belles lettres known as the *humanities*.

By art is meant the overt expression of impulses in line, form, color, rhythm, and tone, as in drawing, painting, sculpture, dance, music, and literature. The impulses are both emotive and rational, but feeling tone predominates over thought.

The basic function of art as art is to release tensions by enabling the artist to externalize some of his emotions and ideas in an objective way. The release of the tensions brings satisfaction and pleasure. The viewers of the art object, if it has meaning to them, are stimulated to sensuous perceptions that likewise produce emotional responses ultimately resolving into pleasurable feelings of euphoria and balance. This is not to deny, however, that the artistic experience may be highly disturbing and may even cause the artist great discomfiture while running its course. The expression of art begins in a state of tension and the process of translation of feelings into high artistic form is not easy.

Thus even from the individualistic point of view, art never exists literally for art's sake alone. It exists for psychophysiologic reasons. And because our scientific knowledge of the physiology of emotion is as yet so crude, we understand little of the workings of the artistic impulses. Aesthetics (the study of beauty), remains almost entirely a branch of philosophy, for beauty is still subjective, as far as our understanding of it goes.

But art may not be seen in its entirety if analyzed only from the individualistic point of view. Art is also a social expression, and inevitably it becomes a part of culture. Further, since man is always a creature of society and the child of culture, art *ipso facto* serves social as well as individual interests and needs. Art is inextricably tied to religion and magic. Yes, and to politics. It cannot help expressing and reflecting social relations and systems. It can serve to sustain them, as Renaissance art served medieval Christianity; or it can strive to destroy them, as does the anarchistic art of the Dadaists who hold modern civilization to be so false and meaningless that the honest artist can only lampoon it with ridiculing combinations of line and color.

### What Is Primitive Art?

The only safe answer to this question is that primitive art is the art of primitive peoples. It is impossible to define primitive art merely as crude art, for some primitive forms of artistic expression are exceedingly complex. It is impossible to label it as "childish," for some primitive art is precocious in technique and sophisticated in ideology. It is impossible to identify it as naturalistic, for some primitive art is highly stylized and conventionalized. The art of primitive peoples runs a wide gamut from technical clumsiness to high skill, from childlike simplicity to confusing complexity, from naturalism and realism to conventionalized abstraction.

Even when we eliminate the more florid forms of primitive art from our consideration and concentrate on the arts of the most primitive of known peoples, this is still true. Bushman art is naturalistic and full of vitality. . . . Australian art is highly stylized and in certain forms is abstract and symbolic. Eskimo art is naturalistic and technically quite sophisticated. . . . Shoshone art is almost nonexistent.

No qualities that universally characterize primitive art can be adduced from the art of primitive peoples, unless it be that no primitives ever solved the problem of perspective—with which most of them never dealt.

The so-called "primitivists" in recent Occidental art are not true primitives. In stripping down their art forms to what they see as essential simplicity, they are not necessarily emulating primitive art, even though they have been consciously influenced by the art of certain primitive peoples, especially African sculpture.

The "primitives" of early American painting cannot be considered truly primitive either. They were only the untutored early representatives of an American offshoot of the European cultural tradition. They are called

The Nootka Indians on Vancouver Island painted the walls of their wooden houses with scenes of tribal legend. The section portrayed here is *Lightning Snake, Wolf, and Thunder Bird on Killer Whale, c.* 1850. Courtesy of the American Museum of Natural History, New York.

*primitives* only because they were early nineteenth century with reference to a very limited art history, and because they were crude in their technique.

Since, as most art students now agree, an art can be aesthetically the art of a culturally primitive people without itself being primitive, primitive art must be defined by extraartistic means, viz., its association with a preliterate culture.

### Decorative Art

Decorative art is the work of the artisan, not the artist. It is the embellishment of an artifact. Plains Indian moccasins were embroidered with dyed porcupine quills. Later, when traders made colored beads available, beadwork replaced quillwork. Basket makers find that variations in twilling produce interesting and pleasing designs within the structure of the basket. They discover that the use of varicolored fibers makes possible tasteful coil and twill work. . . . Potters discover that slips, painting, and sculptural detail make infinite variety a potentiality in ceramic production. Clay vessels can be mere household articles, or, by attention to decorative line and form, they can be transformed into objects of pure beauty. . . . Rawhide boxes could have been left as crude and undecorated as our corrugated shipping cartons. But Plains Indians preferred to decorate them with geometric designs in color.[2] A lime spatula could be a simple stick, but the natives of eastern New Guinea prefer to carve out a handle with painstaking skill. Northern Shoshones were content with roughed-out spoons of mountain-sheep horn, but Northwest Coast Indians worked intricate totemic designs into their handles. . . .

These are all examples of decorative embellishment—superfluous modification in line, form, or color of useful articles—superfluous in the sense that they do not contribute to the utilitarian effectiveness of the article. But they please their owner, impress his guests, and whet the acquisitive appetites of museum collectors.

A valid principle seems to be that as soon as a people solves the fundamental technical problems in the production of an artifact or tool, the artistic impulse begins to assert itself. The more aesthetically endowed individuals begin to play with the surface in an effort to increase the pleasing potentials of the object.

These motifs stem from flat and cylindrical stamps that were often used to decorate pottery. The stamps shown here all represent human figures. From Jorge Encisco, *Design Motifs of Ancient Mexico,* Dover Publications, Inc.

The history of automobile design compresses the whole process within the span of a generation. Motors were first attached to carriages with only as much modification of the erstwhile horse-drawn vehicle as the mechanical needs of the device dictated. The problem was to make a four-wheeled vehicle that was automotive; inventive concern was almost wholly concentrated on mobile power and its problems. By 1935 these problems, so far as the internal-combustion engine is concerned, were for the most part mastered. Creative interest shifted more and more to body design and appearance until by 1940 in Detroit the industrial artist had almost superseded the automotive engineer in importance.

As a rule, technique must first be mastered before decorative art worthy of being called art develops. Beyond mastery of technique, the more leisure the subsistence techniques and resources of a people's culture allow, the greater the likelihood of decorative embellishment. This must not, however, be taken as a bald assertion that leisure produces art. It may or may not. Surplus energies and time may be directed into other channels to satisfy other interests, such as war, trading, or games.

Decorative art may be purely *formal*, or it may be *representative*. Formal decoration is characterized by its concentrated emphasis upon form and design without reference to meaning or thought. Examples of this would be the perfect shaping of a pottery bowl, the turning of a beautiful rim. Designs in coiling, weaving, and twilling that come out of the arrangement of warp and weft, the introduction of decorative bands about the rims of baskets through the process of binding the edges to avoid raveling, are further examples of formal decoration that results primarily from industrial technique. However, formal decoration not imposed by technical needs is world-wide. Decorative bands incised or painted about the neck of a pot or the edges of a box are purely *super-imposed* on the functional structure of the artifact. Such formal design elements are not extensions of technique, but rather expressions of the universal *feeling for form* that prompts man to emphasize the form of his object.

Thus, the ubiquitous formal decorative art that has been so assiduously studied by anthropologists and so generally spurned by art historians ("because it is not *pure* art") springs from two fundamental sources. As Boas has put it, such art "is not necessarily expressive of purposive action," i.e., the artisan is not consciously producing an artistic product, but rather it is based upon "reactions to forms that develop through mastery of technique" and secondly, "the formal interest is directly due to the impression derived from the form. It is not expressive in the sense that it conveys a definite meaning or expresses an aesthetic emotion."[3]

Decorative art may also be representative, i.e., the design or figure may portray some object. It presumes to represent the real thing. If the representation is faithful to the original model, it is said to be *natural*, or naturalistic, as was European cave art, or as are the delightful dancing figures with their long limbs, narrow torsos, and fluid movements conceived by the Bushman. The meaning of *style* in representative art can be quickly grasped by comparing Egyptian naturalistic representation of dancers with the Bushman's. . . .

## Notes

1  O. W. Holmes, Jr., "Law in Science and Science in Law," *Collected Legal Papers*, p. 212.

2  Cf. L. Spier, "Plains Indian Parfleche Designs," *University of Washington Publications in Anthropology*, Vol. 4, No. 3, 1931, pp. 293–322.

3  F. Boas, *Primitive Art* (Oslo, 1929), pp. 62–63.

Kenneth Clark denies that the history of civilization is the history of art, but
he does assert that art is a vital part of civilization. You can generally
believe art, he says. Art tells us something about other peoples as well as
about ourselves.

# Civilization and Art

Kenneth Clark

I am standing on the Pont des Arts in Paris. On one side of the Seine
is the harmonious, reasonable façade of the Institute of France, built as
a college in about 1670. On the other bank is the Louvre, built continuously from the Middle Ages to the nineteenth century: classical
architecture at its most splendid and assured. Just visible upstream is the
Cathedral of Notre Dame—not perhaps the most lovable of cathedrals,
but the most rigorously intellectual façade in the whole of Gothic art.
The houses that line the banks of the river are also a humane and reasonable solution of what town architecture should be, and in front of them,
under the trees, are the open bookstalls where generations of students
have found intellectual nourishment and generations of amateurs have
indulged in the civilized pastime of book collecting. Across this bridge,
for the last one hundred and fifty years, students from the art schools of
Paris have hurried to the Louvre to study the works of art that it contains, and then back to their studios to talk and dream of doing something
worthy of the great tradition. And on this bridge how many pilgrims from
America, from Henry James downwards, have paused and breathed in
the aroma of a long-established culture, and felt themselves to be at the
very center of civilization.

What is civilization? I don't know. I can't define it in abstract terms—
yet. But I think I can recognize it when I see it; and I am looking at it
now. Ruskin said: "Great nations write their autobiographies in three
manuscripts, the book of their deeds, the book of their words and the
book of their art. Not one of these books can be understood unless we
read the two others, but of the three the only trustworthy one is the last."
On the whole I think this is true. Writers and politicians may come out
with all sorts of edifying sentiments, but they are what is known as
declaration of intent. If I had to say which was telling the truth about
society, a speech by a Minister of Housing or the actual buildings put
up in his time, I should believe the buildings.

From pp. 1–7 (excluding illustrations) in *Civilisation* by Kenneth Clark.
Copyright © 1969 by Kenneth Clark. By permission of Harper & Row, Publishers, Inc., and John Murray (Publishers) Ltd./B.B.C. Publications.

But this doesn't mean that the history of civilization is the history of art—far from it. Great works of art can be produced in barbarous societies—in fact the very narrowness of primitive society gives their ornamental art a peculiar concentration and vitality. At some time in the ninth century one could have looked down the Seine and seen the prow of a Viking ship coming up the river. Looked at today in the British Museum it is a powerful work of art; but to the mother of a family trying to settle down in her little hut, it would have seemed less agreeable—as menacing to her civilization as the periscope of a nuclear submarine.

Prow of a Viking ship. Trustees of the British Museum, London.

An even more extreme example comes to my mind, an African mask that belonged to Roger Fry. I remember when he bought it and hung it up, and we agreed that it had all the qualities of a great work of art. I fancy that most people, nowadays, would find it more moving than the head of the Apollo of the Belvedere. Yet for four hundred years after it was discovered the Apollo was the most admired piece of sculpture in the world. It was Napoleon's greatest boast to have looted it from the Vatican. Now it is completely forgotten except by the guides of coach parties, who have become the only surviving transmitters of traditional culture.

Whatever its merits as a work of art, I don't think there is any doubt that the Apollo embodies a higher state of civilization than the mask. They both represent spirits, messengers from another world—that is to say, from a world of our own imagining. To the Negro imagination it is a world of fear and darkness, ready to inflict horrible punishment for the smallest infringement of a taboo. To the Hellenistic imagination it is a world of light and confidence, in which the gods are like ourselves, only more beautiful, and descend to earth in order to teach men reason and the laws of harmony.

Fine words: and fine words butter no parsnips. There was plenty of superstition and cruelty in the Graeco-Roman world. But, all the same, the contrast between these images means something. It means that at certain epochs man has felt conscious of something about himself—body and spirit—which was outside the day-to-day struggle for existence and the night-to-night struggle with fear; and he has felt the need to develop these qualities of thought and feeling so that they might approach as nearly as possible to an ideal of perfection—reason, justice, physical beauty, all of them in equilibrium. He has managed to satisfy this need in various ways—through myths, through dance and song, through systems of philosophy and through the order that he has imposed on the visible world. The children of his imagination are also the expressions of an ideal.

Western Europe inherited such an ideal. It had been invented in Greece in the fifth century before Christ and was without doubt the most extraordinary creation in the whole of history, so complete, so convincing, so satisfying to the mind and the eye, that it lasted practically unchanged for over six hundred years. Of course, its art became stereotyped and conventional. The same architectural language, the same imagery, the same theatres, the same temples—at any time for five hundred years you could have found them all round the Mediterranean, in Greece, Italy, France, Asia Minor, or North Africa. If you had gone into the square of any Mediterranean town in the first century you would hardly have known where you were, any more than you would in an airport today. The so-called Maison Carrée at Nîmes is a little Greek temple that might have been anywhere in the Graeco-Roman world.

A reconstructed model of the interior of the Parthenon with the figure of Athena, which stood forty feet tall. The Metropolitan Museum of Art, The Williard Collection, 1883–1894.

Nîmes isn't very far from the Mediterranean. Graeco-Roman civilization stretched much further than that—right up to the Rhine, right up to the borders of Scotland, although by the time it got to Carlisle it had become a bit rough, like Victorian civilization on the North-West Frontier. It must have seemed absolutely indestructible. And of course some of it was never destroyed. The so-called Pont du Gard, the aqueduct not far from Nîmes, was materially beyond the destructive powers of the barbarians. And a vast mass of fragments remained—the Museum at Arles is full of them. "These fragments have I shored against my ruin." When the spirit of man revived, they were there to be imitated by the masons who decorated the local churches: but that was a long way off.

What happened? It took Gibbon six volumes to describe the decline and fall of the Roman Empire, so I shan't embark on that. But thinking about this almost incredible episode does tell one something about the nature of civilization. It shows that however complex and solid it seems, it is actually quite fragile. It can be destroyed. What are its enemies?

Well, first of all fear—fear of war, fear of invasion, fear of plague and famine, that make it simply not worthwhile constructing things, or planting trees or even planning next year's crops. And fear of the supernatural, which means that you daren't question anything or change anything. The late antique world was full of meaningless rituals, mystery religions, that destroyed self-confidence. And then exhaustion, the feeling of hopelessness which can overtake people even with a high degree of material prosperity. There is a poem by the modern Greek poet, Cavafy, in which he imagines the people of an antique town like Alexandria waiting every day for the barbarians to come and sack the city. Finally the barbarians move off somewhere else and the city is saved; but the people are disappointed—it would have been better than nothing. Of course, civilization requires a modicum of material prosperity—enough to provide a little leisure. But, far more, it requires confidence—confidence in the society in which one lives, belief in its philosophy, belief in its laws, and confidence in one's own mental powers. The way in which the stones of the Pont du Gard are laid is not only a triumph of technical skill, but

Pont du Gard aqueduct at Nîmes. Editorial Photocolor Archives.

shows a vigorous belief in law and discipline. Vigor, energy, vitality: all the great civilizations—or civilizing epochs—have had a weight of energy behind them. People sometimes think that civilization consists of fine sensibilities and good conversation and all that. These can be among the agreeable *results* of civilization, but they are not what make a civilization, and a society can have these amenities and yet be dead and rigid.

So if one asks why the civilization of Greece and Rome collapsed, the real answer is that it was exhausted. And the first invaders of the Roman Empire became exhausted too. As so often happens, they seem to have succumbed to the same weaknesses as the people they conquered. It's misleading to call them barbarians. They don't seem to have been particularly destructive—in fact, they made some quite impressive constructions, like the Mausoleum of Theodoric: a bit heavy and megalithic compared to the little Greek temple at Nîmes—the shallow dome is a single piece of stone—but at least built with an eye to the future. These early invaders have been aptly compared to the English in India in the eighteenth century—there for what they could get out of it, taking part in the administration if it paid them, contemptuous of the traditional culture, except insofar as it provided precious metals. But unlike the Anglo-Indians, they created chaos; and into that chaos came real barbarians like the Huns, who were totally illiterate and destructively hostile to what they couldn't understand. I don't suppose they bothered to destroy the great buildings that were scattered all over the Roman world. But the idea of keeping them up never entered their heads. They preferred to live in pre-fabs and let the old places fall down. Of course, life must have gone on in an apparently normal way for much longer than one would expect. It always does. Gladiators would have continued to fight each other in the amphitheatre of Arles; plays would still have been performed in the theater of Orange. And as late as the year 383 a distinguished administrator like Ausonius could retire peacefully to his estate near Bordeaux to cultivate his vineyard (still known as Chateau Ausone) and write great poetry, like a Chinese gentleman of the T'ang dynasty.

Civilization might have drifted downstream for a long time, but in the middle of the seventh century there appeared a new force, with faith, energy, a will to conquer and an alternative culture: Islam. The strength of Islam was its simplicity. The early Christian Church has dissipated its strength by theological controversies, carried on for three centuries with incredible violence and ingenuity. But Mahomet, the prophet of Islam, preached the simplest doctrine that has ever gained acceptance; and it gave to his followers the invincible solidarity that had once directed the Roman legions. In a miraculously short time—about fifty years—the classical world was overrun. Only its bleached bones stood out against the Mediterranean sky.

The old source of civilization was sealed off, and if a new civilization was to be born it would have to face the Atlantic. What a hope! People sometimes tell me that they prefer barbarism to civilization. I doubt if they have given it a long enough trial. Like the people of Alexandria they are bored by civilization; but all the evidence suggests that the boredom of barbarism is infinitely greater. Quite apart from discomforts and privations, there was no escape from it. Very restricted company, no books, no light after dark, no hope. On one side the sea battering away, on the other infinite stretches of bog and forest. A most melancholy existence, and the Anglo-Saxon poets had no illusions about it:

> A wise man may grasp how ghastly it shall be
> When all this world's wealth standeth waste
> Even as now, in many places over the earth.
> Walls stand wind beaten,
> Heavy with hoar frost; ruined-habitations . . .
> The maker of men has so marred this dwelling
> That human laughter is not heard about it
> And idle stand these old giant works.

Art is not only to be appreciated for its own sake, it is to be used, and the people of the Middle Ages used it in many ways. It was used to fortify the religious need and give elegance to church and ritual, provide the ego with a display of wealth and finery, challenge the imagination with tales of battle and adventure, and please the ear with songs of love and devotion. It added dimension to life, and Professor Huizinga of the University of Leyden in the Netherlands, explains how and why.

# Art and Life

J. Huizinga

## Art and Life

If a man of culture of 1840 had been asked to characterize French civilization in the fifteenth century in a few words, his answer would probably have been largely inspired by impressions from Barante's *Histoire des Ducs de Bourgogne* and Hugo's *Notre Dame de Paris*. The picture called up by these would have been grim and dark, scarcely illuminated by any ray of serenity and beauty.

The experiment repeated today would yield a very different result. People would now refer to Joan of Arc, to Villon's poetry, but above all to the works of art. The so-called primitive Flemish and French masters— Van Eyck, Rogier van der Weyden, Foucquet, Memling, with Claus Sluter, the sculptor, and the great musicians—would dominate their general idea of the epoch. The picture would altogether have changed its color and tone. The aspect of mere cruelty and misery as conceived by romanticism, which derived its information chiefly from the chronicles, would have made room for a vision of pure and naïve beauty, of religious fervor and profound mystic peace.

It is a general phenomenon that the idea which works of art give us of an epoch is far more serene and happy than that which we glean in reading its chronicles, documents, or even literature. Plastic art does not lament. Even when giving expression to sorrow or pain it transports them to an elegiac sphere, where the bitter taste of suffering has passed away, whereas the poets and historians, voicing the endless griefs of life, always keep their immediate pungency and revive the harsh realities of bygone misery.

Now, our perception of former times, our historical organ, so to say, is more and more becoming visual. Most educated people of today owe

From *The Waning of the Middle Ages* by J. Huizinga. Reprinted by permission of Edward Arnold, Ltd.

their conception of Egypt, Greece, or the Middle Ages, much more to the sight of their monuments, either in the original or by reproductions, than to reading. The change of our ideas about the Middle Ages is due less to a weakening of the romantic sense than to the substitution of artistic for intellectual appreciation.

Still, this vision of an epoch resulting from the contemplation of works of art is always incomplete, always too favorable, and therefore fallacious. It has to be corrected in more than one sense. Confining ourselves to the period in question, we first have to take into consideration the fact that, proportionately, far more of the written documents than of the monuments of art have been preserved. The literature of the declining Middle Ages, with some few exception, is known to us fairly completely. We have products of all genres: the most elevated and the most vulgar, the serious and the comic, the pious and the profane. Our literary tradition reflects the whole life of the epoch. Written tradition, moreover, is not confined to literature: official records, in infinite number, enable us to augment almost indefinitely the accuracy of our picture.

Art, on the contrary, is by its very nature limited to a less complete and less direct expression of life. Moreover, we only possess a very special fraction of it. Outside ecclesiastical art very little remains. Profane art and applied art have only been preserved in rare specimens. This is a serious want, because these are just the forms of art which would have most clearly revealed to us the relation of artistic production to social life. The modest number of altar-pieces and tombs teaches us too little in this respect; the art of the epoch remains to us as a thing apart from the history of the time. Now, really to understand art, it is of great importance to form a notion of the function of art in life; and for that it does not suffice to admire surviving masterpieces, all that has been lost asks our attention too.

Art in those times was still wrapped up in life. Its function was to fill with beauty the forms assumed by life. These forms were marked and potent. Life was encompassed and measured by the rich efflorescence of the liturgy: the sacraments, the canonical hours of the day and the festivals of the ecclesiastical year. All the works and all the joys of life, whether dependent on religion, chivalry, trade, or love, had their marked form. The task of art was to adorn all these concepts with charm and color; it is not desired for its own sake, but to decorate life with the splendor which it could bestow. Art was not yet a means, as it is now, to step out of the routine of everyday life to pass some moments in contemplation; it had to be enjoyed as an element of life itself, as the expression of life's significance. Whether it served to sustain the flight of piety or to be an accompaniment to the delights of the world, it was not yet conceived as mere beauty.

One of the more familiar sculptures from the ancient world, King Mycerinus and Queen, c. 2525 B.C., made of painted slate. Courtesy of the Museum of Fine Arts, Boston.

Consequently, we might venture the paradox that the Middle Ages knew only applied art. They wanted works of art only to make them subservient to some practical use. Their purpose and their meaning always preponderated over their purely aesthetic value. We should add that the love of art for its own sake did not originate in an awakening of the craving for beauty, but developed as a result of superabundant artistic production. In the treasuries of princes and nobles, objects of art accumulated so as to form collections. No longer serving for practical use, they were admired as articles of luxury and of curiosity; thus the taste for art was born which the Renaissance was to develop consciously.

In the great works of art of the fifteenth century, notably in the altar-pieces and tombs, the nature of the subject was far more important than the question of beauty. Beauty was required because the subject was sacred or because the work was destined for some august purpose. This purpose is always of a more or less practical sort. The triptych served to intensify worship at the great festivals and to preserve the memory of the pious donors. The altar-piece of the Lamb by the brothers Van Eyck was opened at high festivals only. Religious pictures were not the only ones which served a practical purpose. The magistrates of the towns ordered

A French Gospel Lectionary from the 13th century shows the manner in which lettering and manuscript illustration was a highly developed art in Europe before the invention of the printing press. Trustees of the British Museum, London.

representations of famous judgments to decorate the law courts, in order to solemnly exhort the judges to do their duty. Such are the judgment of Cambyses, by Gerard David, at Bruges; that of the Emperor Otto, by Dirk Bouts, at Louvain; and the lost pictures by Rogier van der Weyden, once at Brussels.

The following example may serve to illustrate the importance attached to the subjects represented. In 1384 an interview took place at Lelinghem for the purpose of bringing about an armistice between France and England. The duke of Berry had the naked walls of the old chapel, where the negotiating princes were to meet, covered with tapestry representing battles of antiquity. But John of Gaunt, duke of Lancaster, as soon as he saw them on entering, demanded that these pictures of war should be removed, because those who aspire to peace ought not to have scenes of combat and of destruction before their eyes. The tapestries were replaced by others representing the instruments of the Passion.

. . .

## The Aesthetic Sentiment

The study of the art of an epoch remains incomplete unless we try to ascertain also how this art was appreciated by contemporaries: what they admired in it, and by what standards they gauged beauty. Now, there are few subjects about which tradition is so defective as the aesthetic sentiment of past ages. The faculty and the need of expressing in words the sentiment of beauty have only been developed in recent times. What sort of admiration for the art of their time was felt by the men of the fifteenth century? Speaking generally, we may assert that two things impressed them especially: first, the dignity and sanctity of the subject; next, the astonishing mastery, the perfectly natural rendering of all the details. Thus we find, on the one hand, an appreciation which is rather religious than artistic; on the other hand, a naïve wonder, hardly entitled to rank as artistic emotion. The first to leave us critical observations on the painting of the brothers Van Eyck and Rogier van der Weyden was a Genoese man of letters, of the middle fifteenth century, Bartolomeo Fazio. Most of the pictures he speaks of are lost. He praises the beautiful and chaste figure of a Virgin, the hair of the archangel Gabriel, "surpassing real hair," the holy austerity expressed by the ascetic face of Saint John the Baptist, and a Saint Jerome who "seems to be alive." He admires the perspective of the cell of Jerome, a ray of light falling through a fissure, drops of sweat on the body of a woman in a bath, an image reflected by a mirror, a burning lamp, and landscape with mountains, woods, villages, castles, human figures, the distant horizon, and, once again, the mirror. The terms he uses to vent his enthusiasm betray merely a naïve curiosity, losing itself in the unlimited wealth of details, without arriving at a judgment on the beauty of the whole. Such is the appreciation of a medieval work by a mind which is still medieval.

*The Annunciation* by Jan van Eyck, *c.* 1441. Formerly an altar wing, this has been transferred to canvas. National Gallery of Art, Washington, D.C., Andrew Mellon Collection.

A century later, after the triumph of the Renaissance, it is just this minuteness in the execution of details which is condemned as the fundamental fault of Flemish art. According to the Portuguese artist, Francesco de Holanda, Michelangelo spoke about it as follows:

> Flemish painting pleases all the devout better than Italian. The latter evokes no tears, the former makes them weep copiously. This is not a result of the merits of this art; the only cause is the extreme sensibility of the devout spectators. The Flemish pictures please women, especially the old and very young ones, and also monks and nuns, and lastly men of the world who are not capable of understanding true harmony. In Flanders they paint, before all things, to render exactly and deceptively the outward appearance of things. The painters choose, by preference, subjects provoking transports of piety, like the figures of saints or of prophets. But most of the time they paint what are called landscapes with plenty of figures. Though the eye is agreeably impressed, these pictures have neither art nor reason; neither symmetry nor proportion; neither choice of values nor grandeur. In short, this art is without power and without distinction; it aims at rendering minutely many things at the same time, of which a single one would have sufficed to call forth a man's whole application.

. . .

Musical sensation was immediately absorbed in religious feeling. It would never have occurred to Denis [a medieval monk of the strict Carthusian Order] that he might admire in music or painting any other beauty than that of holy things themselves.

One day, on entering the church of Saint John at Bois-le-Duc, while the organ was playing, he was instantly transported by the melody into a prolonged ecstasy.

Denis was one of those who objected to introducing the new polyphonous music into the church. Breaking the voice (*fractio vocis*), he says, seems to be the sign of a broken soul; it is like curled hair in a man or plaited garments in a woman: vanity, and nothing else. He does not mean that there are not devout people whom melody stimulates into contemplation, therefore the Church is right in tolerating organs; but he disapproves of artistic music which only serves to charm those who hear it, and especially to amuse the women. Certain people who practiced singing in melodic parts assured him they experienced a certain pleasurable pride, and even a sort of lasciviousness of the heart (*lascivia animi*). In other words, to describe the exact nature of musical emotion the only terms he can find are those denoting dangerous sins.

From the earlier Middle Ages onward many treatises on the aesthetics of music were written, but these treatises, constructed according to the musical theories of antiquity, which were no longer understood, teach us little about the way in which the men of the Middle Ages really enjoyed music. In analyzing musical beauty, fifteenth-century writers do not get beyond the vagueness and naïveness which also characterized their admiration of painting. Just as, in giving expression to the latter, they only praise the lofty character of the treatment and the perfect rendering of nature, so in music only sacred dignity and imitative ingenuity are appreciated. To the medieval spirit, musical emotions quite naturally took the form of an echo of celestial joy. "For music"—says the honest rhetorician Molinet, a great lover of music, like Charles the Bold—"is the resonance of the heavens, the voice of the angels, the joy of paradise, the hope of the air, the organ of the Church, the song of the little birds, the recreation of all gloomy and despairing hearts, the persecution and driving away of the devils." The ecstatic character of musical emotion, of course, did not escape them. "The power of harmony"—says Pierre d'Ailly—"is such that it withdraws the soul from other passions and from cares, nay, from itself."

The heavy Romanesque abbey off the rugged coast of Brittany is dedicated to Saint Michael—Mont-Saint-Michel. It is strong and masculine, like old cognac, says the American essayist Henry Adams, and is quite in contrast to the light and bright Gothic cathedral at Chartres, with its famous stained-glass windows, tall spires, and thin pillars. Chartres is dedicated to the Virgin Mary—Our Lady or Notre Dame in the French—and is delicate and feminine, like sparkling champagne. In this selection by the one-time professor of medieval history at Harvard and a direct descendant of two early American presidents, one experiences two of the arts at the same time: the beautiful and highly imaginative prose of the author and the architectural masterpiece he is describing.

# The Virgin of Chartres

Henry Adams

We must take ten minutes to accustom our eyes to the light, and we had better use them to seek the reason why we come to Chartres rather than to Rheims or Amiens or Bourges, for the cathedral that fills our ideal. The truth is, there are several reasons; there generally are, for doing the things we like; and after you have studied Chartres to the ground, and got your reasons settled, you will never find an antiquarian to agree with you; the architects will probably listen to you with contempt; and even these excellent priests, whose kindness is great, whose patience is heavenly, and whose good opinion you would so gladly gain, will turn from you with pain, if not with horror. The Gothic is singular in this; one seems easily at home in the Renaissance; one is not too strange in the Byzantine; as for the Romans, it is ourselves; and we could walk blindfolded through every chink and cranny of the Greek mind; all these styles seem modern, when we come close to them; but the Gothic gets away. No two men think alike about it, and no woman agrees with either man. The Church itself never agreed about it, and the architects agree even less than the priests. To most minds it casts too many shadows; it wraps itself in mystery; and when people talk of mystery, they commonly mean fear. To others, the Gothic seems hoary with age and decrepitude, and its shadows mean death. What is curious to watch is the fanatical conviction of the Gothic enthusiast, to whom the twelfth century means exuberant youth, the eternal child of Wadsworth, over whom its immortality broods like the day; it is so simple and yet so complicated; it sees so much and so little; it loves so many toys and cares for so few

From *Mont-Saint-Michel and Chartres* by Henry Adams (Boston: Houghton Mifflin, 1933), pp. 87–93. Reprinted by permission of the publishers.

necessities; its youth is so young, its age so old, and its youthful yearning for old thought is so disconcerting, like the mysterious senility of the baby that

> Deaf and silent, reads the eternal deep
> Haunted forever by the eternal mind.

One need not take it more seriously than one takes the baby itself. Our amusement is to play with it, and to catch its meaning in its smile; and whatever Chartres may be now, when young it was a smile. To the Church, no doubt, its cathedral here has a fixed and administrative meaning, which is the same as that of every other bishop's seat and with which we have nothing whatever to do. To us, it is a child's fancy; a toy-house to please the Queen of Heaven—to please her so much that she would be happy in it—to charm her till she smiled.

The Queen Mother was as majestic as you like; she was absolute; she could be stern; she was not above being angry; but she was still a woman, who loved grace, beauty, ornament—her toilette, robes, jewels;—who considered the arrangements of her palace with attention, and liked both light and color; who kept a keen eye on her Court, and exacted prompt and willing obedience from king and archbishops as well as from beggars and drunken priests. She protected her friends and punished her enemies. She required space, beyond what was known in the Courts of kings, because she was liable at all times to have ten thousand people begging her for favors—mostly inconsistent with law—and deaf to refusal. She was extremely sensitive to neglect, to disagreeable impressions, to want of intelligence in her surroundings. She was the greatest artist, as she was the greatest philosopher and musician and theologist, that ever lived on earth, except her Son, Who, at Chartres, is still an Infant under her guardianship. Her taste was infallible; her sentence eternally final. This church was built for her in this spirit of simple-minded, practical, utilitarian faith—in this singleness of thought, exactly as a little girl sets up a doll-house for her favorite blonde doll. Unless you can go back to your dolls, you are out of place here. If you can go back to them, and get rid for one small hour of the weight of custom, you shall see Chartres in glory.

The palaces of earthly queens were hovels compared with these palaces of the Queen of Heaven at Chartres, Paris, Laon, Noyon, Rheims, Amiens, Rouen, Bayeux, Coutances—a list that might be stretched into a volume. The nearest approach we have made to a palace was the Merveille at Mont-Saint-Michel, but no Queen had a palace equal to that. The Merveille was built, or designed, about the year 1200; toward the year 1500, Louis XI built a great castle at Loches in Touraine, and there Queen Anne de Bretagne had apartments which still exist, and which we will visit. At Blois you shall see the residence which served for Catherine de Medicis till her death in 1589. Anne de Bretagne was trebly queen, and Catherine de Medicis took her standard of comfort from the luxury of Florence. At Versailles you can see the apartments which the queens of the Bourbon line occupied through their century of magnificence. All put together, and then trebled in importance, could not rival the splendor of any single cathedral dedicated to Queen Mary in the thirteenth century; and of them all, Chartres was built to be peculariarly and exceptionally her delight.

One has grown so used to this sort of loose comparison, this reckless waste of words, that one no longer adopts an idea unless it is driven in with hammers of statistics and columns of figures. With the irritating demand for literal exactness and perfectly straight lines which lights up every truly American eye, you will certainly ask when this exaltation of Mary began, and unless you get the dates, you will doubt the facts. It is your own fault if they are tiresome; you might easily read them all in the "Iconographie de la Sainte Vierge," by M. Rohault de Fleury, published in 1878. You can start at Byzantium with the Empress Helena in 326, or with the Council of Ephesus in 431. You will find the Virgin acting as the patron saint of Constantinople and of the Imperial residence, under as many names as Artemis or Aphrodite had borne. As Godmother . . . , Deipara . . . , Pathfinder . . . , she was the chief favorite of the Eastern Empire, and her picture was carried at the head of every procession and hung on the wall of every hut and hovel, as it is still wherever the Greek Church goes. In the year 610, when Heraclius sailed from Carthage to dethrone Phocas at Constantinople, his ships carried the image of the Virgin at their mastheads. In 1143, just before the flèche on the Chartres clocher was begun, the Basileus John Comnenus died, and so devoted was he to the Virgin that, on a triumphal entry into Constantinople, he put the image of the Mother of God in his chariot, while he himself walked. In the Western Church the Virgin had always been highly honored, but it was not until the crusades that she began to overshadow the Trinity itself. Then her miracles became more frequent and her shrines more frequented, so that Chartres, soon after 1100, was rich enough to build its western portal with Byzantine splendor. A proof of the new outburst can be read in the story of Citeaux. For us, Citeaux means Saint Bernard, who joined the Order in 1112, and in 1115 founded his Abbey of Clairvaux in the territory of Troyes. In him, the religious emotion of the half-century between the first and second crusades (1095–1145) centered as in no one else. He was a French precursor of Saint Francis of Assisi who lived a century later. If we were to plunge into the story of Citeaux and Saint Bernard we should never escape, for Saint

Bernard incarnates what we are trying to understand, and his mind is further from us than the architecture. You would lose hold of everything actual, if you could comprehend in its contradictions the strange mixture of passion and caution, the austerity, the self-abandonment, the vehemence, the restraint, the love, the hate, the miracles, and the scepticism of Saint Bernard. The Cistercian Order, which was founded in 1098, from the first put all its churches under the special protection of the Virgin, and Saint Bernard in his time was regarded as the apple of the Virgin's eye. Tradition as old as the twelfth century, which long afterwards gave to Murillo the subject of a famous painting, told that once, when he was reciting before her statue the "Ave Maris Stella," and came to the words, "Monstra te esse Matrem," the image, pressing its breast, dropped on the lips of her servant three drops of the milk which had nourished the Savior. The same miracle, in various forms, was told of many other persons, both saints and sinners; but it made so much impression on the mind of the age that, in the fourteenth century, Dante, seeking in Paradise for some official introduction to the foot of the Throne, found no intercessor with the Queen of Heaven more potent than Saint Bernard. You can still read Bernard's hymns to the Virgin, and even his sermons, if you like. To him she was the great mediator. In the eyes of a culpable humanity, Christ was too sublime, too terrible, too just, but not even the weakest human frailty could fear to approach his Mother. Her attribute was humility; her love and pity were infinite. "Let him deny your mercy who can say that he has ever asked it in vain."

Saint Bernard was emotional and to a certain degree mystical, like Adam de Saint-Victor, whose hymns were equally famous, but the emotional saints and mystical poets were not by any means allowed to establish exclusive rights to the Virgin's favor. Abélard was as devoted as they were, and wrote hymns as well. Philosophy claimed her, and Albert the Great, the head of scholasticism, the teacher of Thomas Aquinas, decided in her favor the question: "Whether the Blessed Virgin possessed perfectly the seven liberal arts." The Church at Chartres had decided it a hundred years before by putting the seven liberal arts next her throne, with Aristotle himself to witness; but Albertus gave the reason: "I hold that she did, for it is written, 'Wisdom has built herself a house, and has sculptured seven columns.' That house is the blessed Virgin; the seven columns are the seven liberal arts. Mary, therefore, had perfect mastery of science." Naturally she had also perfect mastery of economics, and most of her great churches were built in economic centers. The guilds were, if possible, more devoted to her than the monks; the bourgeoisie of Paris, Rouen, Amiens, Laon, spent money by millions to gain her favor. Most surprising of all, the great military class was perhaps the most vociferous. Of all inappropriate haunts for the gentle, courteous, pitying Mary, a field of battle seems to be the worst, if not distinctly blasphemous; yet the greatest French warriors insisted on her leading them into battle, and in the actual melee when men were killing each other, on every battlefield in Europe, for at least five hundred years, Mary was present, leading both sides. The battle cry of the famous Constable du Guesclin was "Notre-Dame-Guesclin"; "Notre-Dame-Coucy" was the cry of the great Sires de Coucy; "Notre-Dame-Auxerre"; "Notre-Dame-Sancerre"; "Notre-Dame-Hainault"; "Notre-Dame-Gueldres"; "Notre-Dame-Bourbon"; "Notre-Dame-Bearn";—all well-known battle cries. The King's own battle at one time cried, "Notre-Dame-Saint-Denis-Montjoie"; the Dukes of Burgundy cried, "Notre-Dame-Bourgogne"; and even the soldiers of the Pope were said to cry, "Notre-Dame-Saint-Pierre."

The measure of this devotion, which proves to any religious American mind, beyond possible cavil, its serious and practical reality, is the money it cost. According to statistics, in the single century between 1170 and 1270, the French built eighty cathedrals and nearly five hundred churches of the cathedral class, which would have cost, according to an estimate made in 1840, more than five thousand millions to replace. Five thousand million francs is a thousand million dollars, and this covered only the great churches of a single century. The same scale of expenditure had been going on since the year 1000, and almost every parish in France had rebuilt its church in stone; to this day France is strewn with the ruins of this architecture, and yet the still preserved churches of the eleventh and twelfth centuries, among the churches that belong to the Romanesque and Transition period, are numbered by hundreds until they reach well into the thousands. The share of this capital which was— if one may use a commercial figure—invested in the Virgin cannot be fixed, any more than the total sum given to religious objects between 1000 and 1300; but in a spiritual and artistic sense, it was almost the whole, and expressed an intensity of conviction never again reached by any passion, whether of religion, of loyalty, of patriotism, or of wealth; perhaps never even parallelled by any single economic effort except in war. Nearly every great church of the twelfth and thirteenth centuries belonged to Mary, until in France one asks for the church of Notre Dame as though it meant cathedral; but, not satisfied with this, she contracted the habit of requiring in all churches a chapel of her own, called in English the "Lady Chapel," which was apt to be as large as the church but was always meant to be handsomer; and there, behind the high altar, in her own private apartment, Mary sat, receiving her innumerable suppliants, and ready at any moment to step up upon the high altar itself to support the tottering authority of the local saint.

# Medieval Music

Percy M. Young

Up to the time of the Norman conquest of England [1066] the peoples of Europe were concerned with the reconstruction of the various units of society from the ruins of the formerly powerful Empire of Rome. What was left of that imperialism remained in the attitude and government of the Church, which imposed some sort of uniformity in doctrine and in organization through the medium of Latin. As has been seen there was within the Church some scope for originality of expression at least through the visual arts, in which many regional characteristics were to be found. Such deviation was less easy in music, because of the lack of a means whereby original ideas could be adequately represented in written form, and because of the tight hold kept on music by ecclesiastical authority.

Any organization, whether secular or religious, tends toward a conservative (i.e. conserving) point of view in respect of the arts; for by drawing attention to tradition and by emphasizing its virtues the organization implies its own durability and power. The story of church music in the medieval period is that of those who did not wish for any change in fundamentals and those who did; between those who were suspicious of new ideas and those who welcomed them.

During that period church music also began to lose its privileged position. Nations arose under the leadership of strong kings, round whom developed court rituals and traditions in which music played an important part. Nominally Church and State were one, and medieval Christian monarchs did not appear deliberately to usurp the artistic property of the Church; but royal music stood out more and more in contrast to sacred music. Gradually it made contact with the music of the

From *Music and Its Story* by Percy M. Young (New York: Roy Publishers, n.d.; introduction dated March 1960), pp. 46–51, 53–60. Reprinted by permission of Roy Publishers and Dennis Dobson.

people, and this fusion ultimately led to the enrichment of music as an art.

Between the eleventh and the fifteenth centuries most of the great cathedral churches of Europe were built. The Romansque style was succeeded by the more fluent Gothic, and each city of importance was dominated by the clustered spires that symbolized authority and aspiration. Within the churches windows were filled with brilliant stained glass, such as remains at Chartres or at York; the walls were covered with mural paintings that gave both delight and instruction; sculpture, both in wood and in stone, further indicated a new confidence and zest for living. Such developments were partly the result of a more extensive ceremonial, and partly of a realization of their educational value, but they also derived from a more or less independently enlarged technical capacity.

Bagpiper, Beverly Minster, Yorkshire, England, c. 1325. From *Music and Its Story* by Percy M. Young, Dobson Books, Ltd., London, and Roy Publishers, Inc., New York.

Plainsong, the official music of the Church, was in theory simple, unaccompanied, and in unison. By the tenth century, however, accompaniment was possible, even though the organ often did no more than duplicate the notes of the singers. The great organ at Winchester provided a more ambitious effect, for the rows of pipes operated by the sliders let out simultaneously with the melody notes other notes at a distance of fifth and octave. As a melody proceeded, then, the organ drew a series of parallel tunes.

But the singers themselves were also doing this. Unison singing breaks down when some singers find that certain parts of a melody are too high or too low for comfort. At this point the individual singer sensibly transposes the melody to a more acceptable compass. This is to be found in all early musical culture and the parallel part singing which began to be a regular feature of European church music about the tenth century is also to be found in active folk music.

This form of parallel singing was known as *organum*. By the eleventh century organum was modified so that sometimes there was contrary movement of the parts, the one going up while the other went down. Still the basis of music was the traditional plain-chant melody, even though either one or two extra parts might be added above or below.

The development of music depended on the trained musicians attached to the cathedral and monastic foundations. In the twelfth and thirteenth centuries one of the most important schools of music was in Paris, at Notre Dame. The director of music there in the twelfth century was Leoninus, and eighty of his compositions have survived. These are *organa*, eighty in all, composed for the major feasts of the church. In some of his organa Leoninus gives the main melody in very long notes above which a second voice descants freely in much quicker notes. In others the two parts move, note by note, in the same rhythm. In this case the rhythm is often derived from the secular songs of the troubadours.

After Leoninus came Perotinus, in whose works can be seen the earliest examples of motets. The essence of a motet is that it allowed other words than those given in the fundamental plain chant.

. . .

A striking feature of medieval thought was a chivalrous devotion to women, who—in theory, at least, and in the highest social groups—enjoyed more polite attention than at any other time in European history. Again this partly stemmed from theology, from the cult of the Virgin Mary, to whom many shrines and churches were dedicated, and in whose honor many hymns were composed.

Court life, with its pleasures, encouraged attention to the beauties there assembled, and the invention of suitable poems and songs for their flattery became a prosperous industry. The pioneers of this cult were to be found in France, the land of troubadours and *trouvères* (the former based in the south, the latter in the north). Courtiers kept their hopes of feminine companionship bright by their skill in composition and performance. Naturally they were not all talented artists, and often needed professional advice and assistance. This is where the popular minstrels, outside the jurisdiction of the Church, came into their own; for the clergy could hardly be expected to lend much aid—unless, perhaps, unofficially.

Between them the troubadours, trouvères, and minstrels laid the foundations of secular song and musical form. There were different kinds of songs. Some were proper to Crusaders—for the troubadour art flourished in the time of the Crusades; some were memorials to knights who had died in the wars; some were designed for competitions, like that described in Wagner's opera *Tannhäuser*; some were of a pastoral character; but the great majority were in praise of beauty and of love. Some songs were similar in pattern to hymns, with the same melody for each verse; some were constructed in simpler plainsong manner, with the same melody repeated for each line of poetry; some borrowed from dance forms and of them the most celebrated was the *carol*, from which came the characteristic *rondeau* with alternation between soloist and chorus.

Many of the medieval secular songs were written down, in the same notation as was employed in church music. They were often in the scales or modes of the Church, but sometimes in what in later times came to be known as the major scale. No accompaniments, however, were preserved, for these were extemporized on the indispensable lute.

In the twelfth and thirteenth centuries the greatest patrons of the art of secular song were William, Count of Poitiers, and Thibaut de Champagne, King of Navarre.

The French example spread, and music of the troubadour order was practiced in England (especially in the time of Richard I) and in Germany. In that country the art of the troubadours developed into that of the *Minnesänger* (literally, "love" singers), and the most famous of the *Minnesänger* were Walther von der Vogelweide and Wolfram von Eschenbach.

Walther von der Vogelweide was typical of many medieval minstrels and bards in that he traveled from court to court. At one time he was under the patronage of Hermann of Thuringia, at another of Philip of Swabia, at another of Dietrich of Meissen. Walther was a sturdy and independent character and gained both respect and disapproval for supporting the Emperor against the Pope; in the privileged position enjoyed by medieval secular musicians he was therefore beginning to sow the seeds of discord between Church and State that came to fruition centuries later. Wolfram, a Bavarian who was also in service at the Thuringian Court, adapted a French tale and presented it in German form under the title of *Parzival*. Six centuries later this popular legend of the Middle Ages was read by Richard Wagner, who was thus inspired to compose his music drama on the same subject.

By the thirteenth century there was much more connection between the sacred and secular in music than the more rigorous and conservative of the churchmen would have readily acknowledged. The development of rhythmic part-singing in church was, as we have seen from the music of Perotinus, assisted by troubadour practice. The most attractive and familiar music to show the union of "serious" and "light" is "Summer is i-cumen in," which was written at Reading Abbey in the thirteenth century. The melody is popular in style; its treatment in canon, above the two-part refrain of the lower voices, displays the mastery of the monastic, academic composer experienced in composing in parts. The English words are lively and secular, but there is an alternative and sober set of Latin verses which make a hymn.

King David playing bells, from the St. Omer Psalter, 15th century. From *Music and Its Story* by Percy M. Young, Dobson Books, Ltd., London, and Roy Publishers, Inc., New York.

The connection between the tradition of the Church and the new secular tradition of the court was an emancipating influence in music; for music, together with poetry, now became recognized in its own right and with its own values. But there were often fertilizing influences. Provençal poetry, from which sprang all troubadour art, was at first inspired by Arabic models. Instruments of the lute family were introduced to Europe from Persian, Arabic and Moorish sources through the Moors in Spain and the Saracens in Sicily and Southern Italy. From the Islamic world of the Middle East, visited by so many Crusaders, came other instruments, including oboes and kettle-drums. And in each country of Europe a fresh vitality was arising from the growing skill and political awareness of the mass of the people.

Away from capital cities, the seats of princes, and the rich abbeys, medieval people lived hard and anxious lives; most of them in varying degrees of serfdom. Their main preoccupation was with food and shelter; they lived constantly under the threat of plague, famine, and wars and rarely were they able to travel further than the end of their villages. Music then was a necessity, a release from the bondage of everyday drudgery. This was often the case also in later times and under a different sort of tyranny—especially that imposed by the Industrial Revolution.

In the eleventh and twelfth centuries the ceremonial of the Church was in many places enriched by an increasing repertoire of religious dramas with music. The subjects of these primitive plays were those which attracted oratorio composers of later time, and among them were the stories of the Nativity and the Resurrection, of the wise and foolish virgins, of Daniel and Belshazzar, and of St. Nicholas. These performances were particularly popular in France and Germany. Some of the plays about St. Nicholas were written by Hilarius, a pupil of the Parisian monk-philosopher, Abelard.

Hilarius was one of a group of poets known as Goliards (the name taken from a reputed Bishop Golias). These were students, usually of modest origin, who decided not to proceed with the careers open to them in the Church, the only "safe" careers in those times, but to trade their imagination and their talent in letters and drama—as did the minstrels and jugglers and acrobats theirs—wherever they were welcome. Life being as it was they generally were welcome, for they brought fresh interest to isolated communities, and news of the outside world. Sometimes the plays of the Goliards were in the repertory of traveling groups of players, who were engaged to perform even in monasteries.

The most famous poems of the Goliards, rough and robust, were the collections of *Carmina Burana*—with neumes in the original manuscripts —which are of present interest in that they inspired a striking work of the twentieth century by the German composer Carl Orff.

Minstrels, together with the other entertainers with whom they were generally grouped, were a mixed class. Some were attracted to manorial and princely households. Such was Melioso, the harp player employed by Sir John Matravers. When King Edward I visited Sir John he was taken ill and had to be bled. As the operation was in progress Melioso soothed the monarch's nerves by harp music, for which he was rewarded with a gift—a truly princely gift—of 20 shillings. For the most part, however, minstrels were wanderers and generally under severe criticism by the Church. This criticism was founded on a righteous distaste for the doubtful moral quality of much of their entertainment, and also on their frequent rejection of the clerical careers for which they had been destined. There was another point: the minstrels were able to influence opinion and when they criticized and satirized the rules, whether religious or secular, their words were an effective spur to discontent.

At the beginning of the fourteenth century the minstrels began to band themselves together, as in a union, and the earliest guild which sought to protect the minstrels' interests and to guarantee their skill was the *Corporation des Menestrels* in Paris. Soon afterwards similar bodies were established in other countries.

The junk man recently picked up a jumble of metal outside the door of a house in Chicago. The owner was reported to be beside himself with anxiety over the loss of his work of art, which he valued in the thousands of dollars. This brings up the question, what is art and where is it going? Robert Wraight, an English author, art critic, and collector, has some answers.

# The Art Game

Robert Wraight

That there are probably more easel pictures being painted today than ever before does not alter the fact that this form of art has been dying for fifty years. The present vast quantity being vomited forth may even be the final death throe. Ninety-nine-point-nine recurring percent of them will be absolutely valueless in a hundred years' time. The remainder will probably have found their way into the public art galleries to fill the last gaps in the completed history of easel painting which will have lasted six hundred years. To a not-far-distant-future generation those great art galleries (called "museums" even in Britain by then) will be of no more interest to the general public than the museums of paleontology or ethnography. The art-gamesman's dream of educating the masses to appreciate the precious-object sort of art will long ago have been abandoned, along with the art galleries, to a handful of square eggheads. The masses will have their own sort of art all around them. What sort of art will it be? It will not be anything like the bulk of what passes for avant-garde art today. Not only will the brush-and-paint tradition have been finally played out: with it into oblivion will have gone the rubbish collages made by the legions of would-be neo-Schwitterses, all the old-iron sculptures of imitation Tinguelys, all the drip paintings of imitation Pollocks, the squashed motorcars of John Chamberlain, the outsize prize-winning doodles of Messrs. Hilton and Mundy, the dust-laden combine paintings of Rauschenberg and company, the giant baked-potato and hamburger jokes of Claes Oldenburg, the latter-day ready-mades of Mr. Jim Dine and his followers, the burned books of Mr. John Latham, the burned canvases of Herr Otto Piene and the slashed and torn ones of Signor Fontana and Señor Millares.

It was all fun, even exciting fun, while it lasted, but it was mostly marking time or, at best, consolidating the discoveries of an earlier generation. It was also a jamboree for pseudo innovators. Peggy Guggenheim (whose collection of "modern art" has been described as second to none in private hands) wrote in 1960, not without some justification, that art had gone to hell—not permanently, of course. "One cannot expect every decade to produce genius," she said. "The twentieth century has already produced enough. A field must lie fallow now and then. Artists try too hard to be original. That is why we have all this painting that isn't painting any more."[1]

On reflection, what a very curious statement that is for Miss Guggenheim to have made. Evidently the great champion of the avant-garde of the 1940s has become the reactionary of the 1960s, unable to accept that the day will come when painting as we know it will be practiced, if at all, only as a quaint antique revival, in somewhat the same way as morris dancing survives today. Far from being finished or lying fallow, the art of the twentieth century is now working toward a revolution far greater than that with which it began. In the apparent chaos of today's art the germ of the new art is pulsating. In failing to detect it Miss Guggenheim has aligned herself with the layman, who, although he makes no objection to being rushed along by science that he doesn't understand, demands that art should dawdle along with him, explaining itself as it goes. To say that we have "painting that isn't painting any more" because artists are trying too hard to be original is the wrong answer to the wrong question. The only artists who are trying to be original are the spurious artists who are no more a part of the vital body of living art than are those "artists" who, in the second half of the twentieth century, produce "Impressionist" landscapes. The genuine artist does not strive to be original, he is original involuntarily. If he is young his originality may well take a form that people of Miss Guggenheim's generation, or of mine, find difficult to accept. But rather than accuse the artist of insincerity, of "trying too hard," we should acknowledge that if only because of his youth his art is probably nearer in spirit to the art of the future than we are.

Experience ought to have taught us that in the technological age into which we are now being pushed art will be at least as different from the art of Miss Guggenheim's beloved old men—Picasso, Ernst, Miró—as theirs was from that of their grandfathers' day. We are still inclined today to regard the artist's use of unconventional materials as a gimmick, and so in many cases it undoubtedly is. But there is in this search for new materials a strong pointer to the fundamental way in which the art of the future will differ from that of the present. Technology has already made available to the artist a great variety of new media, and it is in these and, no doubt, the many more to come that the art of the technological age will be created. According to the four young ex-Slade ex-painters who provided the quotation that heads this chapter:

We've had the push-button revolution and the technological takeover. We've been presented with conveyor-belt production, cybernetics, depth psychology, mass communication, instant-packs, supermarkets, glam admanship, man-made fibres, neon, nylon, perspex, plastic, expanding economics and dynamic obsolescence. It's all there—miraculous materials, magical machines, communication techniques and more leisure. And how can the visual artist serve in this social clime? He can avail himself of all these fabulous facilities and use his creative intelligence and imagination to produce inventive and desirable objects, environments and atmospheres. In fact, supply a visual panorama in this new Golden Age in which culture can fulfill its real function and enhance and stimulate the non-functional leisure-time of society.[2]

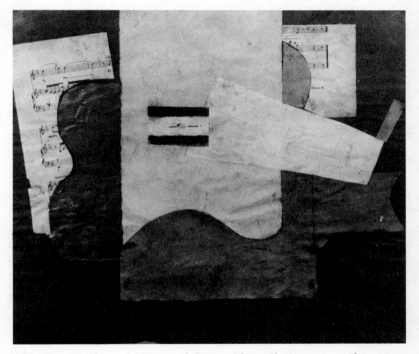

Pablo Picasso, *Sheet of Music and Guitar*. This collage was created in 1912–1913 on gummed paper with pastel. Permission SPADEM 1974 by French Reproduction Rights, Inc., New York City.

Presumably the "inventive and desirable objects" will include not only the motor scooters and electric guitars of the teenagers who, the Fine Artz quartet remind us, are the general public of tomorrow, but also such things as the electrically operated and uncanny mobile sculptures of the Belgian Pol Bury and the magnetically controlled, gravity-defying objects of the Greek sculptor Takis. The "environments and atmospheres" would include the luminodynamic construction of the Hungarian-born French sculptor Nicholas Schöffer, the "luminous pictures" of the English inventor John Healey and the "robot pictures" of P. K. Hoenich. There would be, too, no doubt, examples of the "random art," pioneered by the Italians "Group T" of Milan and "Group N" of Padua, in which iron filings, ping-pong balls, plastic ribbons and other objects are activated electronically.

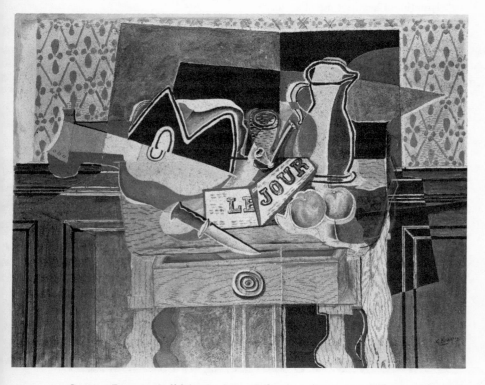

Georges Braque, *Still-life: Le Jour.* Cubism at first entailed the complete disintegration of form, but the years after World War I saw a return to the depiction of everyday objects. National Gallery of Art, Washington, D.C., Chester Dale Collection.

In all these things, it will be noted, the accent is on movement. Fifty-five years ago the Futurists were attempting to express in paint the sensation of motion, but later artists bypassed this problem and offered the spectator real motion in somewhat the same way as Picasso and Braque, realizing the futility of painting imitation wood and newspapers in their still lifes, stuck pieces of wood-patterned wallpaper and scraps of newspaper onto their canvases and so pioneered what has become the elaborate arts of collage and constructivism. The desire for motion in art goes much deeper than that of a few avant-gardists looking for a new gimmick that brings them publicity. The development of moving sculpture from the first mobiles of Alexander Calder, thirty-five years ago, and the development of light-pictures since the attempts, still earlier in the century, to create "color music" will be regarded by the twenty-first century as the most important contributions made to art in the twentieth, not even excluding Cubism.

. . .

To those who believe that art is a substitute for something lacking in life, a religion, a sublimation of a desire that is not directly satisfied, it seems logical to suppose that in an ideal world art (like the State in Marx's ideal Communism) will wither away. That great pioneer of abstract art Piet Mondrian expressed this when he said, "Art will disappear as life gains more equilibrium." But the idea is challenged, surprisingly enough perhaps, by the Marxist philosopher Ernst Fischer. He rejects the belief that art is only a substitute and encouragingly asserts that "art was not merely necessary in the past but will always remain so." On the other hand, if it is true that, as Fischer puts it, "an artist can only experience something which his time and his social conditions have to offer" and "even the most subjective artist works on behalf of society," It is certain that the art of the New Babylon will be vastly different from anything we know today. The several arts will no longer be separated from each other or from science. Art, with a capital *A*, will be collectively created for collective delectation.

So much for speculation. Yet one thing we may be sure of—that the art game as we know it, the "personal art-dealing, private art-collecting and individual artist-enterprising of personalities, privateering art" will disappear as life gains more equilibrium. But keep calm. There is no need yet for alarm, all you actual and would-be collectors, investors, dealers, runners, knockers, auctioneers, experts, critics, art historians, museum wallahs, art-gossipmongers, forgers, fakers, fiddlers, publicists, phony art teachers, culture hawkers, and innumerable other art-etceteras.

The New Babylon won't be coming for a long, long time. When? Poet Stanley Brouwn puts it (pessimistically, I think) at

4000 A.D.
When Science and Art are entirely
Melted together to something new
When the people will have lost their
Remembrance and thus will have
No past, only future.
When they will have to discover everything
Every moment again and again
When they will have lost their need for
Contact with others . . .
. . . Then they will live in a world of only
Colour, Light, Space, Time, Sounds and Movement
Then colour light space time
Sounds and movements will be free
No Music
No Theatre
No Art
No
There will be sound
        COLOUR
        LIGHT
        SPACE
        TIME
        MOVEMENT

Constant Nieuwenhuys, however, believes that the nonworking society will come sooner than most people expect and that it is sufficiently near for artists and others to be doing something about it now. The specific task of the creative man of today is "to prepare a new exciting reality based on the actual possibilities of technical production, instead of depicting and expressing the unsatisfying and stagnant reality that is about to be liquidated." Any activity in the field of art that is not already concerned with this *Homo ludens* can already be called backward.

## Notes

1 Peggy Guggenheim, *Confessions of an Art Addict.*
2 *Ark,* No. 35 (1964).

## Questions

1 What is the function of art?

2 Does a concern for material goods contribute to or detract from the production of art? Why?

3 Henry Adams was distressed by the shoddiness of products in America a hundred years ago. How would he feel today? How do you interpret the contemporary interest in handmade goods?

4 Do you agree with Ruskin that art is the best record of man's past? Why or why not?

5 Does the study of history change history?

6 What is the difference in quality between the written record and the artistic record?

7 What conditions does Henry Adams impose for seeing Chartres "in its glory"? Are these not the basic requirements for the study of history?

8 Compare the minstrels of the Middle Ages with their modern counterparts in both their music and their social criticism.

9 Is music a more important means of communication than words today? Explain.

10 Do you think easel painting is on the way out? Why or why not?

11 What is the task of the artist in the late twentieth century?

# 11

# Individualism in Renaissance Europe

This essay tries to show how the values of society can give forceful direction to the way individuals seek to find self-fulfillment. In contrast with the medieval society, which stressed humility, and even with the Greek classical culture, which emphasized balance as well as concern for the community, Renaissance culture placed such a high premium on individual credits that it did more than merely tolerate the ego trips of its outstanding achievers— it encouraged them. Only by stepping back from the values of one's own cultural period, can one gain the perspective on what it is that is valuable after all. As you seek to evaluate the goals you are pursuing, perhaps you can judge whether you are a free agent in choosing those goals. Or, like so many before us, are we predetermined creatures deluding ourselves that we have free choices? Or, is the truth somewhere in between?

# Ego Trip to Happiness

Melvin Steinfield

There are many roads purporting to lead to self-fulfillment and happiness. Not all of them reach their destination. For the classical Greeks, happiness and self-fulfillment could never be attained if the individual isolated himself from the common concerns of the community. As we pointed out in an earlier chapter on the Greeks, purely selfish pursuit of happiness was doomed by a too-narrow concept of what happiness constituted. Happiness could be attained not only when the individual was successful, but his children and his community were also successful.

In such socialist societies as Russia, China, and the Israeli kibbutzim, theoretically everyone must be willing to contribute to the common good: "From each according to his ability, to each according to his need." It is taboo to hoard one's riches, flaunting one's good health while others suffer, or otherwise exalt one's distinctiveness while others fare poorly.

And in America today there is a growing feeling, among the young especially, that individual fulfillment does not come by the selfish pursuit of Establishment achievement credits. And so encounter groups, communes, and other manifestations of sharing, noncompetitive experiences have developed. And thus, though capitalism and competition, and alienation and isolation, are not dead, there has been some reaction to the purely selfish, isolated pursuit of pleasure that dominates our culture and that intensifies with every technological advance.

During the Middle Ages there were some individuals who were not content with the anonymity of the group, who managed to stand out from the whole. But by and large the Middle Ages, in accordance with Christian traditions, exalted the humble. Did not Christ himself say, "The first shall be last, the last shall be first"? Or, "Blessed are the meek for they shall inherit the earth?" However, as the Middle Ages gave way to the Renaissance, people were encouraged to think of ways to achieve individual greatness.

One of the traits exhibited by Renaissance men was *braggadocio,* or bragging about one's achievements. Instead of being frowned upon, this trait was encouraged. And that's not all. Braggadocio was merely one particular manifestation of the Renaissance ideal of individualism, which helped shape so much of the behavior of Renaissance Man. The Renaissance Man was supposed to develop his talents in as many ways as he could. There were none of the restrictions that were imposed by Greek society.

The Renaissance did, of course, revive some elements of classical antiquity, but it did not restore precisely the same conditions. Lacking a strong sense of polis, Renaissance men were not disturbed by exile as much as the ancient Greeks had been. Lacking a hubris-nemesis doctrine, Renaissance men felt fewer restraints upon individual self-fulfillment than did the hubris-conscious Greeks. Thus while the Renaissance was to a degree a revival of antiquity, it was not a complete duplication of it.

During the Renaissance glory was actively sought. Successes were proudly announced—loudly and often. These behavior traits were part of the accepted quest for attaining that state of well-roundedness known as "uomo universale." The "universal man" must not hide his talents. Rather, he should feel free to boast of them proudly. That was a vital element in the spirit of the Renaissance.

*The Autobiography of Benvenuto Cellini* is replete with statements in praise of the author. They are in keeping with the unabashed and sometimes exaggerated pride felt by Renaissance men who accomplished varied feats. Cellini certainly achieved a lot—and he does not refrain from telling us about it. The opening line of the autobiography leaves no doubt about the absence of Joe Louis-type thoughts in Cellini: "It is a duty incumbent on upright and credible men of all ranks, who have performed any thing noble or praiseworthy, to record, in their own writing, the events of their lives. . . ."[1]

Besides the many statements of his own that praised his works, Cellini frequently reported the praise that others uttered in his behalf. For example, when Cellini had completed work on a silver basin and cup, the author tells us that the French King said: "It is my real opinion that the ancients were never capable of working in so exquisite a taste. I have seen all the masterpieces of the greatest artists of Italy, but never before beheld anything that gave me such high satisfaction."[2]

There were other famous Italians of the Renaissance who shared the self-confidence of Cellini. The great poet Dante had been exiled from the city of Florence for his political activities. After several years, he was offered an opportunity to return, but the terms were not entirely to his liking. Since Renaissance men did not share the deep sense of polis that the ancient Greeks had felt, Dante could afford to take an independent stand without violating any basic Renaissance values. He did just that, as the following excerpt from his reply indicates: "Can I not everywhere behold the light of the sun and the stars; everywhere meditate on the noblest truths, without appearing ingloriously and shamefully before the city and the people? My bread will not fail me."[3]

In classical Greece, that type of behavior would have been considered arrogant and highly intemperate, just as Muhammad Ali's remarks were considered intemperate in his time. But Dante was lucky—he lived in Italy during the Renaissance.

Other trends of the Italian Renaissance can be understood against the backdrop of the all-important concept of individualism. For instance, the sonnet, developed by Petrarch, shows earthy and personal elements that are missing in the poetry of the Middle Ages. The sonnets went much deeper into the love between man and woman than did the lyrics of the Minnesingers when they were celebrating the cult of the Virgin in the late Middle Ages. The sonnet was a long way from the stylized court poetry of the medieval troubadours.

Petrarch and Boccaccio, author of the *Decameron,* demonstrate the new secularism just as the rise of the scientific spirit and the beginnings of the exploration phase do. The early explorers, freed of the medieval spiritual orientation, now moved to discover more about their physical surroundings as well as to express their individual interests in worldly things.

At the core of these related Renaissance trends is the exuberant braggadocio which often took interesting forms. A dramatic visual example is provided in the work of the sculptor, Lorenzo Ghiberti. His famous bronze doors for the baptistery of San Giovanni in Florence contain biblical scenes which are engraved in less than two-inch relief. Embellishing the borders of the doors are busts of prophets, including one of Ghiberti himself, protruding three inches. The scenes are of significant Biblical events, such as Abraham about to slay Isaac, yet Ghiberti allowed his self-portrait to be one of the most prominent features of the doors. What better symbol of unrestrained individualism could one find than that smiling Ghiberti bust positioned in a strategic corner of his greatest work of art? Ghiberti outdid

John Hancock. One is tempted to wonder, how would bold signatures like that be received in American society today? Imagine the Apollo 11 moon plaque with the artist's face embellishing the astronauts names! Ghiberti also inscribed the following at the top of the door: "made by the amazing skill of Lorenzo di Ghiberti."

The beautiful and memorable artistic creations of Cellini and Ghiberti earned them the right to practice braggadocio. Their individual achievements more than made up for their overbearing manner. For during the Italian Renaissance the worth of an individual was not undermined by extraneous factors—not even those such as illegitimate birth or illegitimate accession to political power. Jacob Burckhardt's classic study of the Renaissance describes the prevailing attitude toward illegitimate birth and its relationship to the worth of an individual:

> Closely connected with the political illegitimacy of the dynasties of the fifteenth century was the public indifference to legitimate birth, which to foreigners—for example, to Comines—appeared so remarkable. The two things went naturally together. . . . In Italy . . . there no longer existed a princely house where, even in the direct line of descent, bastards were not patiently tolerated. The Aragonese monarchs of Naples belonged to the illegitimate line, Aragon itself falling to the lot of the brother of Alfonso I. The great Federigo of Urbino was, perhaps, no Montefeltro at all. When Pius II was on his way to the Congress of Mantua (1459), eight bastards of the house of Este rode to meet him at Ferrara, among them the reigning duke Borso himself and two illegitimate sons of his illegitimate brother and predecessor Lionello. The latter had also had a lawful wife, herself an illegitimate daughter of Alfonso I of Naples by an African woman. The bastards were often admitted to the succession where the lawful children were minors and the dangers of the situation were pressing; and a rule of seniority became recognized, which took no account of pure or impure birth. The fitness of the individual, his worth and capacity, were of more weight than all the laws and usages which prevailed elsewhere in the West. It was the age, indeed, in which the sons of the Popes were founding dynasties.[4]

A person of illegitimate birth does not have much chance in American politics; a pervasive Puritanism hovers righteously over the heads of would-be Presidents. Nelson Rockefeller's divorce unquestionably ruined his bid for the Republican presidential nomination in 1964. Adlai Stevenson's divorced status contrasted sharply with

Republican campaign literature, which featured Ike-and-Mamie photos in both campaigns of the 1950's.

Renaissance politics were rough, but at least the politicians' marital status was not a hangup. Of course, Renaissance politicians had to watch their step, too. But the great political realist Machiavelli was not troubled by fears of religious or moral restrictions. His secular attitude was practical and concentrated on what was necessary for the individual in power to survive. As Machiavelli states in *The Prince,* "Therefore it is necessary for a prince, who wishes to maintain himself, to learn how not to be good, and to use this knowledge and not use it, according to the necessity of the case."[5]

*The Prince,* in other words, was another manifestation of the individualism of the Renaissance. The individual Prince, according to Machiavelli, was entitled to engage in all sorts of dishonorable behavior. Indeed, he had to engage in dishonorable behavior in order to survive, to preserve his power. For the furtherance of his own ambitions, he was entitled to step on other people. "Thus it is well to seem merciful, faithful, humane, sincere, religious, and also to be so; but you must have the mind so disposed that when it is needful to be otherwise you may be able to change to the opposite qualities."[6] Often *The Prince* is capsulized by the slogan, "The end justifies the means."

This same self-interest is also revealed in Rabelais' *Gargantua and Pantagruel,* where the rule of the Abbey was DO AS THOU WOULDST. How unlike the somber warnings to the ancient Greek that he not forsake his family or community. How different from the admonishment not to get carried away with one's own importance, or one's own power.

As a matter of fact, Renaissance individualism actively sought to inspire men to the highest pursuits. Thus Leon Battista Alberti wrote: "Men can do all things if they will." There was no limit to the ambition of Renaissance Man. Not polis, not hubris, not humility. Humility was a medieval virtue. It was a Renaissance vice.

Another medieval virtue but Renaissance vice was the idea of this life being merely a preliminary to a more important heavenly life. In the Renaissance the emphasis was on the now. Pico della Mirandola's "Oration on the Dignity of Man" emphasizes the importance of man and his right to seek happiness in this life through varied attainments:

> At last the Best of Artisans ordained that that creature to whom he had been able to give nothing proper to himself should have joint possession of whatever had been the peculiar charac-

teristics of the different creatures. He therefore accorded to Man the function of a form not set apart, and a place in the middle of the world, and addressed him thus: "I have given thee neither a fixed abode nor a form that is thine alone nor any function peculiar to thyself, Adam, to the end that, according to thy longing and according to thy judgment, thou mayest have and possess that abode, that form, and those functions which thou thyself shalt desire. The nature of all other things is limited and constrained within the bounds of laws prescribed by me: thou, coerced by no necessity, shalt ordain for thyself the limits of thy nature in accordance with thine own free will, in whose hand I have placed thee. I have set thee at the world's center, that thou mayest from thence more easily observe whatever is in the world. I have made thee neither of heaven nor of earth, neither mortal nor immortal, so that thou mayest with greater freedom of choice and with more honor, as though the maker and moulder of thyself, fashion thyself in whatever shape thou shalt prefer."[7]

Man is the moulder of his own destiny, and it can be a glorious destiny if he aims high enough, says Pico. Elsewhere Pico encourages man to "let a certain holy ambition invade our souls, so that, not content with the mediocre, we shall pant after the highest. . . . "

It is not by accident that there were many individuals who achieved remarkable virtuosity during the Renaissance. Nor is it coincidental that perhaps the greatest of all well-rounded universal geniuses lived then. Leonardo da Vinci was an unusual person even for Renaissance Italy. His achievements are too well known to cite here. At the age of 30, Leonardo engaged in a bit of braggadocio when he applied for a job. His letter to the Duke of Milan reveals no reluctance to list his talents, among which were: "When a place is besieged I know how to cut off water from the trenches, and how to construct an infinite number of bridges, mantlets, scaling ladders, and other instruments which have to do with the same enterprise."[8] Observe that Leonardo could construct "an infinite" number, not just a whole bunch.

Besides war-making talents, Leonardo possessed peacetime skills, according to his letter, the complete text of which appears in the readings at the end of this chapter. Leonardo's letter ends with:

> In time of peace I believe I can give you as complete satisfaction as anyone else in architecture in the construction of buildings both public and private, and in conducting water from one place to another. Also, I can execute sculpture in marble, bronze, or clay, and also painting, in which my work will stand comparison with that of anyone else, whoever he may be.[9]

Leonardo's letter reached the Duke of Milan. He was hired. Braggadocio paid off again. If not for Muhammad Ali, at least for Leonardo.

This bold and Promethean individualism was reflected in another trend in art: portrait painting and sculptured busts. In contrast with medieval paintings, which tended to subdue the role of the individual as well as to pay little attention to the physical qualities of people and things, Renaissance art highlighted the individual. Very close attention was paid to human anatomy and to other naturalistic features. Because individuals were now being thought of as important in their own right, portrait painting flourished, and people were appearing as the exclusive or main interest in paintings. This contrasts not only with medieval style but also with the more generalized treatment given faces and bodies in the Hellenic Period. And how the medieval artists must have been rolling over in their heavenly berths when they saw those nude statues.

A favorite nude theme for Renaissance sculptors was David, the giant slayer. What greater heights of individual achievement could one hope to attain than killing a giant? Michaelangelo's "David" is one of the most widely acclaimed sculptures in the history of Western Man. It portrays David as the model of self-confident, powerful, dignified individualism. Ah, yes, Alberti said it, and Michaelangelo sculpted it, and Leonardo lived it. *Men can do all things if they will.*

## Notes

1 *The Autobiography of Benvenuto Cellini* (Reading, Pa.: Spencer Press, 1963), p. 1.

2 *Ibid.,* p. 249.

3 Jacob Burckhardt, *The Civilization of the Renaissance in Italy* (London: Phaidon Press, 1955), p. 83.

4 *Ibid.,* p. 12.

5 Niccolo Machiavelli, *The Prince* (New York: New American Library, 1954), p. 92.

6 *Ibid.,* p. 102.

7 Pico della Mirandola, *"Oration on the Dignity of Man,"* Elizabeth L. Forbes, trans. From *Journal of the History of Ideas,* Vol. III (1942), p. 348. Reprinted with permission from the *Journal of the History of Ideas.*

8 *The Literary Works of Leonardo da Vinci,* Irma A. Richter, ed. (New York: Oxford University Press, 1939).

9 *Ibid.*

When one is trying to characterize cultural trends, there is always the danger of oversimplification, and it would be a great oversimplification to say that communes always represent this or that for all of the individuals involved—Escapism, failure to cope with the stresses of urban society, desire to live a more simple life, whatever. Nevertheless, the following report has relevance for a central question raised in this book: What is the best road to happiness and individual self-fulfillment?

# Finding Oneself Through the Group

Bryce Nelson

NEW MEADOW RUN, Pa.—In an era in which many new communes have fallen by the wayside, young people are flocking here to learn why this Christian, passivist community of toymakers has flourished for more than 50 years.

They're all welcome, too, but each must work for his or her board and room by doing the communal chores. Males help make the toys and furniture which the Society of Brothers sells.

The community is composed of people of all ages. No one holds private property. Nor do they vote or serve in the military.

While such beliefs might appeal to the radical Left, the community is traditional in its morals—strongly opposing premarital relations, adultery and divorce, and it supports marriage, the family, and the importance of work.

What the society is attempting is to demonstrate that men can live together in harmony, much as it believes the early Christians did.

"If 200 people can do it, why can't 2 billion eventually learn to live as brothers?" one member asks.

The community, called New Meadow Run, is located on a 160-acre site in the Allegheny Mountains of southwestern Pennsylvania at the edge of the tiny village of Farmington. A sprawling old resort hotel serves as its central building.

Although New Meadow Run is on a major highway (U.S. 40—the Old National Road) its appearance is rustic.

A few sheep graze along the stream that flows through the large meadow. There are four Shetland ponies and four dogs to entertain the 100 children living here. The 4-year-olds sing as they climb the wooded hill to eat a picnic dinner.

From "Commune Achieves Life of Harmony" by Bryce Nelson, *Los Angeles Times*, June 14, 1971, part 1, p. 14. Copyright, 1971, Los Angeles Times. Reprinted by permission.

Conditions were not always so idyllic for the group.

The society—originally named the Bruderhof (place of the brothers)—began in Germany in 1920; the Nazis hounded the group out of the country in the mid-1930s.

The Brothers were forced to move several times—to Liechtenstein, to England, to an impoverished life in Paraguay before finding a more secure footing in the United States in the 1950s.

There are three closely knit branches of the 800-member community. The others are at Norfolk, Conn., and Rifton, N.Y.

The society, which has become economically self sufficient in the last five years, recently purchased land for still another settlement in the south of England.

Like the Israeli kibbutzim, the Bruderhof was an intellectual outgrowth of the German youth movement which was influential for several decades before being crushed in 1933. Of the many collective settlements founded during that period, the Bruderhof is almost the only one to survive.

Its members say that the Bruderhof has survived, not because of the wisdom of its members, but because they have subjected themselves to "the rulership of God."

To the Brothers, it is the community which is important. The individual accepts the discipline of group judgment, and all members must agree before major decisions are implemented.

When speaking, members frequently use the pronoun "we." The use of "I" is much less common than in the outside society.

Students who go to high school in Uniontown 12 miles west or to college for the most part shun organized athletics. "We don't approve of the glorification of the athlete," one brother explained.

They don't regard it as proper for the individual to request the kind of work he wants; he is assigned his task by the work supervisor.

Women prepare the meals, do the cleaning, laundry and sewing, and care for the younger children. Men work in the toy factory or on maintenance, unload the food, wait on tables and wash dishes.

Certain individuals have the responsibility of buying all the food, clothes and other items. The member receives what he needs from the community's storekeeper. It is not up to the individual to determine whether he should have luxuries such as a wristwatch or a bottle of wine.

Claude Nelson, formerly a sportswriter for an Atlanta newspaper, works five days a week in the toy factory. Each Friday, he drives one of the community's 10 automobiles 60 miles northwest to Pittsburgh where he visits churches to sell religious books printed by the community's Plough Publishing House.

"The last thing I thought I would want to be was a book salesman," he explains, "but here I am selling books for the community and I love it."

There are no harsh words uttered. Members tend to be friendly and soft-spoken.

"We don't say things in a pious way—we are weak—we have no reason to be arrogant," says Don Noble. "While we want this to be a place where God reigns, we have to fight for it every day. It's very easy to fall into the trap of becoming different from the world, of feeling superior."

The community does not have a lot of rules. Smoking (most of the men who smoke use pipes) and moderate drinking are acceptable.

Nonetheless, the community's children are isolated from what are regarded as harmful tendencies in the modern world. Members only watch television in groups when there is something special like a presidential address or a cultural event.

Education through the eighth grade is provided here—about 10 students in two grades for each teacher, who is always a community member.

The society does not run a high school, both because secondary education is more specialized and because the community wants the children to experience the outside world in order to help them make an informed decision as to whether or not they want to become members.

Children are sent to college for two years to prepare them to make their living on the outside if they decide not to join. Like marriage, joining the community is regarded as a lifetime commitment. Thus they are expected to take their time in deciding. Those who join give all their property to the community.

Not only is all property owned in common, but most activities are done together.

Children are regarded as a blessing. Big families are commended.

All children are cared for from infancy until school age in the "Children's House" where they also eat their lunch and dinners. In large families, a single woman from the community is often assigned to help the mother; this woman becomes an adopted member of the family.

Families are assigned space according to the number of persons living in the unit. A married couple might live in one room; one of the large families with 10 children might have six or seven rooms. There are no television sets or telephones in individual units.

Some young adults leave the society.

Many decide to stay and become members. Those who do lead a life that seems so tranquil as to be unreal to the visitor from the hectic outside world.

The following selection from Jacob Burckhardt's The Civilization of the
Renaissance in Italy discusses individualism in its many facets. It also
includes a short biography of one of the Renaissance giants, Leon
Battista Alberti.


# The Many-Sided Man

Jacob Burckhardt


Despotism, as we have already seen, fostered in the highest degree
the individuality not only of the tyrant or Condottiere himself, but
also of the men whom he protected or used as his tools—the secretary,
minister, poet, and companion. These people were forced to know
all the inward resources of their own nature, passing or permanent;
and their enjoyment of life was enhanced and concentrated by the
desire to obtain the greatest satisfaction from a possibly very brief
period of power and influence.

But even the subjects whom they ruled over were not free from
the same impulse. Leaving out of account those who wasted their
lives in secret opposition and conspiracies, we speak of the majority
who were content with a strictly private station, like most of the urban
population of the Byzantine empire and the Mohammedan States. No
doubt it was often hard for the subjects of a Visconti to maintain the
dignity of their persons and families, and multitudes must have lost
in moral character through the servitude they lived under. But this
was not the case with regard to individuality; for political impotence
does not hinder the different tendencies and manifestations of private
life from thriving in the fullest vigor and variety. Wealth and culture, so far as display and rivalry were not forbidden to them, a muni-
cipal freedom which did not cease to be considerable, and a Church
which, unlike that of the Byzantine or of the Mohammedan world,
was not identical with the State—all these conditions undoubtedly
favored the growth of individual thought, for which the necessary
leisure was furnished by the cessation of party conflicts. The private
man, indifferent to politics, and busied partly with serious pursuits,
partly with the interests of a *dilettante*, seems to have been first fully
formed in these despotisms of the fourteenth century. Documentary
evidence cannot, of course, be required on such a point. The novelists,
from whom we might expect information, describe to us oddities in
plenty, but only from one point of view and in so far as the needs of
the story demand. Their scene, too, lies chiefly in the republican cities.

From *The Civilization of the Renaissance in Italy* by Jacob Burckhardt
(London: Phaidon Press, 1955), pp. 82–87.

In the latter, circumstances were also, but in another way, favorable to the growth of individual character. The more frequently the governing party was changed, the more the individual was led to make the utmost of the exercise and enjoyment of power. The statesmen and popular leaders, especially in Florentine history, acquired so marked a personal character that we can scarcely find, even exceptionally, a parallel to them in contemporary history, hardly even in Jacob van Arteveldt.

The members of the defeated parties, on the other hand, often came into a position like that of the subjects of the despotic States, with the difference that the freedom or power already enjoyed, and in some cases the hope of recovering them, gave a higher energy to their individuality. Among these men of involuntary leisure we find, for instance, an Agnolo Pandolfini (d. 1446), whose work on domestic economy is the first complete program of a developed private life. His estimate of the duties of the individual as against the dangers and thanklessness of public life is in its way a true monument of the age.

Banishment, too, has this effect above all, that it either wears the exile out or develops whatever is greatest in him. "In all our more populous cities," says Gioviano Pontano, "we see a crowd of people who have left their homes of their own free will; but a man takes his virtues with him wherever he goes." And, in fact, they were by no means only men who had been actually exiled, but thousands left their native place voluntarily, because they found its political or economic condition intolerable. The Florentine emigrants at Ferrara and the Lucchese in Venice formed whole colonies by themselves.

The cosmopolitanism which grew up in the most gifted circles is in itself a high stage of individualism. Dante, as we have already said, finds a new home in the language and culture of Italy, but goes beyond even this in the words, "My country is the whole world." And when his recall to Florence was offered him on unworthy conditions, he wrote back: "Can I not everywhere behold the light of the sun and the stars; everywhere meditate on the noblest truths, without appearing ingloriously and shamefully before the city and the people? Even my bread will not fail me." The artists exult no less defiantly in their freedom from the constraints of fixed residence. "Only he who has learned everything," says Ghiberti,[1] "is nowhere a stranger; robbed of his fortune and without friends, he is yet the citizen of every country, and can fearlessly despise the changes of fortune." In the same strain an exiled humanist writes: "Wherever a learned man fixes his seat, there is home."[2]

An acute and practiced eye might be able to trace, step by step, the increase in the number of complete men during the fifteenth century. Whether they had before them as a conscious object the harmonious development of their spiritual and material existence, is hard to say; but several of them attained it, so far as is consistent with the imperfection of all that is earthly. It may be better to renounce the attempt at an estimate of the share which fortune, character, and talent had in the life of Lorenzo il Magnifico. But look at a personality like that of Ariosto, especially as shown in his satires. In what harmony are there expressed the pride of the man and the poet, the irony with which he treats his own enjoyments, the most delicate satire, and the deepest goodwill!

When this impulse to the highest individual development was combined with a powerful and varied nature, which had mastered all the elements of the culture of the age, then arose the "all-sided man"— "l'uomo universale"—who belonged to Italy alone. Men there were of encyclopedic knowledge in many countries during the Middle Ages, for this knowledge was confined within narrow limits; and even in the twelfth century there were universal artists, but the problems of architecture were comparatively simple and uniform, and in sculpture and painting the matter was of more importance than the form. But in Italy at the time of the Renaissance, we find artists who in every branch created new and perfect works, and who also made the greatest impression as men. Others, outside the arts they practiced, were masters of a vast circle of spiritual interests.

Dante, who, even in his lifetime, was called by some a poet, by others a philosopher, by others a theologian,[3] pours forth in all his writings a stream of personal force by which the reader, apart from the interest of the subject, feels himself carried away. What power of will must the steady, unbroken elaboration of the *Divine Comedy* have required! And if we look at the matter of the poem, we find that in the whole spiritual or physical world there is hardly an important subject which the poet has not fathomed, and on which his utterances —often only a few words—are not the most weighty of his time. For the visual arts he is of the first importance, and this for better reasons than the few references to contemporary artists—he soon became himself the source of inspiration.[4]

The fifteenth century is, above all, that of the many-sided men. There is no biography which does not, besides the chief work of its hero, speak of other pursuits all passing beyond the limits of dilettantism. The Florentine merchant and statesman was often learned in both the classical languages; the most famous humanists read the

Ethics and Politics of Aristotle to him and his sons; even the daughters of the house were highly educated. It is in these circles that private education was first treated seriously. The humanist, on his side, was compelled to the most varied attainments, since his philological learning was not limited, as it is now, to the theoretical knowledge of classical antiquity, but had to serve the practical needs of daily life. While studying Pliny, he made collections of natural history; the geography of the ancients was his guide in treating of modern geography, their history was his pattern in writing contemporary chronicles, even when composed in Italian; he not only translated the comedies of Plautus, but acted as manager when they were put on the stage; every effective form of ancient literature down to the dialogues of Lucian he did his best to imitate; and besides all this, he acted as magistrate, secretary and diplomatist—not always to his own advantage.

But among these many-sided men, some, who may truly be called all-sided, tower above the rest. Before analyzing the general phases of life and culture of this period, we may here, on the threshold of the fifteenth century, consider for a moment the figure of one of these giants—Leon Battista Alberti (b. 1404, d. 1472). His biography, which is only a fragment, speaks of him but little as an artist, and makes no mention at all of his great significance in the history of architecture. We shall now see what he was, apart from these special claims to distinction.

In all by which praise is won, Leon Battista was from his childhood the first. Of his various gymnastic feats and exercises we read with astonishment how, with his feet together, he could spring over a man's head; how, in the cathedral, he threw a coin in the air till it was heard to ring against the distant roof; how the wildest horses trembled under him. In three things he desired to appear faultless to others, in walking, in riding, and in speaking. He learned music without a master, and yet his compositions were admired by professional judges. Under the pressure of poverty, he studied both civil and canonical law for many years, till exhaustion brought on a severe illness. In his twenty-fourth year, finding his memory for words weakened, but his sense of facts unimpaired, he set to work at physics and mathematics. And all the while he acquired every sort of accomplishment and dexterity, cross-examining artists, scholars, and artisans of all descriptions, down to the cobblers, about the secrets and peculiarities of their craft. Painting and modelling he practiced by the way, and especially excelled in admirable likenesses from memory. Great admiration was excited by his mysterious "camera obscura,"[5] in which he showed at one time the stars and the moon rising over rocky hills, at another wide landscapes with mountains and gulfs receding into dim perspective, and with fleets advancing on the waters in shade or sunshine. And that which others created he welcomed joyfully, and held every human achievement which followed the laws of beauty for something almost divine. To all this must be added his literary works, first of all those on art, which are landmarks and authorities of the first order for the Renaissance of Form, especially in architecture; then his Latin prose writings—novels and other works—of which some have been taken for productions of antiquity; his elegies, eclogues, and humorous dinner-speeches. He also wrote an Italian treatise on domestic life in four books; and even a funeral oration on his dog. His serious and witty sayings were thought worth collecting, and specimens of them, many columns long, are quoted in his biography. And all that he had and knew he imparted, as rich natures always do, without the least reserve, giving away his chief discoveries for nothing. But the deepest spring of his nature has yet to be spoken of— the sympathetic intensity with which he entered into the whole life around him. At the sight of noble trees and waving cornfields he shed tears; handsome and dignified, old men he honored as "a delight of nature," and could never look at them enough. Perfectly formed animals won his goodwill as being specially favored by nature; and more than once, when he was ill, the sight of a beautiful landscape cured him. No wonder that those who saw him in this close and mysterious communion with the world ascribed to him the gift of prophecy. He was said to have foretold a bloody catastrophe in the family of Este, the fate of Florence and that of the Popes many years beforehand, and to be able to read in the countenances and the hearts of men. It need not be added that an iron will pervaded and sustained his whole personality; like all the great men of the Renaissance, he said, "Men can do all things if they will."

And Leonardo da Vinci was to Alberti as the finisher to the beginner, as the master to the *dilettante*. Would only that Vasari's work were here supplemented by a description like that of Alberti! The colossal outlines of Leonardo's nature can never be more than dimly and distantly conceived.

### Notes

1 In *secondo commentario*, being Ghiberti's autobiography; see the complete translation of it in the Phaidon Edition of *Ghiberti*. The paragraph to which Burckhardt refers is actually a quotation from Vitruvius's *Architecture*, VI, 2.

2 *Codri Urcei Vita,* Bologna, 1502.

3 Boccaccio, *Vita di Dante.* (English translation by Philip H. Wicksteed, in *The King's Classics,* London, 1904.)

4 The angels which he drew on tablets at the anniversary of the death of Beatrice (*Vita Nuova*) may have been more than the work of a dilettante. Leonardo Aretino says he drew "egregiamente" and was a great lover of music.

5 Other inventions, especially an attempt at a flying-machine, had been made about 880 by the Andalusian Abul Abbas Kasim ibn Firnas. (See Guayangos, *History of the Muhammedan Dynasties in Spain,* London, 1840, Vol. I, p. 148 *et seq.* and 425−7.)

Despite the conspiracy by men against women's active participation in society, some women have achieved top positions as heads of state. Queen Elizabeth I of England reigned for forty-five years and presided over one of the most brilliant periods of English culture. The Elizabethan Renaissance was the fullest expression of the European Renaissance north of Italy. In 1588, in the thirtieth year of her reign, the invasion of England by the Spanish Armada was defeated by the British fleet and the weather, and England became the undisputed mistress of the high seas. Here is Elizabeth's speech to her subjects that launched the British ships in that fateful year. Note the ironic touches of woman-man role playing—for example, "I know I have the body but of a weak and feeble woman."

# A Powerful Renaissance Woman

Queen Elizabeth I

My loving People,—

We have been persuaded by some that are careful of our safety, to take heed how we commit ourselves to armed multitudes, for fear of treachery, but I assure you, I do not desire to live to distrust my faithful and loving people.

Let tyrants fear; I have always so behaved myself, that, under God, I have placed my chiefest strength and safeguard in the loyal hearts and good will of my subjects, and therefore I am come amongst you, as you see, at this time, not for my recreation and disport, but being resolved in the midst and heat of the battle, to live or die amongst you all, to lay down for my God, and for my kingdoms, and for my people, my honor and my blood, even in the dust.

I know I have the body but of a weak and feeble woman; but I have the heart and stomach of a king, and of a king of England too; and think foul scorn that Parma or Spain, or any prince of Europe should dare to invade the borders of my realm; to which rather than any dishonor shall grow by me, I myself will take up arms, I myself will be your general, judge, and rewarder of every one of your virtues in the field.

I know already for your forwardness you have deserved rewards and crowns; and we do assure you in the word of a prince, they shall be duly paid you. In the meantime my lieutenant-general shall be in my stead, than whom never prince commanded a more noble or worthy subject;

From "Elizabeth I, The Armada Speech, 1588" in Charles W. Colby, ed., *Selections from the Sources of English History* (Harlow: Longmans, Green, 1899), pp. 158–159. Reprinted by permission of Longmans, Green and Co., Ltd.

no doubting but by your obedience to my general, by your concord in the camp, and your valor in the field, we shall shortly have a famous victory over those enemies of my God, of my kingdoms, and of my people.

This is the complete text of the letter that Leonardo da Vinci sent to
Duke Ludovico il Moro of Milan, referred to in the first essay of this chapter.
How was Leonardo caught up with the myth, the canon, and the hangup?

# A Genius Applies for a Job

Leonardo da Vinci

Having now sufficiently seen and considered the proofs of all those
who count themselves masters and inventors of instruments of war,
and finding that their invention and use of the said instruments does
not differ in any respect from those in common practice, I am em-
boldened without prejudice to anyone else to put myself in communication with Your Excellency, in order to acquaint you with my secrets,
thereafter offering myself at your pleasure effectually to demonstrate
at any convenient time all those matters which are in part briefly
recorded below.

1. I have plans for bridges, very light and strong and suitable for
carrying very easily, with which to pursue and at times defeat the
enemy; and others solid and indestructible by fire or assault, easy and
convenient to carry away and place in position. And plans for burning and destroying those of the enemy.

2. When a place is besieged I know how to cut off water from the
trenches, and how to construct an infinite number of bridges, mantlets, scaling ladders, and other instruments which have to do with
the same enterprise.

3. Also if a place cannot be reduced by the method of bombard-
ment, either through the height of its glacis or the strength of its
position, I have plans for destroying every fortress or other strong-
hold unless it has been founded upon rock.

4. I have also plans for making cannon, very convenient and easy
of transport, with which to hurl small stones in the manner almost of
hail, causing great terror to the enemy from their smoke, and great
loss and confusion.

5. Also I have ways of arriving at a certain fixed spot by caverns
and secret winding passages, made without any noise, even though
it may be necessary to pass underneath trenches or a river.

6. Also I can make armored cars, safe and unassailable, which will
enter the serried ranks of the enemy with their artillery, and there is

From *The Literary Works of Leonardo da Vinci* by Jean Paul Richter, edited,
enlarged, and revised by Jean Paul Richter and Irma A. Richter (New York:
Oxford University Press, 1939), pp. 92–93.

no company of men at arms so great that they will not break it. And behind these the infantry will be able to follow quite unharmed and without any opposition.

7. Also, if need shall arise, I can make cannon, mortars, and light ordnance, of very beautiful and useful shapes, quite different from those in common use.

8. Where it is not possible to employ cannon, I can supply catapults, mangonels, *trabocchi* [old war engines: trébuchets], and other engines of wonderful efficacy not in general use. In short, as the variety of circumstances shall necessitate, I can supply an infinite number of different engines of attack and defense.

9. And if it should happen that the engagement is at sea, I have plans for constructing many engines most suitable either for attack or defense, and ships which can resist the fire of all the heaviest cannon, and powder and smoke.

10. In time of peace I believe that I can give you as complete satisfaction as anyone else in architecture in the construction of buildings both public and private, and in conducting water from one place to another.

Also I can execute sculpture in marble, bronze, or clay, and also painting, in which my work will stand comparison with that of anyone else, whoever he may be.

Moreover, I would undertake the work of the bronze horse, which shall perpetuate with immortal glory and eternal honor the auspicious memory of the Prince your father and of the illustrious house of Sforza.

And if any of the aforesaid things should seem impossible or impracticable to anyone, I offer myself as ready to make trial of them in your park or in whatever place shall please Your Excellency, to whom I commend myself with all possible humility.

Just as the ancient Spartans carried regimentation to an extreme that killed individualism, Machiavelli's practical handbook on how to be a successful despot in Renaissance Italy, The Prince, condoned tactics that were ruthless and vicious. By justifying inhumane methods to achieve a greater good, Machiavelli was countering the humanistic thrust of the Renaissance. Machiavelli did not invent this kit of dirty tricks, but in advocating bluntly that they be used with skill, he revealed a cynical realism that was counter-productive to the development of individual aspirations. For, in an atmosphere of political repression, censorship of the arts was an inevitable next step.

# Individualism to the Point of Ruthlessness

Niccolò Machiavelli

### Of the Things for Which Men, and Especially Princes, Are Praised or Blamed

It now remains to be seen what are the methods and rules for a prince as regards his subjects and friends. And as I know that many have written of this, I fear that my writing about it may be deemed presumptuous, differing as I do, especially in this matter, from the opinions of others. But my intention being to write something of use to those who understand, it appears to me more proper to go to the real truth of the matter than to its imagination; and many have imagined republics and principalities which have never been seen or known to exist in reality; for how we live is so far removed from how we ought to live, that he who abandons what is done for what ought to be done, will rather learn to bring about his own ruin than his preservation. A man who wishes to make a profession of goodness in everything must necessarily come to grief among so many who are not good. Therefore it is necessary for a prince, who wishes to maintain himself, to learn how not to be good, and to use this knowledge and not use it, according to the necessity of the case.

Leaving on one side, then, those things which concern only an imaginary prince, and speaking of those that are real, I state that all men, and especially princes, who are placed at a greater height, are reputed for certain qualities which bring them either praise or blame. Thus one is considered liberal, another *misero* or miserly (using a Tuscan term, seeing that *avaro* with us still means one who is rapaciously acquisitive and *misero* one who makes grudging use of his own); one a free giver, another rapacious; one cruel, another merciful; one a breaker of his word,

From *The Prince* by Niccolò Machiavelli, translated by Luigi Ricci, revised by E. R. P. Vincent and published by Oxford University Press. Reprinted by permission of the publisher.

another trustworthy; one effeminate and pusillanimous, another fierce and high-spirited; one humane, another haughty; one lascivious, another chaste; one frank, another astute; one hard, another easy; one serious, another frivolous; one religious, another an unbeliever, and so on. I know that every one will admit that it would be highly praiseworthy in a prince to possess all the above-named qualities that are reputed good, but as they cannot all be possessed or observed, human conditions not permitting of it, it is necessary that he should be prudent enough to avoid the scandal of those vices which would lose him the state, and guard himself if possible against those which will not lose it him, but if not able to, he can indulge them with less scruple. And yet he must not mind incurring the scandal of those vices, without which it would be difficult to save the state, for if one considers well, it will be found that some things which seem virtues would, if followed, lead to one's ruin, and some others which appear vices result in one's greater security and well-being.

## Of Liberality and Niggardliness

Beginning now with the first qualities above named, I say that it would be well to be considered liberal; nevertheless liberality such as the world understands it will injure you, because if used virtuously and in the proper way, it will not be known, and you will incur the disgrace of the contrary vice. But one who wishes to obtain the reputation of liberality among men, must not omit every kind of sumptuous display, and to such an extent that a prince of this character will consume by such means all his resources, and will be at last compelled, if he wishes to maintain his name for liberality, to impose heavy taxes on his people, become extortionate, and do everything possible to obtain money. This will make his subjects begin to hate him, and he will be little esteemed being poor, so that having by this liberality injured many and benefited but few, he will feel the first little disturbance and be endangered by every peril. If he recognizes this and wishes to change his system, he incurs at once the charge of niggardliness.

A prince, therefore, not being able to exercise this virtue of liberality without risk if it be known, must not, if he be prudent, object to be called miserly. In course of time he will be thought more liberal, when it is seen that by his parsimony his revenue is sufficient, that he can defend himself against those who make war on him, and undertake enterprises without burdening his people, so that he is really liberal to all those from whom he does not take, who are infinite in number, and niggardly to all to whom he does not give, who are few. In our times we have seen nothing great done except by those who have been esteemed niggardly; the others have all been ruined. Pope Julius II, although he had made use of a reputation for liberality in order to attain the papacy, did not seek to retain it afterwards, so that he might be able to wage war. The present King of France has carried on so many wars without imposing an extraordinary tax, because his extra expenses were covered by the parsimony he had so long practiced. The present King of Spain, if he had been thought liberal, would not have engaged in and been successful in so many enterprises.

For these reasons a prince must care little for the reputation of being a miser, if he wishes to avoid robbing his subjects, if he wishes to be able to defend himself, to avoid becoming poor and contemptible, and not to be forced to become rapacious; this niggardliness is one of those vices which enable him to reign. If it is said that Caesar attained the empire through liberality, and that many others have reached the highest positions through being liberal or being thought so, I would reply that you are either a prince already or else on the way to become one. In the first case, this liberality is harmful; in the second, it is certainly necessary to be considered liberal. Caesar was one of those who wished to attain the mastery over Rome, but if after attaining it he had lived and had not moderated his expenses, he would have destroyed that empire. And should any one reply that there have been many princes, who have done great things with their armies, who have been thought extremely liberal, I would answer by saying that the prince may either spend his own wealth and that of his subjects or the wealth of others. In the first case he must be sparing, but for the rest he must not neglect to be very liberal. The liberality is very necessary to a prince who marches with his armies, and lives by plunder, sack, and ransom, and is dealing with the wealth of others, for without it he would not be followed by his soldiers. And you may be very generous indeed with what is not the property of yourself or your subjects, as were Cyrus, Caesar, and Alexander; for spending the wealth of others will not diminish your reputation, but increase it, only spending your own resources will injure you. There is nothing which destroys itself so much as liberality, for by using it you lose the power of using it, and become either poor and despicable, or, to escape poverty, rapacious and hated. And of all things that a prince must guard against, the most important are being despicable or hated, and liberality will lead you to one or the other of these conditions. It is, therefore, wiser to have the name of a miser, which produces disgrace without hatred, than to incur of necessity the name of being rapacious, which produces both disgrace and hatred.

### Of Cruelty and Clemency, and Whether It Is Better to Be Loved or Feared

Proceeding to the other qualities before named, I say that every prince must desire to be considered merciful and not cruel. He must, however, take care not to misuse this mercifulness. Caesar Borgia was considered cruel, but his cruelty had brought order to the Romagna, united it, and reduced it to peace and fealty. If this is considered well, it will be seen that he was really much more merciful than the Florentine people, who, to avoid the name of cruelty, allowed Pistoia to be destroyed. A prince, therefore, must not mind incurring the charge of cruelty for the purpose of keeping his subjects united and faithful; for, with a very few examples, he will be more merciful than those who, from excess of tenderness, allow disorders to arise, from whence spring bloodshed and rapine; for these as a rule injure the whole community, while the executions carried out by the prince injure only individuals. And of all princes, it is impossible for a new prince to escape the reputation of cruelty, new states being always full of dangers. Wherefore Virgil through the mouth of Dido says:

> Res dura, et regni novitas me talia cogunt
> Moliri, et late fines custode tueri.*

Nevertheless, he must be cautious in believing and acting, and must not be afraid of his own shadow, and must proceed in a temperate manner with prudence and humanity, so that too much confidence does not render him incautious, and too much diffidence does not render him intolerant.

From this arises the question whether it is better to be loved more than feared, or feared more than loved. The reply is, that one ought to be both feared and loved, but as it is difficult for the two to go together, it is much safer to be feared than loved, if one of the two has to be wanting. For it may be said of men in general that they are ungrateful, voluble, dissemblers, anxious to avoid danger, and covetous of gain; as long as you benefit them, they are entirely yours; they offer you their blood, their goods, their life, and their children, as I have before said, when the necessity is remote; but when it approaches, they revolt. And the prince who has relied solely on their words, without making other preparations, is ruined; for the friendship which is gained by purchase and not through grandeur and nobility of spirit is bought but not secured, and at a pinch is not to be expended in your service. And men have less scruple in offending one who makes himself loved than one who makes himself feared; for love is held by a chain of obligation which, men being selfish,

---

*"It's a difficult thing, the condition of the realm requires both caution and action."—*Editor's translation.*

is broken whenever it serves their purpose; but fear is maintained by a dread of punishment which never fails.

Still a prince should make himself feared in such a way that if he does not gain love, he at any rate avoids hatred; for fear and the absence of hatred may well go together, and will be always attained by one who abstains from interfering with the property of his citizens and subjects or with their women. And when he is obliged to take the life of any one, let him do so when there is a proper justification and manifest reason for it; but above all he must abstain from taking the property of others, for men forget more easily the death of their father than the loss of their patrimony. Then also pretexts for seizing property are never wanting, and one who begins to live by rapine will always find some reason for taking the goods of others, whereas causes for taking life are rarer and more fleeting.

But when the prince is with his army and has a large number of soldiers under his control, then it is extremely necessary that he should not mind being thought cruel; for without this reputation he could not keep an army united or disposed to any duty. Among the noteworthy actions of Hannibal is numbered this, that although he had an enormous army, composed of men of all nations and fighting in foreign countries, there never arose any dissention either among them or against the prince, either in good fortune or in bad. This could not be due to anything but his inhuman cruelty, which together with his infinite other virtues, made him always venerated and terrible in the sight of his soldiers, and without it his other virtues would not have sufficed to produce that effect. Thoughtless writers admire on the one hand his actions, and on the other blame the principal cause of them.

And that it is true that his other virtues would not have sufficed may be seen from the case of Scipio (famous not only in regard to his own times, but all times of which memory remains), whose armies rebelled against him in Spain, which arose from nothing but his excessive kindness, which allowed more license to the soldiers than was consonant with military discipline. He was reproached with this in the senate by Fabius Maximus, who called him a corrupter of the Roman militia. Locri having been destroyed by one of Scipio's officers was not revenged by him, nor was the insolence of that officer punished, simply by reason of his easy nature; so much so, that some one wishing to excuse him in the senate, said that there were many men who knew rather how not to err, than how to correct the errors of others. This disposition would in time have tarnished the fame and glory of Scipio had he persevered in it under the empire, but living under the rule of the senate this harmful quality was not only concealed but became a glory to him.

I conclude, therefore, with regard to being feared and loved, that men love at their own free will, but fear at the will of the prince, and that a wise prince must rely on what is in his power and not on what is in the power of others, and he must only contrive to avoid incurring hatred, as has been explained.

### In What Way Princes Must Keep Faith

How laudable it is for a prince to keep good faith and live with integrity, and not with astuteness, every one knows. Still the experience of our times shows those princes to have done great things who have had little regard for good faith, and have been able by astuteness to confuse men's brains, and who have ultimately overcome those who have made loyalty their foundation.

You must know, then, that there are two methods of fighting, the one by law, the other by force: the first method is that of men, the second of beasts; but as the first method is often insufficient, one must have recourse to the second. It is therefore necessary for a prince to know well how to use both the beast and the man. This was covertly taught to rulers by ancient writers, who relate how Achilles and many others of those ancient princes were given to Chiron the centaur to be brought up and educated under his discipline. The parable of this semi-animal, semi-human teacher is meant to indicate that a prince must know how to use both natures, and that the one without the other is not durable.

A prince being thus obliged to know well how to act as a beast must imitate the fox and the lion, for the lion cannot protect himself from traps, and the fox cannot defend himself from wolves. One must therefore be a fox to recognize traps, and a lion to frighten wolves. Those that wish to be only lions do not understand this. Therefore, a prudent ruler ought not to keep faith when by so doing it would be against his interest, and when the reasons which made him bind himself no longer exist. If men were all good, this precept would not be a good one; but as they are bad, and would not observe their faith with you, so you are not bound to keep faith with them. Nor have legitimate grounds ever failed a prince who wished to show colorable excuse for the nonfulfillment of his promise. Of this one could furnish an infinite number of modern examples, and show how many times peace has been broken, and how many promises rendered worthless, by the faithlessness of princes, and those that have been best able to imitate the fox have succeeded best. But it is necessary to be able to disguise this character well, and to be a great feigner and dissembler; and men are so simple and so ready to obey present necessities, that one who deceives will always find those who allow themselves to be deceived.

I will only mention one modern instance. Alexander VI did nothing else but deceive men, he thought of nothing else, and found the occasion for it; no man was ever more able to give assurances, or affirmed things with stronger oaths, and no man observed them less; however, he always succeeded in his deceptions, as he well knew this aspect of things.

It is not, therefore, necessary for a prince to have all the above-named qualities, but it is very necessary to seem to have them. I would even be bold to say that to possess them and always to observe them is dangerous, but to appear to possess them is useful. Thus it is well to seem merciful, faithful, humane, sincere, religious, and also to be so; but you must have the mind so disposed that when it is needful to be otherwise you may be able to change to the opposite qualities. And it must be understood that a prince, and especially a new prince, cannot observe all those things which are considered good in men, being often obliged, in order to maintain the state, to act against faith, against charity, against humanity, and against religion. And, therefore, he must have a mind disposed to adapt itself according to the wind, and as the variations of fortune dictate, and, as I said before, not deviate from what is good, if possible, but be able to do evil if constrained.

A prince must take care that nothing goes out of his mouth which is not full of the above-named five qualities, and, to see and hear him, he should seem to be all mercy, faith, integrity, humanity, and religion. And nothing is more necessary than to seem to have this last quality, for men in general judge more by the eyes than by the hands, for every one can see, but very few have to feel. Everybody sees what you appear to be, few feel what you are, and those few will not dare to oppose themselves to the many, who have the majesty of the state to defend them; and in the actions of men, and especially of princes, from which there is no appeal, the end justifies the means. Let a prince therefore aim at conquering and maintaining the state, and the means will always be judged honorable and praised by every one, for the vulgar is always taken by appearances and the issue of the event; and the world consists only of the vulgar, and the few who are not vulgar are isolated when the many have a rallying point in the prince. A certain prince of the present time, whom it is well not to name, never does anything but preach peace and good faith, but he is really a great enemy to both, and either of them, had he observed them, would have lost him state or reputation on many occasions.

## Questions

1 Is the ideal of the Renaissance man still admired today? Why or why not?

2 Is it possible to be a Renaissance man or woman in this age of specialization? Can you think of any person who is, or who comes close? What would be the advantages or disadvantages of being such a person?

3 Bragadoccio, not modesty, was accepted—even **expected** —of Renaissance men. In general, would you prefer honest boasting or false modesty among our political and cultural leaders today? How would you distinguish between those traits and false boasting and honest modesty?

4 Why must the Prince be prepared for all excesses and yet not appear excessive?

5 In psychology, a scale of Machiavellianism (Mach scale) has been constructed with items drawn from Machiavelli's writings. Subjects who agree with his statements, or similar ones, are rated as **high Mach's**—and studies have revealed that these people are more likely to be professionals who control and manipulate people in everyday life, such as lawyers, psychiatrists, and behavioral scientists. Do you react positively or negatively to the likelihood that many politicians are high Mach's? Why or why not?

6 How would you explain the burst of energy and creativity that produced the Renaissance? Would a twentieth-century Renaissance be possible? If so, describe its characteristics. If not, why not?

# 12

# The Protestant Reformation and the Capitalist System

Capitalism, the lifeblood of Western economics, owes a great debt to the
Protestant Reformation. This is ironic because both Martin Luther and John
Calvin were opposed to the materialistic trends that had become widespread
in the Renaissance church. Both urged spiritual reform and so can hardly
be thought of as favoring capitalistic endeavors. Yet some of their followers
did recommend capitalism. They saw in Protestantism an opportunity to
justify their economic activities, which were frowned on by the Catholic
Church. By twisting the doctrines of salvation and predestination, the Puritan
followers of Protestant reformers found that capitalism was the only way
to fly.

# Religious Yearnings and Capitalist Earnings: The Persistence of Puritanism in American Life

Melvin Steinfield

The most significant impact of the Protestant Reformation for Americans today might very well be the spur it gave to capitalism. According
to R. H. Tawney's *Religion and the Rise of Capitalism* and Max Weber's
*The Protestant Ethic and the Spirit of Capitalism*, one consequence of
the reformers' theology was what has come to be known as "the Puritan
work ethic." In sharp contrast with the medieval Catholic Church which
preached the cult of poverty and held moneylending to be a sin (usury),
the Protestant Reformation was a breakthrough for capitalists. Economic
success, instead of being frowned upon, was now seen as a sign from
Providence that the successful businessman was favored by God because
he was successful in his "calling." Thus, seeking his admission into
Heaven, the devout Puritan worked with a frantic compulsion to accumulate riches, not for themselves, but as greater security that it would
guarantee a place in Heaven. The Puritan work ethic is a myth that
still lives on, despite the declining influence of religion in the lives of
Westerners.

The Puritan work ethic finds sloth to be the greatest sin, hard work to
be the greatest good. Thus, Benjamin Franklin—hardly a Puritan in the
religious sense but definitely one in the economic sense—urges everyone:

Waste not, want not.

Early to bed, early to rise . . .

A penny saved is a penny earned . . .

God helps them that help themselves.

Many words won't fill a bushel.

The sleeping fox catches no poultry.

There are no gains without pains.

Be ashamed to catch yourself idle.

The basic message of Franklin's aphorisms was, "Don't let up from the continuous struggle to accumulate profits." This was a long way from the spiritual reforms advocated by Luther and Calvin. How did it happen?

It began in the late Middle Ages with the rise of a middle class during the commercial revolution. Suddenly Europe was populated by people who were neither wealthy, land-based artistocracy nor poor serfs (or free peasants) tied to the medieval manor. Suddenly, as a result of the renewed contact with the East and the growth of mercantilism and capitalism, there was a whole new class, the middle class, which earned its living by banking, financing, insurance, trade, merchandising, shipbuilding, speculating, exploring, discovering, and colonizing.

Living in a society that frowned on wealth in this world—in a society that said, in effect, "The first shall be last, the last shall be first, the meek shall inherit the earth, it is easier for a camel to go through the eye of a needle than for a rich man to get to Heaven"—the new middle class found its entire way of life out of harmony with the medieval-Christian cult of poverty and emphasis on the afterlife. Some religious justification for the new economic practices was needed.

Martin Luther and John Calvin never had in mind a justification for devoting one's life to the pursuit of economic gain, yet their followers were able to distort their original doctrines in such a way as to make it seem that relentless pursuit of material wealth was not only tolerable but incumbent upon good Christians. Since most people are doomed to Hell forever, according to the harsh Calvinistic faith, and only a few are chosen by the grace of God to be of the Elect (who will go to Heaven), there must be some clue given to those on earth to help them recognize who has been chosen. The clue, the hint of probable salvation, of course, became prosperity on earth. If God favored you and allowed you to prosper when you worked hard at your calling, then he most likely was telling you that you had been chosen to enter Heaven.

But the uncertainty remained. The insecurity about how safe the accumulating treasures were from disastrous loss created a work-hard-and-never-rest syndrome that still affects Americans today. Long after the religious reasons for avoiding sloth have dissipated, the secular behavior remains as firmly rooted as ever. The Puritan work ethic, originating in the religious atmosphere of the Protestant Reformation, lives on in the secular world of American capitalism and influences American behavior perhaps more than is customarily acknowledged.

In no country of the world has the Puritan influence been greater than in America, especially with regard to the concept of "rugged individualism." Puritanism shunned dependence upon government aid. It also shunned frivolity, because gambling, sex, and dancing were wastes of time that could be put to more productive ends. Americans are imbued through cultural conditioning and socialization with relentless drive to "get ahead," to never relax about the state of their finances: "You can't stay in the same place or you'll fall behind" is a relic of our Puritan roots.

When the great interpreter of American national character, Alexis de Tocqueville, was trying to explain why Americans seem more in a hurry than anyone else, he wrote: "He who has set his heart exclusively upon the pursuit of worldly welfare is always in a hurry, for he has but limited time to reach, to grasp, and to enjoy it." Rushing around in a religiously ardent fashion has long been observed of Americans. The Puritan work ethic, inspired by the desire to prove oneself favored by God, has been a major contributor.

When those who have followed the Puritan formula (and succeeded at the capitalist game of pulling themselves up by their own bootstraps) examine the pleas of the poor for government assistance, it is not surprising that they frown on Big Brother getting involved. They decry the loss of individual responsibility. They point to their own success as examples for inspiration. They behave as righteous Puritans, impervious to the cries of hunger. Of course, they do not seem so cold hearted to themselves. They see advocates of social welfare as weaker beings who shirk individual responsibility. Thus, many of the hot political issues of today are to a great extent a clash between Puritan rugged individualists, who are labeled conservatives, and their opponents, who are labeled liberals.

Racism is reinforced by Puritan attitudes. If a group of people is poor, it is because they are not of the Elect. Why else have they no clues that they are probably going to end up in Heaven? Either they did not work hard enough, or God, in His justice and wisdom, finds that they are not worthy. Thus the twin concepts of manifest destiny and mission, which played a large role in nineteenth-century expansionism, serve as racist rationalizations for territorial acquisitions from "inferior groups." It is the American "mission" to civilize the world.

Racism did not need Puritanism to come into being, but Puritan attitudes are not out of harmony with racist notions on the matter of the haves and have-nots of society. Together, the Puritan ethic and racist notions help make much of American history seem to be the natural outgrowth of a wealth-accumulating, aggressive, relentless drive for more.

This is not to endorse the radical interpretation of capitalism as necessarily being racist and colonialist. But the Puritan ethic does not discourage such attitudes once they do come into being.

In the first reading selection following this essay, the author tries to show just how influential Puritanism is for Richard Nixon.

Those who survive fraternity hazings might be expected to condemn them, but it doesn't always work out that way. Sometimes the most ardent defenders of the rough-and-tough are those who "proved" themselves playing at it (though it might not have seemed like play at the time). The issue of government-sponsored health insurance is a case in point. As this essayist points out, the Calvinist ethic has overshadowed any other influence that Richard Nixon's adversities might have had. And Edward Kennedy's good fortunes have not stopped him from advocating free medical care for all. As we went to press, the issue was still unresolved.

# Perversity in the Face of Adversity

TRB

- An American woman had a baby in Helsinki the other day. A fine, bouncing child; total cost, $7.50.
- An American tourist had a crisis in London last summer: appendectomy. All well—no charge.
- An embassy official had a letter from his mother in Ottawa last week; she is hospitalized with a tumor requiring cobalt treatment. Her only cost is for the telephone she had installed near her bed. (Bloody lucky she's not *here*.)

The United States is the only industrialized nation that doesn't have some form of national health insurance. Of course it means that taxes in other nations are generally higher; most of them don't think of these health costs as taxes, however (though they are). They think of them as purchase prices for something essential they have to buy.

The American system is different. NBC put on a fine documentary the other night, "What Price Health?" There was this lower-middle-income worker with a heart attack. The hospital took him in, thinking he was covered by California's state health insurance; he wasn't. He cashed his life insurance for $4000 and gave it to the hospital, but he was left with $8000 still to pay. The doctor told him to go home, take it easy, relax, don't worry about anything. Rather hard to stop worrying, isn't it, when your life savings are gone, and you have a bad heart and no coverage.

The health thing is coming up again in Congress and in the President's budget. Mr. Nixon proposes to slash an estimated $1.6 billion from 23 million elderly Americans in Medicare. Mr. Nixon says no new

From "Life or Death," by TRB, *The New Republic*, February 3, 1973, p. 4. Reprinted by permission of *The New Republic*, © 1973 Harrison-Blaine of New Jersey, Inc.

taxes and is pounding Lyndon Johnson's Great Society with the wrecker's ball. There is not a peep in his budget about the four-billion-dollar Family Assistance Plan (guaranteed income) that he offered to the nation as "a new birth of independence" in August 1969. But that was three years ago.

Nevertheless, the idea of national health insurance won't down. Majority Leader Mike Mansfield told UPI reporter Roy McGhee the other day that this Congress will pass it: "It is absolutely necessary, with medical and hospital costs skyrocketing." Representative Wilbur Mills promises to take it up this year after tax reform and hopes for Senate enactment next year.

Young Richard Nixon saw his oldest brother Harold contract tuberculosis and saw him taken to a private sanitarium in Arizona. There he was bedridden for five years. All the time the bills mounted; in the same time the younger brother, Arthur, died, of tubercular meningitis; and then Harold died. The family was left in "catastrophic" straits—Nixon's own words.

The Nixon family rejected charity and outside help; they heroically fought their way out, leaving an indelible impression on Nixon that that's the way it ought to be—uphold the Puritan work ethic, reject hateful bureaucratic aid. There is nobility in this austere creed, without a doubt; but it is Calvinistic to apply the sink-or-swim standard to those who must have help or sink.

Chief backer for the new national health security program is Senator Edward Kennedy. He wasn't self-made; with a wealthy father he went through no such traumatic boyhood as Richard Nixon (though he knows what it is to have a retarded sister, Rosemary). Maybe some of Nixon's discipline would have been good for him, who knows? But the point here is that Kennedy, with Representative Martha Griffiths (D, Mich.), UAW [United Auto Workers] head Leonard Woodcock and representatives of 40 national labor, church, and consumer organizations (including AFL-CIO and Teamsters) are trying to pass a law for a health system at last. They kicked it off here last week; there are citizens lobbies for it now in a score of states, pressuring Congress.

If the law passes they might call it a memorial to Harry Truman; the greatest disappointment of his presidency, he told Edward R. Murrow in a 1957 TV interview, was failure to get a national system of health care. The AMA beat him.

A woman we know went to the hospital recently for an emergency check-up and chose a low-price room; she was discharged two days later—hospital bill, $237.10. The American Hospital Association says a day in a hospital now averages $105.30. Health costs have shot up 40 percent in four years.

It's all right to argue that people should buy health insurance; a lot don't, or can't. The U.S. now spends around $90 billion annually for health care and buys $17 billion of insurance. But the U.S. still ranks 12th to 15th among the world's nations in infant mortality (over 20 per 1000 live births) and it's here that the disparity in income between rich and poor really shows up. In Detroit, for example, in a better suburb, infant mortality is around 12 per 1000; in the poorest Detroit slum, by contrast, it is an incredible 69 per 1000.

While the U.S. is graduating 10,000 doctors a year, the Soviet Union is graduating 35,000, according to Hubert Humphrey. The American doctors are the best in the world, using the finest technique; the problem is to get the doctors and technique out to the people. Here's a town, Nauvoo, Illinois. It had a big sign hanging over the main street for years, "Nauvoo Needs a Doctor." Five thousand U.S. communities have no doctor.

In his [1973] budget message Mr. Nixon said the country has all the hospital beds it needs, so he's suspending the Hill-Burton Act subsidizing hospital construction. Maybe he is right, if the number of beds is averaged, but the present wait in an emergency hospital ward is still several hours.

Everybody agrees something must be done. The Kennedy-Griffiths plan is for a complete national health system costing $60 billion or $70 billion (but absorbing much private health costs). The American Medical Association wants merely a voluntary insurance scheme to protect against catastrophic costs. Mr. Nixon has a bill somewhere in between.

It's a pity Americans don't ever look up to Canada. There are 3000 miles of contiguous border fenced by an iron wall of apathy. Canadians have a reasonably satisfactory health system started in 1958. Virtually everybody is covered. The cost hasn't risen (except to the government). Doctors fought it at first but are generally reconciled.

Maybe "bureaucracy" is bad, but surely it is better than a system where life or death depends on ability to pay medical bills.

Although Puritanism has persisted well into the latter part of the twentieth century, the increased affluence, with its resulting leisure time, has created a conflicting trend. In the following 1972 article, the point is made that although there is a lot of life still left in the work ethic, it is undergoing significant transformation.

# Is the Work Ethic Going Out of Style?

**Time** magazine

In the pantheon of virtues that made the U.S. great, none stands higher than the work ethic. As Richard Nixon defined it in a nationwide radio address: "The work ethic holds that labor is good in itself: that a man or woman at work not only makes a contribution to his fellow man but becomes a better person by virtue of the act of working." Lately the President has so often mentioned the work ethic—and so often suggested that it may be endangered—that its veneration and preservation have become something of a [1972] campaign issue. The President warns ominously: "We are faced with a choice between the work ethic that built this nation's character—and the new welfare ethic that could cause the American character to weaken."

In Nixon's implied demonology, the man who stands for "the welfare ethic" is George McGovern. Candidate McGovern briefly proposed that, as a substitute for some existing federal assistance programs, the Government give a $1,000 grant to every man, woman and child in the land, whether working or not. Yet McGovern, every bit as compulsive a worker as Nixon, is solidly in favor of the work ethic, saying "I have very little patience with people who somehow feel that it is of no consequence if they do not work." He contends that most people share his dedication to toil, and will work if only given the opportunity.

But will they? Or is the work ethic really in trouble?

There are signs aplenty that the ethic is being challenged, and not just by welfare recipients. In offices and factories, many Americans appear to reject the notion that "labor is good in itself." More and more executives retire while still in their 50s, dropping out of jobs in favor of a life of ease. People who work often take every opportunity to escape. In auto plants, for example, absenteeism has doubled since the early 1960s, to 5% of the work force: on Mondays and Fridays it commonly climbs to 15%. In nearly every industry, employees are increasingly refusing over-

From "Is the Work Ethic Going Out of Style?" *Time* Magazine, October 30, 1972, pp. 96–97. Reprinted by permission from *Time*, The Weekly Newsmagazine; Copyright Time Inc.

433

time work; union leaders explain that their members now value leisure time more than time-and-a-half.

Beyond that, an increasing number of Americans see no virtue in holding jobs that they consider menial or unpleasant. More and more reject such work—even if they can get no other jobs. Though unemployment is a high 5.5% of the labor force, shortages of taxi drivers, domestic servants, auto mechanics, and plumbers exist in many places.

Young adults are particularly choosy; many have little interest in the grinding routine of the assembly line or in automated clerical tasks like operating an addressing machine or processing a payroll. The nation's 22.5 million workers under 30, nursed on television and still showing their Spock marks, may in fact be too educated, too expectant and too anti-authoritarian for many of the jobs that the economy offers them. Affluence, the new rise in hedonism, and the antimaterialistic notions expressed in Charles Reich's *The Greening of America* have turned many young people against their parents' dedication to work for the sake of success.

More than the youth are uneasy. A Gallup poll of workers of all ages last year showed that 19% were displeased with their jobs, up from 13% in 1969. Observes Psychiatrist Robert Coles: "Working people with whom I have talked make quite clear the ways they feel cornered, trapped, lonely, pushed around at work, and confused by a sense of meaninglessness."

These developments should not come as too much of a surprise, considering that only fairly recently in human development has man—or woman—had anything but contempt for work. The Greeks, who relied on slaves for their work, thought that there was more honor in leisure—by which they meant a life of contemplation—than in toil. As Aristotle put it: "All paid employments absorb and degrade the mind." Christianity finally bestowed a measure of dignity on work. Slaves and freemen are all one in Christ Jesus, said St. Paul, adding: "If any one will not work, let him not eat." For the medieval monks, work was a glorification of God; the followers of St. Benedict, the father of Western monasticism, set the tone in their rule: *"Laborare est orare"*—to work is to pray. During the Reformation, John Calvin asserted that hard-earned material success was a sign of God's predestining grace, thus solidifying the religious significance of work. Around Calvin's time, a new, commerce-enriched middle class rose. Its members challenged the aristocracy's view that leisure was an end in itself and that society was best organized hierarchically. In its place they planted business values, sanctifying the pursuit of wealth through work.

The Puritans were Calvinists, and they brought the work ethic to

America. They punished idleness as a serious misdemeanor. They filled their children's ears with copybook maxims about the devil finding work for idle hands and God helping those who help themselves. Successive waves of immigrants took those lessons to heart, and they aimed for what they thought was the ultimate success open to them—middle-class status. They almost deified Horatio Alger's fictional heroes, like Ragged Dick, who struggled up to the middle class by dint of hard work.

During the Great Depression, the work ethic flourished because people faced destitution unless they could find something productive to do. World War II intensified the work ethic under the banner of patriotism. While the boys were on the battlefront, the folks on the home front serenaded Rosie the Riveter; a long day's work was a contribution to the national defense. In sum, the American work ethic is rooted in Puritan piety, immigrant ambition and the success ethic: it has been strengthened by Depression trauma and wartime patriotism.

Not much remains of that proud heritage. Today, in a time of the decline of organized churches, work has lost most of its religious significance. Horatio Alger is camp. Only a minority of workers remember the Depression. Welfare and unemployment benefits have reduced the absolute necessity of working, or at least made idleness less unpleasant.

Automation has given many people the ethic-eroding impression that work may some day be eliminated, that machines will eventually take over society's chores. Says John Kenneth Galbraith: "The greatest prospect we face is to eliminate toil as a required economic institution."

Do all these changes and challenges mean that Americans have lost the work ethic? There is considerable evidence that they have not. After all, more than 90% of all men in the country between the ages of 20 and 54 are either employed or actively seeking work—about the same percentage as 25 years ago. Over the past two decades, the percentage of married women who work has risen from 25% to 42%. Hard-driving executives drive as hard as they ever did. Even welfare recipients embrace the work ethic. In a recent study of 4,000 recipients and non-recipients by Social Psychologist Leonard Goodwin, those on welfare said that, given a chance, they were just as willing to work as those not on welfare.

Despite signs to the contrary, young people retain a strong commitment to work. A survey of college students conducted by the Daniel Yankelovich organization showed that 79% believe that commitment to a career is essential, 75% believe that collecting welfare is immoral for a person who can work, and only 30% would welcome less emphasis in the U.S. on hard work.

What is happening is that the work ethic is undergoing a radical transformation. Workers, particularly younger ones, are taking work *more* seriously, not less. Many may have abandoned the success ethic of their elders, but they still believe in work. Young and old are willing to invest more effort in their work, but are demanding a bigger payoff in satisfaction. The University of Michigan Survey Research Center asked 1,533 working people to rank various aspects of work in order of importance. "Good pay" came in a distant fifth, behind "interesting work," "enough help and equipment to get the job done," "enough information to do the job," and "enough authority to do the job."

Indeed in labor contract negotiations expected to begin early next summer [1973] the United Auto Workers intends to make a major point of its demand for increased participation by workers in decision-making within plants. "People look at life in different ways than they used to," says Douglas Fraser, a U.A.W. vice president. "Maybe we ought to stop talking about the work ethic and start talking about the life ethic."

The trouble is that the new humanistic, holistic outlook on life is at odds with the content of many jobs today. Most white collar work involves elemental, mind-numbing clerical operations. Factory work is usually dull and repetitive, and too often dirty, noisy, demeaning, and dangerous as well. It is a national scandal that last year on-the-job accidents killed 14,200 U.S. workers. In most auto assembly plants, a worker must even get permission from his foreman before he can go to the bathroom. The four-day week offers no real prospect for humanizing work; doing a boring job for four days instead of five is still an empty experience. Charles Reich says: "No person with a strongly developed aesthetic sense, a love of nature, a passion for music, a desire for reflection, or a strongly marked independence could possible be happy in a factory or white collar job."

A few enlightened employers have concluded that work, not workers, must change. Says Robert Ford, personnel director at American Telephone & Telegraph: "We have run out of dumb people to handle those dumb jobs. So we have to rethink what we're doing." In restructuring work, corporate experimenters have hit on a number of productive and promising ideas. Among them:

*Give workers a totality of tasks.* In compiling its telephone books, Indiana Bell used to divide 17 separate operations among a staff of women. The company gradually changed, giving each worker her own directory and making her responsible for all 17 tasks, from scheduling to proofreading. Results: work force turnover dropped, and errors, absenteeism, and overtime declined.

*Break up the assembly line.* A potentially revolutionary attempt at change is under way in the Swedish auto industry. Volvo and Saab are taking a number of operations off the assembly line. Some brakes and other subassemblies are put together by teams of workers; each performs several operations instead of a single-repetitive task. In the U.S. Chrysler has used the work team to set up a conventional engine-assembly line; two foremen were given complete freedom to design the line, hand-pick team members, and use whatever tools and equipment they wanted.

*Permit employees to organize their own work.* Polaroid lets its scientists pursue their own projects and order their own materials without checking with a supervisor; film assembly workers are allowed to run their machines at the pace they think best. AT&T eased supervision of its shareholder correspondents and let them send out letters to complainants over their own signatures, without review by higher-ups. Absenteeism decreased and turnover was practically eliminated. Syntex Corp. allowed two groups of its salesmen to set their own work standards and quotas; sales increased 116% and 20% respectively over groups of salesmen who were not given that freedom.

*Let workers see the end product of their efforts.* Chrysler has sent employees from supply plants to assembly plants so they can see where their parts fit into the finished product. The company has also put assembly-line workers into inspection jobs for one-week stints. Said one welder: "I see metal damage, missing welds and framing fits that I never would have noticed before."

*Let workers set their own hours.* In West Germany, some 3,500 firms have adopted "sliding time." In one form of the plan, company doors are open from 7 A.M. until 7 P.M., and factory or office workers can come in any time they like, provided that they are around for "core time," from 10 A.M. to 3 P.M., and they put in a 40-hour week. Productivity is up, staff turnover is down, and absenteeism has fallen as much as 20%.

*Treat workers like mature, responsible adults.* A few firms are attempting to give workers more status and responsibility. In its Topeka, Kans., plant, for example, General Foods has eliminated reserved parking spaces for executives, banished time clocks, made office size dependent not on rank but on need, abandoned the posting of in-plant behavior rules, and put the same carpeting in workers' locker rooms as in executives' offices.

The work ethic is alive, though it is not wholly well. It is being changed and reshaped by the new desires and demands of the people. "The potential of the work ethic as a positive force in American industry is extremely great," says Professor Wickham Skinner of the Harvard Business School. "We simply have to remove the roadblocks stopping individuals from gaining satisfaction on the job. The work ethic is just waiting to be refound."

In the new ethic, people will still work to live, but fewer will live only to work. As Albert Camus put it: "Without work all life goes rotten. But when work is soulless, life stifles and dies." It will be a long while, if ever, before men figure out ways to make the work of, say, a punch-press operator or a file clerk soul-enriching. While waiting for that millennium —which may require entirely new forms of work—bosses who expect loyalty from their employees should try to satisfy their demands for more freedom, more feeling of participation and personal responsibility, and more sense of accomplishment on the job.

In the following set of definitions of terminology employed by St. Paul, Luther reveals the broad, underlying basis in Scripture for the somber, sword-over-the-head doctrine of predestination.

# Sin in Its Broader Context

Martin Luther

The first thing needed is to master the terminology. We must learn what St. Paul means by such words as law, sin, grace, faith, righteousness, flesh, spirit, and the like; otherwise we shall read and only waste our time. You must not understand the term LAW in its everyday sense as something which explains what acts are permitted or forbidden. This holds for ordinary laws, and you keep them by doing what they enjoin, although you may have no heart in it. But God judges according to your inmost convictions; His law must be fulfilled in your very heart, and cannot be obeyed if you merely perform certain acts. Its penalties do indeed apply to certain acts done apart from our inmost convictions, such as hypocrisy and lying. Psalm 117 declares that all men are liars, because no one keeps God's law from his heart; nor can he do so, for to be averse to goodness and prone to evil are traits found in all men. If we do not choose goodness freely, we do not keep God's law from the heart. Then sin enters in, and divine wrath is incurred even though, to outward appearance, we are doing many virtuous works and living an honorable life.

In Chapter 2, St. Paul therefore asserts that the Jews are all sinners. He says that only those who keep the law are righteous in God's eyes, his point being that no one keeps the law by "works." Rather, Paul says to the Jews, "You teach us not to commit adultery, but you commit adultery yourselves, since you do the very things which you condemn." It is as if he were to say, To outward appearance, you observe the law scrupulously, condemning those who do not observe it, and being quick to teach one and all. You see the splinter in the other man's eye, but are unaware of the timber in your own. Granted that, in appearance and conduct, you observe the law, owing to your fear of punishment or hope of reward, yet you do nothing from free choice and out of love for the law, but unwillingly and under compulsion; were there no law, you would rather do something else. The logical conclusion is that, in the depths of your heart, you hate the law. What is the use of teaching others not to steal if you

From "Preface to the Epistle of St. Paul to the Romans" in *Reformation Writings of Martin Luther*, Vol. II, edited by Bertram Lee Woolf (New York: Philosophical Library, 1956), pp. 284–290.

are a thief at heart yourself and, if you dared, would be one in fact? Of course, the outer conduct of this kind is not continued for long by humbugs of this kind. It follows that, if you teach others but not your own selves, you do not know what you teach and have not rightly understood the nature of the law. Nay, the law increases your guilt, as Paul says in Chapter 5. A man only hates the law the more, the more it demands what he cannot perform.

That is why, in Chapter 7, Paul calls the law spiritual; spiritual because, if the law were corporeal, our works would meet its demands. Since it is spiritual, however, no one keeps it, unless everything you do springs from your inmost heart. Such a heart is given us only by God's spirit, and this spirit makes us equal to the demands of the law. Thus we gain a genuine desire for the law, and then everything is done with willing hearts, and not in fear or under compulsion. Therefore, because that law is spiritual when it is loved by hearts that are spiritual, and demands that sort of mind, if that spirit is not in our hearts, sin remains; a grudge abides together with hostility to the law, although the law itself is right and good and holy.

Therefore, familiarize yourself with the idea that it is one thing to do what the law enjoins and quite another to fulfill the law. All that a man does or ever can do of his own free will and strength is to perform the works required by the law. Nevertheless, all such works are vain and useless as long as we dislike the law and feel it a constraint. That is Paul's meaning in Chapter 3 when he says, "Through the works of the law shall no man be justified before God." It is obvious—is it not?—that the sophisticators wrangling in the schools are misleading when they teach us to prepare ourselves for grace by our works. How can anyone use works to prepare himself to be good when he never does a good work without a certain reluctance or unwillingness in his heart? How is it possible for God to take pleasure in works that spring from reluctant and hostile hearts?

To fulfill the law, we must meet its requirements gladly and lovingly; live virtuous and upright lives without the constraint of the law, and as if neither the law nor its penalties existed. But this joy, this unconstrained love, is put into our hearts by the Holy Spirit, as St. Paul says in Chapter 5. But the Holy Spirit is given only in, with, and through faith in Jesus Christ, as Paul said in his opening paragraph. Similarly, faith itself comes only through the word of God, the gospel. This gospel proclaims Christ as the Son of God; that He was man; that He died and rose again for our sakes, as Paul says in Chapters 3, 4, and 10.

We reach the conclusion that faith alone justifies us and fulfills the law; and this because faith brings us the spirit gained by the merits of

Christ. The spirit, in turn, gives us the happiness and freedom at which the law aims, and this shows that good works really proceed from faith. That is Paul's meaning in Chapter 3 when, after having condemned the works of the law, he sounds as if he had meant to abrogate the law by faith; but says that, on the contrary, we confirm the law through faith, i.e., we fulfill it by faith.

The word SIN in the Bible means something more than the external works done by our bodily action. It means all the circumstances that act together and excite or incite us to do what is done; in particular, the impulses operating in the depths of our hearts. This, again, means that the single term, "doing," includes the case where a man gives way completely and falls into sin. Even where nothing is done outwardly, a man may still fall into complete destruction of body and soul. In particular, the Bible penetrates into our hearts and looks at the root and the very source of all sin, i.e., unbelief in the depth of our heart. Just as faith alone gives us the spirit and the desire for doing works that are plainly good, so unbelief is the sole cause of sin; it exalts the flesh, and gives the desire to do works that are plainly wrong, as happened in the case of Adam and Eve in the garden of Eden, Genesis 3.

Christ therefore singled out unbelief and called it sin. In John 16, He says, The spirit will convict the world of sin because they do not believe in me. Similarly, before good or evil works are performed, and before they appear as good or evil fruits, either faith or unbelief must be already in our hearts. Here are the roots, the sap and the chief energy of all sin. This is what the Bible calls the head of the serpent and of the old dragon, which Christ, the seed of the woman, must crush, as was promised to Adam.

The words GRACE and GIFT differ inasmuch as the true meaning of grace is the kindness of favor which God bears toward us of His own choice, and through which He is willing to give us Christ, and to pour the Holy Spirit and His blessings upon us. Paul makes this clear in Chapter 5 when he speaks of the grace and favor of Christ, and the like. Nevertheless, both the gifts and the spirit must be received by us daily, although even then they will be incomplete, for the old desires and sins still linger in us and strive against the spirit, as Paul says in Romans 7 and Galatians 5. Again, Genesis 3 speaks of the enmity between the woman's children and the serpent's brood. Yet grace is sufficient to enable us to be accounted entirely and completely righteous in God's sight, because His grace does not come in portions and pieces, separately, like so many gifts; rather, it takes us up completely into its embrace for the sake of Christ our mediator and intercessor, and in order that the gifts may take root in us.

This point of view will help you to understand Chapter 7, where Paul depicts himself as still a sinner; and yet, in Chapter 8, [he] declares that no charge is held against those who are "in Christ," because of the spirit and the (still incomplete) gifts. Insofar as our flesh is not yet killed, we are still sinners. Nevertheless insofar as we believe in Christ, and begin to receive the spirit, God shows us favor and goodwill. He does this to the extent that He pays no regard to our remaining sins and does not judge them; rather He deals with us according to the faith which we have in Christ until sin is killed.

FAITH is not something dreamed, a human illusion, although this is what many people understand by the term. Whenever they see that it is not followed either by an improvement in morals or by good works, while much is still being said about faith, they fall into the error of declaring that faith is not enough, that we must do "works" if we are to become upright and attain salvation. The reason is that, when they hear the gospel, they miss the point; in their hearts, and out of their own resources, they conjure up an idea which they call "belief," which they treat as genuine faith. All the same, it is but a human fabrication, an idea without a corresponding experience in the depths of the heart. It is therefore ineffective and not followed by a better kind of life.

Faith, however, is something that God effects in us. It changes us and we are reborn from God (John 1). Faith puts the old Adam to death and makes us quite different men in heart, in mind and in all our powers; and it is accompanied by the Holy Spirit. O, when it comes to faith, what a living, creative, active, powerful thing it is. It cannot do other than good at all times. It never waits to ask whether there is some good work to do. Rather, before the question is raised, it has done the deed and keeps on doing it. A man not active in this way is a man without faith. He is groping about for faith and searching for good works, but knows neither what faith is nor what good works are. Nevertheless, he keeps on talking nonsense about faith and good works.

Faith is a living and unshakable confidence, a belief in the grace of God so assured that a man would die a thousand deaths for its sake. This kind of confidence in God's grace, this sort of knowledge of it, makes us joyful, high-spirited and eager in our relations with God and with all mankind. That is what the Holy Spirit effects through faith. Hence the man of faith, without being driven, willingly and gladly seeks to do good to everyone, serve everyone, suffer all kinds of hardships, for the sake of the love and glory of the God who has shown him such grace. It is impossible, indeed, to separate works from faith, just as it is impossible to separate heat and light from fire. Beware, therefore, of wrong conceptions of your own, and of those who talk nonsense while thinking they are pronouncing shrewd judgments on faith and works whereas they are showing themselves the greatest of fools. Offer up your prayers to God, and ask Him to create faith in you; otherwise you will always lack faith, no matter how you try to deceive yourself, or what your efforts and ability.

RIGHTEOUSNESS means precisely the kind of faith we have in mind, and should properly be called "divine righteousness," the righteousness which holds good in God's sight, because it is God's gift and shapes a man's nature to do his duty to all. By his faith, he is set free from sin, and he finds delight in God's commandments. In this way, he pays God the honor that is due to Him, and renders Him what he owes. He serves his fellows willingly according to his ability, so discharging his obligations to all men. Righteousness of this kind cannot be brought about in the ordinary course of nature, by our own free will or by our own powers. No one can give faith to himself, nor free himself from unbelief; how, then, can anyone do away with even his smallest sins? It follows that what is done in the absence of faith on the one hand, or in consequence of unbelief on the other, is naught but falsity, self-deception and sin (Romans 14), no matter how well it is gilded over.

FLESH and SPIRIT must not be understood as if flesh had only to do with moral impurity and spirit only with the state of our hearts. Rather, flesh, according to St. Paul, as also according to Christ in John 3, means everything that is born from the flesh, i.e., the entire self, body and soul, including our reason and all our senses. This is because everything in us leans to the flesh. It is therefore appropriate to call a man "carnal" when, not having yet received grace, he gibbers and jabbers cheerfully about the high things of the spirit in the very way which Galatians 5 depicts as the works of the flesh, and calls hypocrisy and hatred works of the flesh. Moreover, Romans 8 says that the law is weakened by the flesh. This is not said simply of moral impurity, but of all sins. In particular, it is said of lack of faith, which is a kind of wickedness more spiritual in character than anything else.

On the other hand, the term spiritual is often applied to one who is busied with the most outward of works, as when Christ washed His disciples' feet, and when Peter went sailing his boat and fishing. Hence the term "flesh" applies to a person who, in thought and in fact, lives and labors in the service of the body and the temporal life. The term "spirit" applies to a person who, in thought and fact, lives and labors in the service of the spirit and of the life to come. Unless you give these terms this connotation, you will never comprehend Paul's epistle to the Romans, nor any other book of Holy Scripture. Beware then of all teachers who use these terms differently, no matter who they may be, whether Jerome, Augustine, Ambrose, Origen, or their like; or even persons more eminent than they.

In the following summary of his doctrine, written in 1539, Calvin minces no
words. The stern tone reflects the stern attitude, unremitting as God's
manner itself, that was reinforced by the harsh winters faced by the New
England Puritans. Puritan life was characterized by a somber mode of dress
and general appearance, shunning bright and colorful costumes. Puritans
were not known for their jokes or revelry, for that would have belied the
seriousness of their task: To achieve God's will in sober deference to his
mighty power. Consequently, recreational pleasures were usually not indulged
in, even if there was a large surplus of wealth. The fear of God was the
overriding element in the Puritan psyche.

# Doomed to Hell Forever

John Calvin

As Scripture, then, clearly shows, we say that God once established
by His eternal and unchangeable plan those whom He long before determined once for all to receive into salvation, and those whom, on the
other hand, he would devote to destruction. We assert that, with respect
to the elect, this plan was founded upon His freely given mercy, without
regard to human worth; but by His just and irreprehensible but in-
comprehensible judgment He has barred the door of life to those whom
He has given over to damnation. Now among the elect we regard the
call as a testimony of election. Then we hold justification another sign
of its manifestation, until they come into the glory in which the fulfillment of that election lies. But as the Lord seals His elect by call and
justification, so, by shutting off the reprobate from knowledge of His
name or from the sanctification of His Spirit, he, as it were, reveals by
these marks what sort of judgment awaits them. Here I shall pass over
many fictions that stupid men have invented to overthrow predestination.
They need no refutation, for as soon as they are brought forth they
abundantly prove their own falsity. I shall pause only over those which
either are being argued by the learned or may raise difficulty for the
simple, or which impiety speciously sets forth in order to assail God's
righteousness.

From *The Institutes of the Christian Religion*, 1539, by John Calvin.

One of the best examples of the Puritan hell-fire and damnation sermons is this one given in 1741 by colonial preacher Jonathan Edwards. The impact of Edwards's sermons was immediate, with many in the congregation shrieking and becoming highly unsettled because of their literal belief in his words.

# The Evil in Man's Nature

Jonathan Edwards

The bow of God's wrath is bent, and the arrow made ready on the string, and justice bends the arrow at your heart, and strains the bow, and it is nothing but the mere pleasure of God, and that of an angry God, without any promise or obligation at all, that keeps the arrow one moment from being made drunk with your blood. Thus all you that never passed under a great change of heart, by the mighty power of the Spirit of God upon your souls; all you that were never born again, and made new creatures, and raised from being dead in sin, to a state of new, and before altogether unexperienced light and life, are in the hands of an angry God. However you may have reformed your life in many things, and may have had religious affections, and may keep up a form of religion in your families and closets, and in the house of God, it is nothing but his mere pleasure that keeps you from being this moment swallowed up in everlasting destruction. However unconvinced you may now be of the truth of what you hear, by and by you will be fully convinced of it. Those that are gone from being in the like circumstances with you, see that it was so with them; for destruction came suddenly upon most of them; when they expected nothing of it, and while they were saying, Peace and safety: now they see, that those things on which they depended for peace and safety, were nothing but thin air and empty shadows.

The God that holds you over the pit of hell, much as one holds a spider, or some loathsome insect over the fire, abhors you, and is dreadfully provoked: his wrath towards you burns like fire; he looks upon you as worthy of nothing else, but to be cast into the fire; he is of purer eyes than to bear to have you in his sight; you are ten thousand times more abominable in his eyes, than the most hateful venomous serpent is in ours. You have offended him infinitely more than ever a stubborn rebel did his prince; and yet it is nothing but his hand that holds you from falling into the fire every moment. It is to be ascribed to nothing else, that

From "Sinners in the Hands of an Angry God," by Jonathan Edwards, in *The Works of President Edwards,* IV (New York: Robert Carter and Bros., 1881), p. 318.

you did not go to hell the last night; that you was suffered to awake again in this world, after you closed your eyes to sleep. And there is no other reason to be given, why you have not dropped into hell since you arose in the morning, but that God's hand has held you up. There is no other reason to be given why you have not gone to hell, since you have sat here in the house of God, provoking his pure eyes by your sinful wicked manner of attending his solemn worship. Yea, there is nothing else that is to be given as a reason why you do not this very moment drop down into hell.

O sinner! Consider the fearful danger you are in: it is a great furnace of wrath, a wide and bottomless pit, full of the fire of wrath, that you are held over in the hand of that God, whose wrath is provoked and incensed as much against you, as against many of the damned in hell. You hang by a slender thread, with the flames of divine wrath flashing about it, and ready every moment to singe it, and burn it asunder; and you have no interest in any Mediator, and nothing to lay hold of to save yourself, nothing to keep off the flames of wrath, nothing of your own, nothing that you ever have done, nothing that you can do, to induce God to spare you one moment.

**In this brief but succinct passage the reader can see that the new medicine for poverty was capitalism mixed with Puritan attitudes. With these new attitudes, English economist Tawney says, begging and idleness became completely intolerable. Thus, what was accepted without question during the Medieval period was now being condemned.**

# The New Medicine for Poverty

R. H. Tawney

The new attitude [toward poverty] found expression in the rare bursts of public activity provoked by the growth of pauperism between 1640 and 1660. The idea of dealing with it on sound business principles, by means of a corporation which would combine profit with philanthropy, was being sedulously preached by a small group of reformers.[1] Parliament took it up, and in 1649 passed an Act for the relief and employment of the poor and the punishment of beggars, under which a company was to be established with power to apprehend vagrants, to offer them the choice between work and whipping, and to set to compulsory labor all other poor persons, including children without means of maintenance.[2] Eight years later the prevalence of vagrancy produced an Act of such extreme severity as almost to recall the suggestion made a generation later by Fletcher of Saltoun, that vagrants should be sent to the galleys. It provided that, since offenders could rarely be taken in the act, any vagrant who failed to satisfy the justices that he had a good reason for being on the roads should be arrested and punished as a sturdy beggar, whether actually begging or not.[3]

The protest against indiscriminate almsgiving, as the parade of a spurious religion, which sacrificed character to a formal piety, was older than the Reformation, but it had been given a new emphasis by the reformers. Luther had denounced the demands of beggars as blackmail, and the Swiss reformers had stamped out the remnants of monastic charity, as a bribe ministered by Popery to dissoluteness and demoralization. "I conclude that all the large givings of the papists," preached an English divine in the reign of Elizabeth, "of which at this day many make so great brags, because they be not done in a reverent regard of the commandment of the Lord, in love, and of an inward being touched with the calamities of the needy, but for to be well reported of before men whilst they are alive, and to be prayed for after they are dead . . .

are indeed no alms, but pharisaical trumpets."[4] The rise of a commercial civilization, the reaction against the authoritarian social policy of the Tudors, and the progress of Puritanism among the middle classes, all combined in the next half-century to sharpen the edge of that doctrine. Nurtured in a tradition which made the discipline of character by industry and self-denial the center of its ethical scheme, the Puritan moralist was undisturbed by any doubts as to whether even the seed of the righteous might not sometimes be constrained to beg its bread, and met the taunt that the reputation of good works was the cloak for a conscienceless egoism with the retort that the easy-going open-handedness of the sentimentalist was not less selfish in its motives and was more corrupting to its objects. "As for idle beggars," wrote Steele, "happy for them if fewer people spent their foolish pity upon their bodies, and if more showed some wise compassion upon their souls."[5] That the greatest of evils is idleness, that the poor are the victims, not of circumstances, but of their own "idle, irregular and wicked courses," that the truest charity is not to enervate them by relief, but so to reform their characters that relief may be unnecessary—such doctrines turned severity from a sin into a duty, and froze the impulse of natural pity with the assurance that, if indulged, it would perpetuate the suffering which it sought to allay.

A few tricks of the unsophisticated intellect are more curious that the naïve psychology of the business man, who ascribes his achievements to his own unaided efforts, in bland unconsciousness of a social order without whose continuous support and vigilant protection he would be as a lamb bleating in the desert. That individualist complex owes part of its self-assurance to the suggestion of Puritan moralists, that practical success is at once the sign and the reward of ethical superiority. "No question," argued a Puritan pamphleteer, "but it [riches] should be the portion rather of the godly than of the wicked, were it good for them; for godliness hath the promises of this life as well as of the life to come."[6] The demonstration that distress is a proof of demerit, though a singular commentary on the lives of Christian saints and sages, has always been popular with the prosperous. By the lusty plutocracy of the Restoration, roaring after its meat, and not indisposed, if it could not find it elsewhere, to seek it from God, it was welcomed with a shout of applause.

A society which reverences the attainment of riches as the supreme felicity will naturally be disposed to regard the poor as damned in the next world, if only to justify itself for making their life a hell in this. Advanced by men of religion as a tonic for the soul, the doctrine of the danger of pampering poverty was hailed by the rising school of Political Arithmeticians as a sovereign cure for the ills of society. For, if the theme of the moralist was that an easy-going indulgence undermined character, the theme of the economist was that it was economically disastrous and financially ruinous. The Poor Law is the mother of idleness, "men and women growing so idle and proud that they will not work, but lie upon the parish wherein they dwell for maintenance." It discourages thrift; "if shame or fear of punishment makes him earn his daily bread, he will do no more; his children are the charge of the parish and his old age his recess from labor or care." It keeps up wages, since "it encourages wilful and evil-disposed persons to impose what wages they please upon their labors; and herein they are so refractory to reason and the benefit of the nation that, when corn and provisions are cheap, they will not work for less wages than when they were dear."[7] To the landowner who cursed the poor-rates, and the clothier who grumbled at the high cost of labor, one school of religious thought now brought the comforting assurance that morality itself would be favored by a reduction of both.

As the history of the Poor Law in the nineteenth century was to prove, there is no touchstone, except the treatment of childhood, which reveals the true character of a social philosophy more clearly than the spirit in which it regards the misfortunes of those of its members who fall by the way. Such utterances on the subject of poverty were merely one example of a general attitude, which appeared at times to consign to collective perdition almost the whole of the wage-earning population. It was partly that, in an age which worshiped property as the foundation of the social order, the mere laborer seemed something less than a full citizen. It was partly the result of the greatly increased influence on thought and public affairs acquired at the Restoration by the commercial classes, whose temper was a ruthless materialism, determined at all costs to conquer world-markets from France and Holland, and prepared to sacrifice every other consideration to their economic ambitions. It was partly that, in spite of a century of large-scale production in textiles, the problems of capitalist industry and of a propertyless proletariat were still too novel for their essential features to be appreciated. Even those writers, like Baxter and Bunyan, who continued to insist on the wickedness of extortionate prices and unconscionable interest, rarely thought of applying their principles to the subject of wages. Their social theory had been designed for an age of petty agriculture and industry, in which personal relations had not yet been superseded by the cash nexus, and the craftsman or peasant farmer was but little removed in economic status from the half-dozen journeymen or laborers whom he employed. In a world increasingly dominated by great clothiers, iron-masters and mine-owners, they still adhered to the antiquated categories of master and servant, with the same obstinate indifference to economic realities as leads the twentieth century to talk of employers and employed, long after the individual employer has been converted into an impersonal corporation.

## Notes

1 Samuel Hartlib, *London's Charity Inlarged*, 1650, p. i.

2 Firth and Rait, *Acts and Ordinances of the Interregnum*, 1911, vol. ii, pp. 104–10. An ordinance creating a corporation had been passed Dec. 17, 1647 (*ibid.*, vol. i, pp. 1042–5·).

3 *Ibid.*, vol. ii, pp. 1098–9.

4 Stockwood, at Paul's Cross, 1578 (quoted by Haweis, *Sketches of the Reformation*, p. 277).

5 Richard Steele, *The Tradesman's Calling, being a Discourse concerning the Nature, Necessity, Choice, etc., of a Calling in General*, 1684, p. 22.

6 R Younge, *The Poores' Advocate*, 1654 (Thomason Tracts, E. 1452 [3]), p. 6.

7 For these and other passages from Restoration economists to the same effect, see a striking article by Dr. T. E. Gregory on *The Economics of Employment in England* (1660–1713) in *Economica*, no. i, Jan., 1921, pp. 37 *seqq.*, and E. S. Furniss, *The Position of the Labourer in a System of Nationalism*, 1920, chaps. v, vi.

**Tawney has not gone unquestioned since he advanced his theory that the Reformation helped the growth of capitalism. The following selection by a British historian summarizes the connection between Puritanism and capitalism in a way that supports Tawney but adds certain refinements.**

# A Modified View of Tawney

P. C. Gordon Walker

The Calvinist system . . . provided for the lower class [late sixteenth century]; but in some parts (notably Holland and later England) the lower class was powerful enough to play its own part. By now it had lost its early Anabaptist hope of violent emancipation; capitalism was firmly enough established to make labor within the system the only road. The result was that Menno Simon, the complementary contemporary of Calvin, was able to win the Anabaptists back to their earlier non-resistance. He preached an ethic suitable for the working class and therefore similar to that which Calvin preached for the Reprobates; but the Anabaptist retained his silent protest of withdrawal from the affairs of a wicked world; he lacked the Calvinist's interest in politics, his belief in a strong state and his desire to have that state as his servant. From the amalgam of Calvinist and Anabaptist resulted Puritanism, a vague attitude of mind covering every gradation from the obscure sect to the prosperous Calvinist; and with no fixed internal boundaries; for the Protestant ethic led to worldly success and so, often, to the progress of the successful Protestant up the rungs of the social ladder of Puritanism.

Such was the real spirit of capitalism needed by capitalist society and inculcated by the Reformation. Had the Reformation really produced the libertine "spirit of capitalism" it would have endangered, not advanced, capitalism.

Puritanism was clearly an influential factor: the magic mirror described by Tawney, reflecting back the narrow, arid qualities that led the Puritan to success in this world. It set men striving after new virtues, that yesterday had been vices, rather than their actual achievement. But such a superhuman struggle necessarily left a real impress; apart from moral attitudes, Puritan society saved money and developed novel notions of interest; it developed a special attitude towards colonization; and naturally evolved the Puritan Sunday as the only way of securing regular intervals of rest in peoples avidly devoted to work as the highest end.

From "Capitalism and the Reformation," by P. C. Gordon Walker, *Economic History Review*, VIII (1937). Reprinted by permission.

But, though Puritanism was thus bound up with capitalism in the sixteenth century, the relationship between Protestantism and capitalism is not eternal and absolute. The Reformation was the product of peculiar circumstances; it could occur only against the background of Christendom, in a civilization of nations, and under the stress of the special and urgent problems posed by the Price Revolution. From the beginning of the seventeenth century, Protestantism began to lose its special functions and therewith its spiritual position. Two sets of factors brought this about. First, as the class acclimatization which was the highest task of the Reformation was gradually accomplished, Protestantism had to yield ground to other activities which became more important; above all, it had to give place to the secular state and to science.

Secondly, Protestant societies had no monopoly of the advance of capitalism. The Reformation was necessary for the vital first advance in the sixteenth century; but once this advance had been safely made, other countries could follow in the tracks and "step over the Reformation." In such circumstances, certain social devices became important, especially the military-bureaucratic state (e.g., Colbert's France), that were closed to Protestantism, with its depreciation of state and court service. Protestantism ceased to have a monopoly of world capitalist advance and this lowered the prestige it was already losing in its homes; wide concessions were made to the state and to the individual business-man, which Protestantism would have scorned to make in its heyday. Protestantism, of course, has retained considerable social importance; in Protestant countries it is bound up with the achievement and the thought texture of capitalism. But it is noteworthy that the Reformation was the culminating ascetic revival of Christendom; all subsequent revivals have been Protestant, but of steadily decreasing social significance.

To draw the arguments together. The Reformation was a movement divided into two chronological phases, corresponding to the two phases of the Price Revolution; it was also divided laterally throughout its course into Church and Sect; the emphasis shifted from the problem of primary accumulation to the problem of class acclimatization; and there were the expected relations to the state. The movement was diverse and blind, but wonderfully related in its parts; innumerable leaders, Calvin, Menno Simon, Luther, Melanchthon, Martyr, Melchior Hoffman, Bucer, Olivetan, and a host of others, each played his part, though his only guide was his private conscience; behind these was a mass of anonymous followers, each in his own eyes choosing his adherence according to the logic and reasonableness of his particular leader. The inescapable conclusion is the same that we drew from an examination of the inner logic of Christianity, namely that the Reformation was the reaction to a force external to itself. The genius of leaders, the devotion of followers, even apparent accidents, were not so much independent forces controlling the destinies of the Reformation as factors that were present or called into being and made use of by a force greater than themselves. The Reformation corresponded in its various parts so closely to the social needs created by the Industrial Revolution, its effects (if properly conceived) were so apt, that in my submission we are entitled to say that our *prima facie* supposition that the Industrial Revolution was the external force we were looking for is now proven.

The Reformation was not the cause of capitalism; rather it was the result of needs created by capitalist advance at a particular place and time. *For this reason*, once it was in existence and throughout its various stages and forms, the Reformation played an indispensable part, amongst other factors, in the triumph of European capitalism over difficulties that had threatened to overwhelm it.

## Questions

1 In the sixties students rebelled against the work ethic and materialistic goals of their parents' generation. Is the student generation of the seventies continuing this rebellion, or does there appear to be a reacceptance of the Puritan-inspired motivation to succeed?

2 American society seems to have subscribed to the view that racism is unacceptable. Does this offer hope that we can muster public support for the solution of such other problems as poverty, the decline of cities and public services, pollution, and the energy crisis?

3 How would you react today to a "hell-and-damnation" sermon of the type delivered by Jonathan Edwards? With fear, belief, tolerance, amusement, doubt, cynicism—or some combination of these? Why? What characteristics would you ascribe to those who respond differently from you?

4 Do you agree with the idea that "hard times" engender laudable characteristics in a population? What are the laudable characteristics you're thinking of? How would you respond to someone who professed that another depression—with its potential of impoverishing many economically comfortable people—would be a good thing for the moral fiber of our country?

5 Should colleges teach courses in the creative use of leisure time? Why or why not?

# 13

# The Impact of the Scientific Revolution

We avoid describing the dramatic unfolding of the Scientific Revolution of the sixteenth and seventeenth centuries because we assume that students will have at least a textbook familiarity with the collapse of the geocentric world, a collapse that resulted from attacks upon the Ptolemaic system by such figures as Copernicus, Brahe, Bruno, Galileo, Kepler, and Newton. What we do deal with, however, are the relationships between the attitudes generated by the Scientific Revolution and the broader cultural canons developed during the eighteenth century. The theme is the impact of the Scientific Revolution upon the centuries that followed.

# Science, Sex, and Society

Melvin Steinfield

The teenaged couple passionately petting in their automobile at the local drive-in movie personifies a reality of the twentieth century that both Sigmund Freud and Henry Ford helped create: the portable bed in the public boudoir of the permissive society. Without mass production of steel cars from Detroit and sexy films from Hollywood, a popular form of recreation that frequently leads to procreation would not exist as we know it today. Indirectly, then, both Freud and Ford can be blamed for soaring college enrollments and crowded college classrooms.

In an effort to prevent unwanted pregnancies at drive-in movies and elsewhere, medical researchers have produced a pill. The development of the birth-control pill has not only helped reduce the undesired aftereffects of sexual enlightenment but also opened up a Pandora's box of controversial questions. Pompous politicians are proposing, "Can the government require use of The Pill by unmarried mothers who are receiving welfare aid for dependent children?" Pontificating priests are promulgating, "The Pill is evil. Beware!" Paternalistic parents are probing, "Should we buy a year's supply for our daughter?"

The point is that science can make an impact upon man's culture in areas that go far beyond the specialized boundaries of science itself. In the twentieth century there are numerous examples of the far-reaching implications of science for religious values, political decisions, and social customs. For instance, consider the ethical dilemmas and controversial questions that are posed by twentieth-century medical advances. Some of the questions raised by human-heart transplant operations have shaken the roots of medical ethics and challenged ancient canons. They have also had an influence upon general moral concerns. Thus laymen as well as medical men are asking: Do we need to revise our definition of death? At what point does a physician have a right to remove a vital organ from the body of a dying patient for the purpose of transplanting it into the body of another patient? Should the doctor play God with the donor's life?

Just as the startling achievements of modern science in birth-control, heart-transplants, and even moon-landings have opened up panoramic vistas of potential controversy, the achievements of the Scientific Revolution caused man to re-evaluate his basic religious, social, and political institutions. In many cases, then as now, his conclusions contained revolutionary implications.

And then, as now, it was a practical medical decision that focused attention on the broader issues of the scientific achievement. In the 1720's the inoculation and then in the 1790's the vaccination, perfected by Sir Edward Jenner, provided an opportunity to be immunized against the dreaded smallpox germs. But this raised questions about the right of man to tamper with the will of God. Did not the Scriptures state that God visited plagues and diseases upon man as punishment for his sins? Wouldn't it amount to defiance of God's will and wouldn't it be expressly contrary to Scriptures for man to thwart the natural progress of disease? The debate raged.

Is it not written that Woman must suffer pain in childbirth as punishment for having given Adam the forbidden fruit? Is not the administration of anesthesia during childbirth therefore open violation of God's word? These kinds of questions were just as lively and important to men and women of the seventeenth and eighteenth centuries as is the question today of blood transfusions for Jehovah's Witnesses or surgery for Christian Scientists.

The medical decision depends upon an entire attitude toward human nature. If man is evil by nature, then he deserves to suffer and has no right to seek to alleviate his suffering. In the seventeenth century the religious tradition in Europe tended to uphold this view. But the view of the eighteenth century rationalists was founded upon the assumption that man is basically good. They believed that through use of his reason he could discover the beautiful and harmonious laws of nature and apply his discoveries to an increased measure of happiness upon this earth.

What was at stake, then, in the debate on the propriety of the smallpox vaccination, was a complete system of values founded upon an assumption about the nature of man. The traditional religious assumption that man is evil, and the value system that this belief supported, were being challenged by a new system based upon a different assumption about the nature of man. Thus the narrow medical question served as a lead-in to broader questions about man's nature and religion's pronouncements about man's nature.

Not just the question of health, but also the question of government, was affected by the long-range impact of the Scientific Revolution. People reasoned that if there was a universal system of laws governing the physical universe, there must be a similar rational system in the human arena. A surge of faith arose in man's ability to strip away the mysteries of ideal human organization; man came to believe that if he persisted patiently in applying reason to the affairs of government, he would soon discover the most simple and most natural forms of government.

"That government is best which governs least," concluded Thomas Jefferson. He clearly spoke for the Enlightenment generation, which stood for the simplest and most natural form of government. To many, absolute monarchy was not necessarily the simplest or most logical form. Nor did the "divine right of kings" seem to conform to any natural and universal laws. It was not by accident, then, that the men who were seeking to apply the methods and principles of Newtonian science to human affairs soon discovered that some of the most sacred myths of their society were not founded upon a rational base.

These revolutionary implications of eighteenth-century political theory had their roots in John Locke's ideas of the seventeenth century and their fruits in the French and American Revolutions. The connection is a solid one and can be traced directly by comparing Locke's Essay on Civil Government, which was written in 1690, with Jefferson's Declaration of Independence, which was written in 1776.

The search for order in government was stimulated by the orderly searches of science a century earlier. Besides weakening the basis for absolute monarchy, the Enlightenment quest for natural law led to a serious questioning of the authority of Scriptures as well. The strongest blows came from the heavens, or, more precisely, from the speculations about them. Astronomy challenged the Bible as soon as the heliocentric theory of Copernicus was proposed, for is it not written in the Book of Joshua that, contrary to its usual procedure, the sun was made to stand still? If it says in an unimpeachably authoritative source that the sun normally did the moving, how, then, can the earth move? This was a war between two views of the world, and Copernicus knew it. He postponed the publication of his book for twenty years, not for the fun of it, but for his health, which was clearly at stake. Only when he was on his death bed did he permit his heretical views to come forth in print.

Because the Church was so heavily committed to the geocentric theory, it became the most vigorous opponent of the new ideas of the Scientific Revolution. An enduring example of the Church's opposition to the heliocentric theory is the treatment accorded Galileo and Bruno. At the age of 70, Galileo was threatened with torture and forced to recant his view that the sun is the center of the solar system and that the earth revolves around it. His book in support of Copernicus' theory was placed on the Index of Prohibited Books, as were those by Kepler and Copernicus. Not until 1835 were these books removed from the Index. Giordano Bruno also supported the heliocentric theory and was therefore also considered to be a heretic who was threatening the authority of the Church. The heated controversy about the nature of the physical universe spread until it destroyed the possibility that a literal interpretation of Scriptures could remain supported by a majority of Christians much longer.

The two most severely challenged institutions were the Church and the Monarchy, but they certainly were not the only ones. The eighteenth-century application of the principles of reason, order, harmony, and other elements of the Scientific Revolution reached into many corners of human activity. For example, religious tolerance grew into a reality in the eighteenth century. This was a practical necessity because Europe was tearing itself apart with religious wars. But there was another factor that contributed to the spread of tolerance. The *philosophes* of the eighteenth century began to ask: "Is there a truth certain enough to justify persecution?" "Since Scriptures have been proven wrong in astronomy, can they not also be wrong in other areas?"

Freedom of speech also received a powerful thrust from the new attitude, which encouraged expression of all points of view in an atmosphere of free inquiry. Rational men were capable of sorting out the wheat from the chaff, it was believed, without being any worse for the effort—that is, if one believed that man could be exposed to incorrect doctrines without being poisoned or contaminated by them. The Church, of course, still did not share in the positive view of human nature that was held by the eighteenth-century *philosophes*. Rooted in a belief in the fundamental evil of man's nature, the Church would naturally come to rely upon censorship as a protection from harmful doctrines. But the Index ultimately lost out to the first amendment to the American Constitution. One might well wonder, will the opposition to the Pill lose out to the world population explosion? And, if so, what will the effect be on the authority of the Church?

Despite the dampening effect of medieval otherworldliness upon secular happiness in this life, first the Renaissance and then the Scientific Revolution successfully established the legitimacy of concern about the physical universe and man's pleasure. Out of the solemnity of medieval spirituality came a disparagement of learning about the world for its own sake. But the secular spirit of the Renaissance inspired inquiries into the nature of the universe and the physical objects in it. After the Renaissance, a new era of optimism was created by the effects of the Scientific Revolution. This is illustrated by the following statement by d'Alembert, a famous eighteenth-century French philosopher, who could hardly contain his enthusiasm:

> Natural science from day to day accumulates new riches. Geometry, by extending its limits, has borne its torch into the regions of physical science which lay nearest at hand. The true system of the world has been recognized. . . . In short, from the earth to Saturn, from the history of the heavens to that of insects, natural philosophy has been revolutionized; and nearly all other fields of knowledge have assumed new forms . . . the discovery and application of a new method of philosophizing, the kind of enthusiasm which accompanies discoveries, a certain exaltation of ideas which the spectacle of the universe produces in us; all these causes have brought about a lively fermentation of minds. Spreading throughout nature in all directions, this fermentation has swept with a sort of violence everything before it which stood in its way, like a river which has burst its dams. . . . Thus, from the principles of the secular sciences to the foundations of religious revelation, from metaphysics to matters of taste, from music to morals, from the scholastic disputes of theologians to matters of commerce, from natural law to the arbitrary laws of nations . . . everything has been discussed, analyzed, or at least mentioned.[1]

D'Alembert speaks of a general "effervescence of minds," and that is a good way to describe the general tendency of the eighteenth century. Monarchy was liberated from tradition, science was liberated from theology, and culture in general was liberated from a stultifying inheritance.

During the eighteenth century virtually every major institution was closely examined under the bright light of rational inquiry. Some well-known examples of this trend are: references to "natural law" in politics and religion; new conceptions of "God," such as pantheism and Deism; the concept of progress, especially as elucidated in Condorcet's *Sketch for the Historical Picture of the Progress of the*

*Human Mind;* the growth of humanitarian reforms in prisons and insane asylums on the grounds that men are naturally good and no one voluntarily chooses to become a criminal or misfit; deliberate attempts to subdue passions, as evidenced in the refined rococo mannerisms of the wig-wearing, snuff-inhaling, minuet-dancing Enlightenment tough-guys like George Washington; a more cosmopolitan outlook toward the nations of mankind and toward the abilities of individual men; and the belief that became the root of "liberal" theory today, namely, that evil can be corrected by improving the environment, changing the society, spreading education, and in general, bringing human affairs to a rational, orderly, natural state.

In order to achieve these reforms, however, it was first necessary to destroy prevailing institutions, and also those attitudes that supported the institutions. The next three centuries after the Scientific Revolution witnessed the continued wearing-away of faith in inherited absolute values. Today's bewildering pace is largely the result of the long-range effects of the Scientific Revolution, both in its practical technological applications and its broad theoretical revelations.

Despite the shattering of the medieval world-view and its replacement by new concepts generated first by the Renaissance and then by the Scientific Revolution, some things remain as they were long ago. Men still ask: What is the best form of government? Is human nature good or evil? What types of cooperative behavior can the humanities and science develop? What is Man capable of achieving? And the circle is complete. We are still obsessed by problems of love and hate on Planet III, as we stand, with our hangups from way back, poised on the threshold of unprecedented scientific successes.

Or unprecedented social failures.

## Note

1 Ernest Cassirer, *The Philosophy of the Enlightenment* (Boston: Beacon Press, 1955) pp. 46–47. From d'Alembert, *Elements de Philosophie,* 1759.

The heart transplant is not the only medical procedure that raises
fundamental moral questions of how we are to determine what constitutes
death. The following article, written by a neurologist at George Washington
University Hospital in Washington, D.C., points out the new definition of
death that is slowly emerging.

# Is the Doctor God?

Richard Restak

Washington—Martin Carter's daily routine begins with an early morning visit to his son Robert's room in a Pennsylvania hospital. In late
1966 Robert's brain was critically damaged in an auto accident, and
though his eyes sometimes open, he has not regained consciousness in
six years.

Robert's mother believes she has occasionally seen signs of recognition
on Robert's face and several doctors have observed Robert's hands or
feet withdrawing from annoyances such as nail clippers. But never
since his accident has Robert shown any sign of conscious activity. His
heart and lungs continue working normally only because of regular
intravenous feedings; stop these and the organs soon would cease. Is
Robert dead or alive?

This is the anguishing question that Martin Carter has discussed
time and again with Robert's doctor, and it is a terrible question that
society as a whole—individuals, doctors, legislatures, courts, hospitals—
is more and more groping with today. At what moment can a life be
said to end?

Robert's doctor explained to Carter, quite correctly, that his son's
condition was a "coma vigil," a term describing a patient with irreversible
brain destruction who maintains a semblance of conscious activity. Such
patients can appear to be awake when their eyes wander blankly about
a room; they breathe on their own, and some may even swallow food
that is placed in their mouths.

All activities not requiring consciousness may continue, because the
lower portion of the brain necessary for such acts is intact. But the
cerebral cortex, responsible for conscious, meaningful activity, is reduced
to a mush, eliminating any possibility of a return to truly human functions. In Robert's case several medical studies of his brain revealed no
cure for his continuous coma.

From "Doctors Prolong Life Past Point of Death," by Richard Restak, *Boston
Globe*, December 17, 1972, pp. 33, 48. Courtesy of the Boston Globe.

A little over a year ago, after years of deeply painful talks and tests and talks again, Robert's parents and his doctor agreed:

Robert was, for all intents and purposes, dead. They would stop the intravenous feedings.

Martin Carter, who friends say has aged 15 years since his son's accident, remembers the 24 hours after the decision to stop feeding as filled with terror. He dreamed that night that his son was not dead at all, but alive. He could not go through with it. He would not. The next morning he told Robert's doctor and to resume the feedings immediately. The doctor did so, and Robert now 27, continues to lie in his hospital bed today, his condition unchanged.

Robert is only one of a growing number of "the living dead" in this country and abroad. In any sizable U.S. hospital today, there usually are one or two patients whose brains are irreversibly destroyed and who have no chance of recovering consciousness.

Ironically, their number is increasing because of medical advances, chiefly heart-lung machines which, along with intravenous feedings, can maintain such persons' heartbeats, breathing and pulses indefinitely, even though there is no hope they will ever return to anything remotely resembling normal "life."

With their increase have emerged perhaps the most agonizing questions of 20th century medicine: can such patients be declared dead? Can the machines be unplugged? Who is to make such a decision? On what basis? What is death?

What is death? After all these centuries, this is a fundamental question that mankind is still struggling with. Historically, the diagnosis of death has been left pretty much to individual physicians. In a sense, patients are dead when doctors state that they are dead. Despite the overwhelming importance of this judgment, the subject usually is not covered in medical school or in post-graduate medical education.

Presumably, this is because it was taken for granted over the ages that people were dead when they stopped breathing, or when there was no longer a heartbeat or pulse. Indeed, Black's Law Dictionary today still defines death as the "total stoppage of circulation of the blood and cessation of the animal and vital functions consequent thereon, such as respiration and pulse."

But modern medicine has rendered this definition obsolete. Clearly, the functioning of the heart and lungs alone cannot determine the presence or absence of life when they are entirely the work of a machine. The advent of this and other technology has created the need for a new definition, and in fact we are now moving—gradually and with the utmost caution—toward this definition, one that equates death with irreversible destruction of the brain.

A Virginia jury, in judging a lawsuit involving a heart transplant, also accepted the destruction of the heart donor's brain as evidence that death had occurred.

The grim Virginia story began on May 25, 1968, when William E. Tucker, a 47-year-old black shoe repairman from Charlottesville, arrived at the Medical College of Virginia to ask about his brother Bruce. Tucker learned that the previous afternoon Bruce had suddenly fallen over and struck his head hard on a radiator. After being rushed to the Medical Center by ambulance, Bruce underwent surgery for a brain hemorrhage.

Forty-five minutes after surgery, the operating physician wrote in the chart: "The prognosis for recovery is nil and death imminent." One hour later Bruce was examined by a neurologist, who ran a brain wave test that failed to demonstrate evidence of cerebral activity. He concluded that Bruce's brain was dead. At that time Tucker's pulse, blood pressure and temperature were normal, being artifically maintained by a respirator. It was decided to use Bruce Tucker's heart for the 16th transplant in the world and the first in Virginia, and plans were made for the removal of Bruce Tucker's heart.

Descartes and Newton formulated new methods of inquiring after truth. In the two brief selections below, they each explain the simple rules they tried to observe in their own work.

# The New Rules of the Game

René Descartes and Isaac Newton

### Descartes

The *first* was to accept nothing as true which I did not evidently know to be such, that is to say, scrupulously to avoid precipitance and prejudice, and in the judgments I passed to include nothing additional to what had presented itself to my mind so clearly and so distinctly that I could have no occasion for doubting it.

The *second,* to divide each of the difficulties I examined into as many parts as may be required for its adequate solution.

The *third,* to arrange my thoughts in order, beginning with things the simplest and easiest to know, so that I may then ascend little by little, as it were step by step, to the knowledge of the more complex, and, in doing so, to assign an order of thought even to those objects which are not of themselves in any such order of precedence.

And the *last,* in all cases to make enumerations so complete, and reviews so general, that I should be assured of omitting nothing.

### Newton

*Rule I. We are to admit no more causes of natural things than such as are both true and sufficient to explain their appearances.*

To this purpose the philosophers say that Nature does nothing in vain, and more is in vain when less will serve; for Nature is pleased with simplicity, and affects not the pomp of superfluous causes.

*Rule II. Therefore to the same natural effects we must, as far as possible, assign the same causes.*

As to respiration in a man and in a beast; the descent of stones in

From *Problems in Western Civilization*, Ludwig Schaefer, David Fowler, and Jacob Cooke, eds. (New York: Charles Scribner's Sons, 1968), Vol. 1, pp. 373–374. From *Sir Isaac Newton's Mathematical Principles of Natural Philosophy and His System of the World*, translated by Andrew Motte, revised by Florian Cajori, University of California Press, 1934, 1962. Originally published by the University of California Press; reprinted by permission of The Regents of the University of California.

*Europe* and in *America*; the light of our culinary fire and of the sun; the reflection of light in the earth, and in the planets.

> **Rule III.** *The qualities of bodies, which admit neither intensification nor remission of degrees, and which are found to belong to all bodies within the reach of our experiments, are to be esteemed the universal qualities of all bodies whatsoever.*

For since the qualities of bodies are only known to us by experiments, we are to hold for universal all such as universally agree with experiments; and such as are not liable to diminution can never be quite taken away. We are certainly not to relinquish the evidence of experiments for the sake of dreams and vain fictions of our own devising; nor are we to recede from the analogy of Nature, which is wont to be simple, and always consonant to itself. We no other way know the extension of bodies than by our senses, nor do these reach it in all bodies; but because we perceive extension in all that are sensible, therefore we ascribe it universally to all others also. That abundance of bodies are hard, we learn by experience; and because the hardness of the whole arises from the hardness of the parts, we therefore justly infer the hardness of the undivided particles not only of the bodies we feel but of all others. That all bodies are impenetrable, we gather not from reason, but from sensation. The bodies which we handle we find impenetrable, and thence conclude impenetrability to be an universal property of all bodies whatsoever. That all bodies are movable, and endowed with certain powers (which we call the inertia) of persevering in their motion, or in their rest, we only infer from the like properties observed in the bodies which we have seen. The extension, hardness, impenetrability, mobility, and inertia of the whole, result from the extension, hardness, impenetrability, mobility, and inertia of the parts; and hence we conclude the least particles of all bodies to be also all extended, and hard and impenetrable, and movable, and endowed with their proper inertia. And this is the foundation of all philosophy. Moreover, that the divided but contiguous particles of bodies may be separated from one another, is matter of observation; and, in the particles that remain undivided, our minds are able to distinguish yet lesser parts, as is mathematically demonstrated. But whether the parts so distinguished, and not yet divided, may, by the powers of Nature, be actually divided and separated from one another, we cannot certainly determine. Yet, had we the proof of but one experiment that any undivided particle, in breaking a hard and solid body, suffered a division, we might by virtue of this rule conclude that the undivided as well as the divided particles may be divided and actually separated to infinity.

Lastly, if it universally appears, by experiments and astronomical observations, that all bodies about the earth gravitate towards the earth, and that in proportion to the quantity of matter which they severally contain; that the moon likewise, according to the quantity of its matter, gravitates towards the earth; that, on the other hand, our sea gravitates towards the moon; and all the planets one towards another; and the comets in like manner towards the sun; we must, in consequence of this rule, universally allow that all bodies whatsoever are endowed with a principle of mutual gravitation. For the argument from the appearances concludes with more force for the universal gravitation of all bodies than for their impenetrability; of which, among those in the celestial regions, we have no experiments, nor any manner of observation. Not that I affirm gravity to be essential to bodies: by their *vis insita* I mean nothing but their inertia. This is immutable. Their gravity is diminished as they recede from the earth.

*Rule IV*. *In experimental philosophy we are to look upon propositions collected by general induction from phenomena as accurately or very nearly true, notwithstanding any contrary hypotheses that may be imagined, till such time as other phenomena occur, by which they may either be made more accurate, or liable to exceptions.*

This rule must follow, that the argument of induction may not be evaded by hypotheses.

**The influence of the Newtonian World Machine upon the eighteenth century is discussed in detail in the selection below.**

# The Newtonian World Machine

J. H. Randall

In the front of an old edition of the works of Rousseau there is an engraving which beautifully illustrates the intellectual spirit of the eighteenth century. Rousseau is seated at his writing-table, facing a pleasant pastoral landscape of green fields, sheep, and graceful willows—that rationally ordered Nature which he and his contemporaries accorded so respectful an admiration. On his desk are two volumes, which, in the absence of any other books, seem designed to sum up the learning of the age—the *Principia Mathematica* of Isaac Newton, and the *Essay Concerning Human Understanding* of John Locke.

In truth Newton and Locke were the two luminaries of that brilliant Augustan age in which, under William III and Queen Anne, England assumed for a period of some forty years, from 1680 to 1720, the undisputed intellectual leadership of the world, only to lose it again or at least to share it with first France and then Germany. Theirs are beyond doubt the outstanding names in that epoch which, succeeding to the discoveries and the liberations of the Renaissance and the Reformation, and preceding the rapid change and varied currents of the nineteenth century, made so heroic an attempt to order the world on the basis of the new "Physico-Mathematicall Experimental Learning." The significance of these two men, in spite of their own outstanding achievements, lies not so much in what they themselves did, as in what they stood for to that age, and in the very fact that they became to an increasing multitude the symbols for certain great ideas. Under their standards the new science for the first time actually entered into every field of human interest, and captured the mind of every educated man. Under such banners was actually effected that outstanding revolution in beliefs and habits of thought which we sometimes mistakenly associate with the Renaissance—that complete break with the spirit of the Middle Ages that prepared the way for the further growth of the next century. The age that hailed them as acknowledged masters, that introduced the spirit of the

J. H. Randall, *The Making of the Modern Mind.* Copyright © Houghton Mifflin Company, 1940. Reprinted by permission of the publishers.

Renaissance into religion, that placed man squarely in the midst of the new ordered world, that erected a science of man and of social relations, that formulated a complete and rounded philosophical view admirably framed for the middle class which the Industrial and the French Revolutions were so soon to bring into direct control, and which disseminated these ideas among the whole membership of this class—such an age is fittingly styled the "Age of Enlightenment and Reason." It laid the foundations for our present-day beliefs in every field, and it led on naturally to the two great ideas which the nineteenth century has added to the achievements of its predecessor, evolution and relativity.

In one sense both Newton and Locke were the systematizers of the ideas we have already traced in their formative stage. Newton stands at the end of that row of scientific geniuses who effected the Copernican and the Cartesian revolutions: he finally drew up in complete mathematical form the mechanical view of nature, that first great physical synthesis on which succeeding science has rested, and which has endured unchanged until a present-day revolution bids fair to modify it. Locke stands as apologist and heir of the great seventeenth-century struggles for constitutional liberties and rights and toleration. It is to this expression in systematic form of ideas which had become common property by 1700 that the two owed their immense popularity in the new century. But in another sense both Locke and Newton stand at the threshold of a new era, Newton as the prophet of the science of nature, and Locke as the prophet of the science of human nature. From their inspiration flow the great achievements of the Age of Enlightenment; in their light men went on to transform their beliefs and their society into what we know today.

Possessed of a successful scientific method, a combination of mathematics and experiment, and of a guarantee of truth, that "reason" which was both an individual and a universal authority, men set about the task of discovering a natural order that should be both simple and all-embracing. In the words of Fontenelle, the popularizer of Cartesianism, "The geometric spirit is not so bound up with geometry that it cannot be disentagled and carried into other fields. A work of morals, of politics, of criticism, perhaps even of eloquence, will be the finer, other things being equal, if it is written by the hand of a geometer." Isaac Newton effected so successful a synthesis of the mathematical principles of nature that he stamped the mathematical ideal of science, and the identification of the natural with the rational, upon the entire field of thought. Under the inspiration of Locke, the attempt was made to discover and formulate a science of human nature and human society, and to criticize existing religious and social traditions in the light of what seemed rational and reasonable. The two leading ideas of the eighteenth century, Nature and Reason, as outstanding then as Evolution in the last generation, derived their meaning from the natural sciences, and, carried over to man, led to the attempt to discover a social physics. Man and his institutions were included in the order of nature and the scope of the recognized scientific method, and in all things the newly invented social sciences were assimilated to the physical sciences. There grew up the idea of a simple and all-embracing social order in which free play should be left to the activities of every man. It is this great eighteenth-century synthesis in its most important ramifications that we shall now examine, starting with the rational order of the world, as expressed in the Newtonian system of nature, scientific method, and scientific ideals, and proceeding to trace its applications in religion, and in the comprehensive science of human nature that embraced a rational science of the mind, of society, of business, of government, of ethics, and of international relations.

### The Success of the Mathematical Interpretation of Nature

The outstanding fact that colors every other belief in this age of the Newtonian world is the overwhelming success of the mathematical interpretation of nature. We have seen how Galileo found that he could explain and predict motion by applying the language of mathematics to the book of Nature, and how Descartes generalized from his method and its success a universal principle of scientific investigation and a sweeping picture of the universe as a great machine; how both thinkers arrived at the conception of uniform natural laws that are essentially mechanical in nature. But Descartes' cosmic picture was a sketch which neither the progress of mathematics nor of physical observation enabled him to fill in by the time of his early death. To his disciples he left a system of the world worked out as a provisional hypothesis, which he had not had time to verify by those careful experiments that he increasingly recognized as necessary to determine just what actual phenomena, of the many possible ones that could be deduced from the mechanical principle, really took place. Not to the strict Cartesians, who accepted as final this sketch and did not bother to verify it by the master's method, but to the more original minds who shared Galileo's emphasis on experiment and refrained for a generation from attempting a general hypothesis, were due the discoveries that made Newton's work possible. Especially successful were the triumphs of mathematics in the fields of fluids and gases. Torricelli, Galileo's pupil, in 1643 invented the barometer and weighed the atmosphere, and Pascal confirmed his measurements four years later by his famous experiment of carrying a barometer up a mountain and observing the diminishing atmospheric pressure. To Pascal, too, is due the formulation of the laws of pressure in liquids, while Robert Boyle, who had studied under Galileo, discovered the law of pressure in gases. It is significant that within twenty years these facts had been used in machines for raising water, and that by the end of the century Newcomen's steam engine had begun the application of steam power to industry. To light, too, mathematics was astoundingly applied, and the science of optics, originated by Kepler and Descartes, was systematically developed by the Dutch Huygens and by Newton, who gave it its classic formulation; in 1695, Roemer actually measured the speed of light.

In all this work, mathematics and experimentation were successful allies. The spirit of the new science is exemplified in the foundation of the Royal Society in London in 1662 "for the promoting of Physico-Mathematicall Experimental Learning." This institution for that scientific cooperation so urgently demanded by Descartes, was largely inspired by Bacon's vision of a great scientific establishment; but it wisely followed the mathematical methods of Galileo rather than the purely experimental searching of the Elizabethan. Science rested on experiment, but its main object, for another century at least, was to connect the observed processes of nature with mathematical law. The leading member of the Royal Society, Robert Boyle, shares with Huygens the distinction of being the greatest investigator between Galileo and Newton; he managed to draw together the threads of alchemy and mathematical physics, and his generalization of Galileo's method of mathematical experimentation strongly influenced Newton. Mayow, another member, in 1674 discovered oxygen, although it was a century before Priestley and Lavoisier were able to fit it into a chemical science.

### The Mathematical Synthesis of Newton

All this experimental work, together with much advance in mathematical theory, took place in the single generation after Descartes' death. But the great formulator of seventeenth-century science, the man who realized Descartes' dream, was born in 1642, the very year of Galileo's death. Though he did not publish his immortal work, the *Philosophia Naturalis Principia Mathematica,* till 1687, Newton made his chief discoveries when he was but twenty-three years of age. At that time, he tells us, he discovered:

> . . . first the binomial theorem, then the method of fluxions [the calculus], and began to think of gravity extending to the orb of the moon, and having found out how to estimate the force with which a globe, revolving within a sphere, presses the surface of the sphere, from Kepler's rule I deduced that the forces which keep the planets in their orb must be reciprocally as the squares of their distances from their centres: and thereby compared the force requisite to keep the moon in her orb with the force of gravity at the surface of the earth, and found them to answer pretty nearly. All this was in the two plague years of 1665 and 1666, for in those days I was in the prime of my age for invention and minded Mathematicks and Philosophy more than at any time since.

The thirty years that had passed since Galileo published his *Dialogue on the Two Systems* had seen an enormous intellectual change. Where Galileo was still arguing with the past, Newton ignores old discussions, and, looking wholly to the future, calmly enunciates definitions, principles, and proofs that have ever since formed the basis of natural science. Galileo represents the assault; after a single generation comes the victory. Newton himself made two outstanding discoveries: he found the mathematical method that would describe mechanical motion, and he applied it universally. At last what Descartes had dreamed was true: men had arrived at a complete mechanical interpretation of the world in exact, mathematical, deductive terms. In thus placing the keystone in the arch of seventeenth-century science, Newton properly stamped his name upon the picture of the universe that was to last unchanged in its outlines till Darwin; he had completed the sketch of the Newtonian world that was to remain through the eighteenth century as the fundamental scientific verity.

That Newton invented the calculus is perhaps an accident; Leibniz, building on Descartes' analytic geometry, arrived at it independently, while several other mathematicians, like Pascal, seemed almost on the verge of it. Be that as it may, it was inevitable that after the Frenchman had brought algebra and geometry together, men should advance and apply algebra also to motion. Descartes had shown how to find the equation that would represent any curve, and thus conveniently and accurately measure it and enable calculated prediction to be applied to all figures; but the science of mechanics, and with it any measurement of the processes of change in the world, demands a formula for the law of the growth or falling-off of a curve, that is, the direction of its movement at any point. Such a method of measuring movement and continuous growth Newton discovered; he had arrived at the most potent instrument yet found for bringing the world into subjection to man. Since any regular motion, be it of a falling body, an electric current, or the cooling of a molten mass, can be represented by a curve, he had forged the tool by which to attack, not only the figures, but the processes of nature—the last link in the mathematical interpretation of the world. By its means a Lagrange in the eighteenth or a Clerk-Maxwell in the nineteenth century could bring all measurable phenomena into the unified world of mathematics, and calculate, predict, and control light, heat, magnetism, and electricity.

Newton himself used it to formulate the general laws governing every body in the solar system. Kepler had arrived at the law of planetary motion by induction from observed facts, Galileo had similarly discovered the laws of falling bodies upon the earth. Newton united both in one comprehensive set of principles, by calculating that the deflection of the moon from a straight path, that is, her fall towards the earth, exactly corresponded with the observed force of terrestrial gravitation; and he further showed that on his hypothesis Kepler's law of planetary motion followed mathematically from the law of gravitation. The significance of this lay in the proof that the physical laws which hold good on the surface of the earth are valid throughout the solar system. What Galileo divined, what Descartes believed but could not prove, was both confirmed and made more comprehensive. This meant, on the one hand, that the secrets of the whole world could be investigated by man's experiments on this planet; and on the other, that the world was one huge, related, and uniform machine, the fundamental principles of whose action were known. One law could describe the whirling planet and the falling grass blade; one law could explain the action of every body in the universe. Newton expressed this fundamental principle in a famous rule:

> We are to admit no more causes of natural things than such as are both true and sufficient to explain their appearances. Therefore, to the same natural effects we must, as far as possible, assign the same causes. The qualities of bodies that cannot be diminished or increased, and are found to belong to all bodies within the reach of our experiments, are to be esteemed the universal qualities of all bodies whatsoever. For since the qualities of bodies are only known to us by experiments, we are to hold for universal all such as universally agree with experiments. . . .

We are certainly not to relinquish the evidence of experiments for the sake of dreams and vain fictions of our own; nor are we to recede from the analogy of Nature, which uses to be simple, and always consonant with itself. . . . We must, in consequence of this rule, universally allow, that all bodies whatsoever are endowed with a principle of mutual gravitation.

Using this principle and his new mathematical tool, Newton proceeded "to subject the phenomena of nature to the laws of mathematics." "I am induced by many reasons to suspect," he says, "that all the phenomena of nature may depend upon certain forces by which the particles of bodies, by some causes hitherto unknown, are either mutually impelled towards each other, and cohere in regular figures, or are repelled and recede from each other." Every event in nature is to be explained by the same kind of reasoning from mechanical principles: the whole program of science is "from the phenomena of motions to investigate the forces of nature, and then from these forces to demonstrate the other phenomena." The world is a vast perpetual motion machine, and every event in it can be deduced mathematically from the fundamental principles of its mechanical action; the discovery of these mathematical relations is the goal of science. The universe is one great harmonious order not, as for Thomas and the Middle Ages, on ascending hierarchy of purposes, but a uniform mathematical system.

The universal order, symbolized henceforth by the law of gravitation, takes on a clear and positive meaning. This order is accessible to the mind, it is not preestablished mysteriously, it is the most evident of all facts. From this it follows that the sole reality that can be accessible to our means of knowledge, matter, nature, appears to us as a tissue of properties, precisely ordered, and of which the connection can be expressed in terms of mathematics.

Newton's great mathematical system of the world struck the imagination of the educated class of his time, and spread with amazing swiftness, completing what Descartes had begun. Prior to 1789 some eighteen editions of the difficult and technical *Principia* were called for; British universities were teaching it by the end of the seventeenth century, and Newton was accorded a royal funeral when he died in 1727. In 1734, Bernoulli won the prize of the French Academy of Sciences with a Newtonian memoir; in 1740 the last prize was granted to an upholder of Descartes' physics. Voltaire was struck by Newtonianism during his visit to England in 1726–1728, and popularized him in France in his *English Letters,* in 1734, and his *Elements of the Newtonian Philosophy* in 1738; thenceforth Newton reigned in France as in England. From the presses there poured forth an immense stream of popular accounts for those unable or unwilling to peruse the classic work. His conclusions and his picture of the world were accepted on authority. By 1789 there had appeared about the *Principia* forty books in English, seventeen in French, three in German, eleven in Latin, one in Portuguese, and one in Italian, many of them, like those of Desaguliers, Benjamin Martin, Ferguson's *Lectures for Ladies and Gentlemen,* and Count Alogrotti's *Le Newtonianisme pour les Dames,* running through edition after edition. Newton's name became a symbol which called up the picture of the scientific machine-universe, the last word in science, one of those uncriticized preconceptions which largely determined the social and political and religious as well as the strictly scientific thinking of the age. Newton *was* science, and science was the eighteenth-century ideal.

### The Method of Newtonian Science

Hence the method of the new physical science became all important, for men proceeded to apply it in every field of investigation. Just as the success of biology under Darwin led to the importation of the biological method into all the social sciences, and the more recent success of psychology has led to the wider application of its methods, so the social sciences, which, in the absence of any sure method of their own, always borrow from the striking science of the day, were in the Age of Enlightenment almost completely under the domination of the physico-mathematical method.

The influence of the Scientific Revolution upon religion is clearly brought
out in the selection below, which discusses the rise of Deism in the
eighteenth century.

# Science and Religion

Peter Gay

The philosophical and the scientific revolutions of the seventeenth
century were one and the same, and it was essentially this great revolution, though not led by deists, that gave rise to modern deism. It
began with Bacon, Galileo, and Descartes early in the century: it produced such mavericks as Hobbes and Spinoza; and it culminated in
the writings of Newton and Locke at the end of the century.

## Bacon, Galileo, Descartes

It is fashionable to pit Bacon, the prophet of empiricism, against
Descartes, the pioneer of modern rationalism—and both Bacon and
Descartes, the philosophers, against Galileo, the superb practitioner.
Differences in emphasis, mood, and even philosophy certainly existed
among these three men, but from a larger perspective it is clear that
they were allies. All, each in his own way, were the philosophical
prophets of the new science. All agreed with Bacon's ambitious formulation: mankind must do nothing less than undertake "a total reconstruction of sciences, arts, and all human knowledge, raised upon
proper foundations." And it was the business of these thinkers to discover those proper foundations, for one thing was clear—these foundations had not been laid by the Scholastics or the philosophers of the
Renaissance.

> The knowledge whereof the world is now possessed [Bacon
> insisted] especially that of nature, extendeth not to magnitude
> and certainty of works. The Physician pronounceth many dis-
> eases incurable, and faileth oft in the rest. The Alchemists wax
> old and die in hopes. The Magicians perform nothing that is
> permanent and profitable. The mechanics take small light from
> natural philosophy, and do but spin on their own little threads.

What was needed, therefore, was not a new discovery, or even a host
of new discoveries, but a new method. And that method, Bacon said,

From *Deism: An Anthology* by Peter Gay. © 1968. Reprinted by permission of Van Nostrand Reinhold Company.

and Galileo and Descartes said with him, was the method of the sciences: the mixture of mathematical intuition and laborious empirical enquiry, the fashioning of mechanical and intellectual instruments that would enable the researcher to probe more deeply into the mysteries of nature than had been possible before and (which was more significant) to develop a systematic intellectual procedure that would enable successive generations of scientists to confirm and correct the findings of their predecessors. Bacon, Galileo, and Descartes sought to make science cumulative and self-correcting.

This was essential work for the deists, for, despite their own intentions, the scientific revolutionaries threw doubt on most of the accepted stories of Christianity. They did so neither directly nor deliberately. But they were developing a method that would construct a body of knowledge on which all men could agree—and if there was anything certain in the world, it was that theologians did not agree, and could not agree, and would never agree.

### Hobbes and Spinoza

In the midst of this revolution, a number of intellectuals turned quite directly to the claims of the theologians and pronounced them all unproved, unprovable, and probably false. Some of these radicals were modern Epicureans, citing their favorite text, Lucretius' *De rerum natura*. These had little influence. But there were also two thinkers of stature, Hobbes and Spinoza, despised and rejected—and read.

Thomas Hobbes (1588–1679) is a complicated and in some respects a shadowy figure: the precise nature of his own religious beliefs remains a matter of some dispute. But it is clear that his influence was on the side of disbelief, and it is certain that the deists learned much from him. "The philosopher of Malmesbury," Bishop Warburton wrote in the eighteenth century, "was the terror of the last age, as Tindal and Collins are of this." He might have added that the terrors of his own day were much indebted to their illustrious predecessor.

Hobbes himself argued steadfastly that he believed in a God, and that reason would discover him to any man ready to trust his reason. There are even occasional—very occasional—passages in which he speaks of the truths of revelation and the "blessed Savior Jesus Christ." But for the most part, his God is a remote and philosophical figure, and, while his writings against the Roman Catholic Church—"the Kingdom of Darkness"—are cast in the approved style of Protestant polemics against Papists, his specific teachings on the credibility (or rather incredibility) of tales of revelation gave good Protestants little comfort and earned him the reputation of an atheist. It was not so much that Hobbes openly denied the possibility of revelation; it was, rather, that in his persuasive epistemological writings he managed to throw doubt on nearly all the methods that Christians had used to proclaim that a revelation had taken place. If a man claims, for instance, that God has revealed something to him, there is no way for him to prove that the revelation is genuine; if he claims that the revelation came to him in a dream, this means no more than that a man dreamed that God had spoken to him. "So that though God Almighty can speak to a man by dreams, visions, voice, and inspiration; yet he obliges no man to believe he hath done so to him that pretends it; who, being a man, may err, and, which is more, may lie." Here was a prescription for skepticism that the deists would take up, at interminable length, in the decades after Hobbes's death.

Beyond this, Hobbes raised some difficult questions both as to the authorship and the authenticity of the Scriptures. Clearly—and here too the deists would read him with great profit—the church that had long been dominant in Europe had been corrupt, mendacious, power-hungry, and Reformers had effectively demolished many of their inincredible tales of miracle-working saints and divinely blessed relics. How much more, Hobbes asked, might not a reasonable man do with, or to, the miracles that remained? It was an uncomfortable question.

Hobbes raised other questions, equally uncomfortable. In some remarkable pages of his *Leviathan,* he offered a natural history of the religious sentiment, and concluded that the "natural seed of religion" consisted of "opinion of Ghosts, ignorance of second causes, devotion toward what men fear, and taking of things casual for prognostics." In essence, this was an ancient procedure: the Greeks had already speculated on the reason why men were religious. But Hobbes went beyond them to offer a brilliant, if incomplete, psychological account of the religious impulse; nothing among the many subversive things he did was more subversive than this.

Hobbes was a master of the English language, and constantly enmeshed in controversy. Spinoza wrote as a rigorous mathematical logician, chiefly in Latin, and his influence was therefore less marked than Hobbes's. Yet he too became notorious as an atheist, and his writings were required reading for radicals in his time—most of whom did not read him well. But while the pantheism of his *Ethics* (1677) had to await the late eighteenth century before it was clearly seen and fully appreciated, the theological position of his *Theological-Political Treatise* (1670) was perfectly transparent from the beginning. The *Treatise* is a prescient masterpiece of the higher criticism, written long before scholars had, as it were, invented this discipline. Spinoza points out that once the Bible is confronted as any other book is confronted—as a book written by human authors and subject to the ordinary canons of consistency—it becomes evident that it is not the work of a single, but the work of many hands, and that many tales, especially the tales of miracles, are interpolations into earlier stories. In the *Ethics,* Spinoza had indicated his conviction that there could be no miracles, because God (who is nature) does not violate the laws of which He is Himself an embodiment; in the *Treatise,* Spinoza indicates just how the reports of miracles were written and inserted into the holy text. It was a fruitful hypothesis, and the deists made the best of it.

### Newton and Locke

Neither Isaac Newton (1642–1727) nor John Locke (1632–1704) was a deist, yet both were indispensable to the deist cause. Newton gathered the scattered laws of physics and astronomy into a single imposing system, and while there was room in that system for divine intervention—God, Newton thought, set the universe right once in a while when it threatened to run down—the Newtonians could safely disregard this kind of theology as a personal idiosyncrasy. What mattered was that the regularity of the universe had been reduced to system and, in a modest way, explained. What mattered, also, was that Newton did not merely embody the empirical method of the sciences, he also wrote about it with conviction, and convincingly. "I do not feign hypotheses" (*Hypotheses non fingo*), he wrote in a much-quoted pronouncement. He refused to go beyond the evidence; he rejected systems that must be spun out of the head of the ambitious philosopher; he relied upon experiment, observation, and mathematical generalization alone. This was, as I have said, not a deist tenet, but it encouraged men to move in the direction of deism: Newton's prestige as a sage—the world's greatest man, as Voltaire admiringly called him—lent weight to speculations in which miracles, supernatural interventions, and priestcraft, had no place.

It was, finally, in the work of Locke that the groundwork of deism was completed. Locke was above all an empiricist: man acquires knowledge by his sensations upon which his reflection plays. He achieves authentic certainty only in the way of the "natural philosopher," which is to say, the scientist. In his great *Essay Concerning Human Understanding* (1690), Locke drew the consequences of this position: revelation is but reason extended; if it is anything else, if it subverts or contradicts reason, it is not authentic revelation, but a deception.

Yet Locke in his own way was a Christian, though he was sharply criticized for being something less, and something worse, in his own time. *"The Reasonableness of Christianity"* (a book Locke had published in 1695), and *"Christianity not Mysterious,"* (the deist book Toland published in the following year), "these two Titles," a critic wrote in 1706, "are different in Sound, but agree in Sense."

There we are back at the beginning. That critic was both right and wrong. Locke, in the *Reasonableness of Christianity,* had driven the call for a simple, an optimistic, a philosophical, and a reasonable piety, to as great lengths as it would go: he indicated that all a Christian need believe—but this he must believe—is that Christ is the Messiah. This was not much; it was too little for most Christians. But it was not yet deism. In this sense, the critic was wrong. But in the sense that it was indeed too little for most Christians, and that while the step from Locke to Toland was across an abyss it was still only a single, and not very surprising step, the critic was right. Liberal Protestantism was not deism, but it helped to make deism inevitable.

This selection shows the personal side of a famous contributor to the Scientific Revolution. Here we see the intellectual conflict within the participant himself as well as the dramatic confrontation between old and new. How does the dilemma of Galileo compare with that of the doctor who perfected the birth-control pill?

# Dilemma of a Heretic

Angus Armitage

All his life Galileo was a devout Catholic. It distressed him to find that the opinions to which he was irresistibly led as a scientist were condemned by the Church of which he considered himself a loyal son. Accordingly, he was forced to think out for himself the relations between science and scripture. His position was one in which Christians have been placed from time to time. For example, in the middle of the nineteenth century, difficulties were felt in reconciling Darwin's theory of evolution with the Biblical account of the creation of living things. It seemed then as if man were to be deprived of his unique central position in the world of life, just as in the sixteenth century man's home, the Earth, had been deprived of its unique, central position in the Universe.

One way of getting over the difficulty is to say that the Bible is not a textbook of astronomy (or of biology), intended to teach us things that we can discover for ourselves. It reveals spiritual truths which we could not have found out for ourselves. But it expresses these truths in ways natural to the people to whom, and through whom, they were originally revealed. That was roughly Galileo's position. It did not upset him to find that the Bible pictured the world in ways natural to the early Hebrews.

Soon after Galileo had explained his views on this matter, his enemies seized upon a little book he had written on sunspots. They extracted from it a statement of the principles of the Copernican theory, and they submitted them to a committee of the Inquisition for an opinion. This committee reported that, to make the Sun the fixed center of the world was absurd and heretical; while to say that the Earth was not the center and was in motion was absurd and, if not heresy, at least a wrong belief. This report did not, in itself, make the Copernican theory a heresy, for it was never proclaimed so by the Pope. But it provided grounds on which Galileo, in 1616, was warned not to defend the theory. At the same time Copernicus's *Revolutions* was placed on the *Index*—the list of books that Catholics were not allowed to read without special permission—until it was "corrected." The corrections would have had the effect of reducing the theory to a mere device for calculating tables, as Osiander long since had claimed it to be.

However, some years later, when the storm had died down, Galileo wrote a great book which was really meant to be a defense of the Copernican theory. In order to keep to the letter of the command laid upon him in 1616, Galileo threw his book into the form of a debate between the supporters of the Ptolemaic and of the Copernican theories respectively.

The book is entitled *Dialogue Concerning the Two Chief Systems of the World;* and it relates how three friends meet on four successive days to discuss the two rival theories of the Universe, ignoring that of Tycho Brahe. They range over all the arguments on both sides. One of the characters acts as the spokesman of Galileo himself. He puts forward the fresh evidence based upon the telescopic discoveries. The book is written with great literary skill; and it is in Italian, so that other people besides scholars could read it.

On the first day the three friends debate whether heavy bodies fall in order to reach the fixed center of the *Universe* or (as Galileo supposed) in order to reach the center of the moving *Earth*. On the second day they discuss the Earth's daily turning on its axis. The point is made that the Earth could hardly remain at rest if everything outside were being carried round in a vast daily whirl, whereas, on the Copernican view, the Earth is so small in comparison with the rest of the Universe that it could easily rotate without affecting anything outside itself. On the third day they argue for and against the view that the Earth revolves round the Sun, just as the little moons revolve round Jupiter; and for the last day Galileo provides an explanation of the tides which later proved to be mistaken.

Although the weight of evidence goes in favor of Copernicus, Galileo did not dare to press the debate to a decision. He thus managed to get the book past the Censor. But immediately it was published in 1632, Galileo was attacked by the Jesuits on the ground that he had been commanded, in 1616, not to *teach* the Copernican theory, and that he had concealed this fact from the Censor. Thus, it was argued, he had obtained permission to publish his book on false pretences. The Pope set up a Commission which considered the book in secret and produced a record of the command not to teach. Galileo could remember only being told not to *hold* or *defend* the theory; and he had done neither of these in his book. Whether his memory was at fault, or whether the record was a mistake, or a forgery, may never be cleared up. On the strength of the Commission's report, Galileo, now an invalid of close on seventy, was summoned to Rome to face the Inquisition in the winter of 1633. He was kept in close confinement until the summer, being questioned from time to time, but apparently not physically ill treated as things went in those days. However, he was allowed none of the facilities for legal self-defense normally granted to any criminal by the courts of a civilized state. He was tried in his absence, and brought up for sentence on June 22, 1633. But by that time his age and ill health, the depression born of confinement, the prolonged mental bullying to which he had been subjected, and the confusion of ideas between the spiritual authority of the Church and the testimony of experience—all these had done their work and had reduced Galileo to the condition in which he was prepared, on his knees, to renounce the Copernican theory. The sentence of the Inquisition upon him was one of perpetual imprisonment; but this was relaxed in time to a kind of "house arrest" in which he was able to continue his scientific work, in some measure, until his death.

Galileo is remembered today, however, not because he went down at the last before the forces of darkness, but because he fought so long and so successfully against them. There is even a legend that, as he rose to his feet after his forced submission to the Inquisition, and his denial of the Earth's motion, Galileo muttered something to the effect that the Earth *does* move all the same! Whatever the truth of the story, the words have become a sort of proverb implying that "the truth is great and shall prevail," despite all foolish attempts to suppress it in the interests of this or that school of thought. So it was with the truth of the Copernican theory. By his reformation of mechanics, by his telescopic discoveries, and by his battle against the ignorance of the learned men of his day, Galileo had brought the Copernican theory nearer to its final triumph than he could have dreamed in the moment of his downfall. For the year 1642, which saw the death of Galileo in captivity, saw also the birth of Isaac Newton.

## Questions

1  Science and technology have created or helped to create many of today's problems. Should the scientists and technicians be given the task of solving these problems? Should they be given assistance in setting priorities?

2 Can science and technology be trusted to create work-able solutions? Do we have any choice?

3 This essay mentions The Pill and heart transplants as scientific advances that changed behavior and caused controversy. Name several other such advances (not just in medicine) that have been made in the last twenty years or that may be perfected in the next twenty years that will similarly change accepted or traditional values and create controversy. What are your recommendations for handling the potential problems?

4 Which of our canons are based upon myths? Take two canons and see if you can figure out how they could have developed logically from myth.

5 What are the main scientific hangups of Western civili-zation? Why do you consider your selections hangups?